Seventeenth-century England: A Changing Culture

Volume 1: Primary Sources

Seventeenth-century England: A Changing Culture

Volume 1: Primary Sources

Edited by Ann Hughes
at the Open University

Ward Lock Educational
in association with
The Open University

ISBN 0 7062 4088 X paperback
0 7062 4090 1 hardback

First Published 1980

Set in 10 on 11 point Garamond by
Jubal Multiwrite Ltd, London SE13
and printed by Biddles of Guildford
for Ward Lock Educational
47 Marylebone Lane, London W1M 6AX
A member of the Pentos Group

Contents

SECTION SEVEN: THE PROPAGANDA WAR

SECTION EIGHT: CIVIL WAR ADMINISTRATION

SECTION NINE: THE DIARY OF RALPH JOSSELIN, 1645–1660

SECTION TEN: RELIGIOUS UPHEAVAL, 1642–1659

SECTION ELEVEN: THE LEVELLERS

SECTION TWELVE: THE ARMY LEADERSHIP AND THE KING, NOVEMBER 1648

SECTION THIRTEEN: GERRARD WINSTANLEY, 1609–1676

SECTION FOURTEEN: POLITICAL SETTLEMENTS IN THE 1650s

SECTION FIFTEEN: THE DEBATE OVER EDUCATION

SECTION SIXTEEN: JAMES HARRINGTON: PROPERTY AND POLITICAL POWER

SECTION SEVENTEEN: THE RESTORATION

SECTION EIGHTEEN: POLITICS AND RELIGION AFTER 1660

SECTION NINETEEN: SOME EXAMPLES OF ENGLISH PROSE

SECTION TWENTY: JOHN DRYDEN

SECTION TWENTY-ONE: SCIENTIFIC DEVELOPMENTS

SECTION TWENTY-TWO: SIR CHRISTOPHER WREN, 1632–1723

SECTION TWENTY-THREE: JOHN LOCKE, 1632–1704

Acknowledgments

Most of the extracts that follow were selected by the authors of the teaching material for the A203 Course: Joan Bellamy, Tim Benton, Stuart Brown, Noel Coley, Diane Collinson, Simon Eliot, Margot Heinemann, Christopher Hill, J.R. Jones, Anne Laurence, Rosemary O'Day, John Purkis, Nick Rowling, Colin Russell and Kevin Wilson. I would like to thank all of them for their help, especially for their cheerful cooperation when the original selection had to be cut by half. I am grateful to Noel Coley, John Purkis and Colin Russell for advice on particular notes and introductions. I would like to thank Hazel Ball for her efficient typing of many extracts; Sue Staig who also helped with typing; and Irene Hatt for general secretarial assistance and many kindnesses. Above all, I am grateful to the editor of the companion volume, Bob Owens, and to the successive leaders of the course team, Christopher Hill and Anne Laurence, whose consistent advice and encouragement have made the compilation of this anthology so enjoyable.

A.H.

List of Illustrations

General Introduction

In this anthology we examine seventeenth-century developments through the words of the men who participated in them. The extracts take a variety of forms. Many are official or semi-official documents, public pronouncements taken from legislation, constitutional programmes, parliamentary speeches and sermons. There are selections from the vast propagandist pamphlet literature of the century, and material from contemporary histories and surveys. Some are conscious 'literary' works: poetry, drama and prose are all included. Finally, the private voice of the seventeenth century is represented by extracts from letters and diaries.

The topics covered range widely. We concentrate on the major political and religious controversies of the period, but the anthology was produced for the Open University interdisciplinary arts course, A203, *Seventeenth-Century England: A Changing Culture 1618–1689*, which also explores changes in the economy, education, architecture, painting, music, science and literature. Most of these aspects of the period are touched on in the extracts that follow. The revolutionary decades of the 1640s and 1650s are given special emphasis. The collapse of the censorship in 1640 led to a massive rise in the number of works published; comparatively ordinary people had an exceptional opportunity to get into print and an unprecedented freedom to express radical opinions. It seemed in these years as if the world could be made anew: as Oliver Cromwell said disapprovingly (and with some exaggeration) there was 'nothing in the hearts and minds of men but overturning, overturning, overturning' (extract 99).

This volume is not a comprehensive selection of material on seventeenth-century politics, society and culture. Several important aspects are missing because they are covered in other set books for the Open University course: this consideration accounts for the exclusion of Francis Bacon's philosophical works, John Bunyan, Thomas Hobbes, John Milton, Jacobean and Restoration drama and metaphysical poetry. However, we believe that the anthology presents material that a wider readership interested in seventeenth-century England will work through and enjoy. As well as some of the familiar 'documents' of the period, it includes much that is not easily available, and some material that has not been reproduced since its initial publication.

The individual sections have been organized on a combination of topical and chronological criteria. They are not completely self-contained as one aim of the Open University course for which the anthology has been compiled is to explore the connections between changes in different aspects of seventeenth-century life. Some possible links are suggested in the detailed introductions to each section; readers will probably discover more.

Editorial Note

Spelling and punctuation have been modernized in all cases. Omissions from the original are indicated by . . . and editorial additions by [ ]. Introductory material and notes have been kept to a minimum. I have tried to avoid presenting my interpretations of extracts in the expectation that readers will arrive at their own views. A brief introduction is provided for each section, setting the individual pieces in context, although it has sometimes been necessary to add a headnote to particular extracts. No attempt has been made to annotate the copious biblical allusions found in much seventeenth-century writing except where the biblical reference adds significantly to the understanding of the passage. Words found in *The Concise Oxford Dictionary* have not been noted except where there is some ambiguity.

SECTION ONE: ECONOMY, SOCIAL STRUCTURE AND SOCIAL LIFE

[This short section illustrating economic and social life includes extracts from three literary accounts discussing sixteenth-century developments, such as the price rise, social mobility and the increasingly active landmarket, which profoundly affected the early seventeenth century (extracts 1, 3, 5). Probate inventories, revealing the often meagre possessions which smaller landholders and craftsmen of Essex owned at their deaths, offer some corrective to the general optimism of the literary sources, particularly Harrison (extract 6). Francis Bacon's blueprint for a great house contrasts with the inventories and with Harrison's account of gradual improvement in living standards, but the 'prodigy' houses built by some wealthy men in the early years of the century illustrate Bacon's ideas (extract 4).

Gregory King's 'Table' is an attempt to classify the population and wealth of England in 1688 (extract 2). Wilson had included statistical estimates but King, one of the most important figures in the development of the science of statistics, seems to have a more systematic approach. King was, however, a conservative – 'a thorough, divine right Tory' – and his status categories were the outmoded ones of a static, agricultural society. He underestimated the number of families in his wealthier categories, and grossly underestimated the incomes of those above the poverty line, probably because he did not believe England could afford her involvement in the European wars of the 1690s. The 'Table' remains 'an extraordinary pioneering feat, a creation of awesome scale and of the boldest originality'.[1]

Changes in the relationships between landlords and tenants are illustrated in extracts 7 and 8. A Lancashire gentleman, Edward Moore, wrote a description of his estates for his son, including many proposals for their more efficient exploitation. In his last work, Richard Baxter appealed for more charitable relationships in the countryside. This tract was suppressed after Baxter's death, and not published until the twentieth century.

Finally we include an extract from the 1651 Navigation Act, a landmark in government encouragement for shipping and trade (extract 9) and one of the few pieces of Commonwealth legislation to be continued after the Restoration.]

Note

1 These comments are taken from G.S. Holmes, 'Gregory King and the Social Structure of Pre-Industrial England'. *Transactions of the Royal Historical Society* (1977).

1 Sir Thomas Wilson: England in 1600

[*Source*: F.J. Fisher, editor (1936) *The State of England, 1600* by Sir Thomas Wilson (The Camden Society, Third Series LII, Miscellany volume 16), pp. 18–25.]

The ability and state of the common people of England
It cannot be denied but the common people are very rich, albeit they be much decayed from the states they were wont to have, for the gentlemen, which were wont to addict themselves to the wars, are now for the most part grown to become good husbands and know as well how to improve their lands to the uttermost as the farmer or countryman, so that they take their farms into their hands as the leases expire, and either till themselves or else let them out to those who will give most; whereby the yeomanry of England is decayed and become servants to gentlemen, which were wont to be the glory of the country and good neighbourhood and hospitality; notwithstanding there are yet some store of those yeomen left who have long leases of such lands and lordships as they hold, yea, I know many yeomen in divers provinces in England which are able yearly to dispend betwixt three or five hundred pound yearly by their lands and leases and some twice and some thrice as much; but my young masters the sons of such, not contented with their states of their fathers to be counted yeoman and called John or Robert (such an one), but must skip into his velvet breeches and silken doublet and, getting to be admitted into some Inn of Court or Chancery, must ever after think scorn to be called any other than gentlemen; which gentlemen indeed, perceiving them unfit to do them that service that their fathers did, when their leases do expire, turn them out of their lands, which was never wont to be done, the farmer accounting his state as good as inheritance in times past, and let them to such as are not by their bad pennyworths able to gentleman it as others have done.

Commonalty
Notwithstanding this that the great yeomanry is decayed, yet by this means the commonalty is increased 20 now perhaps with their labour and diligence, living well and wealthily of that land which our great yeoman held before, who did no other good but maintain beef and brews for such idle persons as would come and eat it, a fine daughter or 2 to be married after with 10,000*l*. to some covetous mongrel gentleman. Of these yeomen of the richest sort . . . there are accounted to be about 10,000 in country villages besides citizens.

There are, moreover, of yeomen of meaner ability which are called freeholders, for that they are owners of lands which hold by no base service of any lord or superior, such as are able to keep 10 or 11 or 8 or 6 milch kine, 5 or 6 horses to till their ground, besides young beasts and sheep and are accounted to be worth each of them in all their substance and stock betwixt 3 and 5 hundred pounds sterling more or less, of these, I say, there are reckoned to be in England and Wales about the number of 80,000, as I have seen in sheriffs' books.

The rest are copyholders and cottagers, as they call them, who hold some land and tenements of some other lord which is parcel of the demesne of his seignory or manor at the will of the lord, and these are, some of them, men of as great ability as any of the rest; and some poor, and live chiefly upon country labour working by the day for meat and drink and some small wages . . . The number of this latter sort is uncertain because there is no books or records kept of them . . .

The state of citizens

These, by reason of the great privileges they enjoy, every city being, as it were, a commonwealth among themselves, no other officer of the Queen nor other having authority to intermeddle amongst them, must needs be exceeding well to pass. They are not taxed but by their own officers of the[ir] own brotherhood, every art having one or two of his own which are continually of the council of the city in all affairs to see that nothing pass contrary to their profit; besides they are not suffered to be idle in their cities as they be in other parts of Christendom, but every child of 6 or 7 years old is forced to some art whereby he gaineth his own living and some thing besides to help to enrich his parents or master . . . [In Norwich] I have known in my time 24 aldermen which were esteemed to be worth 20,000*l.* apiece, some much more, and the better sort of citizens the half; but if we should speak of London and some other maritime places we should find it much exceeding this rate, it is well known that at this time there are in London some merchants worth 100,000*l.* and he is not accounted rich that cannot reach to 50,000 or near it . . .

The state of the nobility and the number

. . . [Of] earls some daily decay, some increase according to the course of the world, but . . . still the total sum groweth much to one reckoning and that is to 100,000*l.* rent yearly, accounting them all in gross to avoid prolixity. If a man would proportion this amongst 19 earls and a marquis it would be no great matter, to every one 5,000*l.* rent, but as some exceed that much, so many come short of it.

The 39 barons and 2 viscounts do not much exceed that sum, their revenue is reckoned together to amount to 120,000*l.* yearly.

The bishops' revenues amount to about 22,500*l.* yearly altogether whereof 3 of them, viz. Canterbury, Winchester, and Ely, receive rent per annum betwixt 2,000*l.* and 3,000*l.*, the rest betwixt 1,000*l.* and 500*l.* and some less.

The deans are the chief ecclesiastical persons of every cathedral church; . . . their revenue is not much, the best not exceeding 300*l.* yearly, and the rest some 200, some 100, and many less, their whole revenue accounted through England amounted to the sum of 4,500*l.*

yearly or thereabouts.

But this must be understood, that the state of the clergy is not altogether so bare as may perhaps be conjectured by the smallness of their revenue, for that they never raise nor rack their rents nor put out tenants as the noblemen and gentlemen do to the uttermost penny; but do let their lands as they were let 100 years since, reserving to themselves and their successors some commodities besides the bare rent, as corn, muttons, beef, poultry, or such like; but to say the truth, their wings are well clipped of late by courtiers and noblemen and some quite cut away, both feather, flesh, and bone.

These are the states of the nobility, both clergy and lay, which are called *nobilitas maior*; there rests to touch those of the meaner nobility, which are termed *nobilitas minor* and are either knights, esquires, gentlemen, lawyers, professors, and ministers, archdeacons, prebends, and vicars.

The state and number of knights

There are accounted to be in England about the number of 500 knights as I have reckoned them, both by divers commissions of every several shire remaining in the Chancery Office for making of justices of peace, of which commission all knights to be unless they be put by for religion or some particular disfavour . . . These for the most part are men for living betwixt 1,000 and 2,000*l*. yearly, and many of them equal the best barons and come not much behind many earls . . .

The number and state of gentlemen

Those which we call esquires are gentlemen whose ancestors are or have been knights, or else they are the heirs and eldest of their houses and of some competent quantity of revenue fit to be called to office and authority in their country where they live; of these there are esteemed to be in England, as I have seen by the book of musters of every several shire, to the number of 16,000 or thereabout, whereof there are of them in commissions of the peace about 1,400 in every province – in some 40, in some 50, some 30, more or less; these are men in living betwixt 1,000*l*. and 500*l*. rent. Especially about London and the counties adjoining, where their lands are set to the highest, he is not counted of any great reckoning unless he be betwixt 1,000 marks or 1,000*l*., but northward and far off a gentleman of good reputation may be content with 300*l*. and 400*l*. yearly. These are the elder brothers.

The state of great younger brethren

I cannot speak of the number of younger brothers, albeit I be one of the number myself, but for their estate there is no man hath better cause to know it, nor less cause to praise it; their state is of all stations for gentlemen most miserable, for if our fathers possess 1,000 or 2,000*l*. yearly at his death, he cannot give a foot of land to his younger children in inheritance, unless it be by lease for 21 years or for 3 lives (or unless his land be socage tenure whereof there is little, or gavelkind, such as is only in one province, in Kent), or else be purchased by himself and not descended. Then he may demise as much as he thinks good to his younger children, but such a fever hectic hath custom brought in and inured amongst fathers, and such fond desire they have to leave a great shew of the stock of their house, though the branches be withered, that they will not do it, but my elder brother forsooth must be my master. He must have all, and all the rest, that which the cat left on the malt heap, perhaps some small annuity during his life or what please our elder brother's worship to bestow upon us if we please him, and my mistress his wife. This I must confess doth us good someways, for it makes us industrious to apply ourselves to letters or to arms, whereby many times we become my master elder brothers' masters, or at least their betters in honour and reputation, while he lives at home like a mome [fool] and knows the sound of no other bell but his own.

The estate of common lawyers

This sort and order of people within these 40 or 50 years, since the practice of civil law hath been as it were wholly banished and abrogated, and since the clergy hath been trodden down by the taking away of church livings, and since the long continuance of peace hath bred an inward canker and rest in men's minds, the people doing nothing but jar and wrangle one with another, these lawyers by the ruins of neighbours' contentions are grown so great, so rich, and so proud, that no other sort dare meddle with them; their number is so great now that, to say the truth, they can scarcely live one by another, the practice being drawn into a few hand[s] of those which are most renowned, and all the rest live by pettifogging, seeking means to set their neighbours at variance whereby they may gain on both sides. This is one of the greatest inconveniences in the land, that the number of the lawyers are so great they undo the country people and buy up all the lands that are to be sold, so that young gentlemen or others newly coming to their livings, some of them prying into his evidence will find the means to set him at variance with some other, or some other with him, by some pretence or quiddity, and when they have half consumed themselves in suit they are fain to sell their land to follow the process and pay their debts, and then that becomes a prey to lawyers.

For the greatness of some of them it is incredible not to speak of the 12 chief judges and the multitude of sergeants, which are most of them counted men of 20,000 or 30,000*l*. yearly, there is one at this day of a meaner degree, viz. the Queen's attorney, [Sir Edward Coke-Wilson's note] who, within this 10 years in my knowledge was not able to dispend above 100*l*. a year and now by his own lands, his coins, and his office he may dispend betwixt 12 and 14 thousand.

There are in number of sergeants about 30, counsellers about 2,000, and as many attorneys, besides solicitors, and pettifoggers an infinite number, there being no province, city, town, nor scarce village free from them, unless the Isle of Anglesey, which boast they never had lawyers nor foxes.

2 Gregory King: The Income and Expense of the Families of England in 1688

[*Source*: George E. Barnett, editor (1936) *Two Tracts by Gregory King* (The Johns Hopkins Press, Baltimore), p. 31.]

Number of Families	Ranks, Degrees, Titles, and Qualifications	Heads per Family	Number of Persons	Yearly Income per Family		Total of the Estates or Income	Yearly Income per Head		Expense per Head			Increase per Head			Total Increase per annum
				£	s.	£	£	s.	£	s.	d.	£	s.	d.	
160	Temporal Lords	40	6,400	2800	0	448,000	70	0	60	0	0	10	0	0	£64,000
26	Spiritual Lords	20	520	1300	0	33,800	65	0	55	0	0	10	0	0	5,200
800	Baronets	16	12,800	880	0	704,000	55	0	51	0	0	4	0	0	51,200
600	Knights	13	7,800	650	0	390,000	50	0	46	0	0	4	0	0	31,200
3,000	Esquires	10	30,000	450	0	1,200,000	45	0	42	0	0	3	0	0	90,000
12,000	Gentlemen	8	96,000	280	0	2,880,000	35	0	32	10	0	2	10	0	240,000
5,000	Persons in offices	8	40,000	240	0	1,200,000	30	0	27	0	0	3	0	0	120,000
5,000	Persons in offices	6	30,000	120	0	600,000	20	0	18	0	0	2	0	0	60,000
2,000	Merchants and traders by sea	8	16,000	400	0	800,000	50	0	40	0	0	10	0	0	160,000
8,000	Merchants and traders by sea	6	48,000	200	0	1,600,000	33	0	28	0	0	5	0	0	240,000
10,000	Persons in the law	7	70,000	140	0	1,400,000	20	0	17	0	0	3	0	0	210,000
2,000	Clergymen	6	12,000	60	0	120,000	10	0	9	0	0	1	0	0	12,000
8,000	Clergymen	5	40,000	45	0	360,000	9	0	8	0	0	1	0	0	40,000
40,000	Freeholders	7	280,000	84	0	3,360,000	12	0	11	0	0	1	0	0	280,000
140,000	Freeholders	5	700,000	50	0	7,000,000	10	0	9	10	0		10	0	350,000
150,000	Farmers	5	750,000	44	0	6,600,000	8	15	8	10	0		5	0	187,500
16,000	Persons in sciences and liberal arts	5	80,000	60	0	960,000	12	0	11	10	0		10	0	40,000
40,000	Shopkeepers and tradesmen	4½	180,000	45	0	1,800,000	10	0	9	10	0		10	0	90,000
60,000	Artisans and handicrafts	4	240,000	40	0	2,400,000	10	0	9	10	0		10	0	120,000
5,000	Naval officers	4	20,000	80	0	400,000	20	0	18	0	0	2	0	0	40,000
4,000	Military officers	4	16,000	60	0	240,000	15	0	14	0	0	1	0	0	16,000
511,586 Fam.				£	s.		£	s.	£	s.	d.		s.	d.	£
		5¼	2,675,520	67	0	34,495,800	12	18	12	0	0		18	0	2,447,100

Number of Families	Ranks, Degrees, Titles, and Qualifications	Heads per Family	Number of Persons	Yearly Income per Family	Total of the Estates or Income	Yearly Income per Head	Expense per Head	Decrease per Head	Total Decrease per annum
				£ s.	£	£ s.	£ s. d.	£ s. d.	
50,000	Common seamen	3	150,000	20 0	1,000,000	7 0	7 10 0	10 0	£75,000
364,000	Labouring people and outservants	3½	1,275,000	15 0	5,460,000	4 10	4 12 0	2 0	127,500
400,000	Cottages and paupers	3¼	1,300,000	6 10	2,000,000	2 0	2 5 0	5 0	325,000
35,000	Common soldiers	2	70,000	14 0	490,000	7 0	7 10 0	10 0	35,000
849,000 Fams.		3¼	2,795,000	10 10	8,950,000	3 5	3 9 0	4 0	£562,000
	Vagrants		30,000		60,000	2 0	3 0 0	1 0 0	60,000
				£ s.					
849,000		3¼	2,825,000	10 10	9,010,000	3 3	3 7 6	4 6	£622,000

So the General Account is.

Number of Families	Ranks, Degrees, Titles, and Qualifications	Heads per Family	Number of Persons	Yearly Income per Family	Total of the Estates or Income	Yearly Income per Head	Expense per Head	Decrease per Head	Total Decrease per annum
				£ s.	£	£ s.	£ s. d.	£ s. d.	
511,586 Fam.	increasing the wealth of the kingdom	5¼	2,675,520	67 0	34,495,800	12 18	12 0 0	18 0	£2,447,100
849,000 Fam.	decreasing the wealth of the kingdom	3¼	2,825,000	10 10	9,010,000	3 3	3 7 6	4 6	622,000
1,360,586 Fam.	Neat totals	4 1/20	5,500,520	32 0	43,505,800	7 18	7 11 3	6 9	£1,825,100

3 William Harrison: The Manner of Building and Furniture of our Houses, 1587

[*Source*: F.J. Furnivall, editor (1877) *Harrison's Description of England in Shakspere's Youth* (The New Shakspere Society) Part One, pp. 233–42.]

The greatest part of our building in the cities and good towns of England consisteth only of timber, for as yet few of the houses of the commonalty, except here and there in the west country towns, are made of stone, although they may, in my opinion, in divers other places be built so good cheap of the one as of the other. In old time the houses of the Britons were slightly set up with a few posts and many raddles [slender rods], with stable and all offices under one roof, the like whereof almost is to be seen in the fenny countries and northern parts unto this day, where for lack of wood they are enforced to continue this ancient manner of building. It is not in vain therefore in speaking of building to make a distinction between the plain and woody soils: for as in these, our houses are commonly strong and well timbered – so that in many places there are not above four, six or nine inches between stud and stud – so in the open champaign countries they are enforced for want of stuff to use no studs at all, but only frank posts, raisins, beams, prick posts, groundsels, summers (or dormants), transoms,[1] and such principals, with here and there a girding, whereunto they fasten their splints or raddles, and then cast it all over with thick clay to keep out the wind, which otherwise would annoy them. . . .

The walls of our houses on the inner sides . . . be either hanged with tapestry, arras work, or painted cloths, wherein either divers histories, or herbs, beasts, knots and such like are stained, or else they are sealed with oak of our own, or wainscot brought hither out of the east countries, whereby the rooms are not a little commended, made warm and much more close than otherwise they would be. . . . [It] also hath been common in England, contrary to the customs of all other nations, and yet to be seen, for example, in most streets of London, that many of our greatest houses have outwardly been very simple and plain to sight, which inwardly have been able to receive a duke with his whole train and lodge them at their ease. Hereby, moreover, it is come to pass that the fronts of our streets have not been so uniform and orderly built as those of foreign cities, where, to say truth, the utterside of their mansions and dwellings have oft more cost bestowed upon them than all the rest of the house, which are often very simple and uneasy within, as experience doth confirm. Of old time, our country houses, instead of glass, did use much lattice, and that made either of wicker or fine rifts of oak in chequerwise. . . . But . . . our lattices are also grown into less use, because glass is come to be so plentiful and within a very little so good cheap, if not better than the other. . . .

Moreover, the mansion houses of our country towns and villages (which in champaign ground stand altogether by streets, and joining one to another, but in woodland soils [are] dispersed here and there, each one upon the several grounds of their owners) are built in such sort generally as that they have neither dairy, stable nor brew-house annexed unto them under the same roof, as in many places beyond the sea and some of the north parts of our country, but all separate from the first, and one of them from another. And yet for all this, they are not so far distant in sunder, but that the goodman lying in his bed may lightly hear what is done in each of them with ease, and call quickly unto his meinie [servant] if any danger should attack him.

The ancient manors and houses of our gentlemen are yet, and for the most part, of strong timber, in framing whereof our carpenters have been and are worthily preferred before those of like science among all other nations. Howbeit such as be lately built are commonly either of brick or hard stone, or both; their rooms large and comely, and houses of office further distant from their lodgings. Those of the nobility are likewise wrought with brick and hard stone, as provision may best be made, but so magnificent and stately as the basest house of a baron doth often match, in our days, with some honours of princes in old time. . . .

The furniture of our houses also exceedeth, and is grown in manner even to passing delicacy; and herein I do not speak of the nobility and gentry only, but likewise of the lowest sort, in most places of our south country, that have anything at all to take to. Certes, in noblemen's houses it is not rare to see abundance of arras, rich hangings of tapestry, silver vessel, and so much other plate, as may furnish sundry cupboards, to the sum oftentimes of a thousand or two thousand pounds at the least, whereby the value of this and the rest of their stuff doth grow to be almost inestimable. Likewise in the houses of knights, gentlemen, merchantmen, and some other wealthy citizens, it is not geason [extraordinary] to behold generally their great provision of tapestry, turkey-work, pewter, brass, fine linen and thereto costly cupboards of plate, worth five or six hundred, or a thousand pounds, to be deemed by estimation. But as herein all these sorts do far exceed their elders and predecessors, and in neatness and curiosity the merchant all other; so, in time past, the costly furniture stayed there, whereas now it is descended yet lower, even unto the inferior artificers and many farmers who, by virtue of their old and not of their new leases, have, for the most part, learned also to garnish their cupboards with plate, their joined beds with tapestry and silk hangings, and their tables with carpets and fine napery, whereby the wealth of our country (God be praised therefore, and give us grace to employ it well) doth infinitely appear. . . .

There are old men yet dwelling in the village where I remain, which have noted three things to be marvellously altered in England within their sound remembrance, and other three things, too, too much increased. One is, the multitude of chimneys lately erected, whereas in their young days there were not above two or three, if so many, in most uplandish towns of the realm (the religious houses and manor places of their lords always excepted, and peradventure some great personages) but each one made his fire against a reredos in the hall, where he dined and dressed his meat.

The second is the great, although not general, amendment of lodging for, said they, our fathers, yea, and we ourselves also have lain full oft upon straw pallets, on rough mats covered only with a sheet, under coverlets made of dagswain or hopharlots (I use their own terms) and a good round log under their heads instead of a bolster or pillow. If it were so that our fathers, or the goodman of the house, had within seven years after his marriage purchased a mattress or flock-bed, and thereto a sack of chaff to rest his head upon, he thought himself to be as well lodged as the lord of the town, that peradventure lay seldom in a bed of down or whole feathers; so well were they contented and with such base kind of furniture which also is not very much amended as yet in some parts of Bedfordshire, and elsewhere further off from our southern parts. Pillows, said they, were thought meet only for women in childbed. As for servants, if they had any sheet above them, it was well, for seldom had they any under their bodies, to keep them from the pricking straws that ran oft through the canvas of the pallet and razed their hardened hides.

The third thing they tell of, is the exchange of vessel, as of treen platters into pewter and wooden spoons into silver or tin. For so common were all sorts of treen stuff in old time, that a man should hardly find four pieces of pewter, of which one was peradventure a salt, in a good farmer's house, and yet for all this frugality, if it may so be justly called, they were scarce able to live and pay their rents at their days without selling of a cow or a horse, or more, although they paid but four pounds at the uttermost by the year. Such also was their poverty, that if some one odd farmer or husbandman had been at the alehouse, a thing greatly used in those days, amongst six or seven of his neighbours, and there in a bravery to show what store he had, did cast down his purse and therein a noble or six shillings in silver unto them (for few such men then cared for gold because it was not so ready payment and they were oft enforced to give a penny for the exchange of an angel) it was very likely that all the rest could not lay down so much against it. Whereas in my time, although peradventure four pounds of old rent be improved to forty, fifty or a hundred pounds, yet will the farmer, as another palm or date tree, think his gains very small toward the end of his term, if he have not six or seven years rent lying by him, therewith to purchase a new lease, besides a fair garnish of pewter on his cupboard with so much more in odd vessel going about the house, three or four featherbeds, so many coverlets and carpets of tapestry, a silver salt, a bowl for wine, if not a whole nest, and a dozen of spoons to furnish up the suit. This also he taketh to be his own clear, for what stock of money soever he gathereth and layeth up in all his years, it is often seen that the landlord will take such order with him for the same, when he reneweth his lease, which is commonly eight or six years before the old be expired (sith it is now grown almost to a custom, that if he come not to his lord so long before another shall step in for a reversion and so defeat him outright) that it shall never trouble him more than the hair of his beard, when the barber hath washed and shaved it from his chin.

And as they commend these, so beside the decay of house-keeping whereby the poor have been relieved, they speak also of three things that are grown to be very grievous unto them: to wit, the enhancing of rents, lately mentioned; the daily oppression of copyholders, whose lords seek to bring their poor tenants almost into plain servitude and misery, daily devising new means, and seeking up all the old, how to cut them shorter and shorter, doubling, trebling, and now and then seven times increasing their fines; driving them also for every trifle to lose and forfeit their tenures, by whom the greatest part of the realm doth stand and is maintained, to the end they may fleece them yet more, which is a lamentable hearing. The third thing they talk of is usury, a trade brought in by the Jews, now perfectly practised almost by every Christian, and so commonly, that he is accounted but for a fool that doth lend his money for nothing.

Note

1 'Frank posts . . . transoms': various kinds of beams used in building.

4 Francis Bacon: Of Building

[*Source*: First published in the 1625 edition of Bacon's *Essayes*; here taken from James Spedding, Robert L. Ellis and Douglas D. Heath, editors (1858) *The Works of Francis Bacon* volume six, pp. 481–5.]

Houses are built to live in, and not to look on; therefore let use be preferred before uniformity, except where both may be had. Leave the goodly fabrics of houses, for beauty only, to the enchanted palaces of the poets; who build them with small cost. He that builds a fair house upon an ill seat, committeth himself to prison. Neither do I reckon it an ill seat only where the air is unwholesome; but likewise where the air is unequal; as you shall see many fine seats set upon a knap of ground, environed with higher hills round about it; whereby the heat of the sun is pent in, and the wind gathereth as in troughs; so as you shall have, and that suddenly, as great diversity of heat and cold as if you dwelt in several places. Neither is it ill air only that maketh an ill seat, but ill ways, ill markets: and, if you will consult with Momus,[1] ill neighbours. I speak not of many more; want of water; want of wood, shade, and shelter; want of fruitfulness, and mixture of grounds of several natures; want of prospect; want of level grounds; want of places at some near distance for sports of hunting, hawking, and races; too near the sea, too remote; having the commodity of navigable rivers, or the discommodity of their overflowing; too far off from great cities, which may hinder business, or too near them, which lurcheth all provisions, and maketh every thing dear; where a man hath a great living laid together, and where he is scanted: all which, as it is impossible perhaps to find together, so it is good to know them, and think of them, that a man may take as many as he can; and if he have several dwellings, that he sort them so, that what he wanteth in the one he may find in the other. Lucullus answered Pompey well;[2] who, when he saw his stately galleries, and rooms so large and lightsome, in one of his houses, said, *Surely an excellent place for summer, but how do you in winter?* Lucullus answered, *Why, do you not think me as wise as some fowl are, that ever change their abode towards the winter?*

To pass from the seat to the house itself; we will do as Cicero[3] doth in the orator's art; who writes books *De Oratore*, and a book he entitles *Orator*; whereof the former delivers the precepts of the art, and the latter the perfection. We will therefore describe a princely palace, making a brief model thereof. For it is strange to see, now in Europe, such huge buildings as the Vatican and Escurial and some others be, and yet scarce a very fair room in them.

First therefore, I say you cannot have a perfect palace, except you have two several sides; a side for the banquet, as is spoken of in the book of Hester,[4] and a side for the household; the one for feasts and triumphs, and the other for dwelling. I understand both these sides to be not only returns, but parts of the front; and to be uniform without, though severally partitioned within; and to be on both sides of a great and stately tower in the midst of the front, that, as it were, joineth them together on either hand. I would have on the side of the banquet, in front, one only goodly room above stairs, of some forty foot high; and under it a room for a dressing or preparing place at times of triumphs. On the other side, which is the household side, I wish it divided at the first into a hall and a chapel, (with a partition between;) both of good state and bigness; and those not to go all the length, but to have at the further end a winter and a summer parlour, both fair. And under these rooms, a fair and large cellar sunk under ground; and likewise some privy kitchens, with butteries and pantries, and the like. As for the tower, I would have it two stories, of eighteen foot high a piece, above the two wings; and a goodly leads upon the top, railed with statuas [statues] interposed; and the same tower to be divided into rooms, as shall be thought fit. The stairs likewise to the upper rooms, let them be upon a fair open newel, and finely railed in with images of wood, cast into a brass colour; and a very fair landing-place at the top. But this to be, if you do not point any of the lower rooms for a dining place of servants. For otherwise you shall have the servants' dinner after your own: for the steam of it will come up as in a tunnel. And so much for the front. Only I understand the height of the first stairs to be sixteen foot, which is the height of the lower room.

Beyond this front is there to be a fair court, but three sides of it, of a far lower building than the front. And in all the four corners of that court fair stair-cases, cast into turrets, on the outside, and not within the row of buildings themselves. But those towers are not to be of the height of the front, but rather proportionable to the lower building. Let the court not be paved, for that striketh up a great heat in summer, and much cold in winter. But only some side alleys, with a cross, and the quarters to graze, being kept shorn, but not too near shorn. The row of return on the banquet side, let it be all stately galleries: in which galleries let there be three, or five, fine cupolas [rounded vaults or domes] in the length of it, placed at equal distance; and fine coloured windows of several works. On the household side, chambers of presence and ordinary entertainments, with some bed-chambers; and let all three sides be a double house, without thorough lights on the sides, that you may have rooms from the sun, both for forenoon and afternoon. Cast it also, that you may have rooms both for summer and winter; shady for summer, and warm for winter. You shall have sometimes fair houses so full of glass, that one cannot tell where to become to be out of the sun or cold. For inbowed windows, I hold them of good use; (in cities, indeed, upright do better, in respect of the uniformity towards the street;) for they be pretty retiring places for conference; and besides, they keep both the wind and sun off; for that which would strike almost thorough the room doth scarce pass the window. But let them be but few, four in the court, on the sides only.

Beyond this court, let there be an inward court, of the same square and height; which is to be environed with the garden on all sides, and in the inside, cloistered on all sides, upon decent and beautiful arches, as high as the first story. On the under story, towards the garden, let it be turned to a grotta, or place of shade, or estivation [summer house]. And only have opening and windows towards the garden; and be level upon the floor, no whit sunken under ground, to avoid all dampishness. And let there be a fountain, or some fair work of statuas in the midst of this court; and to be paved as the other court was. These buildings to be for privy lodgings on both sides; and the end for privy galleries. Whereof you must foresee that one of them be for an infirmary, if the prince or any special person should be sick, with chambers, bed-chamber, antecamera, and recamera [ante chamber and inner chamber], joining to it. This upon the second story. Upon the ground story, a fair gallery, open, upon pillars; and upon the third story likewise, an open gallery, upon pillars, to take the prospect and freshness of the garden. At both corners of the further side, by way of return, let there be two delicate or rich cabinets, daintily paved, richly hanged, glazed with crystalline glass, and a rich cupola in the midst; and all other elegancy that may be thought upon. In the upper gallery too, I wish that there may be, if the place will yield it, some fountains running in divers places from the wall, with some fine avoidances. And thus much for the model of the palace; save that you must have, before you come to the front, three courts. A green court plain, with a wall about it, a second court of the same, but more garnished, with little turrets, or rather embellishments, upon the wall; and a third court, to make a square with the front, but not to be built, nor yet enclosed with a naked wall, but enclosed with tarrasses [terraces], leaded aloft, and fairly garnished, on the three sides; and cloistered on the inside, with pillars, and not with arches below. As for offices, let them stand at distance, with some low galleries, to pass from them to the palace itself.

Notes

1 'Momus': the Greek god of mockery, who commented on a house built by Minerva, the goddess of wisdom, that it should have been made on wheels to escape bad neighbours.

2 'Lucullus answered Pompey . . .': Lucullus and Pompey were Roman generals of the first century B.C.; the anecdote is from Plutarch's life of Lucullus, in his *Lives*.

3 'Cicero': Roman orator, philosopher and statesman.

4 'book of Hester': Esther 1. 3–5.

5 John Stow: London, 1603

[*Source*: C.L. Kingsford, editor (1908) *A Survey of London by John Stow* (Oxford, The Clarendon Press) volume 1, p. 127; volume 2, pp. 70–2, 74–5.]

Spitalfields: within these forty years had on both sides fair hedgerows of elm trees, with bridges and easy stiles to pass over into the pleasant fields, very commodious for citizens therein to walk, shoot, and otherwise to recreate and refresh their dulled spirits in the sweet and wholesome air; which is now within a few years made a continual building throughout, of garden-houses and small cottages, and the fields on either side be turned into garden plots, tenter yards,[1] bowling alleys and such like, from Hounsditch in the west so far as Whitechapel and further towards the east. . . .

The Suburbs without the Walls: From this precinct of St Katherine to Wapping in the west, the usual place of execution for hanging of pirates and sea rovers, at the low water mark there to remain till three tides had over-flowed them, was never a house standing within these forty years; but since the gallows being after removed farther off, a continual street, or filthy straight passage, with alleys of small tenements or cottages built, inhabited by sailors' victuallers, along by the river of Thames, almost to Radcliff, a good mile from the Tower . . .

Also without the bars [the gates of the City] both the sides of the street be pestered with cottages and alleys, even up to Whitechapel church and almost half a mile beyond it, into the common field, all which ought to lie open and free for all men. But this common field . . . is so encroached upon by building of filthy cottages and with other purprestors [enroachers], enclosures and laystalls, notwithstanding all Proclamations and Acts of Parliament made to the contrary, that in some places it scarce remaineth a sufficient highway for the meeting of carriages and droves of cattle; much less is there any fair, pleasant or wholesome way for people to walk on foot; which is no small blemish to so famous a city, to have so unsavoury and unseemly an entry or passage thereunto . . .

[In Shoreditch] was one row of proper small houses with gardens for poor decayed people, there placed by the Prior of the . . . hospital, everyone tenant whereof paid one penny rent by the year at Christmas, and dined with the Prior on Christmas Day; after the suppression of the hospital, these houses, for want of reparations, in a few years were so decayed, that it was called Rotten Row, and the poor worn out, for there came no new in their place. The houses, for a small portion of money, were sold from Goddard to Russell, a draper, who new built them and let them out for rent enough, taking also large fines of the tenants, near as much as the houses cost him purchase and building; for he made his bargains so hardly with all men that both carpenter, bricklayer and plasterer were by that work undone. And yet in honour of his name it is now called Russell's Row.

Note

1 'Tenter yards': where cloth is stretched.

6 Essex Inventories

[*Source*: F.W. Steer, editor (1950) *Farm and Cottage Inventories of Mid Essex 1635–1749* (Essex Record Office Publications, 8, published by Essex County Council, Chelmsford), pp. 72–3, 81–4.]

John Burrag, the elder, of Roxwell, husbandman, taken 3rd March 1638.

One bed, one bolster and one pillow,	26s 8d
Two old coverings, one old blanket and an old bolster,	3s 4d
A mortar and a pestle,	1s 8d
Pewter,	4s 6d
His wearing apparel,	11s 0d
Two pillow-beres [i.e. cases]	4s 0d
One chest and one box,	6s 0d
One brass kettle,	13s 8d
Old brass,	6s 8d
One old iron pot and one old pail,	2s 0d
Two old scythes,	8d
Three broken chairs and one old cushion,	1s 0d
Working tools,	6s 8d
One old barrel and one old kneading trough,	2s 0d
Two old bottles, one brush and old, old sickle,	1s 0d

One bedstead and two old tubs, 6s 8d
Received since of Jeremy Danish of White Notley,
being parcel of the goods of the said testator, £5 0s
Total – £9-17-6d
An inventory of the goods of John Burrag, deceased, remaining in his house in Black Notely . . . amount to the value of thirty two shillings . . .

Received in money being in a cupboard at his said house, 19s 9d.
Total – £2-11-9d

Bennett Gue of Writtle, 21 April 1638

In the Chamber–one feather bed and bolster,	£3-15s
Two pair of sheets,	18s 0d
One brass pot,	7s 0d
Two posnets [small cooking pots]	5s 0d
One chest,	6s 8d
One salt box with other small things,	12d
In malt, 28 quarters – bushels,	£60-4s
Six sacks,	16s 0d
His wearing apparel,	40s 0d
In money in his purse,	£13-6-8d
In bonds and other good debts,	£26-0-8d
In desperate debts,	£6-0-0d
Debts due by him to others	10s 10d, 6s 8d
Total –	£113-2-6d

[The appraisers wrongly calculated the total at £112-18s.]

Thomas Rainbeard of Roxwell, weaver, 28 January 1639

In the Hall – one table and a frame, 2 forms, two little join[ed] stools, the bench and bench board, one little plain table, one fire shovel, a pair of tongs, two cob-irons, 2 pot hooks, one pair of bellows, the painted cloths with other implements appraised at £1-13-4d.

In the Parlour – one half-headed bedstead, one old feather bed with stripped feathers, one bolster, one pillow, 2 blankets, one coverlet at £2; one press cupboard, 13s 4d; 20lb weight of pewter, 6s 8d; 3 earthern dishes and 3 glasses at 1s; one join[ed] chest and 2 plain chests, one chair with other implements in the parlour, 13s 4d.

In the Chamber over the Hall – one plain bedstead, one flock-bed, one bolster, one pillow, 2 blankets, with other implements at £1.

In the Buttery – two little barrels, one kneading trough, two little tubs, one little trough, the shelves with other implements at £1.

The Brass – three kettles, one little brass pot, one little posnet, one frying pan, one gridiron at £1-10s.

In the Shop – three old looms with all other implements belonging to them at £5-10s.

One old cow and one bullock at £5.

One pig and the hay, £1.
Linen – 3 pair of sheets, 4 pillow-beres, 4 table napkins, one table-cloth, 2 small towels, £1.
His wearing apparel, £1-6-8d.
Sum' is £22-14-4d.

John Taverner of Writtle, husbandman, 13 February 1639
Two old chests, one bolster, one spade, one cupboard, his wearing apparel with other implements, 10s.
In money £11 14s.
Total – £12-4s.

[Another copy of Taverner's inventory includes a shovel as well as his other goods.]

John George, yeoman of Writtle, 1638 [no other date]
In the Hall – one joined table with a frame, one joined form and 7 joined stools, £1-10s; one square table, 2 foot-stools, one joined stool, 5s; 3 bench boards, 2s 6d; one wainscot press, £1-4s; eight chairs and one form, 6s 8d; two pair of andirons, 5s; two pair of tongs, one fire fork, one fire shovel, one fire iron, 3s 6d; two pair of trammels, 5s; a jack, 10s; one musket, one birding piece with furniture, £1-6-8d; one pound of yarn with other implements, 2s; 5 cushions, one painted cloth with other implements, 8s; one *Book of Martyrs* [by John Foxe], £2; other books, 4s.
In the Parlour – one fair joined bedstead and trundle-bed, £2-6-8d; one feather bed, 2 bolsters, 2 pillows, £3-10s; one green rug, 2 blankets, £1-6-8d; one pair of valance curtains, £1; one wainscot press, one cupboard cloth, 16s; one square table and 3 stools and one box, 14s; one glass case with glasses, 5s; two chairs, 6s 8d; 14 pound of yarn, £1-1s; 71 pound of pewter, £3-5s; 2 brass candlesticks, 6s.
In the Buttery in the Hall – 3 shelves, one little form, one little barrel, 2 jugs, one strainer with other implements, 6s 8d.
In the great Buttery – one cupboard, one livery table, 4s; three hogsheads, 10s; one shelf, one dish case with other implements, 9s.
In the Kitchen – two brass pots and one brass posnet and one iron pot, £2; five brass kettles and one brass pan, £1-10s; 4 brass skillets, 4s 6d; one iron dripping pan, 5 spits, 2 gridirons, 17s; one brass skimmer, one cleaver, one ladle, one mortar, one chopping knife, one basting ladle, 5s 10d; one frying pan, one quern, one pair of andirons, 5s; one dish case, two planks with other implements, 14s 4d.
In the Brew-house – one brewing lid, £1; 4 brewing vessels and one cooler, one under fat, £2-10s; one quern, one cheese press, one kneading trough, one meal trough, one cheese tub with 7 cheese mats and 2 breads, £2-5-6d; one old kettle, one coop with other implements, 11s.
In the Milk-house – one salting trough, 8s; one table and two churns,

10s; two powdering tubs, 6s 8d; seven kimnels [tubs] 11s; one chopping block, one plank, 2 forms, 2 shelves, 4s; 5 old tubs, one butter basket with other implements, 3s 6d.

In the Servants' Chamber – one trundle bed, one boarded bed, 8s; two flock beds, two bolsters, £1-10s; two coverlets [?illegible], two blankets, 16s; two leather bottles, one broome hook [for cutting grass], one pair of winch pins with other implements, 6s 8d.

In the Chamber over the servants' chamber – one table with trestles, 7s; one corn bin, one bushel, one peck, one half peck, 14s 8d; 4 tubs, 3 riddles, one sieve, 5s 6d; eight pitchforks, one dew-rake [for raking stubble], 4 meadow-rakes with weeding hooks, 9s 4d; one two-hand-saw with other iron work, 15s 4d; one old trough, 3 barrels, 4s 6d; two pair of scales and weights, 8s.

In the Cheese-loft – cheese, £3-6s; one cheese plank with trestles, 4s 6d; onions, 3s; shelves, 2s 6d.

In the Chamber over the Parlour – one standing bed, 13s 4d; one feather bed and two feather bolsters, one flock bolster, 2 pillows, £4-15s; curtains and fringe, 10s; one coverlet, one blanket, £1-6-8d; one press, £1-10s; six pair of sheets, £2-8s; six pillow beres, 10s; one dozen of napkins, 6s; half a dozen of napkins, 3s; 5 table cloths, 8s 8d; towels, 3s; 3 wallets, 2s 4d; 3 bags, 1s 6d; one chest, two trunks, 16s; 2 hampers, one basket, 4s 6d.

In the Chamber over the Buttery – one standing bedstead, 13s; one feather bed and bolster, £3-10s; one flock bed and bolster, 13s 4d; one coverlet and blanket, £1-6-8d; curtains and fringe, 13s 4d; one warming pan, 5s; one chair, one trunk, 8s.

In the Chamber over the Kitchen – 2 half-headed beds, 18s; 2 feather beds, 2 bolsters, and 2 flock bolsters, £5; two coverlets, 2 blankets, £1-6-8d; two sheets, 2 chairs, one old trunk, 11s; one one-boarded cradle, 1s 8d; one standing still, 12s.

In the Chamber over the Brew-house – two flax wheels, one coop with other implements, 5s.

In the Yards – one wagon, £4; one load chart, £5; one load cart body, 8s; two dung carts, £2-6-8d; two cart ropes, 6s 8d; six gates, 2 cribs, 5s; wood, 3 load, £1-10s; one pair of winch pins, 2s; 2 ropes, one axe, 5s 10d; 2 scythe snaths and cradles, 1s 6d; one horse block, 2s.

In the Barn – one barn cloth, one shovel, one sieve, 10s; 6 sacks, 2 [winnowing] fans, 14s; five cows and two bullocks, £26; 24 sheep, £12; eight lambs, £2-13-4d.

In the Stable – three cart collars, with their harness, and four pair of harness with their furniture, £1; one cart saddle, one collar with 2 pair of fill-bells [for the shaft of a cart], 5s; four plough collars with harness, one pair of new harness, 9s; [word illegible] bit halters, 8s; three collar halters with iron reins, 2s 6d; one pair of fetters, one pair of couplings, 2 barlings [poles], 2s 6d; one saddle, one bridle, one panel, 12s; one corn hutch and 1 chaff bin, 6s 8d; one plough, one pair of harness and one coulter, 2 plough sha-[rest torn] with chains, 14s. His wearing apparel and money in his purse,

£6-13-4d.
In the Hay-barn – thirty loads of hay, £25.
Four cart horses and one colt, £30; two hogs, £2-10s. Fifteen acres of wheat, £47-10s; eight acres of oats and pease, £16; fourteen acres, barley, pease and oats, £18-13-4d; five acres of fallow in Broadfield, 16s 8d; fourteen acres and a half fallow, Priestfield, £2-8-6d.
Owing the Testator by bond – £100.
Total – £389-4-6d.

7 Edward Moore and his Tenants, 1668

[*Source*: Thomas Heywood, editor (1847) *The Moore Rental* (Chetham Society, Manchester, volume 12), from pp. 11–12, 50–1, 72, 86–9, 96–7, 119.]

Liverpool
Old Hall Street
Take this notice from me: what you expect your tenants should do, let them be well bound to in their leases; otherwise riches and pride is so predominant over them in this town, together with a perfect antipathy they have against all gentlemen – much more your family, in regard they know your interest is always able to curb them – I know this by experience, that they are the most perfidious knaves to their landlords in all England; therefore I charge you, in the name of God, never to trust them . . .

There is no such thing as truth or honesty in such mercenary fellows, but what tends to their own ends. And this observe as a general rule, civility will do no good, but make them contemn you for a kind fool. And likewise observe for a certain rule, although you be never so great enemies, yet, if you be but a justice, and have power in the country, or once mayor of the town, they will be like spaniels at your feet . . ..

Castle Street: Horse Mill
Where you find a great brewer that is none of your tenant, that doth not grind with you, try if they will be your tenant for one or more lands in the field, and for the same oblige them to grind with you. But remember you set as few lands to one tenant as you can, by which you will have lands to satisfy all; and never set more houses to a tenant than one; then will you have more customers and more votes, and upon all occasions more strength by how many tenants you have. Observe the rule above said exactly, and if ever you be mayor and a justice of peace in the country, you may very easily make this mill worth twenty measures a week, which, at a

crown a measure, is five pounds a week, many of your tenants brewing thirty measures a week . . .

Dale Street
If once you are of the council, your oath obliges you to care for the good of the town; and if you be not, your interest is so involved with theirs, that take this as a warning from me, that if they prosper you must thrive, and if the town sink you must drown; so as where a finger be cut, the whole body feels it; so you, in your interest, being a member of that body, it can receive not the least sear either in loss or repute, but your estate or person will be damnified thereby. Therefore, in the name of God, let them love you, and you them, and twenty of the greatest men in the county cannot wrong you; but if you quarrel, you are easily broken. God bless you both. Amen . . .

More Street
So long as the town and you holds closely together, your interest, as a gentleman, to countenance them before the king, the privy council, or in any place or court of England, and their purse, discreetly managed, to back you, I must tell you, (my experience hath found it,) and dare tell to the face of the greatest enemy the town of Liverpool hath in England, we value their malice not of a farthing, for nothing can destroy so great a body but faction . . . This you may boldly and truly say, the corporation and you have lived together this four hundred and odd years . . . There hath not been a parliament this two hundred and fifty years, but one of your ancestors have been burgess for that town; and in man's memory, my father, John Moore, my grandfather, Edward Moore, and my great grandfather, William Moore, have been parliament men. These truths considered, there is nothing like self interest to keep all things well and good correspondence betwixt you. For if you serve God, keep your estate in that town, and be honest to them, let your enemies do what they can, time will weather them . . . If they will have their town preserved, and their privileges kept inviolable, it must be by your two friendships; for if you flee from them and put your interest in the other scale, it is of that weight, of my knowledge, will bring down the balance; I mean as to matter of law, you being the greatest charterer or freeholder in the town . . . The proudest man in Liverpool cannot live there, if he go but into the town field, or indeed anywhere else about the town, but they must trespass upon you; and those that are your friends, you are able to privilege them to fish, fowl, or hunt, for three miles or more end-ways, in despite of any man in England, if God bless the king and the laws; and when wise men understands this, their own self interest will make them great with you . . .

Dorothy Hardman
Make this rent one pound, and twenty pounds fine. They are orphans; be good to them; but if they should die, so that some others would have it, take at least thirty pounds fine, and one pound yearly rent. They pay now three rent hens at Christmas, three days shearing, and old rent 14s. . .

Robert Johnson
An arrant knave, one that grinds from my mill very often. He hath played me twenty slippery tricks; trust him not. Make him pay one pound rent and ten pounds fine, for he is but a poor knave, and mercy must be had to his children; only, for being such a knave, make him to slate his house, as the whole street is besides himself . . .

Fenwick Alley: Widow Harrison
Remember, notwithstanding all my civility of giving this house to her for no fine to speak of, yet when I came to desire but a small part of her back side to make Fenwick Street withal . . . she was worse than a Turk, for I must either give her two children's lives in, or I should not have a foot there, upon which I was forced to grant it, which was better to them than fifty pounds. Thus you may see what you must expect from a tenant, as use them never so well. Therefore, serve God and make much of your own; and as these new leases fall out, raise your old rents according to my directions, that you may have something to live on like other neighbour gentlemen.

8 Richard Baxter: The Poor Husbandman, 1691

[*Source*: F.J. Powicke, editor (1926) 'The Reverend Richard Baxter's Last Treatise', *Bulletin of the John Rylands Library* (Manchester) volume 10, pp. 179–83, 185, 192–7, 210–12, 214–18.]

The old custom was to let lands for lives or for long terms of years, and to take a fine at first and a small yearly rent afterwards; and so, when a man with his marriage portion had taken a lease, he lived comfortably afterward and got somewhat for his children. But now in most countries (counties) the custom is changed into yearly rack-rents; or, if a man takes a lease for many years, it is yearly to pay as much as the tenement is worth and that is as much as any man will give for it . . .

The labour of these men is great, and circular or endless, insomuch that their bodies are almost in constant weariness and their minds in constant care or trouble. Yet for all this I pity not their bodies much because their labour is usually recompensed with health . . .

They are usually so poor that they cannot have time to read a chapter in the Bible or to pray in their families. They come in weary from their labours so that they are fitter to sleep than to read or pray; and their servants are so heavy with early rising and hard working that they cannot attend to what they hear. The soul is here so tied to the body that it hath constant need of its right temperament for its due operation: a heavy body tired with labour is like a tired horse to a traveller or a lute out of tune to a musician or a knife or tool to cut or work with that wants an edge . . .

This ignorant rabble are everywhere the greatest enemies against Godly ministers and people. And if they can but get a literate, malignant prelate or priest out of faction and enmity to encourage them, they will be ready for any mischievous designs. If any would raise an army to extirpate knowledge and religion, the tinkers and sowgaters [sowgelders?] and crate-carriers and beggars and bargemen and all the rabble that cannot read, nor ever use the Bible, will be the forwardest to come in to such a militia. And they will join with those that cry up the Church, if it may but tend to pull down the Church and all serious church-work and interest. If Papists or foreign enemies or rebels would raise insurrections these are fit to serve them, if they get but advantage by some great landlords and hypocrite, malicious clergymen to seduce them. And poverty, causing ignorance, turneth men to barbarians like the wild Americans and then into brutes and then into devils . . .

Among merchants, mercers, drapers, and other corporation-tradesmen, and among weavers, tailors, and such like labourers, yea among poor nailers and such like, there is usually found more knowledge and religion than among the poor *enslaved* husbandmen. I may well say *enslaved* for none are so servilely dependent (save household servants and ambitious expectants) as they are on their landlords. They dare not displease them lest they turn them out of their houses or increase their rents. I believe that their great landlords have more command of them than the King hath . . .

No doubt but the poor themselves are the chief causes of their own calamity. Did not their sin provoke God to afflict them, he would have saved them from oppression . . . But this is no excuse to the oppressors . . . The love of money, the root of all evil, so blindeth and hardeneth them that they can scarce feel any evil in anything that tendeth to increase their wealth. Let them have never so much, they would have more . . . The atheistical misconceit of their property hardeneth them. They think they may please themselves with their own as they list. As if they knew not that there is no absolute propriety but God's. Only He that made and maintaineth all is the absolute owner of all, or anything. No man hath any other propriety than that of a trusted servant or steward, or a child in minority who is at his father's will . . .

When worldlings can enjoy no more for themselves, their last self-deceit is to think that, whatever it cost their poor tenants, they must leave their children as great and dangerous a temptation of riches as they were undone by themselves . . .

Few scruple raising rents to as much as they can get, when poor men, rather than beg and have no dwelling, will promise more than they can pay; and then, with care and toil, make shift as long as they can, and then run away and do so in another country, i.e. county. And so the gentlemen lose more by their racking than they get, whereas if they would abate a third part, and let their tenants live a comfortable life, they might have their rents constantly paid, and have the people's love, and partake of the comforts of those that are benefited or comforted by them . . .

Objection: 'All this is but from the levelling spirit of popularity, and by lifting up the vulgar to take down the nobility and gentry and, at last, the king, and to teach the people to cry down monarchy and cry up a commonwealth.' . . .

Answer: It's such as you that foolishly and fraudulently endeavour to set up democracy or anarchy, while you make the people's burden heavy, and make them groan as the Israelites in Egypt. You force them to discontent and to desire a change. Uneasiness and pain will put men still to look every way about them for some relief and ease . . . There is no standing before the multitude if they be but armed with despair. While you coop them up in your pens, they are, as always, looking to get out. And if a turn of affairs do give them opportunity, you will feel it. Interest ruleth the world. Use the people so well that they feel that peace and obedience and the kingdom's defence is their interest, and you take the most probable way of public safety. But how miserable is that nation that is ridden by such fools as think they ride not well but on a tired horse, because a pampered horse may cast them; and that think a kingdom's best and safest when it is unmanned and serves as slaves in chains and fetters . . .

Advice to Poor Unrelieved Husbandmen

Because the knowledge of the wickedness of the world persuades me that it is not the most of rich landlords that all this will prevail with, yea that there is little hope that they will so much as read it, I will speak to you for yourselves . . .

Understand . . . what advantages your poverty giveth you, above the rich and prosperous worldlings; and then you will find that the benefit will weigh down all your losses.

Think of these following:

Is it not a comfort to be so far conformed to Christ who for our sakes became poor that we, by his poverty, might be made rich . . .

How great a help have you, to escape the too much love of this present world, and to drive you most seriously to seek a better . . .

You little know how great a mercy it is that you have not the constant strong temptations to fleshly pleasures, drunkenness and fornication, and fleshly lust and brutish sensuality, as those have that live with the continual baits of those sins before them, that are every day at a full table of flesh and wines . . .

Add not to your poverty by indiscretion, idleness, or gaming, or excess.

Flatter not yourselves with the thoughts of long life, but spend every day in preparation for death; and in all your business remember whither you are going and where you must dwell for ever. Take not Christ's redemption and the promises of heaven for doubtful things. May the firm belief of heavenly glory possess you souls, how comfortably may you suffer and live and die!

9 The Navigation Act 9 October 1651

[*Source*: S.R. Gardiner editor (1906, third edition) *Constitutional Documents of the Puritan Revolution*, pp. 468–9.]

Goods from Foreign parts by whom to be imported

For the increase of the shipping and the encouragement of the navigation of this nation, which under the good providence and protection of God is so great a means of the welfare and safety of this Commonwealth: be it enacted by this present Parliament, and the authority thereof, that from and after the first day of December, one thousand six hundred fifty and one, and from thence forwards, no goods or commodities whatsoever of the growth, production or manufacture of Asia, Africa or America, or of any part thereof; or of any islands belonging to them, or which are described or laid down in the usual maps or cards of those places, as well of the English plantations as others, shall be imported or brought into this Commonwealth of England, or into Ireland, or any other lands, islands, plantations, or territories to this Commonwealth belonging, or in their possession, in any other ship or ships, vessel or vessels whatsoever, but only in such as do truly and without fraud belong only to the people of this Commonwealth, or the plantations thereof, as the proprietors or right owners thereof; and whereof the master and mariners are also for the most part of them of the people of this Commonwealth, under the penalty of the forfeiture and loss of all the goods that shall be imported contrary to this act; as also of the ship (with all her tackle, guns and apparel) in which the said goods or commodities shall be so brought in and imported; the one moiety to the use of the Commonwealth, and the other moiety to the use and behoof of any person or persons who shall seize the goods or commodities, and shall prosecute the same in any court of record within this Commonwealth . . .

[The Act also laid down that imports from Europe could be carried only in English ships or in ships of the country of origin of the commodities imported; and barred foreign ships from participation in the domestic coastal trade.

After the Restoration, the measure was re-enacted in a strengthened form, applying to exports to the colonies as well as to imports.]

SECTION TWO: KING AND PARLIAMENT 1603–1629

[In 1628, John Pym, who became the dominant figure of the early years of the Long Parliament, managed the impeachment of the clergyman Roger Manwaring (extract 14). Yet Pym also held an official post as a receiver of Crown lands until the 1630s. This is one indication among many that it is misleading to read back the alignments of the civil war into the earlier seventeenth century. Few people in the 1620s saw politics in terms of two 'sides'. Tensions between the King and the 'political nation' can be discerned, however, and some are indicated in this section. In general, the high claims for kingship made by James I (extract 10), existed uncomfortably alongside the belief of many that the 'fundamental law' should govern the monarch's actions (extracts 13 and 14). This belief emerged most strongly in the 1628 Parliament with the opposition to the measures taken by Charles I to organize and finance the war against France and Spain. The Petition of Right was intended to prevent the recurrence of these policies which Parliament considered to be illegal. Specific causes of friction are also illustrated: confusion and disagreement over foreign policy (extract 11); opposition to Charles's attempts to raise revenue without Parliament's consent (extracts 12, 13, and 15); and the early alarm over the King's religious policy (extracts 14 and 15). Most of the extracts show that it is hard to separate economic, religious and political issues. Although this section focuses on Parliament, it is important to emphasize that in the 1620s the burdens of war and frequent Parliaments (and elections) brought many outside the gentry and mercantile classes into political activity. The dilemma over the 'forced loan' was faced by all who paid national taxation, while one historian has suggested that the popular rejoicing that accompanied the Petition of Right was as significant in the long run as the measure itself (Conrad Russell, *Parliaments and English Politics* (Oxford 1979) p. 389).]

10 James I on the Monarchy

[*Source*: James I (1616) *Workes*: (a) pp. 201–3, 208–9; (b) pp. 529–31.]

a The True Law of Free Monarchies, 1598

The kings therefore in Scotland were before any estates or ranks of men within the same, before any Parliaments were holden, or laws made; and by them was the land distributed, which at the first was whole theirs, states erected and discerned, and forms of government devised and established. And so it follows of necessity, that the kings were the authors and makers of the laws, and not the laws of the kings . . .

And according to these fundamental laws already alleged, we daily see that in the Parliament, which is nothing else but the head court of the king and his vassals, the laws are but craved by his subjects and only made by him at their rogation, and with their advice. For albeit the king made daily statutes and ordinances, enjoining such pains thereto as he thinks meet, without any advice of Parliament or estates, yet it lies in the power of no Parliament to make any kind of law or statute without his sceptre be to it, for giving it the force of a law. And although divers changes have been in other countries of the blood royal and kingly house, the kingdom being reft by conquest from one to another as in our neighbour country in England, which was never in ours, yet the same ground of the king's right over all the land, and subjects thereof remaineth alike in all other free monarchies, as well as in this. For when the Bastard of Normandy came into England and made himself king, was it not by force and with a mighty army? Where he gave the law and took none; changed the laws; inverted the order of government; set down the strangers, his followers, in many of the old possessors' rooms as, at this day well appeareth, a great part of the gentlemen of England being come of the Norman blood; and their old laws, which to this day they are ruled by, are written in his language and not in theirs. And yet his successors have with great happiness enjoyed the Crown to this day, whereof the like was also done by all them that conquested them before . . .

And as ye see it manifest, that the king is overlord of the whole land so is he master over every person that inhabiteth the same, having power over the life and death of every one of them. For although a just prince will not take the life of any of his subjects without a clear law, yet the same laws whereby he taketh them are made by himself or his predecessors, and so the power flows always from himself. As by daily experience we see, good and just princes will from time to time make new laws and statutes, adjoining the penalties to the breakers thereof, which, before the law was made, had been no crime to the subject to have committed. Not that I deny the old definition of a king and of a law, which makes the king to be a speaking law and the law a dumb king. For certainly a king that governs not by his law can neither be

[ac]countable to God for his administration nor have a happy and established reign. For albeit it be true that I have at length proved that the king is above the law, as both the author and giver of strength thereto, yet a good king will not only delight to rule his subjects by the law, but even will conform himself in his own actions thereunto, always keeping that ground that the health of the commonwealth be his chief law . . .

Yet is he not bound thereto but of his good will, and for good example giving to his subjects . . . A king at his coronation, or at the entry to his kingdom, willingly promiseth to his people to discharge honourably and truly the office given him by God over them. But presuming that thereafter he breaks his promise unto them never so inexcusab[ly]; the question is, who should be the judge of the break . . . Now in this contract, I say, betwixt the king and his people God is doubtless the only judge, both because to him only the king must make [ac]count of his administration, as is oft said before, as likewise by the oath in the coronation, God is made judge and revenger of the breakers. For in his presence, as only judge of oaths, all oaths ought to be made. Then since God is the only judge betwixt the two parties contractors, the cognition and revenge must only appertain to him . . .

And it is here likewise to be noted, that the duty and allegiance which the people sweareth to their prince, is not only bound to themselves but likewise to their lawful heirs and posterity, the lineal succession of crowns being begun among the people of God, and happily continued in divers Christian commonwealths. So as no objection either of heresy, or whatever private statute or law may free the people from their oath giving to their king, and his succession, established by the old fundamental laws of the kingdom.

b From James's speech to the Parliament 21 March 1610

The state of monarchy is the supremest thing upon earth; for kings are not only God's lieutenants upon earth, and sit upon God's throne, but even by God himself they are called gods. There be three principal similitudes that illustrates the state of monarchy: one taken out of the word of God; and the two other out of the grounds of policy and philosophy. In the Scriptures kings are called gods and so their power after a certain relation compared to the divine power. Kings are also compared to fathers of families for a king is truly *Parens Patriae* [father of his country], the politic father of his people. And lastly, kings are compared to the head of this microcosm of the body of man.

Kings are justly called gods for that they exercise a manner or resemblance of divine power upon earth. For if you will consider the attributes to God, you shall see how they agree in the person of a king. God hath power to create or destroy, make or unmake at his pleasure, to give life or send death, to judge all and to be judged nor accountable to none, to raise low things and to make high things low at his pleasure, and to God are both soul and body due. And the like power have kings:

they make and unmake their subjects; they have power of raising and casting down; of life and of death; judges over all their subjects, and in all causes, and yet accountable to none but God only. They have power to exalt low things, and abase high things, and make of their subjects like men at the chess – a pawn to take a bishop or a knight – and to cry up or down any of their subjects as they do their money. And to the king is due both the affections of the soul and the service of the body of his subjects . . .

A father may dispose of his inheritance to his children at his pleasure, yea, even disinherit the eldest upon just occasions and prefer the youngest, according to his liking; make them beggars or rich at his pleasure; restrain, or banish out of his presence as he finds them give cause of offence; or restore then in favour again with the penitent sinners. So may the king deal with his subjects.

And lastly, as for the head of the natural body, the head hath the power of directing all the members of the body to that use which the judgement in the head thinks most convenient. It may apply sharp cures or cut off corrupt members, let blood in what proportion it thinks fit and as the body may spare, but yet is all this power ordained by God *ad aedificationem, non ad destructionem* [for construction, not destruction] . . .

In the first original of kings, whereof some had their beginning by conquest and some by election of the people, their wills at that time served for law. Yet how soon kingdoms began to be settled in civility and policy, then did kings set down their minds by laws which are properly made by the king only, but at the rogation of the people, the king's grant being obtained thereunto. And so the king became to be *Lex Loquens* [a speaking law] after a sort, binding himself by a double oath to the observation of the fundamental laws of the kingdom: tacitly, as by being a king and so bound to protect as well the people, as the laws of his kingdom; and expressly, by his oath at his coronation. So, as every just king in a settled kingdom is bound to observe that paction [agreement] made to his people by his laws, in framing his government agreeable thereunto, according to that paction which God made with Noah after the deluge, 'Hereafter seed time and harvest, cold and heat, summer and winter, and day and night shall not cease, so long as the earth remains' [Genesis 8.22]. And therefore a king governing in a settled kingdom leaves to be a king and degenerates into a tyrant, as soon as he leaves off to rule according to his laws . . . As for my part, I thank God I have ever given good proof that I never had intention to the contrary, and I am sure to go to my grave with that reputation and comfort, that never king was in all his time more careful to have his laws duly observed, and himself to govern thereafter, than I . . .

I will not be content that my power be disputed upon, but I shall ever be willing to make the reason appear of all my doings, and rule my actions according to my laws.

Frontispiece from James I *Workes* (1616) showing 'Religion and Peace' (Bodleian Library)

11 The House of Commons Debates English Foreign Policy, 26 November 1621

[*Source*: W. Notestein, F.H. Relf, H. Simpson, editors (1935) *Commons Debates 1621* (Yale University Press) volume II, pp. 447–8, 451; volume III, pp. 445–6, 452–5, 471; volume V, pp. 216–17.]

[In 1619 James I's son in law, Frederick, Elector Palatine, accepted the throne of Bohemia, traditionally held by the Austrian Habsburgs. By 1621, Frederick had not only been driven from Bohemia but had lost a large part of the Palatinate which had been invaded by Spanish and Imperial troops. The Emperor had granted the Palatinate to the Elector of Bavaria. The 1621 Parliament was called by James to discuss this situation, but the government's intentions were unclear. The King seems to have hoped that the calling of a Parliament in itself would bring Spain to negotiations, or, failing this, that a limited war in the Palatinate would be enough. Others in the Privy Council and in Parliament wished for a general war against Spain, in alliance with the Dutch, whose truce with the Spaniards ended in March 1621. The Parliament was adjourned in December and dissolved in January 1622, when James took offence at the Commons' advice that Prince Charles should marry a Protestant.

The following extract has been compiled from several contemporary diaries and descriptions of the debate.]

SIR DUDLEY DIGGES [MP for Tewkesbury, linked to the Pembroke-Abbott wing of the Privy Council, which was strongly in favour of a general war. Digges had served as a diplomat, and was one of the most active members of the Commons.]

Let us fall upon what is to be done in this case. And the King hath called us to this end and hath taken hold of our proposition to maintain the army in the Palatinate. The King hath sent £40,000 already; there is a desire of more, for fear that the Count M[ansfield] [the General of Frederick's army in the Palatinate] should revolt and spoil.

Now for the estate of Christendom, look first to religion, where the Catholic and Reformed. Spain and Italy are the centre of defence of the Catholic; we and the islands near, of the Reformation. Now in a balance of state we should have none but the Protestant, as they of the Catholic.[1] Germany is part of the Catholic, France part, Poland all. I leave out Sweden, because part of Germany, Bohemia, Moravia, Silesia are mixed. Brandenburg, Saxony, much true religion before these troubles, now the House of Austria carries the balance as much as they can the other way. So that the Spanish of one, we of the other. The end of the King of Spain is wise, viz. to keep religion as he can and pray God not land too.[2] His Majesty doth so too; but his way is peace, Spain's war . . .

SIR ROBERT PHELIPS [MP for Bath, one of the most important MPs; throughout the 1620s Phelips attempted to perform a balancing act, looking for favour at court, but also trying to keep the support of his Somerset constituents.]

The duty I owe to my King and country calleth me up. The propositions are two: 1, for the present supply; 2, for future war. First the states that hinder our projects are the Catholic states of Germany, and the great wheel of Spain. Those that may help us are the princes of our profession in Germany, the Protestants in France and the United Provinces in the Low Countries. And how unlike[ly] those are to help us. And the German confederates are fallen away, seeing we look aside, and the Low Countries are more naturally pendent upon us. They cannot consist [i.e. subsist] without us, no more than our well being without them. Thirdly, for France, the King doth cut the throats of his own subjects,[3] which God open his eyes to see that the western monarchy [i.e. France] may rise; (the Emperor did say) that he took the Palatinate to restore it. If the King of Spain be our friend we cannot but prosper. The Duke of Bavaria is but a petty prince to the other [i.e. The Emperor and the King of Spain] who will not move but with their motion and centre. First, for the honour of our country. If we had kept the crown on the King of Bohemia's head we had made equal the state of our religion with theirs. Secondly, our abilities, the want of trade and moneys wherein the care of the Lords of the [Privy] Council hath not produced so good effect. We have many enemies even within our own bowels which call us the Protestant faction . . . How bold they are in their disputations, openly hoping great matters. Therefore some course is to be taken with them, lest that we repent too late. Therefore I like of the war and would have it openly proclaimed thereby to unite the princes unto it, but yet I would not presently give too much until our next meeting because our own kingdom may have some content in lieu of their subsidies already given.[4] For we must take care that we give not such advantages for the future, that our country may find fault with us. That this may be made a session, that acts may pass, yet let us not strive to do too much lest as those that strive to go out of a door too fast we hinder one another . . .

SIR EDWARD GILES [MP for Totnes, prominent Devon gentleman.]

. . . We must fortify ourselves both abroad and at home. Papists increase and grow braving and outfacing . . . Their chief aim is at England and in England at the King and the Prince. Consider we have abroad to do with Spain. The walls of our Kingdom are the navy, which being employed as it may be would make us one of the greatest and richest kingdoms in the world . . .

SIR GEORGE HASTINGS [Puritan MP for Leicestershire, brother of the fifth earl of Huntingdon.]

. . . Let the merchants go with swords and bullets and make way through the sea. Let's have 20 or 30,00[0] men in Flanders between this and Christmas, and every parish to maintain a man, which would be an easy charge . . . And the younger brothers and the merchants may stop the passages of Spain and enrich ourselves as the Queen [Elizabeth] did, and enable us to maintain a war. Supply the Palatinate, and that we may have this first proposition soon effected and sith the King will take our sword in his hand, I wish the scabbard were thrown away.

SIR GEORGE MORE [Veteran MP for Surrey, father in law of John Donne; an active member of the Commons.]

We can hardly keep our words within these walls, but our acts must pass out. For religion martyred in Bohemia, wounded in France, scattered in Germany, we sit yet in peace. The King's children in danger to be dispossessed. Their enemies, the Duke Bavaria, Spain the Emperor, the Princes of the Union.[5] . . . Would not this blemish us and our religion, and 'twill grieve me that we should do nothing at this time . . .

MR THOMAS CREW [Puritan MP for Northampton; Speaker in the Parliaments of 1624 and 1625.]

Let the West Indies be open to us as they are shut, we shall be able to keep as many armies as the King of Spain. If we might have some assurance from his Majesty that we might see the Prince matched to one of the same religion, how glad would it make us and willing to give. I say if we might know our adversary, have the Jesuits banished, our bills passed, the pardon enlarged, our ships well furnished, we might promise it now, and some rich citizens lay it down . . .

SIR RICHARD GROSVENOR [Puritan MP for Cheshire.]

. . . To have an army maintained in the Palatinate is the desire of the enemy, because it will be a means to consume us. It is better and easier to begin in the Low Countries. For the manner of the supply, I like no new ways, but think it not seasonable to give till it please the King to let us know our enemy . . .

SIR RICHARD WESTON [Chancellor of the Exchequer, MP for Arundel, Sussex. Weston had recently returned from a diplomatic mission to Brussels and the princes of the Empire.]

. . . The King's counsels have been more for the peace of Christendom than for the affairs of his children. The King owes nothing now to the peace of Christendom, he hath discharged his part. I know this house will not defer to begin their help till the wound be incurable and when confusion will precipitate our counsels . . .

SIR DUDLEY DIGGES

I know not what we have done these two days, but only showed our love, hearts full for want of vent by Parliaments. The Palatinate, Queen, Christendom, Religion.[6] . . .

Notes

1 'a balance of state': Digges is referring to the internal religious composition of the states of Europe.
2 'not land too': i.e. Digges hopes the King of Spain will not keep all the lands he has; another diary recorded this passage as, 'the end of the King of Spain is both to keep all the lands he hath gotten and all that he hath brought to his religion' (*Commons Debates* VI, p. 195).
3 'the King doth cut . . .': a civil war between Louis XIII of France and his Protestant subjects, the Huguenots, broke out in spring 1621.
4 'subsidies already given': James was granted two subsidies in the first session of the Parliament.
5 'Princes of the Union': the Union of the Protestant princes of the Empire had withdrawn from helping Frederick in spring 1621.
6 Modern historians disagree over the significance of these debates: for contrasting interpretations see Conrad Russell, *Parliaments and English Politics 1621–1629* (1979) and Simon Adams, 'Foreign Policy and the Parliaments of 1621 and 1624' in Kevin Sharpe, editor, *Faction and Parliament* (1978).

12 Clarendon: The 'Forced Loan'

[*Source*: W. Dunn Macray, editor (1888) *The History of the Rebellion and Civil Wars in England* by Edward, Earl of Clarendon (Oxford, The Clarendon Press) volume I, p. 6.]

In the second Parliament [1626] there was a mention, and intention declared, of granting five subsidies, a proportion (how contemptible soever in respect of the pressures now every day imposed) never before heard of in Parliament. And that meeting being, upon very unpopular and unplausible reasons, immediately dissolved, those five subsidies were exacted throughout the whole kingdom with the same rigour, as if, in truth, an Act had passed to that purpose. And very many gentlemen of prime quality, in all the several counties of England, were, for refusing to pay the same, committed to prison, with great rigour and extraordinary circumstances. And could it be imagined, that these men would meet again in a free convention of Parliament without a sharp and severe expostulation, and inquisition into their own right, and the power that had imposed upon that right? And yet all these provocations, and many other, almost of as large an extent, produced no other resentment than the Petition of Right, (of no prejudice to the Crown,) which was likewise purchased at the price of five more subsidies, and, in a very short time after that supply granted, that Parliament was likewise, with strange circumstances of passion on all sides, dissolved.

13 The Petition of Right, June 1628

[*Source*: S.R. Gardiner (1906, Third edition) *Constitutional Documents of the Puritan Revolution*, pp. 66–70.]

To the King's Most Excellent Majesty.

Humbly show unto our Sovereign Lord the King, the Lords Spiritual and Temporal, and Commons in Parliament assembled, that . . . your subjects have inherited this freedom, that they should not be compelled to contribute to any tax, tallage, aid, or other like charge, not set by common consent in Parliament.

Yet nevertheless, of late divers commissions directed to sundry Commissioners in several counties with instructions have issued, by means whereof your people have been in divers places assembled, and required to lend certain sums of money unto your Majesty, and many of them upon their refusal so to do, have had an oath administered unto them, not warrantable by the laws or statutes of this realm, and have been constrained to become bound to make appearance and give attendance before your Privy Council, and in other places, and others of them have been therefore imprisoned, confined, and sundry other ways molested and disquieted: and divers other charges have been laid and levied upon your people in several counties, by Lords Lieutenants, Deputy Lieutenants, Commissioners for Musters, Justices of Peace and others, by command or direction from your Majesty or your Privy Council, against the laws and free customs of this realm.

And where also by the statute called, 'The Great Charter of the Liberties of England,' it is declared and enacted, that no freeman may be taken or imprisoned or be disseised of his freeholds or liberties, or his free customs, or be outlawed or exiled; or in any manner destroyed, but by the lawful judgment of his peers, or by the law of the land. . . .

Nevertheless, against the tenor of the said statutes, and other the good laws and statutes of your realm, to that end provided, divers of your subjects have of late been imprisoned without any cause showed, and when for their deliverance they were brought before your Justices, by your Majesty's writs of Habeas Corpus, there to undergo and receive as the Court should order, and their keepers commanded to certify the causes of their detainer; no cause was certified, but that they were detained by your Majesty's special command, signified by the Lords of your Privy Council, and yet were returned back to several prisons, without being charged with anything to which they might make answer according to the law.

And whereas of late great companies of soldiers and mariners have been dispersed into divers counties of the realm, and the inhabitants against their wills have been compelled to receive them into their houses, and there to suffer them to sojourn, against the laws and customs of this realm, and to the great grievance and vexation of the people.

And whereas also by authority of Parliament, in the 25th year of the reign of King Edward the Third, it is declared and enacted, that no man shall be forejudged of life or limb against the form of the Great Charter, and the law of the land . . . nevertheless of late divers commissions under your Majesty's Great Seal have issued forth, by which certain persons have been assigned and appointed Commissioners with power and authority to proceed within the land, according to the justice of martial law against such soldiers and mariners, or other dissolute persons joining with them . . .

They do therefore humbly pray your Most Excellent Majesty, that no man hereafter be compelled to make or yield any gift, loan, benevolence, tax, or such like charge, without common consent by Act of Parliament; and that none be called to make answer, or take such oath, or to give attendance, or be confined, or otherwise molested or disquieted concerning the same, or for refusal thereof; and that no freeman, in any such manner as is before-mentioned, be imprisoned or detained; and that your Majesty will be pleased to remove the said soldiers and mariners, and that your people may not be so burdened in time to come; and that the foresaid commissions for proceeding by martial law, may be revoked and annulled; and that hereafter no commissions of like nature may issue forth to any person or persons whatsoever, to be executed as aforesaid, lest by colour of them any of your Majesty's subjects be destroyed or put to death, contrary to the laws and franchise of the land.

All which they most humbly pray of your Most Excellent Majesty, as their rights and liberties according to the laws and statutes of this realm: and that your Majesty would also vouchsafe to declare, that the awards, doings, and proceedings to the prejudice of your people, in any of the premises, shall not be drawn hereafter into consequence or example: and that your Majesty would be also graciously pleased, for the further comfort and safety of your people, to declare your royal will and pleasure, that in the things aforesaid all your officers and ministers shall serve you, according to the laws and statutes of this realm, as they tender the honour of your Majesty, and the prosperity of this kingdom.

[The King's first answer to the petition came on 2 June:]

The King willeth that right be done according to the laws and customs of the realm; and that the statutes be put in due execution, that his subjects may have no cause to complain of any wrong or oppressions, contrary to their just rights and liberties, to the preservation whereof he holds himself as well obliged as of his prerogative.

[This answer was not acceptable to parliament, which was only satisfied when, on 7 June, the King answered with the words of the Royal Assent to a bill.]

14 John Pym: The Laws of England, 4 June 1628

[*Source*: John Rushworth (1721) *Historical Collections* volume 1, p. 596.]

[An extract from Pym's speech at the impeachment of Dr Roger Manwaring who had preached that the King's power was not limited by human law, and that the people were obliged by God's law to pay all taxes (and specifically to pay the forced loan). Manwaring was convicted, but in the interval between the 1628 and 1629 sessions of the Parliament he was pardoned by Charles and became a royal chaplain.]

The law of England, whereby the subject was exempted from taxes and loans not granted by common consent of Parliament, was not introduced by any statute, or by any charter or sanction of princes, but was the ancient and fundamental law, issuing from the first frame and constitution of the kingdom . . . There are plain footsteps of those laws in the government of the Saxons; they were of that vigour and force as to overlive the Conquest, nay, to give bounds and limits to the Conqueror, whose victory gave him first hope. But the assurance and possession of the Crown he obtained by composition, in which he bound himself to observe these and the other ancient laws and liberties of the kingdom, which afterwards he likewise confirmed by oath at his coronation. From him the said obligation descended to his successors. It is true they have been often broken, they have been often confirmed by charters of kings, by acts of parliaments, but the petitions of the subjects upon which those charters and acts were founded were ever petitions of right, demanding their ancient and due liberties, not suing for any new . . .

15 The Protestation of the Commons, 2 March 1629

[*Source*: S.R. Gardiner editor (1906, Third edition) *Constitutional Documents of the Puritan Revolution*, pp. 82–3.]

1 Whosoever shall bring in innovation of religion, or by favour or countenance seek to extend or introduce Popery or Arminianism, or other opinion disagreeing from the true and orthodox Church, shall be reputed a capital enemy to this Kingdom and Commonwealth.

2 Whosoever shall counsel or advise the taking and levying of the

subsidies of Tonnage and Poundage, not being granted by Parliament, or shall be an actor or instrument therein, shall be likewise reputed an innovator in the Government, and a capital enemy to the Kingdom and Commonwealth.

3 If any merchant or person whatsoever shall voluntarily yield, or pay the said subsidies of Tonnage and Poundage, not being granted by Parliament, he shall likewise be reputed a betrayer of the liberties of England, and an enemy to the same.'

SECTION THREE: BEN JONSON, COURT AND COUNTRY

[Both contemporaries and modern historians have regarded the division between 'court' and 'country' as fundamental in the early seventeenth century. The country believed the court was corrupt, wasteful, innovative and, under Charles I, popishly inclined, while the country was innocent, frugal and the upholder of traditional standards in government, religion and social relationships. The division existed within the minds of individuals as much as between different groups however – as these Jonson poems suggest. 'Penshurst' is one of the most famous expositions of country ideals, while the 'Expostulation' deals with the typical manifestation of court culture, the masque. Jonson's quarrel with the architect and designer, Inigo Jones, led him to write bitterly of masques but he had collaborated with Jones in their production for some twenty-five years.]

16 To Penshurst

[*Source*: Ian Donaldson editor (1975) Ben Jonson, *Poems*, pp. 87–91.]

[Probably written before the death of Prince Henry in 1612 (see line 77). Penshurst, in Kent, was the home of Robert Sidney (1563–1626) Earl of Leicester and younger brother of the poet Sir Philip Sidney.]

Thou art not, Penshurst, built to envious show
  Of touch[1] or marble, nor canst boast a row
Of polished pillars, or a roof of gold;
  Thou hast no lantern whereof tales are told,
Or stair, or courts; but stand'st an ancient pile,
  And these grudged at, art reverenced the while.
Thou joy'st in better marks, of soil, of air,
  Of wood, of water; therein thou art fair.
Thou hast thy walks for health as well as sport:
  Thy Mount, to which the dryads do resort,
Where Pan and Bacchus their high feasts have made,
  Beneath the broad beech and the chestnut shade;
That taller tree, which of a nut was set
  At his great birth, where all the muses met.[2]
There, in the writhed bark, are cut the names
  Of many a sylvan taken with his flames;
And thence the ruddy satyrs oft provoke
  The lighter fauns to reach thy lady's oak.
Thy copse, too, named of Gamage,[3] thou hast there,
  That never fails to serve the seasoned deer
When thou wouldst feast or exercise thy friends.
  The lower land, that to the river bends,
Thy sheep, thy bullocks, kine and calves do feed;
  The middle grounds thy mares and horses breed.
Each bank doth yield thee conies, and the tops,
  Fertile of wood, Ashour and Sidney's copse,
To crown thy open table, doth provide
  The purpled pheasant with the speckled side;
The painted partridge lies in every field,
  And for thy mess is willing to be killed.
And if the high-swoll'n Medway fail thy dish,
  Thou hast thy ponds that pay thee tribute fish:
Fat, aged carps, that run into thy net;
  And pikes, now weary their own kind to eat,
As loath the second draught or cast to stay,
  Officiously, at first, themselves betray;
Bright eels, that emulate them, and leap on land
  Before the fisher, or into his hand.

Then hath thy orchard fruit, thy garden flowers,
  Fresh as the air and new as are the hours:
The early cherry, with the later plum,
  Fig, grape and quince, each in his time doth come;
The blushing apricot and woolly peach
  Hang on thy walls, that every child may reach.
And though thy walls be of the country stone,
  They're reared with no man's ruin, no man's groan;
There's none that dwell about them wish them down,
  But all come in, the farmer and the clown,
And no one empty-handed, to salute
  Thy lord and lady, though they have no suit.
Some bring a capon, some a rural cake,
  Some nuts, some apples; some that think they make
The better cheeses, bring 'em; or else send
  By their ripe daughters, whom they would commend
This way to husbands; and whose baskets bear
  An emblem[4] of themselves, in plum or pear.
But what can this (more than express their love)
  Add to thy free provisions, far above
The need of such? whose liberal board doth flow
  With all that hospitality doth know!
Where comes no guest but is allowed to eat
  Without his fear, and of thy lord's own meat;
Where the same beer and bread and self-same wine
  That is his lordship's shall be also mine;
And I not fain to sit, as some this day
  At great men's tables, and yet dine away.
Here no man tells my cups, nor, standing by,
  A waiter, doth my gluttony envy,
But gives me what I call, and lets me eat;
  He knows below he shall find plenty of meat,
Thy tables hoard not up for the next day.
  Nor, when I take my lodging, need I pray
For fire or lights or livery: all is there,
  As if thou then wert mine, or I reigned here;
There's nothing I can wish, for which I stay.
  That found King James, when, hunting late this way
With his brave son, the Prince, they saw thy fires
  Shine bright on every hearth as the desires
Of thy Penates had been set on flame
  To entertain them; or the country came
With all their zeal to warm their welcome here.
  What (great, I will not say, but) sudden cheer
Didst thou then make 'em! and what praise was heaped
  On thy good lady then! who therein reaped
The just reward of her high housewifery:
  To have her linen, plate, and all things nigh

When she was far; and not a room but dressed
As if it had expected such a guest!
These, Penshurst, are thy praise, and yet not all.
Thy lady's noble, fruitful, chaste withal;
His children thy great lord may call his own,
A fortune in this age but rarely known.
They are and have been taught religion; thence
Their gentler spirits have sucked innocence.
Each morn and even they are taught to pray
With the whole household, and may every day
Read in their virtuous parents' noble parts
The mysteries of manners, arms and arts.
Now, Penshurst, they that will proportion thee
With other edifices, when they see
Those proud, ambitious heaps, and nothing else,
May say, their lords have built, but thy lord dwells.

Notes

[Only brief notation has been provided. The Donaldson edition gives a full commentary, including details of Jonson's classical models, and comparisons with other 'country house' poetry of the seventeenth century. Numbers in brackets refer to the lines of the poem.]

1 (2) 'touch': black marble.
2 (13–14) 'That taller tree . . .': an oak at Penshurst is said to have grown from an acorn planted on the day of Sir Philip Sidney's birth in 1554.
3 (19) 'Gamage': the maiden name of Leicester's wife.
4 (56) 'emblem', of sexual maturity.

17 An Expostulation with Inigo Jones

[*Source*: Donaldson editor (1975) Jonson, *Poems*, pp. 319–24.]

[Written in or shortly after July 1631. The quarrel between Jonson and Jones was superficially about precedence – whose name should appear first on the title pages of the court masques on which they collaborated; but Jonson presents it as a fundamental division over the relative importance of the visual and the verbal elements in the masque.]

Master Surveyor,[1] you that first began
From thirty pound in pipkins, to the man
You are: from them leaped forth an architect
Able to talk of Euclid, and correct
Both him and Archimede; damn Archytas,[2]
The noblest engineer that ever was;

Control Ctesibius,[3] overbearing us
With mistook names out of Vitruvius;[4]
Drawn Aristotle on us: and thence shown
How much architectonike[5] is your own!
(Whether the building of the stage or scene,
Or making of the properties it mean,
Vizors or antics, or it comprehend
Something your sirship doth not yet intend!)
By all your titles and whole style at once
Of Tire-man, Mountebank, and Justice[6] Jones
I do salute you! Are you fitted yet?
Will any of these express your place or wit?
Or are you so ambitious 'bove your peers,
You would be an asinigo,[7] by your ears?
Why, much good do't you! Be what beast you will,
You'll be, as Langley said, an Inigo still.[8]
What makes your wretchedness to bray so loud
In town and court; are you grown rich and proud?
Your trappings will not change you: change your mind.
No velvet sheath you wear will alter kind;
A wooden dagger[9] is a dagger of wood,
Though gold or ivory hafts would make it good.
What is the cause you pomp it so? (I ask)
And all men echo, You have made a masque.
I chime that too; And I have met with those
That do cry up the machine, and the shows,
The majesty of Juno in the clouds,
And peering-forth of Iris in the shrouds![10]
The ascent of Lady Fame, which none could spy,
Not those that sided her, Dame Poetry,
Dame History, Dame Architecture, too,
And Goody Sculpture, brought with much ado
To hold her up. O shows! Shows! Mighty shows!
The eloquence of masques! What need of prose,
Or verse, or sense, to express immortal you?
You are the spectacles of state! 'Tis true
Court hieroglyphics, and all arts afford
In the mere perspective of an inch-board.
You ask no more than certain politic eyes,
Eyes that can pierce into the mysteries
Of many colours, read them, and reveal
Mythology there painted on slit deal.
Oh, to make boards to speak! There is a task!
Painting and carpentry are the soul of masque.
Pack with your peddling poetry to the stage:
This is the money-get, mechanic age!
To plant the music where no ear can reach,
Attire the persons as no thought can teach

Sense what they are: which, by a specious, fine
Term of the architects, is called *design*!
But in the practised truth destruction is
Of any art beside what he calls his.
Whither, O whither will this tire-man grow?
His name is εκευοπόιος [11] we all know,
The maker of the properties, in sum,
The scene, the engine! But he now is come
To be the music-master, fabler, too;
He is, or would be, main Dominus Do-
All in the work! And so shall still, for Ben:
Be Inigo the whistle, and his men.
He's warm on his feet[12] now, he says, and can
Swim without cork:[13] why, thank the good Queen Anne.[14]
I am too fat to envy him; he too lean
To be worth envy. Henceforth I do mean
To pity him, as smiling at his feat
Of lantern-lurry:[15] with fuliginous[16] heat
Whirling his whimsies, by a subtlety
Sucked from the veins of shop-philosophy.
What would he do now, giving his mind that way,
In presentation of some puppet-play
Should but the king his justice-hood employ
In setting-forth of such a solemn toy?
How would he firk,[17] like Adam Overdo
Up and about, dive into cellars, too,[18]
Disguised, and thence drag forth enormity:
Discover vice, commit absurdity
Under the moral?[19] Show he had a pate
Moulded, or stroked up, to survey a state?
O wise surveyor! Wiser architect!
But wisest Inigo! Who can reflect
On the new priming of thy old sign-posts,
Reviving with fresh colours the pale ghosts
Of thy dead standards; or (with miracle) see
Thy twice-conceived, thrice-paid-for imagery
And not fall down before it, and confess
Almighty architecture: who no less
A goddess is, than painted cloth, deal-boards,
Vermillion, lake, or cinnabar[20] affords
Expression for; with that unbounded line
Aimed at in thy omnipotent design.
What poesy e'er was painted on a wall
That might compare with thee? What story shall,
Of all the Worthies, hope to outlast thy one,
So the materials be of Purbeck stone?
Live long the Feasting Room![21] And ere thou burn
Again, thy architect to ashes turn!

Whom not ten fires nor a parliament can,
With all remonstrance, make an honest man.

Notes

Detailed references to the particular masques discussed by Jonson will be found in the Donaldson edition. Numbers in brackets refer to the lines of the poem.

1 (1) 'Master Surveyor': Jones became Surveyor of the King's Works in 1615.
2 (5) 'Archytas': Greek philosopher and mathematician of the fifth century B.C.
3 (7) 'Ctesibius': Alexandrian engineer of the third century B.C.
4 (8) 'Vitruvius': Roman architect and writer of the first century B.C.
5 (10) 'architectonike': the term used by Aristotle to denote the ultimate end to which all knowledge is directed, i.e. virtuous action.
6 (16) 'Justice': Jones was a Justice of the Peace in Westminster.
7 (20) 'asinigo': little ass (from the Spanish).
8 (22) 'Langley': Francis Langley, builder of the Swan theatre, London; 'Inigo': a pun on the Italian word for wicked or unrighteous.
9 (27) 'wooden dagger': traditionally carried by the Vice in masque interludes.
10 (34) 'shrouds': fly-ropes.
11 (60) '*εκευοποίος* : maker of stage properties.
12 (67) 'warm on his feet': doing nicely.
13 (68) 'Swim without cork': get on without the help of others.
14 (68) 'Queen Anne', wife of James I, patronized the masque but also gave Jones several architectural commissions, particularly that for the Queen's House, Greenwich.
15 (72) 'lantern-lurry': an effect of moving lights.
16 (72) 'fuliginous': sooty, but also thick, poisonous vapours that trouble the head, and hence it refers to Jones himself as well as to his invention.
17 (79) 'firk': move briskly.
18 (79–80) 'Adam Overdo . . .': in 1630 Jones and other Westminster JPs were empowered to inspect houses for signs of plague; Jonson compares this to the officiousness of Justice Overdo in his play *Bartholomew Fair.*
19 (83) 'Under the moral': commissioned by the King.
20 (94) 'cinnabar': crimson.
21 (101) 'the Feasting Room': the Banqueting House, Whitehall, which was rebuilt by Jones after it had been burnt down in 1619.

SECTION FOUR: THE PERSONAL RULE OF CHARLES I 1629–1640

[After 1629 Charles I resolved to rule without Parliament. He made peace with Spain and France and resorted to a series of expedients to finance his government. The most profitable, and ultimately the most controversial of these was ship money, traditionally an emergency levy from coastal areas only. From 1635, however, ship money was raised annually from all the counties of England. In 1637 the legality of the levy was challenged by John Hampden, a Buckinghamshire gentleman, but in 1638 the judges decided narrowly in the King's favour (extracts 21 and 22). Charles also increased his revenue from wardship to the alarm of the country's leading landowners (extracts 19 and 20). If a minor inherited land which was held from the King by feudal tenure, the King gained custody of the heir (the ward) and the estates, and had the right to arrange the ward's marriage. The King's promotion of Laud's religious policies, and the enforcement of Laudian ceremonial and doctrine through the ecclesiastical court of High Commission (extract 26) and the prerogative court of Star Chamber (extract 25) probably did the most to alienate the staunchly Protestant gentry, fearful of the growth of popery. Prynne, Burton and Bastwick, cruelly punished in Star Chamber for attacks on the bishops like Bastwick's *Letany* (extracts 24 and 25), became popular martyrs, cheered on their way to remote prisons. All three men had a history of suffering under the Laudian regime: Bastwick and Prynne were in prison when they wrote the works for which they were punished in 1637, while Prynne had already had his ears cropped by the Star Chamber in 1634 for his work, *Histriomastix*, an attack on the theatre. Laud's promotion of bishops to high secular office especially offended men who felt their own social positions qualified them for political power (extracts 27 and 28). Finally we include an extract from the Canons issued by the 1640 Canterbury Convocation (the clerical equivalent of a Parliament) which vividly illustrates the links between Laudian religion and divine right monarchy. (For the reaction to these religious developments in 1640 see extracts 30 and 33, in Section Five.]

18 John Selden: The King and the Law

[*Source*: *Table Talk: Being the Discourses of John Selden, Esq.* (1689), p. 29.]

The king's oath is not security enough for our property, for he swears to govern according to law; now the judges, they interpret the law, and what judges can be made to do, we know.

19 Clarendon

[*Source*: W. Dunn Macray, editor (1888) *The History of the Rebellion and Civil Wars in England* by Edward Earl of Clarendon (Oxford, The Clarendon Press) volume I, pp. 198–9.]

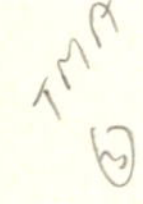

Besides being Chancellor of the Exchequer, he [i.e. Francis, Lord Cottington] was likewise Master of the Wards, and had raised the revenue of that court to the King to be much greater than it had ever been before his administration; by which husbandry, all the rich families of England, of noblemen and gentlemen, were exceedingly incensed, and even indevoted to the Crown, looking upon what the law had intended for their protection and preservation to be now applied to their destruction; and therefore resolved to take the first opportunity to ravish that jewel out of the royal diadem, though it was fastened there by the known law upon as unquestionable a right as the subject enjoyed any thing that was most his own.

20 Bishop Goodman

[*Source*: Godfrey Goodman (1839) *The Court of King James the First* volume I, p. 271.]

All the lands in the kingdom either mediately or immediately were held from the crown; insomuch that I heard a very honest and a very understanding man say, that he heard my Lord Chancellor Egerton deliver this in Chancery,–that if men's estates were looked into, he did not know that man in all England whose land was not liable to wardship. And here the Court of Wards was such a tie upon the subject as no king in the world ever had the like: and how much this Court of Wards hath been improved may appear by this, – that the register's office there was of six times greater value than it was. At my knowledge, a feodary's[1] place, which in my remembrance was but the place of a servant, and for which was usually given not above thirty or forty pieces, came after to be sold for three or four hundred pounds; and, as I have been credibly informed, the last master of the Wards took seven hundred pounds.

Note

1 feodary: the official who undertook the court's work in each county.

Ship Money

21 The Hampden Case

[*Source*: S.R. Gardiner (1906) *Constitutional Documents of the Puritan Revolution*, pp. 112, 114–15, 121–3.]

[From the speech of one of Hampden's lawyers, Oliver St John, who became one of the leaders of Parliament during the civil war (November 1637).]

And as without the assistance of his Judges, who are his settled counsel at law, His Majesty applies not the law and justice in many cases unto his subjects; so likewise in other cases: neither is this sufficient to do it without the assistance of his great Council in Parliament; if an erroneous judgment was given before the Statute of 27 Eliz. in the King's Bench, the King could not relieve his grieved subjects any way but by Writ of Error in Parliament; neither can he out of Parliament alter the old laws, nor make new, or make any naturalizations or legitimations, nor do some other things; and yet is the Parliament His Majesty's Court too, as well as other his Courts of Justice. It is His Majesty that gives life and being to that, for he only summons, continues, and dissolves it, and he by his *le volt* [the words of the royal consent to Parliamentary legislation] enlivens all the actions of it; and after the dissolution of it, by supporting his Courts of Justice, he keeps them still alive, by putting them in execution: and although in the Writ of Wast, and some other writs, it is called *Commune Concilium Regni* [The Common Council of the kingdom], in respect that the whole kingdom is representatively there; and secondly, that the whole kingdom have access thither in all things that concern them, other Courts affording relief but in special causes; and thirdly, in respect that the whole kingdom is interested in, and receive benefit by the laws and things there passed; yet it is *Concilium Regni* no otherwise than the Common Law is *Lex Terrae* [the law of the land], that is *per modum Regis* [through the means of the King] whose it is; if I may so term it in a great part, even in point of interest, as he is the head of the Commonwealth, and whose it is wholly in trust for the good of the whole body of the realm; for he alone is trusted with the execution of it. . . .

My Lords, the Parliament, as it is best qualified and fitted to make this supply for some of each rank, and that through all the parts of the kingdom being there met, His Majesty having declared the danger, they best knowing the estates of all men within the realm, are fittest, by comparing the danger and men's estates together, to proportion the aid accordingly.

And secondly, as they are fittest for the preservation of that fundamental propriety which the subject hath in his lands and goods, because each subject's vote is included in whatsoever is there done; so that it cannot be done otherwise, I shall endeavour to prove to your Lordships both by reason and authority.

My first reason is this, that the Parliament by the law is appointed as the ordinary means for supply upon extraordinary occasions, when the ordinary supplies will not do it: if this in the writ therefore may, without resorting to that, be used, the same argument will hold as before in resorting to the extraordinary, by [exclusion?] of the ordinary, and the same inconvenience follow.

My second reason is taken from the actions of former Kings in this of the defence.

The aids demanded by them, and granted in Parliament, even for this purpose of the defence, and that in times of imminent danger, are so frequent, that I will spare the citing of any of them: it is rare in a subject, and more in a prince, to ask and take that of gift, which he may and ought to have of right, and that without so much as a *salvo*, or declaration of his right. . . .

My Lords, it appears not by anything in the writ [for ship money] that any war at all was proclaimed against any State, or that if any His Majesty's subjects had taken away the goods of any prince's subjects in Christendom, but that the party might have recovered them before your Lordships in any His Majesty's Courts; so that the case in the first place is, whether in times of peace His Majesty may, without consent in Parliament, alter the property of the subject's goods for the defence of the realm.

[From the argument of Sir Robert Berkeley, Justice of the King's Bench, giving judgment in the Hampden case, 1638.]

Where Mr Holborne [one of Hampden's lawyers] supposed a fundamental policy in the creation of the frame of this kingdom, that in case the monarch of England should be inclined to exact from his subjects at his pleasure, he should be restrained, for that he could have nothing from them, but upon a common consent in Parliament.

He is utterly mistaken herein. I agree the Parliament to be a most ancient and supreme court, where the King and Peers, as judges, are in person, and the whole body of the Commons representatively. There Peers and Commons may, in a fitting way, *parler lour ment* [speak their mind] and show the estate of every part of the kingdom; and amongst other things, make known their grievances (if there be any) to their sovereign, and humbly petition him for redress.

But the former fancied policy I utterly deny. The law knows no such king-yoking policy. The law is of itself an old and trusty servant of the King's; it is his instrument or means which he useth to govern his people by . . .

There are two maxims of the law of England, which plainly disprove Mr Holborne's supposed policy. The first is, 'That the King is a person trusted with the state of the commonwealth.' The second of these maxims is, 'That the King cannot do wrong.' Upon these two maxims the *jura summae majestatis* [highest rights of majesty] are grounded, with which none but the King himself (not his high court of Parliament without leave) hath to meddle, as, namely, war and peace, value of coin, Parliament at pleasure, power to dispense with penal laws, and divers others; amongst which I range these also, of regal power to command provision (in case of necessity) of means from the subjects, to be adjoined to the King's own means for the defence of the commonwealth, for the preservation of the *salus reipublicae* [health of the state]. Otherwise I do not understand how the King's Majesty may be said to have the majestical right and power of a free monarch . . .

Though I have gone already very high, I shall go yet to a higher contemplation of the fundamental policy of our laws: which is this, that the King of mere right ought to have, and the people of mere duty are bound to yield unto the King, supply for the defence of the kingdom. And when the Parliament itself doth grant supply in that case, it is not merely a benevolence of the people, but therein they do an act of justice and duty to the King. I know the most solemn form of Parliament, and of the humble expression of the Commons, of their hearty affection and goodwill to their King, in tendering to him their bills of subsidies or fifteenths.

22 Clarendon

[*Source*: Macray, editor, *History of the Rebellion* volume I, pp. 85–7.]

Lastly, for a spring and magazine that should have no bottom, and for an everlasting supply of all occasions, a writ is framed in a form of law, and directed to the sheriff of every county of England, to provide a ship of war for the King's service, and to send it, amply provided and fitted, by such a day to such a place; and with that writ were sent to each sheriff instructions that, instead of a ship, he should levy upon his county such a sum of money, and return the same to the Treasurer of the Navy for his majesty's use, with direction in what manner he should proceed against such as refused: and from hence that tax had the denomination of *Ship-Money*, a word of a lasting sound in the memory of this kingdom; by which for some years really accrued the yearly sum of two hundred thousand pounds to the King's coffers, and was in truth the only project that was accounted to his own service. And, after the continued receipt of it for four years together, was at last (upon the refusal of a private gentleman to pay thirty shillings as his share) with great solemnity publicly argued before all the judges of England in the Exchequer-chamber, and by the major part of them the King's right to impose asserted, and the tax adjudged lawful; which judgment proved of more advantage and credit to the gentleman condemned, Mr Hambden, than to the King's service. . .

It is notoriously known that pressure was borne with much more cheerfulness before the judgment for the King than ever it was after; men before pleasing themselves with doing somewhat for the King's service, as a testimony of their affection, which they were not bound to do; many really believing the necessity, and therefore thinking the burden reasonable; others observing that the access to the King was of importance, when the damage to them was not considerable; and all assuring themselves that when they should be weary, or unwilling to continue the payment, they might resort to the law for relief and find it. But when they heard this demanded in a court of law as a right, and found it by sworn judges of the law adjudged so, upon such grounds and reasons as every stander-by was able to swear was not law, and so had lost the pleasure and delight of being kind and dutiful to the King; and instead of giving were required to pay, and by a logic that left no man any thing which he might call his own; they no more looked upon it as the case of one man but the case of the kingdom, nor as an imposition laid upon them by the King but by the judges; which they thought themselves bound in conscience to the public justice not to submit to.

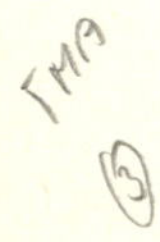

23 John Selden: Puritans and Arminians

[*Source*: *Table Talk* (1689), p. 20.]

The Puritans who will allow no freewill at all, but God does all, yet will allow the subject his liberty to do, or not to do, notwithstanding the King, the God upon earth. The Arminians, who hold we have freewill, yet say, when we come to the King, there must be all obedience, and no liberty to be stood for.

24 John Bastwick: Laud

[*Source*: *The Letany of John Bastwick* (1637), pp. 5–6.]

But see the prelate of Canterbury, in his ordinary garb, riding from Croydon to Bagshot, with forty or fifty gentlemen, well mounted, attending upon him; two or three coaches, with four and six horses apiece in them, all empty, waiting on him; two or three dainty steeds of pleasure, most rich in trappings and furniture, likewise led by him; and wherever he comes, his gentlemen ushers and his servants crying out, 'Room, room for my lord's grace. Gentlemen, be uncovered, my lord's grace is coming.' And all this is true, if *vox populi* and fame may be credited, which is a good plea in their court. Now what, I pray, could be done more to the King's majesty, or Queen, or the Prince of Wales, or to the royal blood?

Behold him, I beseech you again, not only in his journeys, but in his hourly passing from Lambeth to the court, and look upon his attendance and train, and the reverence the King's household and all men give unto him; and listen to the crying out of his waiters to the people, for the making of him way, and to be uncovered, and you would think it were the King himself, if you saw not the priest.

Again, if you should meet him coming daily from the Star Chamber, and see what pomp, grandeur and magnificence he goeth in; the whole multitude standing bare wherever he passeth; having also a great number of gentlemen and other servants waiting on him, all uncovered; some of them carrying up his tail, for the better breaking and venting of his wind, and easing of his holy body (for it is full of holes); others going before him, and calling to the folk before them to put off their hats, and to give place, crying, 'Room, room, my lord's grace is coming'; tumbling down and thrusting aside the little children aplaying there; flinging and tossing the poor coster-mongers' and sauce-wives' fruit and puddings, baskets and all, into the Thames (though they hindered not their passage), to show the greatness of his state, and the promptitude of their service, to the utter undoing and perishing of those already indigent creatures; I say, you would think, seeing and hearing all this, and also the speed and haste they make, that it were some mighty proud Nimrod, or some furious Jehu, running and marching for a kingdom, rather than a meek, humble and grave priest. Which spectacle, though in itself merciless, yet one can scarce keep from laughter, to see the grollery [foolishness] of it, and considering the whole passages of the business, with the variety of the actions; hearing on the one side the noise of the gentlemen, crying, 'Room', and cursing all that meet them, and that but seem to hinder their passage; and, on the other side, seeing the wailing, mourning, and lamentation the women make, crying out, 'Save my puddings, save my codlings, for the Lord's sake'; the poor tripes and apples, in the meantime, swimming like frogs about the Thames, making way for his grace to go home again. On the other side, hearing the diversity of all men's discourses, concerning the pride, arrogancy, barbarousness, and cruelty of the prelates – it would, I say, move laughter to men, though disposed otherwise to seriosity. Most certain it is, his most excellent Majesty goeth not in greater state, neither doth he suffer such insolency to be done to his poor subjects, wherever he becometh. And this, I say, is the ordinary deportment of the prelate.

25 The Sentence on Prynne, Burton and Bastwicke, 30 June 1637

[*Source*:John Rushworth (1706, abridged edition) *Historical Collections* volume two, pp. 293–4.]

Dr Bastwick spake first, and (among other things) said, had he a thousand lives he would give them all up for this cause. Mr Prynne . . . showed the disparity between the times of Queen Mary and Queen Elizabeth, and the times then (of King Charles), and how far more dangerous it was now to write against a bishop or two than against a King or Queen: there at the most there was but six months imprisonment in ordinary prisons, and the delinquent might redeem his ears for £200, and had two months' time for payment, but no fine; here they are fined £5,000 a piece, to be perpetually imprisoned in the remotest castles, where no friends must be permitted to see them, and to lose their ears without redemption. There no stigmatizing, here he must be branded on both cheeks . . . He challenged the prelates to a fair dispute, and he would maintain against them, that their prelatical jurisdiction over presbyters and their calling is not *jure divino* [by divine right]; as he would maintain also against all the lawyers that the issuing of writs and process in the prelates' own names, and under their own seals, is against law, and entrenches on the king's prerogative and the subject's liberty. He said, if the people but knew into what times they were cast, and what changes of laws, religion and ceremonies had been made of late by one man [Archbishop Laud], they would look about them. They might see that no degree or profession was exempted from the prelates' malice; here is a divine for the soul, a physician for the body, and a lawyer for the estates,[1] and the next to be censured in Star Chamber is likely to be a bishop . . . The Archbishop of Canterbury, being informed by his spies what Mr Prynne said, moved the Lords then sitting in the Star Chamber that he might be gagged and have some further censure to be presently executed on him; but that motion did not succeed. Mr Burton . . . spake much while in the pillory to the people. The executioner cut off his ears deep and close, in a cruel manner, with much effusion of blood, an artery being cut, as there was likewise of Dr Bastwick. Then Mr Prynne's cheeks were seared with an iron made exceeding hot; which done, the executioner cut off one of his ears and a piece of his cheek with it; then hacking the other ear almost off, he left it hanging and went down; but being called up again he cut it quite off.

Note

1 'a divine for the soul' . . .: Burton was a minister, Bastwick a physician and Prynne a barrister.

26 Clarendon: The High Commission

[*Source*: Macray, editor (1888) *History of the Rebellion* volume I, p. 125.]

Persons of honour and great quality, of the court and of the country, were every day cited into the High Commission court, upon the fame of their incontinence, or other scandal in their lives, and were there prosecuted to their shame and punishment: and as the shame (which they called an insolent triumph upon their degree and quality, and levelling them with the common people) was never forgotten, but watched for revenge, so the fines imposed there were the more questioned and repined against because they were assigned to the rebuilding and repairing St. Paul's church, and thought therefore to be the more severely imposed, and the less compassionately reduced and excused; which likewise made the jurisdiction and rigour of the Star Chamber more felt and murmured against, which sharpened many men's humours against the bishops before they had any ill intention towards the Church.

27 Lord Brooke

[*Source*: Robert Greville, Lord Brooke (second edition, 1642) *A Discourse Opening the Nature of that Episcopacie which is exercised in England* pp. 34–7; printed also in William Haller, editor, *Tracts on Liberty in the Puritan Revolution* (1934, reprinted 1965).]

I humbly propound, as worthy mature consideration, how fit these spiritual lords may be to sit as law-makers in that highest court [i.e. the House of Lords], by whose fundamental orders, as also by the law of nature, none ought to have vote, but free men.

And how can they possibly be deemed free, that wholly depend on another's thought (for I need not say, beck, smile or frown) not only for their first creation, but continual preservation in this state and power of giving vote in that court? . . .

There is a vast difference between those who cannot but still be affected with noble, generous, and most virtuous deportment-being still to live in their names, honours, posterity; and those, who in their height are but as meteors, that must quickly blaze out, vanish, fall and be no more. Between those whose birth and breeding hath filled their veins with heroic, noble blood, and those that are so much disadvantaged both by their birth and breeding; though their birth is nothing so ignoble as their education, compared with that breeding a true statesman should have.

For, will any wise man living think them fit to give counsel in princes' closets; to make laws in Parliament; and sit judges in the highest tribunals of civil justice; that all their lifetime, before the *conge d' elire* [nomination to a bishopric] diverted their thoughts, were wholly taken up in turning, rather than reading, *Aquinas* and *Scotus* [medieval scholastic philosophers], with some other school triflers, before they came to some church benefice; where ever since they have spent all their time, that might be spared from tithing, in liturgies or canons, except some new scruple with some of their neighbours, have called them to peruse some author *de Decimis* [concerning tenths, i.e. tithes]? . . .

Though the birth, blood, thoughts, breeding, and all of a bishop were as noble as any one, or all, of the peers, which none dare say; yet are not, cannot bishops be possibly so free (and so, not so fit to sit and vote in Parliament) as other lords and members of that great body.

For first, they that have large estates by inheritance, and [are] to continue their names and families to the same inheritance, are in all reason probable, with more impartial freedom, to provide for the good of the Commonwealth in general than those that, having little or no estate of their own (at least, to leave to posterity), are not like much to look after the weal-public, or good of posterity; but rather will seek to humour the present times, being truly *filii unius horae* (men of a short continuance),[1] especially to insinuate themselves into more and more favour with their creator and preserver, on whose smile wholly depends more than their *bene esse*, their welfare . .

Though all the branches of nobility first sprouted out from the root of royalty, (honours being in all good states, appendices to majesty, and wholly disposed by the royal hand); yet estates and revenues did not, which are the partiments [parts] and supporters of noble honours. And these also in bishops, depend on the prince's will.

Yea, our honours and baronies, though first they were granted by the king, yet now being so invested in our blood and become hereditary, they cannot be revoked. In this, therefore, we are freer than any bishop, whose baronies are only annexed to their office, and not invested in them by blood . . .

Now, to what unworthiness will not ambition and avarice carry them? When they look upon themselves as peers and grandees of the kingdom, and again reflect on their wives and children, as those which, after their decease, must soon be reduced from such a height (like falling stars) into their first principles; must not this be a great temptation by any means, right or wrong, to seek the private enrichment of themselves and families, even before the public good of the commonwealth, which is never more injur'd, than when it is made to stoop and vail to the boundless ambition of some private, low, base, sordid, spirit.

Note

1 'of a short continuance' – Brooke's gloss; the Latin literally translates as 'sons of a single hour'.

28 Clarendon

[*Source*: Macray, editor (1888) *History of the Rebellion* volume I, pp. 131–2.]

The Treasurer's is the greatest office of benefit in the kingdom, and the chief in precedence next the archbishop and the Great Seal, so that the eyes of all men were at gaze who should have this great office; and the greatest of the nobility who were in the chiefest employments looked upon it as the prize of one of them, such offices commonly making way for more removes and preferments: when on a sudden the staff was put into the hands of the bishop of London, [William Juxon, who became Treasurer in March 1636] a man so unknown that his name was scarce heard of in the kingdom, who had been within two years before but a private chaplain to the King and the president of a poor college in Oxford [St John's]. This inflamed more men than were angry before, and no doubt did not only sharpen the edge of envy and malice against the archbishop [Laud], (who was the known architect of this new fabric,) but most unjustly indisposed many towards the Church itself, which they looked upon as the gulph ready to swallow all the great offices, there being others in view, of that robe, who were ambitious enough to expect the rest.

* * * * * * * * * * *

29 The Canons of June 1640

[*Source*: J. P. Kenyon (1966) *The Stuart Constitution 1603–1688: Documents and Commentary*, pp. 166–8.]

. . . Forasmuch as we are given to understand that many of our subjects, being misled against the rites and ceremonies now used in the Church of England, have lately taken offence at the same, upon an unjust supposal that they are not only contrary to our laws but also introductive unto Popish superstitions; whereas it well appeareth unto us . . . that the authors and fomenters of these jealousies, though they colour the same with a pretence of zeal, and would seem to strike only at some supposed iniquity in the said ceremonies, yet, as we have cause to fear, aim at our own royal person, and would fain have our good subjects imagine that we ourselves are perverted, and do worship God in a superstitious way, and that we intend to bring in some alteration of the religion here established . . .

We therefore, out of our princely inclination to uniformity and peace, in matters especially that concern the holy worship of God, . . and . . ., having fully advised herein with our metropolitan, and with the commissioners authorised under our Great Seal for causes ecclesiastical, have thought good to give them free leave to treat in Convocation, and agree upon certain other canons necessary for the advancement of God's glory, the edifying of his Holy Church, and the due reverence of his blessed Mysteries and Sacraments . . .

[The parish clergy were to read the following 'explanations of the regal power' at morning prayers, once in every quarter.]

The most high and sacred Order of Kings is of Divine Right, being the ordinance of God himself, founded in the prime laws of nature, and clearly established by express texts both of the Old and New Testaments. A supreme power is given to this most excellent Order by God himself in the Scriptures, which is, that kings should rule and command in their several dominions all persons of what rank or estate soever, whether ecclesiastical or civil, and that they should restrain and punish with the temporal sword all stubborn and wicked doers.

The care of God's Church is so committed to kings in the Scripture that they are commended when the Church keeps the right way, and taxed when it runs amiss, and therefore her government belongs in chief unto kings; for otherwise one man would be commended for another's care, and taxed but for another's negligence, which is not God's way.

The power to call and dissolve Councils, both national and provincial, is the true right of all Christian kings within their own realms and territories; and when in the first times of Christ's Church prelates used this power, it was therefore only because in those days they had no Christian kings; and it was then so only used as in times of persecution, that is, with supposition (in case it were required) of submitting their very lives unto the very laws and commands even of those pagan princes that they might not so much as seem to disturb their civil government, which Christ came to confirm, but by no means to undermine.

For any person or persons to set up, maintain or avow in any their said realms or territories respectively, under any pretence whatsoever, any independent coactive power, either papal or popular (whether directly or indirectly), is to undermine their great royal office, and cunningly to overthrow that most sacred ordinance which God himself hath established, and so is treasonable against God as well as against the King.

For subjects to bear arms against their kings, offensive or defensive, upon any pretence whatsoever, is at least to resist the powers which are ordained of God; and though they do not invade but only resist, St Paul tells them plainly they shall receive to themselves damnation.

And although tribute, and custom, and aid, and subsidy, and all manner of necessary support and supply be respectively due to kings from their subjects by the Law of God, Nature and Nations, for the public defence, care and protection of them; yet nevertheless subjects have not only possession of but a true and just right, title, and property to and in all their goods and estates, and ought to have. And these two are so far from crossing one another that they mutually go together for the honourable and comfortable support of both. For as it is the duty of the subjects to supply their king so it is part of the kingly office to support his subjects in the property and freedom of their estates . . .

SECTION FIVE: PARLIAMENTARY REFORM AND POPULAR UPHEAVAL

[The Parliament that was to be dubbed the 'Long Parliament' opened on 3 November 1640 with most of its members united against the abuses of the Personal Rule. A series of reforming measures followed, among them the ending of unparliamentary taxation and the abolition of the prerogative courts like the Star Chamber (extract 34). By the winter of 1641–2, consensus no longer existed and a 'royalist party' was emerging among MPs. This section includes extracts by Edward Hyde, later Earl of Clarendon, the most eminent of the MPs who supported the early reforms of the Long Parliament, but believed Charles I had the best of the case by November 1641 (extracts 30 and 36); and highlights some of the pressures that fractured the unity of the Commons. Conflict over religion was one factor: most MPs probably preferred a reformed episcopacy but the London petition calling for 'root and branch' policies (extract 33) opened a debate that could not be halted. MPs differed too in their reactions to the popular upheaval of 1640–2. The reception of the Laudian martyrs showed the popular enthusiasm for the Parliament's cause (extract 30) and the hostility of the London crowd towards Charles I's government was crucial in several crises, pressurizing the King into acceptance of Strafford's execution (May 1641) and ultimately forcing him to leave London (January 1642). The collapse of the censorship in 1640 led to the emergence of a flourishing anti-court literature. Our examples are from two pamphlets attributed to Richard Overton, the future Leveller leader (extracts 31 and 32; see also Section Eleven). Their form, inspired by popular drama, suggests that 'Puritan' hostility to the theatre has been exaggerated or misconstrued. Parliament closed the theatres as the war began but perhaps the reasons it gave should be taken at face value (extract 40). The fear of many MPs that the 'people' were pushing them further than they wanted to go in their opposition to the King, was a major reason for the divisions of late 1641; this alarm is revealed very clearly in the conflict over the Grand Remonstrance. The Remonstrance was an attempt by John Pym to recover the consensus of 1640 in the atmosphere of panic following the news of the Irish rebellion. Its 204 paragraphs and the accompanying petition (extract 38) gave a partisan history of the reign of Charles I and proposed far-reaching reforms. Contrary to usual procedure the House of Lords was not consulted and the Remonstrance was an implicit appeal to the people – an appeal that became explicit with the proposal for its printing. Far from restoring consensus, the passing of the Remonstrance by just eleven votes showed how deeply the Commons was divided (extracts 35–37). Charles's reply, influenced by advisers like Hyde, was the first of a series of constitutional manifestos designed to appeal to the middle ground (extract 39; see also extract 50 below). But Charles's actions often contradicted his declarations, as with the attempt to arrest the 'Five Members' a few weeks later.]

30 Prynne and Burton Return from Prison, November 1640

[*Source*: W. Dunn Macray, editor (1888) *The History of the Rebellion and Civil Wars in England* by Edward, Earl of Clarendon, volume I, pp. 268–9.]

Prynne and Burton being neighbours (though in distinct islands)[1] landed at the same time at Southampton; where they were received and entertained with extraordinary demonstration of affection and esteem, attended by a marvellous conflux of company, and their charges not only borne with great magnificence, but liberal presents given to them. And this method and ceremony kept them company all their journey, great herds of people meeting them at their entrance into all towns, and waiting upon them out with wonderful acclamations of joy. When they came near London multitudes of people of several conditions, some on horseback, others on foot, met them some miles from the town, very many having been a day's journey; and so they were brought, about two of the clock in the afternoon, in at Charing Cross, and carried into the city by above ten thousand persons with boughs and flowers in their hands, the common people strewing flowers and herbs in the ways as they passed, making great noise and expressions of joy for their deliverance and return, and in those acclamations mingling loud and virulent exclamations against the bishops, 'who had so cruelly prosecuted such godly men.'

Note

1 'in distinct islands': Prynne had been imprisoned in Jersey, Burton in Guernsey.

31 The Cardinal's Conspiracy

[*Source*: Richard Overton (?) (1640 or 1641) *Vox Borealis or the Northern Discoverie* sig B2]

[From *Vox Borealis*, probably Overton's earliest pamphlet. It takes the form of a dialogue in the camp of the English army at Berwick in 1640 between Jamie, a Scotsman, and Willie, an English soldier, who both hate the bishops. Jamie has recently visited London and is reporting the latest news; the following extract is based on an incident in May 1639 when an anti-Laudian play at the Fortune was suppressed.]

In the meantime let me tell ye a lamentable tragedy acted by the prelacy against the poor players of the 'Fortune' playhouse which made them sing, 'Fortune my foe, why dost thou frown on me?' . . . They having gotten a new old play called *The Cardinal's Conspiracy* whom they brought upon the stage in as great state as they could, with altars, images, crosses, crucifixes and the like to set forth his pomp and pride. But woeful was the sight to see how in the midst of all their mirth the pursuivants came and seized upon the poor Cardinal and all his consorts and carried them away. And when they were questioned for it, in the High Commission Court, they pleaded ignorance and told the Archbishop that they took those examples of their altars, images and the like from heathen authors. This did somewhat assuage his anger, that they did not bring him on the stage; but yet they were fined for it and after a little imprisonment got their liberty. And having nothing left them but a few old swords and bucklers they fell to act *The Valiant Scot*,[1] which they played five days with great applause which vexed the bishops worse than the other, insomuch as they were forbidden playing it any more, and some of them prohibited ever playing again.

Note

1 '*The Valiant Scot*': the title of a real play, but here intended as a reference to the victory of the Scots in the Bishops' Wars of 1639–40.

32 A New Play called Canterbury his Change of Diet

[*Source*: Richard Overton (?) (1641) *A New Play Called Canterburie His Change of Diot* (in full).]

[This satire was perhaps suggested to Overton by a feast given by Laud for the King and Queen at Oxford in 1636. The festivities included a play that mocked the mutilated Prynne.]

1 Act: the Bishop of Canterbury having variety of dainties is not satisfied till he be fed with tippets of men's ears.
2 Act: he hath his nose held to the grindstone.
3 Act: he is put into a bird cage with the confessor.
4 Act: the jester tells the king the story.

THE FIRST ACT

Enter the Bishop of Canterbury and with him a Doctor of Physic, a lawyer and a divine, who being set down, they bring him variety of dishes to his table.

Canterbury: Is here all the dishes that are provided?

Doctor: My Lord there is all, and 'tis enough, were't for a prince's table; there's 24 several dainty dishes and all rare.

Cant: Are these rare? No, no, they please me not. Give me a carbinadoed cheek or a tippet of a coxcomb. None of all this, here is meat for my palate.

Lawyer: My Lord, here is both cock and pheasant, quail and partridge, and the best varieties the shambles yield.

Cant: Shambles, I am not tied to such a strait; give not me common things that are in the shambles; let me have of the rarest dainties, dressed after the Italian fashion.

Divine: My Lord, here are nothing but rarities; please you to give me leave to crave a blessing that your Lordship may fall too and eat. My Lord, is it your pleasure I shall?

Cant: You vex me; ho, ho, come away, these rascals torment me.

He knocking, there enters divers bishops with muskets on their necks, bandoleers and swords by their sides.

A Bishop: What is the matter my Lord? Wherefore do you call us?

Cant: Call you, quoth I? It is time to call I think when I am fain to wait. Nay, call and ask, yet cannot have what I desire.

A Bishop: What would you have my Lord?

Cant: Them fellows, bring them to me.

The Doctor is brought to him.

Doctor: What will your Lordship do with me?

Cant: Only cut off your ears.

Doctor: That would be an unchristian action, a practice without a precedent. (*He cuts off his ears*). O cruelty, tyranny! Hold me, hold me or else I die. Heavens support me under this tyrant.

Cant: Come, lawyer, your two ears will make me four. That is almost a little dish for rarity. (*He cuts off the lawyer's ears. Then he cuts off the divine's ears.*)

Divine: Will your Lordship be so cruel? Our blood will be required at your hands.

Cant: This I do, to make you examples, that others may be more careful to please my palate. Henceforth, let my servants know that what *I* will, *I* will have done.
Whate'er is under heaven's sun.

He sends them all away and commands the ears to be dressed for his supper, and after a low curtsey, follows himself.
Exeunt.

THE SECOND ACT

Enter the Bishop of Canterbury into a carpenter's yard by the waterside, where he is going to take water, and seeing a grindstone, draweth his knife and goeth thither to whet it, and the carpenter follows him.

Carpenter: What makes your Grace here my Lord?
Cant: My knife is something dull friend. Therefore I make bold to sharpen it here because an opportunity is here so ready.
Carp: Excuse me, sir, you shall not do it. What reason have you to sharpen your knife on my stone?
You serve me as you did the other three? No, stay!
I'll make you free of the grindstone, before you go away.

He ties his nose to the grindstone.

Cant: O man, what do you mean?
Carp: Hold down your head, it will blood you bravely. By the brushing of your nostrils you shall know what the paring of an ear is. Turn boy.

The carpenter's boy turns the stone and grinds his nose.

Cant: O, hold, hold, hold. Turn qd [quoth?] I, here is turning indeed, such turning will soon deform my face. O, I bleed, I bleed and am extremely sore.
Carp: But who regarded hold before? Remember the cruelty you have used to others whose blood cries out for vengeance. Were not their ears to them as precious as your nostrils can be to you. If such dishes must be your fare let me be your cook, I'll invent you rare sippets.

Enter a Jesuit, a confessor, and washeth his face with holy water and binds up his sore in a cloth.

Jesuit: Right Reverend Sir, what makes your grace in such a sad condition?
Cant: 'Tis sad indeed. Time was, when all the land was swayed by me,
But I am now despised, bound fast and scorned you see.
What shall I do for ease?
Jesuit: I'll try conclusions for you. I'll go in to him and to his wife. I'll woo them both, I'll speak them fair, I'll tell them things they never knew, and if I can, I will procure your liberty that so your grace may escape this danger.
Cant: There will be great difficulty in it? What shall I do, my joys are gone, my face defaced and all my comforts [have] left.
Jesuit: Fear not, there is yet hope, comfort yourself. I have a force

may chance make Rome to flourish that your gray hairs may once more sit in glory which England little dreams of.

The carpenter unties the Bishop and leads him away.

THE THIRD ACT

Enter the Bishop of Canterbury, the Jesuit and the carpenter's wife with a great birdcage in her hand, and a fool standing by and laughing at them, 'Ha, ha, ha, ha, who is the fool now?'

Carpenter's wife:
O, good husband, put in these cormorants into this cage; they that have cut off ears at the first bout, God knows what they may cut off next. Put them in, put them in.

He takes the cage and puts them into it.

Cant: What mean you by this?
Carp: Only to teach you to sing.
Jesuit: Alas, we cannot sing, we are not nightingales.
Carpenter's wife:
Come, come husband; we'll make them sing before they come out again. A blackbird and a canary bird will sing best together.
Cant: Why should they be so strict to us?
Jesuit: Yet if we still abide it, though we die, we die in honour. Our merits we shall leave for others' wants, when we are gone.
Carp: Merits quoth I: if Tower Hill and Tyburn had their due we should have less Jesuits and fewer mass priests. There is many a man that have merited a rope that have not yet met with a halter.
Exeunt.

THE FOURTH ACT

Enter the king and his jester.

Jester: O my king, ha, ha, ha, ha, ha, I cannot forbear laughing.
King: Why, what is the matter sirrah?
Jester: O, the strangest sight that ever I saw. They have put the Bishop of Canterbury and the Confessor into a cage together. Did you ever see the like, the one looks like a crow and the other like a magpie. I waited long to hear them sing, at last they began to chatter.
King: What note did they sing?
Jester: What note? I am sure it was nine notes and a half lower

than they use to sing at court.
King: What was the song?
Jester: One sung thus: 'I would I was at court again for me'. Then the other answered, 'I would I was at Rome again with thee'.
King: Well sirrah, you will never leave your flouts.
Jester: If I should, my liege, I were not fit to be a jester.
Exeunt.

[Epilogue]

The jig between a Paritor[1] and the Fool.

Paritor: What news, sir, what news, I pray you know you,
Fool: Correction doth wait sir, to catch up his due,
Paritor: His due sir, what's that, I pray you tell me,
Fool: Not blue cap, nor red cap, but cap of the see,
Paritor: What caps are these, pray you, shall I never know?
Fool: The caps that would us and our church overthrow.
Both Together:
O welladay, welladay, what shall we do then?
We'll wear tippet fool caps and never undo men.
Paritor: Did you never hear, pray, of Lambeth great fair,
Where white puddings were sold for two shillings a pair?
Fool: Yes, sir, I tell you I heard it and wept,
I think you are broke e'er since it was kept.
Paritor: Broke I am not, you fool I am poor,
Fool: Your master is sick, you are turned out of door,
Both: O welladay, welladay etc.
Paritor: I might have been Jester once as well as you,
Fool: You jested too much which now you do rue,
Paritor: Wherein have I jested, like a fool in place?
Fool: To work projects for such who practise disgrace.
Paritor: You fool, will not profit make anything done?
Fool: Such profit make fools soon after to run,
Both: O welladay, welladay etc.

Note
1 'Paritor': apparitor, an official of the church courts.

Enter the Bishop of Canterbury, and with him a Doctor of Physicke, a Lawyer, and a Divine; who being set downe, they bring him variety of Dishes to his Table.

C*Anterbury*, is here all the dishes, that are provided?
Doct. My Lord there is all: and 'tis enough, wert for a Princes table,
Ther's 24. severall dainty dishes, and all rare.

Laud dining off the ears of Prynne etc. from *Canterbury his Change of Diot* (1641) (Bodleian Library)

33 The Root and Branch Petition

[*Source*: S.R. Gardiner (1906, Third Edition) *Constitutional Documents of the Puritan Revolution*, pp. 137–44.]

[Presented to the Commons 11 December 1640]

The humble Petition of many of His Majesty's subjects in and about the City of London, and several counties of the Kingdom,

Showeth,

That whereas the government of archbishops and lord bishops, deans and archdeacons, etc., with their courts and ministrations in them, have proved prejudicial and very dangerous both to the Church and Commonwealth, they themselves having formerly held that they have their jurisdiction or authority of human authority, till of these later times, being further pressed about the unlawfulness, that they have claimed their calling immediately from the Lord Jesus Christ, which is against the laws of this kingdom, and derogatory to His Majesty and his state royal. And whereas the said government is found by woeful experience to be a main cause and occasion of many foul evils, pressures and grievances of a very high nature unto His Majesty's subjects in their own consciences, liberties and estates, as in a schedule of particulars hereunto annexed may in part appear.

We therefore most humbly pray, and beseech this honourable assembly, the premises considered, that the said government, with all its dependencies, roots and branches, may be abolished, and all laws in their behalf made void, and the government according to God's Word may be rightly placed amongst us: and we your humble suppliants, as in duty we are bound, will daily pray for His Majesty's long and happy reign over us, and for the prosperous success of this high and honourable Court of Parliament.

A particular of the manifold evils, pressures, and grievances caused, practised and occasioned by the prelates and their dependents.

1 The subjecting and enthralling all ministers under them and their authority, and so by degrees exempting them from the temporal power; whence follows,

2 The faint-heartedness of ministers to preach the truth of God, lest they should displease the prelates; as namely, the doctrine of predestination, of free grace, of perseverance, of original sin remaining after baptism, of the sabbath, the doctrine against universal grace, election for faith foreseen, free-will against antichrist, non-residents, human inventions in God's worship; all which are generally withheld from the people's knowledge, because not relishing to the bishops.

3 The encouragement of ministers to despise the temporal magistracy, the nobles and gentry of the land; to abuse the subjects, and live contentiously with their neighbours, knowing that they, being the bishops' creatures, shall be supported.

4 The restraint of many godly and able men from the ministry, and thrusting out of many congregations their faithful, diligent, and powerful ministers, . . .

5 The suppressing of that godly design[1] set on foot by certain saints, and sugared with many great gifts by sundry well-affected persons for the buying of impropriations, and placing of able ministers in them, maintaining of lectures, and founding of free schools, which the prelates could not endure, lest it should darken their glories, and draw the ministers from their dependence upon them.

6 The great increase of idle, lewd and dissolute, ignorant and erroneous men in the ministry, which swarm like the locusts of Egypt over the whole kingdom . . .

7 The discouragement of many from bringing up their children in learning; the many schisms, errors, and strange opinions which are in the Church; great corruptions which are in the Universities; the gross and lamentable ignorance almost everywhere among the people; the want of preaching ministers in very many places both of England and Wales; the loathing of the ministry, and the general defection to all manner of profaneness.

8 The swarming of lascivious, idle, and unprofitable books and pamphlets, play-books and ballads . . .

9 The hindering of godly books to be printed, the blotting out or perverting those which they suffer, all or most of that which strikes either at Popery or Arminianism . . .

10 The publishing and venting of Popish, Arminian, and other dangerous books and tenets . . .

11 The growth of Popery and increase of Papists, Priests and Jesuits in sundry places . . .

12 The multitude of monopolies and patents, drawing with them innumerable perjuries; the large increase of customs and impositions upon commodities, the ship-money, and many other great burthens upon the Commonwealth, under which all groan.

13 . . . The offices and jurisdictions of archbishops, lord bishops, deans, archdeacons, being the same way of Church government, which is in the Romish Church, and which was in England in the time of Popery, little change thereof being made (except only the head from whence it was derived) . . .

14 The great conformity and likeness both continued and increased of our Church to the Church of Rome, in vestures, postures, ceremonies and administrations, . . .

19 . . . Also the canons made in the late Sacred Synod,[2] as they call it, wherein are many strange and dangerous devices to undermine the Gospel and the subjects' liberties, to propagate Popery, to spoil God's people, ensnare ministers, and other students, and so to draw all into an absolute subjection and thraldom to them and their government, spoiling both the King and the Parliament of their power. . .

21 Profanation of the Lord's Day, pleading for it, and enjoining ministers to read a Declaration[3] set forth (as it is thought) by their

procurement for tolerating of sports upon that day, suspending and depriving many godly ministers for not reading the same only out of conscience, because it was against the law of God so to do, and no law of the land to enjoin it.

22 The pressing of the strict observation of the saints' days, whereby great sums of money are drawn out of men's purses for working on them; a very high burthen on most people, who getting their living on their daily employments, must either omit them, and be idle, or part with their money, whereby many poor families are undone, or brought behindhand; . . .

24 The general abuse of that great ordinance of excommunication, which God hath left in His Church as the last and greatest punishment which the Church can inflict upon obstinate and great offenders . . .

28 The exercising of the oath *ex officio*[4] and other proceedings by way of inquisition, reaching even to men's thoughts . . . And from hence followed amongst others these dangerous consequences.

1 The general hope and expectation of the Romish party, that their superstitious religion will ere long be fully planted in this kingdom again . . .

2 The discouragement and destruction of all good subjects, of whom are multitudes, both clothiers, merchants and others, who being deprived of their ministers, and overburthened with these pressures, have departed the kingdom to Holland, and other parts, and have drawn with them a great manufacture of cloth and trading out of the land into other places where they reside, whereby wool, the great staple of the kingdom, is become of small value, and vends not; trading is decayed, many poor people want work, seamen lose employment, and the whole land is much impoverished, to the great dishonour of this kingdom and blemishment to the government thereof.

3 The present wars and commotions happened between His Majesty and his subjects of Scotland, wherein His Majesty and all his kingdoms are endangered, and suffer greatly . . .

All which we humbly refer to the consideration of this Honourable Assembly, desiring the Lord of Heaven to direct you in the right way to redress all these evils.

Notes

1 'that godly design': the project of the Feoffees for Impropriations, who bought up impropriations (tithes held by laymen) and used the proceeds to fund ministers and lecturers of whom they approved. In 1633 the Feoffees were dissolved by order of the Exchequer Court.

2 'the canons made . . .': the canons of the 1640 Convocation, see pp. 58–59.

3 'a Declaration': in 1618 James I issued a Declaration encouraging dancing and sports on a Sunday; Charles I reissued this Book of Sports in 1633, with an order that all ministers should read it from the pulpit.

4 'the oath *ex officio*', used in the Court of High Commission, obliged people to incriminate themselves, a contravention of common law practice.

34 The Abolition of the Court of Star Chamber

[*Source*: Gardiner (1906, Third edition) *Constitutional Documents*, pp. 181–3.]

[From the Act of July 1641]

Forasmuch as all matters examinable or determinable before the said Judges, or in the Court commonly called the Star Chamber, may have their proper remedy and redress, and their due punishment and correction by the common law of the land, and in the ordinary course of justice elsewhere, and forasmuch as the reasons and motives inducing the erection and continuance of that Court do now cease, and the proceedings, censures and decrees of that Court have by experience been found to be an intolerable burden to the subjects, and the means to introduce an arbitrary power and government: and forasmuch as the Council Table hath of late times assumed unto itself a power to intermeddle in civil causes and matters only of private interest between party and party, and have adventured to determine of the estates and liberties of the subject contrary to the law of the land and the rights and privileges of the subject, by which great and manifold mischiefs and inconveniences have arisen and happened, and much uncertainty by means of such proceedings hath been conceived concerning men's rights and estates: for settling whereof and preventing the like in time to come, be it ordained and enacted by the authority of this present Parliament, that the said Court commonly called the Star Chamber . . . be . . . clearly and absolutely dissolved, taken away, and determined . . .

Be it likewise declared and enacted . . . that neither His Majesty nor his Privy Council have or ought to have any jurisdiction, power or authority by English bill, petition, articles, libel, or any other arbitrary way whatsoever, to examine or draw into question, determine or dispose of the lands, tenements, hereditaments, goods or chattels of any the subjects of this kingdom, but that the same ought to be tried and determined in the ordinary Courts of Justice and by the ordinary course of the law.

35 Sir Edward Dering

[*Source*: John Rushworth (1721) *Historical Collections* volume four, p. 425.]

This Remonstrance is now in progress upon its last foot in this House; I must give a vote unto it, one way or other. My conscience bids me not to dare to be affirmative: so sings the bird in my breast and I do cheerfully believe the tune to be good.

This Remonstrance, whensoever it passeth, will make such an impression and leave such a character behind, both of his Majesty, the people, the Parliament and of this present church and state, as no time shall ever eat it out whilst histories are written and men have eyes to read them . . .

To what end do we decline thus to them that look not for it? Wherefore is this descension from a Parliament to a people? They look not up for this so extraordinary courtesy? The better sort think best of us; and why are we told that the people are expectant for a declaration?

I did never look for it of my predecessors in this place, nor shall do from my successors. I do here profess that I do not know any one soul in all that country [the county of Kent], for which I have the honour to serve, who looks for this at your hands. They do humbly and heartily thank you for many good laws and statutes already enacted, and pray for more; that is the language best understood of them and most welcome to them. They do not expect to hear any other stories of what you have done, much less promises of what you will do.

Mr Speaker, when I first heard of a Remonstrance, I presently imagined that like faithful councillors, we should hold up a glass unto his Majesty: I thought to represent unto the King the wicked counsels of pernicious councillors; the restless turbulency of practical Papists; the treachery of false judges; the bold innovations and some superstition brought in by some pragmatical bishops and the rotten part of the clergy.

I did not dream that we should remonstrate downward, tell stories to the people and talk of the King as of a third person.

The use and end of such Remonstrance I understand not; at least, I hope I do not.

36 John Pym

[*Source*: John Bruce, editor (1845) *Verney Papers: Notes of Proceedings in the Long Parliament* by Sir Ralph Verney, knight (Camden Society, volume 31), pp. 122–3.]

The honour of the king lies in the safety of the people, and we must tell the truth; the plots have been very near the king, all driven home to the court and the popish party.

Let a law be made against sectaries. Ministers driven out of England for not reading the Book of Sports,[1] and they are now separatists beyond sea.

The popish lords and bishops do obstruct us. No breach of privilege [of the House of Lords] to name these, for we have often complained of lords being away, and lords' miscarriages.

Nothing but a declaration can take away the accusations that lie upon us.

We have suffered so much by councillors of the king's choosing, that we desire him to advise with us about it, and many of his servants move him about them, and why may not the Parliament?

A peace was made with Spain without consent of Parliament, though King James promised the contrary.

Altar-worship is idolatory, and that was enjoined by the bishops in all their cathedrals.

Learning will be better provided for in the general.

The declaration [the Grand Remonstrance] doth not prophesy, but say what is fit, and may easily be done.

The English courts have usurped an unjust and arbitrary jurisdiction.

The matter of the declaration is not fit for the Lords, for the matters were only agitated in this House, and again many of them are accused by it.

Remonstrances are not directed either to the king or the people, but show the acts of this House.

This declaration will bind the people's hearts to us, when they see how we have been used.

Note

1 'the Book of Sports': see p. 71, Note 3.

37 Clarendon

[*Source*: Macray, editor (1888) *History of the Rebellion* volume I, pp. 419–20.]

The next morning, the debate being entered upon about nine of the clock in the morning, it continued all that day; and candles being called for when it grew dark, (neither side being very desirous to adjourn it till the next day; though it was evident very many withdrew themselves out of pure faintness, and disability to attend the conclusion,) the debate continued till after it was twelve of the clock, with much passion; and the House being then divided upon the passing or not passing it, it was carried for the affirmative by nine voices[1] and no more: and as soon as it was declared, Mr Hampden[2] moved 'that there might be an order entered for the present printing it;' which produced a sharper debate than the former. It appeared then, that they did not intend to send it up to the House of Peers for their concurrence, but that it was upon the matter an appeal to the people, and to infuse jealousies into their minds. It had never been the custom to publish any debates or determinations of the House which [were] not regularly first transmitted to the House of Peers, nor was it thought, in truth, that the House had authority to give warrant for the printing of any thing; all which was offered by Mr Hyde with some warmth, as soon as the motion was made for the printing it; and he said he did believe the printing it in that manner was not lawful, and he feared it would produce mischievous effects, and therefore desired the leave of the House that, if the question should be put and carried in the affirmative, he might have liberty to enter his protestation. Which he no sooner said than Geoffrey Palmer[3] (a man of great reputation, and much esteemed in the House) stood up and made the same motion for himself, that he might likewise protest, when immediately together many afterwards, without distinction and in some disorder, cried out, 'They did protest:' so that there was after scarce any quiet and regular debate.

Notes
1 'nine voices': the majority was in fact eleven.
2 'Mr Hampden': John Hampden, M.P. for Buckinghamshire; the man who challenged the legality of ship money (see pp. 49–52).
3 'Geoffrey Palmer': M.P. for Stamford, Lincolnshire; he had supported the early reforms of the Parliament, but this attempt to protest earned him a spell in the Tower.

38 The Remonstrance

[*Source*: Gardiner (1906, Third edition) *Constitutional Documents*, pp. 202–5.]

a. The Petition Accompanying the Grand Remonstrance
[Presented to the King 1 December 1641]

Most Gracious Sovereign, your Majesty's most humble and faithful subjects, the Commons in this present Parliament assembled, do with much thankfulness and joy acknowledge the great mercy and favour of God, in giving your Majesty a safe and peaceable return out of Scotland into your kingdom of England,[1] where the pressing dangers and distempers of the State have caused us with much earnestness to desire the comfort of your gracious presence, and likewise the unity and justice of your royal authority, to give more life and power to the dutiful and loyal counsels and endeavours of your Parliament, for the evention of that eminent ruin and destruction wherein your kingdoms of England and Scotland are threatened. The duty which we owe to your Majesty and our country, cannot but make us very sensible and apprehensive, that the multiplicity, sharpness and malignity of those evils under which we have now many years suffered, are fomented and cherished by a corrupt and ill-affected party, who amongst others their mischievous devices for the alteration of religion and government, have sought by many false scandals and imputations, cunningly insinuated and dispersed amongst the people, to blemish and disgrace our proceedings in this Parliament, and to get themselves a party and faction amongst your subjects, for the better strengthening themselves in their wicked courses, and hindering those provisions and remedies which might, by the wisdom of your Majesty and counsel of your Parliament, be opposed against them.

For preventing whereof, and the better information of your Majesty, your Peers and all other your loyal subjects, we have been necessitated to make a declaration of the state of the kingdom, both before and since the assembly of this Parliament, unto this time, which we do humbly present to your Majesty, without the least intention to lay any blemish upon your royal person, but only to represent how your royal authority and trust have been abused, to the great prejudice and danger of your Majesty, and of all your good subjects.

And because we have reason to believe that those malignant parties, whose proceedings evidently appear to be mainly for the advantage and increase of Popery, is composed, set up, and acted by the subtile practice of the Jesuits and other engineers and factors for Rome, and to the great danger of this kingdom, and most grievous affliction of your loyal subjects, have so far prevailed as to corrupt divers of your Bishops and others in prime places of the church, and also to bring divers of these instruments to be of your Privy Council, and other employments of trust and nearness about your Majesty, the Prince, and the rest of your royal children.

And by this means have had such an operation in your counsel and the most important affairs and proceedings of your government, that a most dangerous division and chargeable preparation for war betwixt your kingdoms of England and Scotland, the increase of jealousies betwixt your Majesty and your most obedient subjects, the violent distraction and interruption of this Parliament, the insurrection of the Papists in your kingdom of Ireland, and bloody massacre of your people, have been not only endeavoured and attempted, but in a great measure compassed and effected.

For preventing the final accomplishment whereof, your poor subjects are enforced to engage their persons and estates to the maintaining of a very expensive and dangerous war, notwithstanding they have already since the beginning of this Parliament undergone the charge of £150,000 sterling, or thereabouts, for the necessary support and supply of your Majesty in these present and perilous designs. And because all our most faithful endeavours and engagements will be ineffectual for the peace, safety and preservation of your Majesty and your people, if some present, real and effectual course be not taken for suppressing this wicked and malignant party:–

We, your most humble and obedient subjects, do with all faithfulness and humility beseech your Majesty,–

1. That you will be graciously pleased to concur with the humble desires of your people in a parliamentary way, for the preserving the peace and safety of the kingdom from the malicious designs of the Popish party:–

For depriving the Bishops of their votes in Parliament, and abridging their immoderate power usurped over the clergy, and other your good subjects, which they have perniciously abused to the hazard of religion, and great prejudice and oppression to the laws of the kingdom, and just liberty of your people:–

For the taking away such oppressions in religion, church government and discipline, as have been brought in and fomented by them:–

For uniting all such your loyal subjects as join in the same fundamental truths against the Papists, by removing some oppressive and unnecessary ceremonies by which divers weak consciences have been scrupled, and seem to be divided from the rest, and for the due execution of those good laws which have been made for securing the liberty of your subjects.

2. That your Majesty will likewise be pleased to remove from your council all such as persist to favour and promote any of those pressures and corruptions wherewith your people have been grieved; and that for the future your Majesty will vouchsafe to employ such persons in your great and public affairs, and to take such to be near you in places of trust, as your Parliament may have cause to confide in; that in your princely goodness to your people you will reject and refuse all mediation and solicitation to the contrary, how powerful and near soever.

3. That you will be pleased to forbear to alienate any of the forfeited and escheated lands in Ireland which shall accrue to your Crown by reason of this rebellion, that out of them the Crown may be the better supported, and some satisfaction made to your subjects of this kingdom for the great expenses they are like to undergo [in] this war.

Which humble desires of ours being graciously fulfilled by your Majesty, we will, by the blessing and favour of God, most cheerfully undergo the hazard and expenses of this war, and apply ourselves to such other courses and counsels as may support your real estate with honour and plenty at home, with power and reputation abroad, and by our loyal affections, obedience and service, lay a sure and lasting foundation of the greatness and prosperity of your Majesty, and your royal posterity in future times.

Note

1 'a safe and peaceable return . . .': Charles spent August–November 1641 in Scotland, attempting to gain support.

b. From the Preamble to the Grand Remonstrance

[*Source*: Gardiner (1906, Third edition) *Constitutional Documents*, p. 207.]

[The commons accused the papists, the 'Bishops and the corrupt part of the clergy', and some of the King's councillors of a plot to subvert the fundamental laws of the kingdom. They then described their methods.]

First, to maintain continual differences and discontents between the King and the people, upon questions of prerogative and liberty, that so they might have the advantage of siding with him, and under the notions of men addicted to his service, gain to themselves and their parties the places of greatest trust and power in the kingdom.

A second, to suppress the purity and power of religion and such persons as were best affected to it, as being contrary to their own ends, and the greatest impediment to that change which they thought to introduce.

A third, to conjoin those parties of the kingdom which were most propitious to their own ends, and to divide those who were most opposite, which consisted in many particular observations.

To cherish the Arminian part in those points wherein they agree with the Papists, to multiply and enlarge the difference between the common Protestants and those whom they call Puritans, to introduce and countenance such opinions and ceremonies as are fittest for accommodation with Popery, to increase and maintain ignorance, looseness and profaneness in the people; that of those three parties, Papists, Arminians and Libertines, they might compose a body fit to act such counsels and resolutions as were most conducible to their own ends.

A fourth, to disaffect the King to Parliaments by slander and false imputations, and by putting him upon other ways of supply, which in show and appearance were fuller of advantage than the ordinary course of subsidies, though in truth they brought more loss than gain both to the King and people, and have caused the great distractions under which we both suffer.

39 From the King's Answer to the Petition, 23 December 1641

[*Source*: Gardiner (1906, Third edition) *Constitutional Documents*, pp. 234–6.]

To the petition, we say that although there are divers things in the preamble of it which we are so far from admitting that we profess we cannot at all understand them, as of 'a wicked and malignant party prevalent in the government'; of 'some of that party admitted to our Privy Council and to other employments of trust, and nearest to us and our children'; of 'endeavours to sow among the people false scandals and imputations, to blemish and disgrace the proceedings of the Parliament'; all, or any of them, did we know of, we should be as ready to remedy and punish as you to complain of, so that the prayers of your petition are grounded upon such premises as we must in no wise admit; yet, notwithstanding, we are pleased to give this answer to you.

To the first, concerning religion, consisting of several branches, we say that, for preserving the peace and safety of this kingdom from the design of the Popish party, we have, and will still, concur with all the just desires of our people in a parliamentary way: that, for the depriving of the Bishops of their votes in Parliament, we would have you consider that their right is grounded upon the fundamental law of the kingdom and constitution of Parliament. This we would have you consider; but since you desire our concurrence herein in a parliamentary way, we will give no further answer at this time.

As for the abridging of the inordinate power of the clergy, we conceive that the taking away of the High Commission Court hath well moderated that; but if there continue any usurpations or excesses in their jurisdictions, we therein neither have nor will protect them.

Unto that clause which concerneth corruptions (as you style them) in religion, in church government, and in discipline, and the removing of such unnecessary ceremonies as weak consciences might check at: that for any illegal innovations which may have crept in, we shall willingly concur in the removal of them: that, if our Parliament shall advise us to call a national synod, which may duly examine such ceremonies as give just cause of offence to any, we shall take it into consideration, and apply ourself to give due satisfaction therein; but we are very sorry to hear, in such general terms, corruption in religion objected, since we are persuaded in our consciences that no Church can be found upon the earth that professeth the true religion with more purity of doctrine than the Church of England doth, nor where the government and discipline are jointly more beautified and free from superstition, than as they are here established by law, which, by the grace of God, we will with constancy maintain (while we live) in their purity and glory, not only against all invasions of Popery, but also from the irreverence of those many schismatics and separatists, wherewith of late this kingdom and this city abounds, to the great dishonour and hazard both of Church and State, for the suppression of whom we require your timely aid and active assistance.

To the second prayer of the petition, concerning the removal and choice of councillors, we know not any of our Council to whom the character set forth in the petition can belong: that by those whom we had exposed to trial, we have already given you sufficient testimony that there is no man so near unto us in place or affection, whom we will not leave to the justice of the law, if you shall bring a particular charge and sufficient proofs against him; and of this we do again assure you, but in the meantime we wish you to forbear such general aspersions as may reflect upon all our Council, since you name none in particular.

That for the choice of our councillors and ministers of state, it were to debar us that natural liberty all freemen have; and as it is the undoubted right of the Crown of England to call such persons to our secret counsels, to public employment and our particular service as we shall think fit, so we are, and ever shall be, very careful to make election of such persons in those places of trust as shall have given good testimonies of their abilities and integrity, and against whom there can be no just cause of exception whereon reasonably to ground a diffidence; and to choices of this nature, we assure you that the mediation of the nearest unto us hath always concurred.

To the third prayer of your petition concerning Ireland, we understand your desire of not alienating the forfeited lands thereof, to proceed from much care and love, and likewise that it may be a resolution very fit for us to take; but whether it be seasonable to declare resolutions of that nature before the events of a war be seen, that we much doubt of. Howsoever, we cannot but thank you for this care, and your cheerful engagement for the suppression of that rebellion; upon the speedy affecting whereof, the glory of God in the Protestant profession, the safety of the British there, our honour, and that of the nation, so much depends; all the interests of this kingdom being so involved in that business, we cannot but quicken your affections therein, and shall desire you to frame your counsels, to give such expedition to the work as the nature thereof and the pressures in point of time require; and whereof you are put in mind by the daily insolence and increase of those rebels.

* * * * * * * * * * *

40 Order for Stage Plays to Cease, 2 September 1642

[*Source*: *Journals of the House of Lords* volume five, p. 336.]

Whereas the distressed estate of Ireland, steeped in her own blood, and the distracted estate of England, threatened with a cloud of blood by a civil war, call for all possible means to appease and avert the wrath of God appearing in these judgements; among which fasting and prayer having been often tried to be very effectual, have been lately and are still enjoined; and whereas public sports do not well agree with public calamities, nor public stage plays with the seasons of humiliation, this being an exercise of sad and pious solemnity, and the other being spectacles of pleasure, too commonly expressing lascivious mirth and levity; it is therefore thought fit and ordained by the Lords and Commons in this Parliament assembled that, while these sad causes and set times of humiliation do continue, public stage plays shall cease and be forborn; instead of which are recommended to the people of this land the profitable and seasonable considerations of repentance, reconciliation and peace with God, which probably may produce outward peace and prosperity and bring again times of joy and gladness to these nations.

SECTION SIX: THE TAKING OF SIDES

[Civil war did not erupt with a single great explosion, but developed gradually through diverse, fragmented struggles in the counties as each side sought control of the local militias, the only substantial armed force in England. In March 1642 Parliament passed the Militia Ordinance which put Lords Lieutenant believed to be sympathetic to Parliament in charge of the county militias. (It was an ordinance rather than an act because the King did not give his consent to the measure.) Parliament did not begin to implement the Militia Ordinance until June, and in the same month the King reacted by issuing the Commission of Array, a medieval device which empowered the King's supporters to raise forces in each county. The extracts in this section (especially 42–45) describe the events of the summer of 1642 in several counties, but they also introduce some of the contemporary debate about the motives which influenced side-taking in 1642: the contrasting views of Selden and Baxter on the importance of religion is one example (extracts 41 and 47). The question of how far the political division between King and Parliament corresponded to a social division has been a major concern of modern historiography, and it was an issue that also exercised seventeenth-century commentators: we include the analyses of the royalist Clarendon and the moderate Parliamentarian Baxter (extracts 46 and 47) and an example of an independent political initiative by the 'middling sort' in Yorkshire (extract 42). Through recent historical work, particularly in local history, we are coming to realize the horror many felt at the thought of civil war in 1642 and the strength of the moves to remain apart from the conflict. Clarendon (extract 43) describes a neutrality pact in Yorkshire (though he sees it as a Parliamentarian stratagem) while Thomas Knyvett (extract 48) represents the bewildered local gentleman who hoped against hope for a consensus between King and Parliament that would free him from the necessity of commitment to one side.]

41 John Selden: Religious Motivation

[*Source*: *Table Talk: Being the Discourses of John Selden* (1689), p. 52.]

If men would say they took arms for anything but religion, they might be beaten out of it by reason; out of that they never can, for they will not believe you whatever you say.

The very *arcanum* of pretending religion in all wars is that something may be found out in which all men may have interest. In this the groom has as much interest as the lord. Were it for land, one has one thousand acres, and the other but one; he would not venture so far as he that has a thousand. But religion is equal to both. Had all men land alike by a *lex agraria* [agrarian law], then all men would say they fought for land.

42 The Protestation of the Yorkshire Freeholders, 13 May 1642

[*Source*: *A Letter from the Right Honourable Ferdinando Lord Faifax . . . with the Freeholders Protestation inclosed* (1642); a slightly different version is printed in Mildred Campbell *The English Yeoman* (New Haven, 1942).]

[In spring 1642 Charles travelled to Yorkshire to gather support. After an unsuccessful attempt to seize Hull, he summoned the county's gentry to discuss the raising of an armed guard. A group of lesser landholders stormed the meeting to protest at their exclusion, and issued the following Protestation. As a result the King called three meetings of the Yorkshire freeholders.]

Whereas his Majesty hath been pleased to give summons to the gentry of this county to attend him at his court at York the 12th of May instant, to advise with him in some particulars concerning the honour and safety of his Majesty's person and the well being and peace of this our county, and in the same summons was pleased to omit the freeholders of this county, out of a tender respect of putting them to any extraordinary charge; yet we, conscious of our sincere loyalty to his Majesty our gracious sovereign, and conceiving ourselves according to the proportions of our estates equally interested in the common good of the county, did take boldness to come in person to York, and were ready to attend his Majesty's pleasure there. And whereas his Majesty was pleased there to propound several things to the purpose aforesaid, at the meeting of the country to consider a fit answer to return to his Majesty thereupon, the doors of the meeting house were shut against us, we utterly excluded, and in our absence a referee[1] of knights and gentlemen chosen without our knowledge or consent to draw up the said answer. We the freeholders who petitioned his Majesty the day abovesaid, conceiving ourselves abundantly injured in the election (not knowing any warrant by writ or otherwise for the same) of the said referee, and that we ought not however to be concluded by any resolution of theirs, without our assent in their election, do absolutely protest and declare against the said election; and as far as concerns us disavow whatsoever shall be the result of their consultation thereupon, and do desire a new and fair election of a referee may be made, we admitted to our free votes in the same, and some one or more to be nominated by us allowed to deliver our sense for us at another meeting. And that we shall not make good in the least respect anything whatsoever which shall otherwise be concluded upon.

Note

1 'a referee': a committee of twelve was appointed to consider the King's request for a guard. The committee could not decide on an answer, six of the members agreeing to the King's request, six advising him to seek Parliament's protection.

43 Clarendon

[*Source*: W. Dunn Macray editor (1888) *The History of the Rebellion and Civil Wars in England* by Edward, Earl of Clarendon, volume two, pp. 461–4.]

Truly I believe there was scarce one conclusion that hath contributed more to the continuance and length of the war, than that general received opinion in the beginning that it would be quickly at an end. Hereupon, there being but one visible difference like to beget distractions in the country, which was about the militia, the King appointing it to be governed and disposed by the commission of array, and the Parliament by its ordinance, for the composing [thereof] the gentlemen of the several opinions proposed between themselves that neither the one nor the other should be meddled with, but that all should be contented to sit still, without engagement to either party. This seemed very reasonable to the Parliament party, who were rather carried away with an implicit reverence to the name of a Parliament (the fatal disease of the whole kingdom) than really transported with the passion and design of the furious part of it, and who plainly discerned that by much the greatest part of the persons of honour, quality, and interest in the country would cordially oppose their proceedings: for, besides the lord Fairfax,[1] there were in truth few of good reputation and fortune who ran that way. On the other hand, the King's party thought their work done by it . . .

They thought they had nothing to do but to keep the country in such a peace . . . concluding as the other did, that the decision between the King and Parliament would be at the first encounter. Upon these deliberations, articles were solemnly drawn up, consented to, and subscribed by the lord Fairfax and Harry Belasyse, the heir apparent of the lord Fauconberg, who were the two knights who served in Parliament for Yorkshire, nearly allied together, and of great kindness till their several opinions and affections had divided them in this quarrel, the former adhering to the Parliament, the latter, with great courage and sobriety, to the King.

With them, the principal persons of either party subscribed the articles . . . The Parliament no sooner was informed of this transaction than they expressed their detestation of it, and gently in words (though scornfully in matter) reprehending the lord Fairfax and his party for being cozened and overreached by the other . . . Upon this declaration and vote [of Parliament against the neutrality agreement] not only young Hotham[2] fell to the practice of acts of hostility with all license out of the garrison at Hull, but the lord Fairfax himself, and all the gentlemen of that party who had with that protestation signed the articles, instead of resenting the reproach to themselves, tamely submitted to those unreasonable conclusions, and, contrary to their solemn promise and engagement, prepared themselves to bear a part in the war, and made all haste to levy men.

The present disadvantage of this rupture was greater to the King's party there than to the other. For, (besides that many who concurred with them very frankly and solicitously in the neutrality separated themselves from them now there was a necessity of action) they had neither money to raise men nor arms to arm them; so that the strength consisted in the gentlemen themselves and their retinue, who, by the good affections of the inhabitants of York, were strong enough to secure one another within the walls of that city. Then, the earl of Cumberland, in whom the chief power of command was to raise men and money in a case of necessity, though he was a person of entire devotion to the King, was in his nature inactive, and utterly unexperienced in affairs and exigents of that nature.

On the other hand, the opposite party was strengthened and enabled by the strong garrison of Hull, whence young Hotham on all occasions was ready to second them with his troop of horse, and to take up any well affected person who was suspected to be loyal; which drove all resolved men from their houses into York, where they only could be safe. They could have what men more they desired from London, and both ready money from thence to Hull and ordinances to raise what they would in the county to pay them. Leeds, Halifax, and Bradford, three very populous and rich towns, (which depending wholly upon clothiers naturally maligned the gentry,) were wholly at their disposition. . . . So that if Sir John Hotham's[3] wariness had not kept him from being active, and his pride and contempt of the lord Fairfax, upon whom the country chiefly depended, hindered him from seconding and assisting his lordship, or if any man had had the entire command of those parts and forces to have united them, the Parliament had with very little resistance been absolute masters of all Yorkshire, and as easily of the city itself. But their want of union in the by, though they agreed too well in the main, gave the King's party time to breathe, and to look about for their preservation.

Notes

Individuals have not been noted unless relevant additional information is available.

1 'Lord Fairfax': Ferdinando Fairfax, father of Sir Thomas Fairfax who became Commander of the New Model Army.

2 'young Hotham': John Hotham, son of Sir John. The Hothams secured Hull for the Parliament in 1642 and refused Charles entry to the city. In 1643 father and son attempted to change sides but they were arrested by Parliament and executed in 1645.

3 'Sir John Hotham': see Note 2.

* * * * * * * * * *

44 Clarendon: Somerset

[*Source*: Macray editor (1888) *History of the Rebellion* volume two, pp. 296–7.]

For though the gentlemen of ancient families and estates in that county were for the most part well affected to the King, and easily discerned by what faction the Parliament was governed, yet there were a people of an inferior degree, who, by good husbandry, clothing, and other thriving arts, had gotten very great fortunes, and, by degrees getting themselves into the gentlemen's estates, were angry that they found not themselves in the same esteem and reputation with those whose estates they had; and therefore, with more industry than the other, studied all ways to make themselves considerable. These from the beginning were fast friends to the Parliament, and many of them were now intrusted by them as deputy-lieutenants in their new ordinance of the militia; and having found when the people were ripe, gathered them together, with a purpose on a sudden, before there should be any suspicion, to surround and surprise the marquis[1] at Wells. For they had always this advantage of the King's party and his counsels, that their resolutions were no sooner published than they were ready to be executed, there being an absolute implicit obedience in the inferior sort to those who were to command them, and their private agents, with admirable industry and secrecy, preparing all persons and things ready against a call. Whereas all the King's counsels were with great formality deliberated before concluded: and then, with equal formality and precise caution of the law, executed; there being no other way to weigh down the prejudice that was contracted against the Court but by the most barefaced publishing all conclusions, and fitting them to that apparent justice and reason that might prevail over the most ordinary understandings.

Note

1 'the marquis': William Seymour, Marquis of Hertford, Charles's leading supporter in the west country.

45 Clarendon: Lancashire and Cheshire

[*Source*: Macray editor (1888) *History of the Rebellion* volume two, pp. 470–2.]

The fair expectation of Cheshire was clouded by the storms that arose in Lancashire, where men of no name and contemned interest, by the mere credit of the Parliament and frenzy of the people, on a sudden snatched that large and populous county from their devotion to the great earl of Derby.[1]

The town of Manchester had from the beginning (out of that factious humour which possessed most corporations, and the pride of their wealth) opposed the King and declared magisterially for the Parliament. But as the major part of the county consisted of Papists, of whose insurrections they had made such use in the beginning of the Parliament, when they had a mind to alarm the people with dangers, so it was confidently believed that there was not one man of ten throughout that province who meant not to be dutiful and loyal to the King: yet the restless spirit of the seditious party was so sedulous and industrious, and every one of the party so ready to be engaged and punctually to obey, and on the other hand the earl of Derby so unactive, and through greatness of mind so uncomplying with those who were fuller of alacrity and would have proceeded more vigorously against the enemy, or through fear so confounded, that, instead of countenancing the King's party in Cheshire, which was expected from him, the earl insensibly found Lancashire to be almost possessed against him; the rebels every day gaining and fortifying all the strong towns, and surprising his troops, without any considerable encounter. And yet, so hard was the King's condition, that, though he knew those great misfortunes proceeded from want of conduct and of a vigorous and expert commander, he thought it not safe to make any alteration, lest the earl might be provoked, out of disdain to have any superior in Lancashire, to manifest how much he could do against him, though it appeared he could do little for him. Yet it was easily discerned that his ancient power there depended more upon the fear than love of the people, there being very many now in this time of liberty engaging themselves against the King that they might not be subject to that lord's commands. . . .

[In Cheshire] it is true . . . [the Parliamentarians] had no other straits and difficulties to struggle with than what proceeded from their enemy, being always supplied with money to pay their soldiers and with arms to arm them; whereby it was in their power not to grieve and oppress the people; and thereby (besides the spirit of faction that much governed) the common people were more devoted to them, and gave them all intelligence of what might concern them. Whereas they who were intrusted to govern the King's affairs had intolerable difficulties to pass through, being to raise men without money, to arm them without weapons, (that is, they had no magazine to supply them,) and to keep them together without pay; so that the country was both to feed and clothe the soldier, which quickly inclined them to remember only the burden and forget the quarrel.

Note

1 'earl of Derby': James Stanley, seventh earl of Derby, the dominant figure in Lancashire.

Social Differences Between the Two Sides

46 Clarendon

[*Source*: Macray editor (1888) *History of the Rebellion* volume three, p. 177.]

[The following comment was occasioned by the deaths of the royalist Earls of Sunderland and Caernarvon at the first battle of Newbury, September 1643.]

On which side soever the marks and public ensigns of victory appeared most conspicuous, certain it is, that, according to the unequal fate that attended all skirmishes, and conflicts with such an adversary, the loss on the King's side was in weight much more considerable and penetrating; for whilst some obscure, unheard of, colonel or officer was missing on the enemy's side, as some citizen's wife bewailed the loss of her husband, there were above twenty officers of the field and persons of honour and public name slain upon the place, and more of the same quality hurt.

47 Richard Baxter

[*Source*: Richard Baxter (1696) *Reliquiae Baxterianae*, edited by Matthew Sylvester, pp. 30–31.]

A great part of the Lords forsook the Parliament, and so did many of the House of Commons, and came to the King; but that was for the most of them after Edgehill fight [October 1642], when the King was at Oxford. A very great part of the knights and gentlemen of England in the several counties (who were not Parliament men) adhered to the King; except in Middlesex, Essex, Suffolk, Norfolk, Cambridgeshire, etc. where the King with his army never came. And could he have got footing there, it's like that it would have been there as it was in other places. And most of the tenants of these gentlemen, and also most of the poorest of the people, whom the other called the rabble, did follow the gentry and were for the King.

On the Parliament's side were (besides themselves) the smaller part, as some thought, of the gentry in most of the counties, and the greatest part of the tradesmen and freeholders, and the middle sort of men, especially in those corporations and countries which depend on clothing and such manufactures.

If you ask the reasons of this difference, ask also why in France it is not commonly the nobility nor the beggars, but the merchants and middle sort of men that were Protestants. The reasons which the party themselves gave was because, say they, the tradesmen have a correspondency with London, and so are grown to be a far more intelligent sort of men than the ignorant peasants that are like brutes, who will follow any that they think the strongest, or look to get by. And the freeholders, say they, were not enslaved to their landlords as the tenants are: the gentry, say they, are wholly by their estates and ambition more dependent on the King than their tenants on them; and many of them envied the honour of the Parliament, because they were not chosen members themselves. The other side said, that the reason was because the gentry, who commanded their tenants, did better understand affairs of state than half-witted tradesmen and freeholders do.

But though it must be confessed, that the public safety and liberty wrought very much with most, especially with the nobility and gentry who adhered to the Parliament; yet it was principally the differences about religious matters that filled up the Parliament's armies, and put the resolution and valour into their soldiers, which carried them on in another manner than mercenary soldiers are carried on. Not that the matter of bishops, or no bishops was the main thing (for thousands that wished for good bishops were on the Parliament's side) though many called it *Bellum Episcopale* [the Bishops' War], and with the Scots that was a greater part of the controversy. But the generality of the people through the land (I say not all, or everyone) who were then called Puritans, Precisians, religious persons, that used to talk of God, and heaven, and Scripture, and holiness, and to follow sermons, and read books of devotion, and pray in their families, and spend the Lord's day in religious exercises, and plead for mortification and serious devotion, and strict obedience to God, and speak against swearing, cursing, drunkenness, prophaneness, etc. I say, the main body of this sort of men, both preachers and people, adhered to the Parliament. And on the other side, the gentry that were not so precise and strict against an oath, or gaming, or plays, or drinking, nor troubled themselves so much about the matters of God, and the world to come, and the ministers and people that were for the King's book,[1] for dancing and recreations on the Lord's days; and those that made not so great a matter of every sin, but went to church and heard Common Prayer, and were glad to hear a sermon which lashed the Puritans, and which ordinarily spoke against this strictness and preciseness in religion, and this strict observation of the Lord's day, and following sermons, and praying *ex tempore*, and talking so much of scripture and the matters of salvation, and those that hated and derided them to take these courses, the main body of these were against the Parliament. Not but that some such for money, or a landlord's pleasure, served them; as some few of the stricter sort were against them, or not for them (being neuters); but I speak of the notable division through the land.

Note

1 'the King's book': the Book of Sports, issued in 1618 and again in 1633 – see p. 71, Note 3.

* * * * * * * * * * *

48 A Reluctant Participant: Thomas Knyvett to his wife, 18 May 1642

[*Source*: B. Schofield, editor (1949) *The Knyvett Letters 1620–1644* (Norfolk Record Society volume XX), pp. 101–4; a similar extract is printed in J.S. Morrill (1976) *The Revolt of the Provinces: Conservatives and Radicals In the English Civil War 1630–1650*.]

I cannot let any opportunity pass without telling of thee how I do; and I praise Almighty God I am able to tell thee I am at this present as well as I was these seven years. I would to God I could write thee any good news, but that is impossible so long as the spirit of contradiction reigns between King and Parliament higher still than ever, and 'tis to be feared this threatening storm will not be allayed without some showers (I pray God, not a deluge) of blood. The one party now grows as resolute as the other is obstinate . . . Oh, sweetheart, I am now in a great strait what to do. Walking this other morning at Westminster, Sir John Potts[1] . . . saluted me with a commission from the Lord of Warwick[2] to take upon me, by virtue of an ordinance of Parliament, my company and command [as a Captain in the Norfolk county militia] again. I was surprised what to do, whether to take or refuse. 'Twas no place to dispute, so I took it and desired some time to advise upon it. I had not received this many hours, but I met with a Declaration point blank against it [the militia ordinance] by the King. This distraction made me to advise with some understanding men what condition I stand in, which is no other than a great many men of quality do. What further commands we shall receive to put this ordinance in execution, if they run in a way that trenches upon my obedience against [to] the King, I shall do according to my conscience; and this is the resolution of all honest men that I can speak with. In the meantime I hold it good wisdom and security to keep my company as close to me as I can in these dangerous times, and to stay out of the way of my new masters till these first musterings be over . . . Poor King, he grows still in more contempt and slight here every day . . . and no wonder when the reverence and worship of the king of kings comes to be construed superstitious and idolatrous, yet no worship too much for the sons of men . . . This I heard more than ever, that since the King deserts his coming near them, and disclaims passing of anything until he hath satisfaction and justice in the business of Hull, they are now resolved to go on without him[3] by ordinance of Parliament; but how legal another age must resolve, for sure this dares not . . . I wish myself in thy arms every night most cordially, and all the Potts in Christendom shall not keep me from thee long.

Notes

1 'Sir John Potts': M.P. for Norfolk in the Long Parliament; a moderate Parliamentarian who helped to organize a local pacification with the Norfolk royalists in July 1642.

2 'the Lord of Warwick': Robert Rich, Earl of Warwick, Lord Lieutenant of Norfolk under the Militia Ordinance.

3 'to go on without him': Parliament had decided to legislate without obtaining the royal consent.

SECTION SEVEN: THE PROPAGANDA WAR

[Parliament urgently needed theoretical justification for taking up arms against the King. Philip Hunton wrote in answer to Dr Henry Ferne, a royal chaplain who denied that subjects could ever justly resist their king, but Hunton's own view of the English constitution led him into a logical impasse that was little help to the Parliament (extract 52). Others though argued that government should aim at the good of the governed and moved towards the idea of Parliamentary sovereignty (extracts 51 and 53). This idea was implicit in the practical proposals suggested by Parliament for the ending of the conflict: extract 55 is an example. On the royalist side the restraint of the reply to the Grand Remonstrance (extract 39 above) was continued. The settlement proposed by Parliament on the eve of war (the Nineteen Propositions) elicited an answer that was so moderate that even Hyde doubted its wisdom. Extract 50 was written by the Secretary of State Lord Falkland and the Chancellor of the Exchequer, Sir John Colepeper, two of the constitutionalist advisers appointed by Charles in January 1642. It draws on classical republican theory to portray the king as one of three estates in a mixed monarchy. Sir Robert Filmer presented a very different view of kingship in his 1648 critique of Hunton's mixed monarchy theories (extract 54). *Patriarcha*, Filmer's fullest articulation of absolutist theories, was not published until 1680 and his approach was found more serviceable by the supporters of Charles I's sons.]

49 John Selden: Contracts

[*Source*: *Table Talk: Being the Discourses of John Selden* (1689), p. 15.]

If our fathers have lost their liberty, why may not we labour to regain it? Answer: we must look to the contract, if that be rightly made we must stand to it. If we once grant we may recede from contracts upon any inconveniency that may afterwards happen, we shall have no bargain kept. If I sell you a horse and do not like my bargain, I will have my horse again.

50 Charles I: Reply to the Nineteen Propositions, 18 June 1642

[*Source*: J.P. Kenyon (1966) *The Stuart Constitution: Documents and Commentary*, pp. 21–3.]

There being three kinds of government among men, absolute monarchy, aristocracy and democracy, and all these having their particular conveniences and inconveniences, the experience and wisdom of your ancestors hath so moulded this out of a mixture of these as to give to this kingdom (as far as human prudence can provide) the conveniences of all three, without the inconveniences of any one, as long as the balance hangs even between the three estates, and they run jointly on in their proper channel (begetting verdure and fertility in the meadows on both sides) and the overflowing of either on either side raise no deluge or inundation. The ill of absolute monarchy is tyranny, the ill of aristocracy is faction and division, the ills of democracy are tumults, violence and licentiousness. The good of monarchy is the uniting a nation under one head to resist invasion from abroad and insurrection at home; the good of aristocracy is the conjunction of counsel in the ablest persons of a state for the public benefit; the good of democracy is liberty, and the courage and industry which liberty begets.

In this kingdom the laws are jointly made by a king, by a house of peers, and by a House of Commons chosen by the people, all having free votes and particular privileges. The government, according to these laws, is [en]trusted to the King; power of treaties of war and peace, of making peers, of choosing officers and councillors for state, judges for law, commanders for forts and castles, giving commissions for raising men, to make war abroad, or to prevent or provide against invasions or insurrections at home, benefit of confiscations, power of pardoning, and some more of the like kind are placed in the King. And this kind of regulated monarchy, having this power to preserve that authority without which it would be disabled to preserve the laws in their force and the subjects in their liberties and properties, is intended to draw to him such a respect and relation from the great ones, as may hinder the ills of division and faction, and such a fear and reverence from the people as may hinder tumults, violence and licentiousness.

Again, that the prince may not make use of this high and perpetual power to the hurt of those for whose good he hath it, and make use of the name of public necessity for the gain of his private favourites and followers, to the detriment of his people, the House of Commons (an excellent convener of liberty, but never intended for any share in government, or the choosing of them that govern) is solely entrusted with the first propositions concerning the levy of money (which is the sinews as well of peace as of war), and the impeaching of those who for their own ends, though countenanced by any surreptitiously gotten command of the King, have violated the law, which he is bound (when he knows it) to protect; and to the prosecution of which they are bound to advise him, at least not to serve him to the contrary. And the Lords, being trusted with a judicatory power, are an excellent screen and bank between the prince and people, to assist each against any encroachments of the other, and by just judgements to preserve that law which ought to be the rule of every one of the three . . .

Since therefore the power, legally placed in both houses, is more than sufficient to prevent and restrain the power of tyranny, and without the power which is now asked from us we shall not be able to discharge that trust which is the end of monarchy, since this would be a total subversion of the fundamental laws, and that excellent constitution of this kingdom which hath made this nation so many years both famous and happy to a great degree of envy, since to the power of punishing (which is already in your hands according to law) if the power of preferring be added, we shall have nothing left for us but to look on, since the encroaching of one of these estates upon the power of the other is unhappy in the effects, both to them and all the rest, since this power of at most a joint government in us with our councillors (or rather, our guardians) will return us to the worst kind of minority, and make us despicable both at home and abroad, and beget eternal factions and dissensions (as destructive to public happiness as war) both in the chosen, and in the houses that chose them, and the people who chose the choosers, since so new a power will undoubtedly intoxicate persons who were not born to it, and beget not only divisions among them as equals, but in them contempt of us, as become an equal to them, and insolence and injustice toward our people, as now so much their inferiors, which will be the more grievous unto them, as suffering from those who were so lately of a nearer degree to themselves, and being to have redress only from those that placed them, and fearing they may be inclined to preserve what they have made, both out of kindness and policy, since all great changes are extremely inconvenient, and almost infallibly beget yet greater changes, which beget yet greater inconveniences.

Since as great a one in the Church must follow this of the Kingdom, since the second estate would in all probability follow the fate of the first, and by some of the turbulent spirits jealousies would soon be raised against them, and the like propositions for reconciliations of differences would then be sent to them as they now have joined to send to us till (all power being vested in the House of Commons, and their number making them incapable of transacting affairs of state with the necessary service and expedition, these being retrusted to some close committee) at last the common people (who in the meantime must be flattered, and to whom licence must be given in all their wild humours, how contrary soever to established law, or their own real good) discover this *arcanum imperii* [secret of command], that all this was done by them, but not for them, and grow weary of journey-work, and set up for themselves, call parity and independence liberty, devour that estate which had devoured the rest, destroy all rights and proprieties, all distinctions of families and merit, and by this means this splendid and excellently distinguished form of government end in a dark, equal chaos of confusion, and the long line of our many noble ancestors in a Jack Cade or a Wat Tyler.[1]

Note

1 'a Jack Cade or a Wat Tyler': Cade led a popular rising in 1450; Tyler was a leader of the Peasants' Revolt (1381).

51 The End of Government

[*Source*: Anon. (1643) *Touching the Fundamentall Laws*, pp. 10 and 13.]

God and nature hath ordained government for the preservation of the governed. This is a truth so undeniable, as that none will gainsay it, saving in practice; which therefore being taken for granted, it must needs follow that to what end government was ordained, it must be maintained, for that it is not in the power of particular persons or communities of men to depart with self-preservation by any covenant whatsoever, nor ought it to be exacted by any superiors from their inferiors, either by oath or edict, because neither oaths nor statutes are obligatory further than they agree with the righteous laws of God and nature; further than so they ought neither to be made nor kept.

Let it be supposed then for argument sake, that the Militia of the Kingdom, is in the power of the King, yet now, as the case stands, it is lawful for the Parliament to re-assume it, because though they passed it into his hands for the people's preservation, yet it was never intended that by it he might compass their destruction, contrary to the law of nature, whereby every man, yea every thing is bound to preserve itself . . .

The representative body of the Commonwealth [i.e. the Parliament] which is all men *conjunctim* [together] . . . may not only oppose the person [of the King] and his will, but even the office and authority itself when abused, and are bound to it both in conscience to God when he gives them opportunity, and in discharging of their trust to them that employed them. For first God calls to have the wicked removed from the throne; and whom doth he call upon to do it but upon the people, in case the King will not, or their trustees; for as he hath originally founded all authority in the people, so he expects a discharge of it from them for his glory, and the public weal, which are the ends of government, from which God and nature hath ordained it.

52 Philip Hunton

[*Source*: Philip Hunton (1643) *A Treatise of Monarchie*, published anonymously. (a) pp. 39–41; (b) pp.27–9.]

a. England as a Mixed Monarchy

I conceive it a clear and undoubted truth, that the authority of this land is of a compounded and mixed nature in the very root and constitution thereof. And my judgement is established on these grounds.

First, it is acknowledged to be a monarchy mixed with aristocracy in the house of Peers, and democracy in the House of Commons . . .

Secondly, that monarchy where the legislative power is in all three, is in the very root and essence of it compounded and mixed of those three, for that is the height of power . . .

Thirdly, that monarchy in which the three estates are constituted to the end that the power of one should moderate and restrain from excess the power of the other is mixed in the root and essence of it . . .

The never enough to be admired wisdom of the architects and contrivers of the frame of government in this realm, whoever they were, have found a . . . way by which they have conserved the sovereignty of the Prince, and also made an excellent provision for the people's freedom, by constituting two estates of men, who are for their condition subjects, and yet have that interest in the government that they can both moderate and redress the excesses and illegalities of the royal power; which, I say, cannot be done but by a mixture: that is, by putting into their hands a power to meddle in acts of the highest function of government; a power not depending on his will, but radically their own, and so sufficient to moderate the sovereign's power.

b. Resistance in a Mixed Monarchy

Concerning the extent of the Prince's power and the subject's duty in a mixed monarchy . . . it is a general rule in this matter: such as the constitution of government is, such is the ordinance of God; such as the ordinance is, such must our subjection be. No power can challenge an obedience beyond its own measure; for if it might, we should destroy all rules and differences of government, and make all absolute and at pleasure . . .

In such a composed state, if the monarch invade the power of the other two [estates] or run in any course tending to the dissolving of the constituted frame, they ought to employ their power in this case to preserve the state from ruin; yea, that is the very end and fundamental aim in constituting all mixed policies: not that they by crossing and jarring should hinder the public good, but that if one exorbitate, the power of restraint and providing for the public safety should be in the rest . . . For such other estates, it is not only lawful to deny obedience and submission to illegal proceedings, as private men may, but it is their duty, and by the foundations of government, they are bound to prevent dissolution of the established frame.

. . . The person of the monarch, even in these mixed forms . . . ought to be above the reach of violence in his utmost exorbitances: for when a people have sworn allegiance, and invested a person or line with supremacy, they have made it sacred, and no abuse can divest him of that power, irrevocably communicated . . .

One inconvenience must necessarily be in all mixed governments . . . There can be no constituted, legal, authoritative judge of the fundamental controversies arising betwixt the three estates. If such do arise, it is the fatal disease of these governments, for which no salve can be prescribed, for the established being of such authority would *ipso facto* overthrow the frame and turn it into absoluteness. So that if one of these, or two, say their power is invaded, and the government assaulted by the other, the accused denying it, it doth become a controversy: of this question there is no legal judge; it is a case beyond the possible provision of such a government. The accusing side must make it evident to every man's conscience. In this case, which is beyond the government, the appeal must be to the community as if there were no government; and as by evidence men's consciences are convinced, they are bound to give their utmost assistance. For the intention of the frame in such states justifies the exercise of any power conducing to the safety of the universality and government established.

53 Henry Parker

[*Source*: Henry Parker, (Second edition, 1642) *Observations upon some of his Majesties late Answers and Expresses* (a) p. 1; (b) pp. 5, 8, 24, 30 and 45.]

a. On the Origins of Political Power

The King attributeth the original of his royalty to God and the law, making no mention of the grant, consent or trust of man therein, but the truth is, God is no more the author of regal, than of aristocratical power, nor of supreme, than of subordinate command; nay, that dominion which is usurped and not just, yet whilst it remains dominion, and till it be legally again divested, refers to God as to its author and donor, as much as that which is hereditary. And that law which the King mentioneth, is not to be understood to be any special ordinance, sent from heaven by the ministry of angels or prophets (as amongst the Jews it sometimes was): it can be nothing else amongst Christians but the pactions [contracts] and agreements of such and such politic corporations. Power is originally inherent in the people, and it is nothing else but that might and vigour which such or such a society of men contains in itself; and when by such or such a law of common consent and agreement, it is derived into such and such hands, God confirms that law; and so man is the free and voluntary author, the law is the instrument, and God is the establisher of both.

b. On the Role of Parliaments

Two things especially are aimed at in Parliament, not to be attained to by any other means. First, that the interest of the people might be satisfied; secondly, that kings might be better counselled . . .

The people then having entrusted their protection into the king's hands irrevocably, yet have not left that trust without all manner of limits: some things they have reserved to themselves out of Parliament, and something in Parliament . . .

Parliamentary government being used as physic, not diet, by the intermission of due spaces of time has in it all that is excellent in all forms of government whatsoever. If the king be an affector of true liberty, he has in Parliament a power as extensive as ever the Roman Dictator's was for the preventing of all public distresses. If the king be apt to intrude upon the common liberties, the people have hereby many democratical advantages to preserve themselves; if war be, here is the unitive virtue of monarchy to encounter it; here is the admirable counsel of aristocracy to manage it; if peace be, here is the industry and courage of democracy to improve it[1] . . .

If kings be so inclinable to follow private advice rather than public, and to prefer that which closes with their natural, impotent ambition before that which crosses the same, [and] are without all limits, then they may destroy their best subjects at pleasure, and all charters and laws of public safety and freedom are void, and God hath not left human nature any means of sufficient preservation. But, on the contrary, if there be any benefit in laws to limit princes when they are seduced by privados [favourites], and will not hearken to the great council of the land, doubtless there must be some court to judge of that seducement, and some authority to enforce that judgement, and that court and authority must be the Parliament . . .

Parliaments . . . may judge of public necessity without the king, and dispose of anything. They may not desert the king, but being deserted by the king, when the kingdom is in distress, they may judge of that distress, and relieve it, and are to be accounted, by the virtue of representation, as the whole body of the state.

Note

1 Based on the first paragraph of the extract from Charles I's answer to the Nineteen Propositions, see p. 94, above.

54 Sir Robert Filmer: A defence of the Divine Right of Kings

[Source: Sir Robert Filmer (1648) *The Anarchy of a Limited or Mixed Monarchy*, pp. 6–7, 12–13, originally published anonymously.]

Neither Eve nor her children could either limit Adam's power, or join others with him in the government, and what was given unto Adam was given in his person to his posterity . . . Now if this supreme power was settled and founded by God himself in the fatherhood, how is it possible for the people to have any right or title to alter and dispose of it otherwise? What commission can they show that gives them power either of limitation or mixture? It was God's ordinance, that supremacy should be unlimited in Adam, and as large as all the acts of his will; and as in him, so in all others that have supreme power . . .

As the Scripture teacheth us, that supreme power was originally in the fatherhood without any limitation, so likewise reason doth evince it, that if God ordained that supremacy should be, that then supremacy must of necessity be unlimited, for the power that limits must be above that power which is limited: if it be limited it cannot be supreme . . .

The monarchical power of Adam, the father of all flesh, being by a general binding ordinance settled by God in him and his posterity by right of fatherhood, the form of monarchy must be preferred above other forms, except the like ordinance for other forms can be showed . . .

If it be objected, that kings are not now (as they were at the first planting or peopling of the world) the fathers of their people, or kingdoms, and that the fatherhood hath lost the right of governing; an answer is, that all kings that now are, or ever were, are, or were either fathers of their people, or the heirs of such fathers, or usurpers of the right of such fathers. It is a truth undeniable that there cannot be any multitude of men whatsoever, either great or small, though gathered together from the several corners and remotest regions of the world, but that in the same multitude considered by itself, there is one man amongst them that in nature hath a right to be the king of all the rest, as being the next heir to Adam, and all the others subject unto him; every man by nature is a king or a subject: the obedience which all subjects yield to kings is but the paying of that duty which is due to the supreme fatherhood. Many times by the act either of an usurper himself, or of those that set him up, the true heir of a crown is dispossessed, God using the ministry of the wickedest men for the removing and setting up of kings. In such cases the subject's obedience to the fatherly power must go along and wait upon God's providence who only hath right to give and take away kingdoms, and thereby to adopt subjects into the obedience of another fatherly power . . .

However the natural freedom of the people be cried up as the sole means to determine the kind of government and the governors, yet, in the close, all the favourers of this opinion are constrained to grant that the obedience which is due to the fatherly power is the true and only cause of the subjection, which we that are now living give to kings; since none of us gave consent to government, but only our forefathers' act and consent hath concluded us.

55 Theory into Practice: The Propositions of Uxbridge, presented to the King, 24 November, 1644

[*Source*: S.R. Gardiner editor (1906, Third edition) *Constitutional Documents of the Puritan Revolution*, pp. 275–7 and 281–5.]

1 That by Act of Parliament in each kingdom respectively all oaths, declarations and proclamations against both or either of the Houses of Parliament of England, and the late Convention of Estates in Scotland . . . or their Ordinances and proceedings or against any for adhering unto them; and all indictments, outlawries and attainders against any for the said causes, be declared null, suppressed and forbidden; and that this be publicly intimated in all parish churches within His Majesty's dominions, and all other places needful.

2 That His Majesty, according to the laudable example of his royal

father of happy memory, may be pleased to swear and sign the late Solemn League and Covenant;[1] and that an Act of Parliament be passed in both kingdoms respectively, for enjoining the taking thereof by all the subjects of the three kingdoms . . .

3 That the Bill be passed for the utter abolishing and taking away of all Archbishops, Bishops, their Chancellors and Commissaries, Deans and Sub-Deans, Deans and Chapters, Archdeacons . . . [etc.] out of the Church of England and dominion of Wales, and out of the Church of Ireland . . .

4 That the Ordinance concerning the calling and sitting of the Assembly of Divines be confirmed by Act of Parliament.

5 The reformation of religion, according to the Covenant, be settled by Act of Parliament, in such manner as both Houses shall agree upon after consultation had with the Assembly of Divines . . .

[Clauses 6–10 dealt with penalties to be imposed on Roman Catholics.]

11 That the King do give his royal assent,
To an Act for the due observation of the Lord's day;
And to the Bill for the suppression of innovations in churches and chapels, in and about the worship of God, and for the better advancement of the preaching of God's Holy Word in all parts of this kingdom;
And to the Bill against the enjoying of pluralities of benefices by spiritual persons, and non-residency;

And to an Act to be framed and agreed upon by both Houses of Parliament, for the reforming and regulating of both Universities, of the Colleges of Westminster, Winchester and Eton;
And to an Act in like manner to be agreed upon for the suppressing of interludes and stage plays: this Act to be perpetual;
And to an Act for the taking the accounts of the kingdom;
And to an Act to be made for relief of sick and maimed soldiers, and of poor widows and children of soldiers;
And to such Act or Acts for raising of moneys for the payment and satisfying of the public debts and damages of the kingdom, and other public uses as shall hereafter be agreed upon by both Houses of Parliament.
And to an Act . . . for taking away the Court of Wards and Liveries . . .
And for the taking away of all tenures by homage . . . and that His Majesty will please to accept, in recompense thereof, £100,000 *per annum* . . .
[And to an Act confirming the proceedings of the Convention of Estates of Scotland.]
[The treaties between the Parliament and the Scots were to be confirmed; the agreements between the King and the Catholic Irish were to be made void; and Parliament was to manage the Irish war.]

[A scale of penalties was laid down for royalist supporters depending on their prominence, and the degree of their commitment. These varied from condemnation as traitors to disqualification from public office, and the confiscation of part of their estates.]

15 That by Act of Parliament the subjects of the kingdom of England may be appointed to be armed, trained and disciplined in such manner as both Houses shall think fit, the like for the kingdom of Scotland . . .

16 That an Act of Parliament be passed for the settling of the admiralty and forces at sea, and for the raising of such moneys for maintenance of the said forces and of the navy, as both Houses of Parliament shall think fit; the like for the kingdom of Scotland . . .

17 An Act for the settling of all forces both by sea and land, in Commissioners to be nominated by both Houses of Parliament, of persons of known integrity, and such as both kingdoms may confide in for their faithfulness to religion and peace of the kingdoms . . .

[These Commissioners, with similar Commissioners for Scotland, were to enforce the peace treaty.]

[All peerages and other honours granted since 20 May 1642 were to be null and void.]

20 That by Act of Parliament the Deputy or Chief Governor, or other Governors of Ireland, be nominated by both Houses of Parliament . . . And that the Chancellor or Lord Keeper, Lord Treasurer, Commissioners of the Great Seal or Treasury, Lord Warden of the Cinque Ports, Chancellors of the Exchequer and Duchy, Secretary of State, Judges of both Benches, and of the Exchequer of the kingdoms of England and Ireland, be nominated by both Houses of Parliament, to continue *quam diu se bene gesserint* [as long as they behave themselves well] . . . the like for the kingdom of Scotland . . .

[Parliament was to control the education and marriages of the King's children.]

[The King was to assent to measures for the restoration of the Palatinate.]

23 That by Act of Parliament the concluding of peace or war with foreign Princes and States, be with advice and consent of both Parliaments . . .

24 That an Act of Oblivion be passed in the Parliaments of both kingdoms . . .

25 That the members of both Houses of Parliament, or others, who have during this Parliament been put out of any place or office, pension or benefit, for adhering to the Parliament, may either be restored thereunto or otherwise have recompense . . .

[The like for Scotland.]

26 That the armies may be disbanded at such time and in such manner as shall be agreed upon by the Parliaments of both kingdoms, or such as shall be authorised by them to that effect.

27 That an Act be passed for the granting and confirming of the charters, customs, liberties and franchises of the City of London . . .

Note

1 'Solemn League and Covenant': the symbol of the Parliament's alliance with the Scots, signed in September 1643. It included commitments to reform the churches of England and Ireland, 'according to the Word of God and the example of the best reformed churches'; and to 'endeavour' to create religious uniformity in the three kingdoms. In effect, the English agreed to a Presbyterian system. The 'laudable example' was a reference to the anti-papist 'Negative Confession' signed by the young James VI in 1581; it formed the preamble to the Scottish National Covenant of 1638.

SECTION EIGHT: CIVIL WAR ADMINISTRATION

[Civil war involved unprecedented duties for local administrators. In Parliamentarian areas committees were established to raise money and organize the war effort. In some counties several specific committees dealt with particular matters, but in others like Staffordshire a single committee covered all aspects of civil war administration (extract 59). The political division within the ruling class allowed comparatively obscure men to gain positions of power in local government, especially as the war went on and moderates withdrew from activity. Taxation was higher than ever before while informal charges on the civilian population, particularly freequarter and plunder, could be more expensive than official levies. Royalist and Catholic landowners (Parliament's papists, delinquents and malignants) suffered the confiscation or 'sequestration' of their estates although from 1644 penitent royalists could recover their estates on the payment of a fine – the process known as 'composition'. Extract 60 illustrates many of these points and shows how wide Parliament's definition of a 'delinquent' could be. Conservatives were highly alarmed at the powers wielded by committees and it was often argued in the later 1640s that Parliament's arbitrary rule was worse than anything done by Charles I in the 1630s. We include two such critics and an example of a justification of Parliament's procedures (extracts 56–58). Radicals like Overton and Winstanley also attacked Parliament's 'tyrannical' rule (extracts 85, 94 and 97 below). We know much less about royalist civil war administration although it has been argued that the royalists were more careful to follow traditional legal methods. Clarendon (extract 44 above) suggests this was the case in Somerset although he hints that it was necessary because the royalists had to make more effort than the parliamentarians to overcome popular hostility.]

General Comments

56 John Selden

[*Source*: *Table Talk: Being the Discourses of John Selden* (1689), p. 53.]

Heretofore the Parliament was wary what subsidies they gave to the King because they had no account, but now they care not how much they give of the subjects' money because they give it with one hand and receive it with the other, and so upon the matter [in fact] give it themselves. In the meantime what a case the subjects of England are in; if the men they have sent to the Parliament misbehave themselves, they cannot help it, because the Parliament is eternal.

57 Clarendon

[*Source*: W. Dunn Macray editor (1888) *The History of the Rebellion and Civil Wars in England* by Edward Earl of Clarendon, volume two, p. 318.]

It was the usual course, (and very few scaped it,) after any man was committed as a *notorious malignant*, (which was the brand,) that his estate and goods were seized or plundered, by an order from the House of Commons or some committee, or [by] the soldiers, (who in their march took the goods of all Catholics and eminent malignants as lawful prize), or by the fury and license of the common people, who were in all places grown to that barbarity and rage against the nobility and gentry, (under the style of *cavaliers*,) that it was not safe for any to live at their houses who were taken notice of as no votaries to the Parliament.

58 John Bryan

[*Source*: John Bryan (1647) *A Discovery of the Probable Sin*, p. 3.]

[From a sermon preached at Coventry, 23 December 1646]

We are displeased and murmur at taxes and impositions whereat we should not quarrel, seeing we enjoy our lives, liberties, privileges, estates and religion (all which were at stake and almost lost; for so great a difference is there betwixt these taxes the Parliament at present imposeth and those which formerly our taskmasters laid upon us. Those were in design to ruin and enslave us to arbitrary power; these are to preserve us from it . . .).

* * * * * * * * * * *

59 A County Committee at Work

[*Source*: *The Committee at Stafford 1643–1645: The Order Book of the Staffordshire County Committee*, edited with an Introduction by D.H. Pennington and I.A. Roots. (Published by Manchester University Press in Association with Staffordshire Record Society, 1957), pp. 236–41.]

[1645] January 9

Whereas Mr Hunter, Corporal under Captain Thacker, having taken a horse from Mr Hart of Uttoxeter Woodlands, hath refused to restore the said horse upon the Committee's order (and given contemptuous words against them, saying he neither cared for the Committee nor their order);[1] it is ordered that for his contempt of the said order he shall be committed to the marshal till he restore the said horse and give satisfaction to the Committee for his contempt.

Mr Allicock's weekly pay to be paid by the Treasurer

Whereas the weekly pay of Acton Trussell is assigned to Lieutenant Colonel Jackson for the pay of his officers and soldiers, and that Mr Thomas Allicock, having lands within the said township, being now in service at Stafford,[2] it is ordered that his lands there shall be freed and discharged from the weekly pay during his service, and that Mr Wilmot, the Treasurer, shall pay the said Lieutenant Colonel the weekly pay for the said lands being 3s 4d weekly.

Whereas it is informed that Mayfield, Butterton, Throwley Woodhouses, Wetton and the third part of Calton is a division whereof Wetton is the third part of the said division and that at the £400,000 assessment[3] it paid answerable as a third part and no more, until now of late Lieutenant Colonel Watson, to whom the weekly pay of that division is assigned, doth demand more of the said township of Wetton than formerly they paid, and of right ought to pay. It is therefore ordered that the said township of Wetton shall pay no more than what formerly they were accustomed to pay according to the said £400,000 assessment, unless the said Lieutenant Colonel Watson, having notice of this order shall show sufficient cause to the contrary.

That a muster of all the horse and foot be taken on Monday next at Rushall, Eccleshall, Tamworth, and the Moorlands.

High Constable
Mr Richard Parker of Diglake in the parish of Audley, High Constable for part of Pirehill hundred for one month next in the room of Mr William Hill of Shelton.

January 11
It is desired by the Committee at Stafford that Mr Edward Mainwaring junior, Mr Samuel Terrick and Mr John Simcox, or any two of them, shall view the Castle of Heighley upon Tuesday next and agree with masons and other labourers at as cheap rates as they can to demolish and pull down the said castle and walls for fear lest an enemy should possess himself of it; and the conductors thereabouts are to summon in the masons and workmen to be ready there upon Tuesday to the end they may be agreed with for the service aforesaid. And the Committee will take care that the money be paid to the workmen for the demolishing of the same . . .
[A first attempt at the next order was deleted here.]

Upon the petition of Richard Backhouse of Stafford, showing that he, being tenant to Mrs Cradock for his house at the yearly rent of eight pounds, Colonel Lewis Chadwick, Lieutenant Colonel Jackson, and others at the taking of the town,[4] seized upon his house for the public use, and have ever since held it upon promise that his rent should be defrayed. It is therefore ordered that the Treasurer shall pay to the said Mr Backhouse, the sum of eight pounds yearly so long as the Committee, their officers and servants shall make use of it; and shall likewise pay the arrears of the rent for the time since first they entered upon it. Signed by [committeemen] Sir William Brereton, Thomas Crompton, Philip Jackson, Henry Stone, William Foxall and William Bendy.

13 January
Whereas Colonel John Bowyer informs that he hath disbursed one hundred and fourscore pounds for ammunition and other things necessary for the garrison of Leek, more than his weekly pay amounts unto, it is ordered, that for the raising of the said money, the said Colonel Bowyer, Lieutenant Colonel John Watson, Mr Edward Hippesley, Captain Thomas Gent and Mr John Smith of Horton, or any three or more of them, shall have power to call before them certain persons within the hundred of Totmonslow that have not advanced moneys upon the Propositions,[5] or have not advanced answerable to their abilities; and shall treat and compound with the said persons, and receive so much money of them as will extend to pay the said one hundred and fourscore pounds; and shall account to the Committee at Stafford what moneys they shall receive of every such person to the end they may have the public faith for the money they so pay. Signed by Colonel [Edward] Leigh, Mr Crompton, Lieutenant Colonel [Philip] Jackson, Captain [Henry] Stone, Mr [Richard] Whitehalgh, Mr [Thomas] Dolman.

Whereas Colonel John Bowyer informs that he hath more soldiers than his weekly pay will satisfy, it is ordered that a muster shall be presently called, and a list taken of his soldiers that if they appear to be more, as is alleged, there may be a speedy course taken for pay for them, or else order to disband part of them. Signed by Mr Crompton, Lieutenant Colonel Jackson, Captain Stone and Mr Whitehalgh.

It is ordered that the tenants and occupiers of the lands of Walter Chetwynd esquire, belonging to the four prebends within Gnosall, shall pay their lewns [taxes] and assessments to the constable there, since the first of June last, and shall continue to pay till further order.

Weston and Steele
Whereas there was complaint made to us by Alice Weston and others against John Steele of Madeley, blacksmith, for violently assaulting her servants and wronging her by taking away her goods out of her own lands by a pretended right; upon hearing and debating of which, it was by us desired that the difference should be referred to the hearing of Nicholas Browne and William Coleclough, gentlemen, to make report to us: who do accordingly certify that they caused a jury to view the meres [limits] and boundaries of the lands, claimed by the said Steele; [and certify the lands] to belong to the said Alice Weston and hath been and continued in the possession of Mr John Weston, her husband, for the space of thirty years or thereabouts; and conceive the said Steele to have done injury to her by hindering her of the quiet possession of her lands, and then not suffering her to take away her wood and other benefits. It is therefore now ordered that the said Steele shall quietly permit and suffer her to enjoy her lands and take her wood and trouse [brushwood] from off the lands without any let or molestation.

L C Watson
It is ordered that Lieutenant Colonel Watson shall have liberty to fetch in any malignant persons, being countrymen, for the exchange of such honest men that are taken prisoners out of his neighbourhood.

L C Watson
Whereas Lieutenant Colonel Watson holds certain grounds of Mr Leonard Hatfield, and the said Mr Hatfield being tenant to Sir William Savile, a delinquent, for a third part of the land he holds; it is ordered that the sequestrators shall pay to the said Mr Hatfield such a proportion of rents for the lands Lieutenant Colonel holds, as the said Mr Hatfield pays for the lands he holds. And the said Mr Hatfield is to pay the sequestrators the arrears of the weekly pay for the lands he holds till the time he was assessed.[6]

Hatfield
Whereas Mr Hatfield was ordered to pay the arrears of his weekly pay till the time of the assessment to the sequestrators, the Committee are content that he shall pay no weekly pay for the lands he holds, but only for the time they have been assessed.[7]

Q Buxtons
It is ordered that Quartermaster Richard Buxtons shall receive twenty

shillings weekly from the Treasurer towards his service as Quartermaster.

Thacker 14 January
Upon the understanding of Mr Bark and Edward Foster that they will, upon Saturday next, deliver again to the Marshal's custody the person of Thomas Thacker, now prisoner here, or in the mean time release Richard Greene, now prisoner at Lichfield, [a royalist garrison] it is ordered that the said Thacker shall be forthwith released.

Twyford
Whereas there is £23 due to John Twyford for his quartering of soldiers, it is ordered that he shall be paid £11 by the solicitors for sequestration, and shall have the public faith of the kingdom for the sum of £12.

Machin
Ordered, that upon the payment of £5 to the treasurer, Humphrey Machin, now prisoner, shall be forthwith released.

Mrs Stanford
Whereas the lands of Edward Stanford, esquire, within the county of Stafford, are sequestered for the use of the King and Parliament,[8] he being a recusant and in arms against them; yet upon Mrs Dorothy Stanford, his wife's petition for maintenance out of the said lands, it is agreed by and between the Committee at Stafford, and the said Mrs Stanford: that Francis Erpe of Lynn, gentleman, and Thomas Jordan of Perry Barr, yeoman shall set and let the lands of the said Mrs Stanford for the best use; a fifth part whereof, both of the profits both of the demesnes and tenants' rents, the Committee do order shall be paid to the said Mrs Stanford for her maintenance as aforesaid, and the rest to the Treasurer at Stafford for the state's use. And because the said Mrs Stanford is destitute of a house, it is ordered that she shall have the hall called Perry Barr Hall, and two closes called Pale Close and Broomie leasow [pasture] upon such a rent as Mr Erpe and Thomas Jordan shall agree upon, which is to be accounted as parcel of the fifth part of the profits of the demesnes allowed her. And the said Mrs Stanford doth undertake to secure the said Mr Erpe from any danger or molestation of the King's party, and the Committee do undertake to secure the said Thomas Jordan from the Parliament forces. It is intended that the said Mrs Stanford shall pay the weekly pay for the lands and profits she holds.

Leacroft
Whereas William Shelley held a tenement of one Leake in Aston upon the yearly rent of £14-10s and weekly pay, and now refuseth to hold it any longer upon the said rent, alleging that it is too dear; and that Thomas Leacroft proffereth to hold it upon the said terms, it is ordered that the said Leacroft shall hold the said tenement from the Annunciation next, for one whole year, upon the rent aforesaid, which he is to pay to the treasurer at Stafford in this manner, viz. the one moiety at

the Annunciation next, and the other moiety at the feast of St Michael the Archangel.

Notes

No attempt has been made to identify individuals unless additional information is necessary to an understanding of the orders.

1 The words in brackets were inserted later.
2 Thomas Allicock served as muster master to the county forces.
3 'The £400,000 assessment': a tax raised in March 1642. It levied a fixed sum on each county and its procedure formed the basis for later parliamentary taxation, especially the 'weekly pay'.
4 Stafford was taken from the royalists in May 1643.
5 'the Propositions': money advanced under Parliament's appeal for a loan in June 1642. Repayment with interest at 8 per cent was promised on the 'Public Faith'. In May 1643 the 'loan' was made compulsory for those of more than a certain wealth.
6 Hatfield was the keeper of the royalist Sir William Saville's park at Alton; Watson the commander of the parliamentary garrison there.
7 This order was inserted at a later date.
8 That is for the use of the Parliament.

60 The Sufferings of William Davenport of Bramhall, Cheshire

[*Source*: *The Commonplace Book of William Davenport*, printed in J.S. Morrill (1976) *The Revolt of the Provinces: Conservatives and Radicals in the English Civil War, 1630–1650*, pp. 190–2.]

A brief summary of my sufferings in some special passages since the beginning of March 1643.

About which time, Sir William Brereton sending his cornet with part of his troop to be quartered with me overnight, next morning came to Bramhall himself, attended with his whole troop, and John Brereton with him, and then he disarmed me of all the arms I had in my house (leaving only a piece for my keeper) viz: eight muskets, eight corslets, besides my horse (being a lancer) and man with their furniture worth forty pounds, besides some seven pounds in money paid to John Brereton. When after some conference I and my wife in the hearing of others had his promise that as he did disarm, so he would defend us from all the Parliament's party whatsoever, he being then chief commissioner for the Parliament and afterwards general.

Ever since that present we have kept our men, wherewith my land is charged, in continual pay at Nantwich [a Parliamentarian garrison] which comes to above three score pounds per annum. My wife paid moreover to Colonel Duckenfield betwixt forty and fifty pounds upon the Propositions[1] of Parliament, which she made with Sir George Booth and the rest of the commissioners for the Parliament.

We have likewise paid all layes [levies] and taxations that have been [illegible], Tamworth and the moorelands

High Const. Mr Richard Parker of Diglake in the parish of Audley high Constable for part of Pirehill hundred for one moneth next in the roome of Mr William Hill of Shelton.

Jan: 11° It is desired by the Committee at Stafford that Mr Edward Mainwaringe junr, Mr Samuell Terricke and John Swinnerton or any two of them shall view the Castle of Healye upon Tuesday next, agree with Masons & other labourers at as cheape rates as they can to demolish & pull downe the said Castle and walls for feare least an Enemie should possesse himselfe of it, the Constables thereabouts are to summon in the Masons & workmen to be readie there upon Tuesday to the end they may be agreed with for the service aforesaid. And the Committee will take care that the money be paid to the workmen for the demolishinge of the same.

~~In answere to a petition of Richard Backhouse sent to Mrs Cradock shewing that he held at the taking of the Col. Lewis Chadwicke, Lieutent Col. Jackson & others seized upon his house & stables &c, which he~~

Upon the petition of Richard Backhouse of Stafford shewing that he being tenant to Mrs Cradocke for his house at the yearely rent of eight pounds Colonell Lewis Chadwicke Lieutent Colonell Jackson & others at the taking of ye Towne seized upon his house for the publique use, & have ever since held it upon promise that his rent should be discharged. It is therefore ordered that the Treasurer shall pay to the said Mr Backhouse the summe of eight pounds yearely so long as the Committee theyr Officers & servants shall make use of it: And shall likewise pay the arreares of the rent for the time since first they entred upon it.

Send Sr Wm. Brereton Tho: Crompton Phil. Jackson Hen: Stone Wm Foxall & Wm Bendy.

A page from the manuscript of *The Order Book of the Staffordshire County Committee* (William Salt Library, Stafford) demanded, given quarter and free entertainment to all the Parliament's soldiers that have come, obeyed their warrants, sustained manifold injuries, losses and indignities as well as by my own tenants as others, yet never any way opposed the Parliament or stood in contention with any of that party. On New Year's day 1644 (Sir William Brereton being about Stockport) Captain Sankey, Captain Francis Duckenfield, with two or three troops came to Bramhall and went into my stable and took out all my horses, then drove all they could find out of the park, taking them quite away with them, above twenty in all, afterwards searched my house for arms again, took my fowling piece, cocking piece, and drum, which Sir William had left me with divers other things; and although by means my wife made to Sir William Brereton, we had a warrant from him to have all my goods restored and had my young horse (which died within a while after) with some other horses again, yet we lost them both horses and other goods, which we could never after get . . .

[Davenport suffered also at the hands of royalist armies.]

In May 1644 . . . came Prince Rupert his army, by whom I lost better than a hundred pounds in linens and other goods at Milesend, besides the rifling and pulling in pieces of my house. By them and my Lord Goring's army I lost eight horses, and besides victuals and other provision they ate me three score bushels of oats. No sooner was the Prince gone but Stanley's cornet, one Lely, and twenty of his troop hastened their return to plunder me of my horses which the Prince had left me, which he did . . . Then came the commission for sequestration.

On Friday the 9th August 1644, information was brought into the sequestrators against me for delinquency, by oath as they say, but by whose malicious instigation I could not yet come to know, but certainly by my own tenants. On Monday following, being the 12th of the said month (notwithstanding all the aforesaid losses and expenses I had suffered on the Parliament's side, and Sir William Brereton's promise to the contrary) there came to Bramhall, William Barret, Captain Edmund Shelmerdine, Richard Button, George Newton, Gerard Hayes, Robert Ridgeway, John Wharmby, William Thomson, my own tenant, Daniel of the lane, William Smith, commissioners deputed by the sequestrators of Macclesfield Hundred . . . with a commission directed to them from the said sequestrators to take an inventory of all my goods both within the house and without, which they in a most strict and severe manner performed, going into every room in the house, narrowly searching every corner causing all boxes and chests to be opened which otherwise they threatened to break up, being in the meantime guarded with a company of musketeers who stood in the park and all about the house with their matches lighted.

On Thursday next ensuing they began their examination of witnesses to prove me a delinquent, not sparing what they could exhort from anyone that might turn to my disadvantage; wherein some of my own tenants showed themselves forward to give evidence against me, but I must not know who they were. About three weeks after I received a warrant from the sequestrators to appear at Stockport in person to answer such objections as they had framed against me, which I accordingly did, where they alleged against me that I had joined with the Commissioners of Array[2] at Hoo Heath, at Knutsford and at Macclesfield, whereunto I affirmatively answered that I was there, and withal gave them such reasons for my being there as might have satisfied them, yet nevertheless I did conceive that my composition made with Sir William Brereton, Sir George Booth and Colonel Duckenfield since then, and my restraint from arms might free me from delinquency in that point, if thereby I had incurred the penalty thereof. With these and such other allegations in defence of myself at that time, I thought I had given them such satisfaction as I should have heard no more from them, till above a month afterward that I received another warrant to appear before them at Stockport again, where they said they had more to charge me withal concerning my delinquency. I accordingly came before them the second time, Colonel Duckenfield being there, and then they demanded if I had taken the National Covenant[3] and pressed me with it, whereunto I desired to have time given me in such weighty matter to advise with some of my friends about it, and at length got ten days respite to answer it at Nantwich, where I in the meantime satisfied the gentlemen and Council of War,[4] and had a certificate from them to the sequestrators to that purpose. They not therewith contented, nor with any reasonable satisfaction I could give them, and neglecting my just allegations in defence of my innocency, proceeded further against me in renewing their commands to my tenants to detain their rents from me, and commanding them to bring their leases before them in viewing and rating all my lands; and in conclusion, unless I would agree to give them five hundred pounds in composition they intended to proceed against me as a delinquent in all rigor and extremity.

This composition of five hundred pounds I was constrained to make with them on Friday the seventh of March 1645,[5] though not as acknowledging myself guilty of delinquency, yet thereby to buy my own peace, and rather than suffer myself and my estate to fall into the hands of them of whose unjust proceedings I have already had sufficient trial . . . [Davenport then resumed his account of his losses from quarter and plunder.]

Notes

All places are in Cheshire; individuals have not been identified as their roles are clear from Davenport's account.

1 'the Propositions': see p. 111, Note 5.

2 'the Commissioners of Array': see the introduction to Section Six, p. 82.

3 'the National Covenant': the Solemn League and Covenant, see p. 104, Note 1.

4 'the gentlemen and Council of War': Davenport is probably referring to the deputy lieutenants of Cheshire who were moderate Parliamentarians; the sequestration administration was dominated by more radical followers of Sir William Brereton.

5 Davenport ultimately paid £250 of this £500 but in 1647 he was fined a further £745 by the central Committee for Compounding. At first he deducted the £250 he had paid locally, but was eventually forced to pay the whole amount. (J.S. Morrill, 'William Davenport and the "silent majority" of early Stuart England'. *Journal of the Chester Archaeological Society*, **58** (1975).)

SECTION NINE: THE DIARY OF RALPH JOSSELIN, 1645–1660

[Ralph Josselin was born into a prosperous Essex yeoman's family in 1617, but his father was an unsuccessful farmer and left his family impoverished on his death in 1636. Ralph was nevertheless educated at Cambridge and after three years job hunting obtained a curacy in Bedfordshire in 1639. In 1640 he obtained a living in Essex and in 1641 became Vicar of Earl's Colne in the same county, where he remained until his death in 1683. Josselin received £80 p.a. as Vicar, a comparatively good salary, half of which came from tithes and half from voluntary contributions. Many aspects of Josselin's life from 1645 until 1660 are covered in extract 61. He accepted the Restoration but opposed the Act of Uniformity (extract 121, below) and did not completely conform to the practices of the Anglican Church after 1660. Despite this, he avoided deprivation although he was frequently in trouble with the ecclesiastical authorities.

The Diary itself has an interesting history, illustrating changes in editorial principles and in the interests of historians. A selective edition of the diary published in 1908 ran to some 70,000 words and concentrated on Josselin's links with the major political developments of his time. The latest and complete edition, from which this short selection is taken, is more than four times as long and covers also Josselin's family life, his dreams and his millenarian beliefs. Our extracts show how a middle of the road, 'middle class' Parliamentarian reacted to, and was affected by the political and religious events of the mid-seventeenth century, but they also provide many insights into Josselin's day-to-day concerns and personal relationships, and illustrate the precarious nature of seventeenth-century life.]

61 Extracts from the diary of Ralph Josselin, 1645–1660

[*Source*: *The Diary of Ralph Josselin 1616–1683*, (1976) edited by Alan Macfarlane. (Published by Oxford University Press for the British Academy: Records of Social and Economic History, New Series III), pp. 35, 41–2, 73, 78–9, 94, 104, 121, 130–3, 138, 155–6, 164–5, 203, 205, 218–19, 223, 243, 253, 257, 302–3, 307–8, 348, 457–8.]

1645 February 26: A day of Public Humiliation, the Lord good to me in the same; oh Lord, never was there more need of personal reformation than now; stir me up to it I humbly intreat thee.

27: Preached at Maplestead. God good to me going and returning, in the word preached in the company of good friends, in the mercies of family, and in my strength notwithstanding my more than ordinary labour, and often exercise in preaching.

Dry February: This month was dry all the time, ways like summer on the 10 and 11 day; upon the 12 it rained, afterwards dry and a little frost, but generally very warm, ushering in the spring; our streets all overdry, ways plain, grounds so hard they could ever remember the like. So it continued until March 3, then it rained. Violets were commonly blown, rose bushes fully leaved, apricots and my melocoton[1] fully blossomed out . . .

June 10, 11, 12: I was out with our regiment, we marched to [Saffron] Walden, mustered, I sung psalms, prayed and spake to our soldiers on the common at Walden and also at Halstead; God was good to us in accommodating us, and preserving us; Mr Josselin of Chelmsford brake his leg at Walden, his horse threw him; our soldiers resolute, some somewhat dissolute, the Colonel[2] was pleased to honour me to be his comrade, I shall never forget his great love and respect. I found my family well, I praise God at my return, abundance of love made my wife grieve, for which I must the more respect and love her. I rid to my sister['s] at Wenden, I had not seen her in divers years, the Lord has made a difference in our outward conditions, I gave her and her children 6s. Lord thou canst do more than return it again to me.

June 14: At my Lady Honywood's,[3] we agreed to meet on Tuesday to seek God for our armies and I went to prayer, dum [while], even while we were in prayer our armies were conquering,[4] the Lord's name be praised and receive the glory of all.

June 15: The Lord was good to us this week in many mercies, we had our weaknesses yet, my eyes troubled with rheume, my daughter with her cough, and my wife ill, the Lord yet gave us our peace, plenty, good to me on his Sabbath. I was stung and swelled much with one of our bees, yet it hindered me not from my work, his name be praised. . . .

1646 October 24: Received a letter from Mr Harrington that my money was ready and that I should have it when I sent for it, for which I bless

God; at night I heard by Major Haynes[5] that our ship wherein my part was about £18 was cast away, three men drowned, but the merchants saved their goods; this was the first frown upon my estate from my first being of age; it is the Lord, let him do what pleaseth him; if I can upon the sense hereof be more faithful in my place, watchful over my ways and vain thoughts, I shall have cause to rejoice. The master of the ship oweth me above £6 for hops, which I doubt [fear] will come in heavily. God hath given me, if he take away shall I not bless him? Shall we receive good and not evil, yes and in every condition be content and bless his name. This is but a loss of worldly things, to have been overtaken with sin against my God hath cut my heart, but this I value not so as to be troubled.

A wonderful sad wet season, much corn in many places abroad, rotted and spoiled in the fields, grass exceedingly trodden under foot and spoiled by cattle through the wet which hath continued almost since the Assizes, work very dead, wool risen 16d in the pound and upwards, butter and cheese, and meat very dear, and corn rising. Little corn sown, and a very sad season still continued, great divisions and fears of our utter ruin in the kingdom. The Lord only able to help, help, for in vain is all other help and assistance . . .

December 9: Mr High Sheriff[6] with me. I drew up a petition for him to the Lords to take off his burthen, he was much afraid it would continue another year. I ventured with him, it would be passed in both Houses [of Parliament] a sheriff for Essex before Christmas, or I was to give him 5s for two books which if, I was to have them for nothing. Mr William Harlakenden went towards London, I gave him 5s to buy me two Hebrew Grammars. His chief occasion was about the sheriff's business.

10: Met with divers of my friends and neighbours at my special friend's house, Mrs [Mary] Church, where we had sweet and good discourse about the love of God to the creature, and truly we know God loves us *partim sensu* [partly through emotion] by experience of the same, in the steps of his gracious providence, and not only by outward good things, and partly by faith, in living upon him for love, as the fountain of it; this spirit witnesseth to us that God loveth us, blessed be the Lord that hath not shut up his compassion towards me, but hath kept me from sins, temptations, not suffered me to lie and live in the same. We pitch upon a method and order for our meeting, to discourse of the principles of religion, and begin with man's creation, in what estate framed, and to what end framed. Appointed our meeting at my house December 25 following.[7] . . .

1647 May 16: This week God was very good to me and mine in the continuance of our peace, health and outward mercies, in keeping my feet in his paths and delivering me from the power of many temptations. The Lord makes me to possess my wants, and surely one end why he shows them unto me, is to make me more earnest in begging a supply for my emptiness out of His fullness; God very good in the mercies of the day, in reading and expounding the

IMPORTANCE OF BIBLE

scripture, and in preaching the word; oh, how sweet is the meditation and apprehension of God a father; oh, how love streams out from thence; God good to me in my family, my eyes also somewhat bettered. Took notice of the rudeness of divers about the congregation, reproved them, and encouraged the officers to punish them. Heard Mr Richard Simons was indifferently recovered out of his distemper,[8] Lord sanctify that dealing and chastisement of thine unto him.

17: Heard high language of the soldiers' intentions and resolutions, though I scarce may credit that they should be so bold, yet I shall observe whether a multitude dare not attempt anything, and learn not to judge hastily of things and persons and [a]wait conclusion of things. Reports of soldiers foot, abusing of women; they are now coming towards us, the Lord be our guard and protection from their violence and insolency. I had some rugged words from one of them, a Lieutenant, about quartering, whereby I perceive how unable poor men are to contain their spirits, if ever they are in employment. . . .

September 20: Meeting at my house. People drive at an arbitrary maintenance of their ministers and upon their courtesy; but seeing the Scripture doth not command this, there is no reason that requireth us to yield to the same.[9] . . .

September 26: This week the Lord was good and merciful to me and mine in our health, peace plenty, and many outward mercies, to his name be praise. My cold finally worn away, the Lord in mercy give me to consider of the vanity of my mind, in earthly imaginations and give me to endeavour faithfully against them, which I confess I have not done, but pleased myself in ruminating on such fooleries. The Lord give me power against every evil for his mercy sake; the Lord good in the season which was very fair, and as fit a seed time as ever came, things are at that rate as never was in our days: wheat 8s, malt 4s, beef 3d, butter 6½d, cheese 4d, candle 7d, currants 9d, sugar 18d and every other thing whatsoever dear. The soldiers also returning to quarter again with us, and that in a great proportion, viz. 25. The Lord was good and merciful unto me in some measure in the duty of the day, the good Lord in mercy accept me, and pardon me; people, especial[ly] poor of both sexes and men are exceeding careless of the Sabbath, profaneness is ready to overrun us. . . .

1648 28–29 March: At night I was ill, yet I had a fine sleep in the morning through mercy, and slept very much in the night and was loose. The next morning I was very sore especially on the outside of my thighs. My uncle Ralph Josselin was with me early on the fast day morning. The day was dry and windy and the sun shone though the morning was tempestuous, the Lord was good and merciful unto me in enabling me to expound and preach. There was the thinnest audience that ever I had, the Lord pardon my sins and accept my soul for his holy and precious name['s] sake.

31: Rid to Colchester, met Mr Newcomen,[10] and divers other ministers, we had much discourse concerning falling into practice;

and in the first place, seeing that elders are to be chosen, by when [whom?] shall it be done; the Parliament proposeth by the people that have taken the Covenant; others as Mr Owen[11] conceived this too broad, and would have first a separation to be made in our parishes, and that by the minister, and those godly that join unto him, and then proceed to choosing.[12] My horse threw me as I returned home, but through the good providence of God, I had no hurt, at all. . . .

August 16: A very great flood with the great rains last day and night, the season sad and threatening; this day I retired myself to seek God by reason of his judgements on us, to bewail not his afflictions which we suffer, but especially the sins whereby he is provoked for he doth not willingly afflict.

The nation's sins are many and sad, Lord let public ones be pardoned; the nation's judgements are continual rains to the spoiling of much grass, and threatening of the harvest. The sad charge by war to the undoing of country; the sad decay of trade in reference to our poor, to our undoing except God find out some other way of subsistence.

The war in the nation, the divisions among ourselves; our cryings out after peace on any terms to save our skins and estates whatsoever become of others, Lord remove these judgements from us for thy name['s] sake.

And in respect of my soul: my heart is full of sinful and vain meditations, not being clean in the eyes of God, my conversation is not even in the sight of God. Oh, give me a clean heart and keep me in uprightness. Oh, make this nation happy in peace and truth, and make me righteous and holy in thy eyes for these things I pour out my soul in thy presence, be gracious, oh Lord, to us we intreat thee . . .

Public Fast, August 30: A wet night, and wettish day, as if God would have called men to his worship. But there was no regard of the same; my thoughts grow strong within me to give over preaching at Colne at Michaelmas, and to declare the same beforehand to the chief inhabitants, Lord direct me what to do, I have given out speeches of my enforcement unto it. I preached once this day on Amos 8. 11–12,[13] concerning the famine of the word, wherein having occasion to speak of the condition of this land, I delivered my thoughts to this purpose:

People, when our armies had conquered all our enemies, my thoughts were sad concerning the displeasure of God remaining towards England, and I told you Essex must not escape, which is come to pass by the marchings of Goring[14] and his army, and plundering many places, persons, the sad ruin of Colchester by fire, the decay of trade by their losses, the charge of the county in maintaining their forces at the siege, and sending in provisions for above 11 weeks for many thousands of horse and foot; my thoughts were and are sad concerning England still, not from the rising of many counties against the Parliament, the strong invasion of the Scots upon us, for my thoughts verily were, God would break them,[15] but when I consider the decay of the power of godliness among Christians, the flightiness of spirit towards God's ordinances, the woeful uncontrollable increase of all manner of wickedness among us, the awe that was on men's hearts towards God and his ways being removed, the slighting all the warnings of God in judgements and by his ministers, maketh me think God is yet angry and he will leave our great Council to their wonted partiality in their ways, and bring more ruin one way or other on the nation, or give us up to the cursed ways of our own hearts, taking away his ministers and saints apace from England, and few arising in their stead . . .

September: This week 20–22 was very wet, the season very sad both in reference to corn and unto fallows, very few lands being fit to be sown upon; some say that divers cattle that feed in the meadows die, their bowels being eaten out with gravel and dirt.

On the 17 August I intimated that it was probable I should not very long stay with them, but truly very few in the town regard it, or that seem to take any notice of it . . .

1649 February 2: Troubled with a great pose [headcold].

3: I had home some wood from my vicarage close worth near 20s but I got a great cold and was much troubled with it.

4: This week I was much troubled with pose, and cold, but through mercy they did not settle in my chest. Otherwise I enjoyed many mercies outward and that in particular in my health. I was much troubled with the black providence of putting the King to death, my tears were not restrained at the passages about his death; the Lord in mercy lay it not as a sin to the charge of the kingdom, but in mercy do us good by the same. The Lord was good to all mine in their healths; the smallpox on some families of the town but spreadeth not, to God be the glory thereof. My vanities of mind returned to my trouble; oh, when shall vain thoughts depart from me. This week I could do nothing neither in my Hebrew nor in my reconciler.[16] The Lord was good to me in the Sabbath in enabling me with strength for the work, the Lord in mercy accept me therein, and bless it to my people, and own soul eternal good.

The death of the King talked much of; very many men of the weaker sort of Christians in divers places passionate concerning it, but so ungroundedly, that it would make any bleed to observe it; the Lord hath some great thing to do, fear and tremble at it, oh England.

Monday it was debated about Kings and Peers; on Tuesday the House of Commons ordered to null the House of Lords as useless, and on the next day to lay aside the government by Kings, and to set up a Council of State.

February 11: This week the Lord was good to me and mine in our peace and plenty. The times are very sad and full of difficulties, and yet God provideth for me and mine, God good to us in our health. My cold causeth me to wheeze in the nights but not much; my children preserved in divers dangers: Jane fell into the fire, her hands only a little hurt; I had more experience of my heart looking back after old vanities than a long time before, I had well nigh slipped, but God upheld me; this week I omitted the study of my Hebrew but observed 6 chapters in Genesis in my reconciler. We had a lusty woman died this week in our town suddenly, I preached at her funeral.

God was good to me in the Sabbath, in carrying me on in the work of it; the good Lord in mercy accept me and pardon for the glory of his own rich name, do me and my people good. The weather was frost, snow and windy which made it very cold, and thus it hath continued about three weeks . . .

April 22: This week the Lord was good and merciful to me and mine in our peace, plenty and health; my navel hath continued well through God's goodness about 6 weeks; and yet I have travailed, sweat, and taken cold; I am exercised with a pose, and wheezing in the night, as if my chest and head were full of rheume; God in his due time will put an end to those illnesses, but through mercy they do not much take me off from my employment. This week I had experience of God's mercy to me, not being led into some temptations as formerly; Lord, I am very apt to sin in many things against thee; oh, keep me for thy name['s] sake. I did not much in any of my studies this week, but only against the Lord's day. My wife held up her head beyond expectation; this week another family afflicted with the smallpox and we hitherto preserved, blessed be his name; this is the fourth family in the town thus dealt with, and yet not any have died. The season was clear, dry, windy, warm and sometimes cool, a most comfortable seed time. The Lord was good to me in the Sabbath, in the duties and exercises of the same, the preaching and expounding the word, my subject was about the future glory of the church of Jesus Christ here in this world . . .

May 5: My dear wife had been very ill for 3 weeks; now towards night pains came fast on her and she was delivered before nine of the clock of her 5th child and third son, God giving us another son instead of my dear Ralph[17] whom he took away; the Lord command grace for my poor infant, and make it his, and perfect his mercy towards my dear wife, and keep me in uprightness that I may fear his name; my wife was alone a great while with our good friends Mrs Mary [Church], and her mother; some few women were with her, but the midwife not, but when God commands deliverance there is nothing hinders it.[18]

I feared my navel this day, there was some lint that stick in it; I think it was by reason of my former sweating; I meddled not with it, but I look up to my God perfectly to heal me. . . .

1650 May 26: This morning all our hopes of Mary's[19] life was gone; to the Lord I have resigned her, and with him I leave her, to receive her into his everlasting arms, when he seeth best; she rests free from much pain, we hope, in regard she maketh no dolour the Lord makes us willing she should be out of her pain, and why are we at any times unwilling, when God is about such a work, that he should take them up into his glory; this day the word was made marvellous comfortable to me; my heart could not but mourn over and for my babe, but I left it with the Lord, and was quiet in my spirit, in God's taking it, to whom I did freely resign it; my little son in all people's eyes is a dying child; Lord thy will be done, thou art better to me than sons and daughters, though I value them above gold and jewels. My navel continued well this week for which I bless God; my bile grew sorer, and my kernels [glands] in my flank, which God, I trust, will ordain for an abundance of good unto me.

27: This day a quarter past two in the afternoon my Mary fell asleep in the Lord, her soul passed into that rest where the body of Jesus, and the souls of the Saints are; she was 8 years and 45 days old when she died; my soul had abundant cause to bless God for her, who was our first fruits, and those God would have offered to him, and this I freely resigned up to him; it was a precious child, a bundle of myrrh, a bundle of sweetness; she was a child of ten thousand, full of wisdom, woman-like gravity, knowledge, sweet expressions of God, apt in her learning, tender hearted and loving, an obedient child to us. It was free from the rudeness of little children; it was to us as a box of sweet ointment, which now it's broken smells more deliciously than it did before; Lord, I rejoice I had such a present for thee; it was patient in the sickness, thankful to admiration; it lived desired and died lamented, thy memory is and will be sweet unto me . . .

June 4: This day my dear friend Mrs Mary Church and my sweet Ralph[20] were buried together in the church; I preached her funeral on Matthew 25: 34 verse;[21] God hath taken from me a choice special friend, the good Lord in mercy sanctify that his dealing unto me, and truly my heart looks wholly to God herein, who is my life, my grace, my all; I am poor and empty. In some respect I see great mercy therein, for Satan lieth in wait to corrupt our affections, and that mine were not, was God's abundant grace, who keeps me that though I fall, yet I am not utterly cast down.

When Mrs Mary died, my heart trembled, and was perplexed in the dealings of the Lord so sadly with us, and desiring God not to proceed on against us with his darts and arrows, looking back into my ways, and observing why God had thus dealt with me; the Lord followed me with that sin no more lest a worse thing happen unto thee, and the intimation of God was he would proceed no farther against me or mine, and he would assist me with his grace if I clave to him with a full purpose of heart, which I resolve; oh, my God help me; oh, my God, fail me not, for in thee do I put my trust . . .

October 23: Dined, and lay at my Lady Honywood's. Mr Harlakenden was very wet in his coming home; it was a good providence to me that I escaped the rain. Mr [Richard] Harlakenden [junior] and his tutor came to Colne [from Cambridge]; the Engagement [22] outs many deserving men from their fellowships; it's thought there will fall a sad blow upon the ministry, the universities, and their means; the report is that one moved whether there should be any standing ministry in England, but that is somewhat too much yet for this early day . . .

December 9: Begun to peruse the Revelation, and Brightman upon it;[23] a great encouragement thereunto is what is written, Rev. 1:3,[24] of the blessedness of them that know, and keep the words of this prophecy. . . .

1651 April 20: This week also the God of my mercies renewed his protection towards me and mine; some others down of the smallpox, my [family] yet preserved for which my soul desireth to be thankful. My navel continued somewhat moist, and foul but not sore; I did not yet dress it. I leave myself to my God who knoweth what is best for me, and I trust he will direct me for the best, and will be health to my navel and marrow to my bones. The season dry and now somewhat cold, inviting unto action; many suppose our Commonwealth lost. Spain and France and Holland against us. Ireland and Scotland heavy work, and not to be effected, the English divided, and worn out with taxes and burthens, the merchants' trade even ruined, and so all tending to poverty. But if the work be God's, there is enough in his arm to effect the same, and up to him his people look to be their salvation. The Lord was good to me in the week past in the frame of my spirit in giving me a submitting heart to him in order to afflictions, and in leaving myself to God with quietness of spirit forasmuch as he seeth what is best for me and mine; the Lord was good to me in the Sabbath, and in the exercises thereof; the Lord in much mercy pardon my sin and accept my sinful soul . . .

August 3: This week past the Lord was good to me and mine in our health, peace, outward mercies; mine still preserved from the smallpox, and God will still preserve them. One other family in the town more is afflicted; it is very sore and heavy at Halstead, and a sad fever also at Coggeshall as they report. Harvest is now begun, the season is very dry, the Lord in mercy remember us therein as he seeth good. My heart was the week past much disquieted with the heedlessness of my servant; Lord make me careful not to do that myself, which I blame in another. The Lord was good to me in the work and duty of the Sabbath; I moved for poor Mighill whose house was burnt down; we gathered near £3 for him; the Lord be blessed for this mercy in my people who gave them a heart to give. The Lord sanctify it to him, and requite their loves into their bosoms . . .

September 19: This Friday morning my wife was very well delivered of her fourth son, and sixth child, much about seven of the clock; I intend to name him John, the Lord be gracious and merciful to him; he was born on a day that we had set apart for a day of thanks, and God begun with me in my family; I preached at Markshall, where was a vast company, and a large dinner; God's hand was towards us for good, exceedingly.

A great Rabbi's saying: if the Messiah's coming be not before 1656 of the Christians' account then expect no other Messiah but the Christians' Messiah.

I am persuaded the present dispensation is the breaking in pieces the kingdoms of the earth which God is entering on, and sometime when this work is advanced will the Jews appear; and then comes in the happy season of the flock . . .

1653 May 1: The week past God good to me and mine, the weather very dry, speaking a drought, yet the field doth not much rain, water exceedingly scarce, all quiet everywhere notwithstanding this great change at hand;[25] most serious men are silent under it, as being an evil time, many rejoice; the Lord stayeth up my heart to rely on him, and leave the issue of all things to him, who taketh care for us; it was general discourse, now down go the ministers, but why should we fear to suffer if God please to have it so. I find my base inward vain thoughts, deadness, and straightness of spirit on me, with a very slothful common heart. Lord how long! I cry, and yet, how long! This day it dewed a little, the former heat abated, and the earth refreshed; the Lord was good to me this day in the work of the Sabbath for which I bless and praise his holy name.

May 4: In regard of the troubles of the times I resolve to buy no more books for present than absolutely needful, until with the money set apart for books and givings, I have paid the £3-9-6d I owe Mr Tompson,[26] and £5-10s to my sister, monies that I owe for books and that I borrowed to give away.

May 5: Lord, I bless thee for inward esteems of thee, and that I can undervalue all these things in comparison of thou. Heard, but not true, Cromwell was made Lord High Protector of England; all apprehend a storm on the ministry. Lord arm me with faith and patience . . .

July 10: In this morning I dreamed, that divers were in a pulpit in a church, and that divers heaved it this way, and that, but could not make it fall; I dreamed that the Mayor, and great men of the place sat at the upper end, but did nothing one way or other; I thought I came in with a rod in my hand and laid it by the wall, divers looked on me; I trust God will take care of me in those church-troubles that are coming on us.

The Lord continueth his shade on my tabernacle, blessed be his name. I want no outward good thing. I find a filthy, wretched heart; shall I never find Christ empowering me to put every imagination under; oh Lord, let thy goodness do this for me, for I am weak, and nothing; this day very hot, God good to me in the work and duty thereof; the Lord was a good God in the season, which suits to the fruits of the earth. Some of the separation called Anabaptists hearing this day. Do they hope to enjoy our meeting places, and therefore will disown their old opinion of abominating the place; come they as spies to catch, or to make way for others to come? Lord, I am not solicitous, I desire only to serve thee singly.

July 12: Had in all my hay out of Dagnal, about 3 good loads, it cost me 5 goings thither; it was inned in very good case; the season is very dry, and hot, fit for the field work. Through mercy I think my crop in

Dagnal this year is a saving crop . . .

1655 July 1: God good to me and mine in the week past; good in my quiet on the Lords Day, when it was likely I should have had a disturbance [from the Quakers] as some of my neighbours had; I bless God for this sweet calm; the Lord prepare me for trouble and let not any evil come upon me unawares as a snare I most humbly intreat thee.

July 3: Preached at Gaines Colne, the Quakers' nest, but no disturbance; God hath raised up my heart not to fear, but willing to bear, and to make opposition to their ways in defence of truth; it is an evil that runs much in all places; some think it will be dangerous to Cromwell's interest, and is so, God knows I do not, yet I think he fears them not, and perhaps the clause in his Declaration[27] not to disturb the minister in exercise, was to hint to them they might do it after if they would, securely, for that is their practice . . .

1660 January 25: This day I spent at Priory in a day of praise to my God at Mr H. [Harlakenden's] desire to whom I spake something from Psal. 50, v.15[28] and heartily prayed to my God in Christ for him; Lord hear and be gracious. When I look back into the world I find nothing but confusions, hopes of a peace between Spain and France, but sad wars in the north, the Swedes bustling as a rod tearing the flesh of the nations, but not advantaging themselves, and our poor England unsettled, and her physicians hitherto leading her into deep waters. Cromwell's family cast down with scorn to the ground, none of them in command or employment, the nation looking more to Charles Stuart, out of love to themselves not him, the end of these things God only knoweth; we have had sad confusions in England, the issue God only knoweth.[29]

Notes

Unless otherwise noted, people mentioned in the diary are Josselin's friends and neighbours in his home village of Earls Colne and nearby; most places are in Essex.

1 'melocoton': a peach tree grafted on a quince.

2 The Colonel of the Essex regiment was Richard Harlakenden of Colne Priory, lord of the manor in Josselin's parish.

3 'Lady Honywood's': Lady Hester Honywood of Markshall, the next parish to Earls Colne.

4 'Our armies were conquering': at Naseby, 14 June 1645.

5 'Major Haynes': Hezekiah Haynes, one of the Josselins' closest friends; major of foot in the Essex forces and later Major General in East Anglia, (see p. 213).

6 'Mr High Sheriff': Richard Harlakenden. The shrievalty was a costly, and not very prestigious county office. Harlakenden did not have to serve for another year, and so Josselin won his wager.

7 From 1646–*c.*1657 Josselin led meetings of a gathered church of the 'godly' at Earls Colne; he continued to minister to the whole parish too.

8 On 9 May, Josselin wrote that Richard Simons was 'sadly distracted' (Diary, p. 93).

9 The meeting of the 'godly' was thus discussing the voluntary maintenance of the clergy.

10 'Mr Newcomen': Matthew Newcomen, member of the Westminster Assembly and lecturer at Dedham, Essex from 1637 until his ejection in 1662.

11 'Mr Owen': John Owen, leading 'Independent' minister, Vice Chancellor of Oxford in the 1650s but in 1648 a minister at Coggeshall, Essex.

12 The ministers were discussing the implementation of the Presbyterian system.
13 Amos 8. 11–12: 'Behold, the days come, saith the Lord God, that I will send a famine in the land, not a famine of bread, nor a thirst for water, but of hearing the word of the Lord:
'And they shall wander from sea to sea, and from the north even to the east, they shall run to and fro to seek the word of the Lord, and shall not find it.'
14 'Goring': Lord George Goring (1608–1657), royalist commander.
15 Josselin is describing the events of the second civil war, which affected Essex particularly severely.
16 'reconciler': a collection of apparently contradictory biblical texts which Josselin attempted to 'reconcile'.
17 'Ralph': Josselin's fourth child, born 11 February, died 21 February 1648.
18 Josselin's wife Jane had ten live births and five miscarriages between 1642 and 1663.
19 'Mary': Josselin's first child, born 12 April 1642.
20 Josselin's youngest son, born 5 May 1649, and his close friend Mary Church both died on 2 June.
21 Matthew 25.34: 'Then shall the King say unto them on his right hand, Come, ye blessed of my Father, inherit the Kingdom prepared for you from the foundation of the world.'
22 'The Engagement': an oath of loyalty to the Republic, imposed on all adult office holders, including fellows of the Universities, in October 1649; and on all adult males in January 1650.
23 'Brightman': Thomas Brightman *A Revelation of the Apocalypse* (1611): the most famous commentary on Revelation, and the source of much millenarian speculation. Josselin was very much concerned with millenarianism from 1647 to 1657, especially from November 1650.
24 Revelation 1.3: 'Blessed is he that readeth, and they that hear the words of this prophecy, and keep those things which are written therein: for the time is at hand.'
25 'this great change at hand': the Rump was dissolved by the army 20 April 1653.
26 'Mr Tompson': Robert Tompson, rector of Copford, Essex from 1639 until his ejection in 1662.
27 'his Declaration': Cromwell's Proclamation on Religious Liberty, February 1655, did not extend to those who disturbed other congregations.
28 Psalm 50.15: 'And call upon me in the day of trouble: I will deliver thee, and thou shalt glorify me.'
29 January 25 was the eve of Josselin's birthday, and as he did in most years, he was summing up his impressions of the world.

SECTION TEN: RELIGIOUS UPHEAVAL, 1642–1659

[As Clarendon pointed out (extract 62) the civil war and its aftermath provided an unprecedented opportunity for ordinary people to participate in radical religious movements. For conservatives, the main problem in this period was to construct a satisfactory State Church to replace the episcopal structure hastily abolished in January 1643. The Assembly of Divines, summoned by Parliament in June 1643 to advise on the formation of a new State Church, was predominantly Presbyterian and the Scots, Parliament's allies from winter 1643, pushed in the same direction. Hence most of Parliament's legislation and proposals on the Church in the 1640s were Presbyterian (extract 66 for example). Varying degrees of toleration were claimed by the Independents and other more radical groups, however; and with the support for toleration in the New Model Army, it proved impossible to re-establish a coercive, all-inclusive State Church (extracts 63–65, 67 and 68). The debate over whether ministers should be a separate caste, specially chosen and trained for their role, was an important part of the discussion of the form a State Church should take, or whether there should be one at all. Radicals and conservatives disagreed sharply over the nature of the ministry, and the debate had serious social and political implications (extracts 69–75; see also Section Fifteen below). Conservatives on these issues included many who had been committed Parliamentarians, but were highly alarmed at the movements unleashed by war: Hall and Edwards are examples (extracts 64, 71 and 76). Hall's defence of the ministry sparked off a wide-ranging debate: our extracts from Collier and Hartley are from pamphlets written expressly to answer Hall (extracts 71–73). The Quakers in the 1650s were not the quietist sect they became after the Restoration and their ideas and activities increased conservative anxiety (extracts 77–80). Hall and Edwards pointed to the lack of sharp boundaries between the various sects, and the last three extracts, illustrating the individual searches for personal salvation and religious truth characteristic of these years, reinforce their point (extracts 81–83). (Material on the religious developments of these years will also be found in Sections Eleven and Thirteen to Fifteen.)]

62 Preface: Clarendon

[Source: W. Dunn Macray, editor, (1888) *The History of the Rebellion and Civil Wars in England* by Edward Earl of Clarendon (Oxford, the Clarendon Press) volume I, p. 269.]

This insurrection (for it was no better) and frenzy of the people was an effect of great industry and policy, to try and publish the temper of the people; and to satisfy themselves in the activity and interest of their tribunes, to whom that province of showing the people was committed. And from this time the license of preaching and printing increased to that degree that all pulpits were freely delivered to the schismatical and silenced preachers, who till then had lurked in corners or lived in New England; and the presses [were] at liberty for the publishing the most invective, seditious, and scurrilous pamphlets that their wit and malice could invent.

The Independents

[In the Assembly of Divines, the supporters of a Presbyterian Church system had an overwhelming majority. In January 1644, five 'Independent' ministers, Thomas Goodwin, Philip Nye, Sidrach Simpson, Jeremiah Burroughs and William Bridge, submitted an alternative to Parliament (and the public) when they issued *An Apologeticall Narration*. Under Laud's ascendancy, all five had ministered to English congregations in Holland, and they pointed to the practice of their churches there as a model for a decentralized English Church.]

63 The Apologetical Narration

[*Source*: *An Apologeticall Narration Humbly Submitted to the Honourable Houses of Parliament* (1644) from pp. 14, 16–17, 19, 23–4, 28. Also printed in William Haller, editor, *Tracts on Liberty in the Puritan Revolution* (1934, reprinted 1965).]

We could not . . . but judge it a safe and an allowed way to retain the government of our several congregations for matter of discipline within themselves, to be exercised by their own elders, whereof we had for the most part of the time we were abroad, three at least in each congregation, whom we were subject to; yet not claiming to ourselves an independent power in every congregation, to give account or be subject to none others; but only a full and entire power complete within ourselves, until we should be challenged to err grossly, such as corporations enjoy, who have the power and privilege to pass sentence for life and death within themselves, and yet are accountable to the state they live in . . .

Our churches did mutually and universally acknowledge and submit to this as a sacred and undoubted principle and supreme law to be observed among all churches, that, as by virtue of that apostolical command, churches, as well as particular men, are bound to give no offence neither to Jew nor Gentile, nor the Churches of God they live amongst. So that in all cases of such offence or difference, by the obligation of the common law of communion of churches, and for the vindication of the glory of Christ which in common they hold forth, the church or churches challenged to offend or differ, are to submit themselves, upon the challenge of the offence or complaint of the person wronged, to the most full and open trial and examination by other neighbour churches offended thereat, of whatever hath given the offence. And further, that by the virtue of the same and like law of not partaking in other men's sins, the churches offended may, and ought, upon the impenitency of those churches, persisting in their error and miscarriage, to pronounce that heavy sentence against them, of withdrawing and renouncing all Christian communion with them until they do repent; and further to declare and protest this, with the causes thereof, to all other churches of Christ, that they may do the like . . . And if the magistrate's power, to which we give as much and, as we think, more than the principles of the Presbyterian government will suffer them to yield, do but assist and back the sentence of other churches denouncing [i.e. announcing] this non-communion against churches miscarrying . . . then, without all controversy, this our way of church proceeding will be every way as effectual as their other can be supposed to be; and, we are sure, more brotherly, and more suited to that liberty and equality Christ hath endowed his churches with . . .

That proud and insolent title of 'Independency' was affixed unto us, as our claim, the very sound of which conveys to all men's apprehensions the challenge of an exemption of all churches from all subjection and dependence, or rather a trumpet of defiance against whatever power, spiritual or civil, which we do abhor and detest. Or else the odious name of Brownism,[1] together with all their opinions as they have stated and maintained them, must needs be owned by us, although, upon the very first declaring our judgements in the chief and fundamental point of all church discipline, and likewise since, it hath been acknowledged that we differ much from them. And we did then, and do here publicly profess, we believe the truth to lie and consist in a middle way betwixt that which is falsely charged on us, Brownism, and that which is the contention of these times, the authoritative Presbyterian government in all the subordinations and proceedings of it . . .

If in all matters of doctrine, we were not as orthodox in our judgements as our [Presbyterian] brethren themselves, we would never have exposed ourselves to this trial and hazard of discovery in this Assembly, the mixture of whose spirits, the quick-sightedness of whose judgements, intent enough upon us, and variety of debates about all sorts of controversies afoot in these times of contradiction, are such as would be sure soon to find us out if we nourished any monsters or serpents of opinions lurking in our bosoms.

Note

1 'Brownism': separatism, after Robert Browne who argued, in the 1580s, that the true Church consisted only of gathered congregations of the elect.

Hostile Views

64 Thomas Edwards

[*Source*: Thomas Edwards (1646) *Gangraena* (Second edition) The first part, pp. 16–7, 61–3.]

And I desire to commend to the reader's serious and sad consideration, three particulars concerning the errors and sects of this time; and the rather, because they were not so common to the sects in the ages before, at least not the two first. That among all these sorts of sects and sectaries, there are hardly now to be found in England (for to this Kingdom, and to these four last years do I confine myself all along in this discourse) any sect that's simple and pure, and not mixed and compounded; that is, any sect, among them all, which holds only the opinions and principles of its own way, without interfering and mingling with the errors of other sects; as for example, where can a man find a Church of simple Anabaptists, or simple Antinomians, or simple pure Independents, each of them keeping to their own principles, as Anabaptists to Anabaptism, Independents to Independency, and holding no other? But rather do we not see by experience, that both the several kinds of sects, and most persons of each kind, are compounded of many, yea, some of all: one and the same society of persons in our times, being both Anabaptistical, Antinomian, Manifestarian, Libertine, Socinian, Millenary, Independent, Enthusiastical? Yea, among the Independents, who are of all the rest accounted best, where can any man show me an Independent Church strictly so called, or a man of them hardly, who symbolizes not with the other sects, holding beside Independency, neither the opinions of the Chiliasts, nor of the Libertines, nor other strange opinions! The Army that is so much spoken of upon all occasions in the news-books, pulpits, conferences, to be Independent (though I conceive upon good information, that upon a true muster of the whole, commanders and common soldiers, there would not be found above one in six of that way); yet of that Army, called by the sectaries, Independent, and of that part of it which truly is so, I do not think there are 50 pure Independents, but higher flown, more seraphical (as a chaplain, who knows well the state of that Army, expressed it) made up and compounded of Anabaptism, Antinomianism, Enthusiasm, Arminianism, Familism; all these errors and more too sometimes meeting in the same persons, strange monsters, having their heads of Enthusiasm, their bodies of Antinomianism, their thighs of Familism, their legs and feet of Anabaptism, their hands of Arminianism, and Libertinism as the great vein going through the whole; in one word, the great religion of that sort of men in the Army, is liberty of conscience, and liberty of preaching . . .

Now for the particular practices of the sectaries, they are many, and it would require a tractate by itself to set them down; indeed, I hardly know any strange practice that hath reference to their ways, but some or other of them are guilty in one kind or another. Most of their practices and ways may be referred to these ten heads:

1 To looseness and liberty in life and conversation.
2 To covetousness, ambition and self-seeking.
3 To policies and subtlety.
4 To activeness, sedulity and nimbleness in the prosecution of their way.
5 To tumultuousness, disorder and confusion.
6 To the disturbance and overthrow of economical, ecclesiastical and political relations and government.
7 To insolencies, pride and arrogancy.
8 To acts of immodesty and incivility.
9 To power and will, carrying all before them, and throwing down all that stands in their way.
10 To hypocrisy under pretences of piety and holiness.

Now for the particular practices of the sectaries, I had drawn up many, to the number of seventy, and provided for every practice instances for proof, and upon some of them I could write a large discourse, even a book upon several of them: as of their behaviour and carriage towards the Parliament, the kingdom of Scotland, the Assembly of Divines, the city of London, the ministry of England, yea, of all the reformed churches; as of their seeking and getting into all sorts of offices and places they are any way capable of, being sequestrators, collectors, receivers, surveyers, excisers, customers, secretaries, clerks, etc; getting places in Court, great towns, dwelling in sequestered houses freely, procuring arrears etc; not a man almost of late coming into any place or office but an Independent or Independentish, there being no kind or sort of preferment, employment, place, but some or other of that way enjoy; as of their plotting and labouring from the first year of the wars to get into their hands the sword and power of arms, by having a considerable army, which they might look upon more particularly as theirs and of their way, by attempting to remove and heave at many gallant commanders, to get the command of the strongest garrisons and places, yea, to make towns of consequence that were no garrisons to have been garrisons, as Yarmouth; but I am necessitated for divers reasons to pass by wholly for the present many of their practices, and others to name only, desiring the reader as he goes along to supply the defects, by calling to mind all particulars he knows and hath heard of upon the several heads.

They use to ascribe and attribute all the success of things, all that's done in [the] field, at leaguers, all victories, brave actions, to their party, crying them up in pulpits, newsbooks, conferences, calling them the saviours of the kingdoms and for this purpose they have certain men that are criers and trumpeters between the army, city and country, who trumpet forth their praises, giving them titles of terrible etc.; a large book would not contain the relation of all the victories, glorious actions, exploits [that] have been given to the Army called Independent.

They give out and boast their party to be more and greater than they are; some of them will speak in all places as if all were theirs, all for them; they have given out as if Parliament, armies, city of London, country, all the godly, wise, judicious, understanding men were theirs, and will be theirs . . .

They appropriate to themselves the name of the godly and well-affected party, the title of Saints, calling themselves the Saints; that they only preach Jesus Christ; and though they be Anabaptists, Seekers etc., yet they are the Saints. This is common in printed books, petitions, sermons, discourses; what, speak against the Saints? Be against a toleration for the Saints? – meaning themselves only.

They pretend one thing, when they intend quite another, and 'tis usual for them to pretend the public good, the benefit of the state, when 'tis evident they intend their own interest, and strengthening of their party; they will pretend peace, love, forbearing of all names of difference, to make the Presbyterians secure, negligent, and to forbear all means of settling things; and yet at the same time go quite contrary, using all means and ways for promoting their own party.

65 Richard Baxter

[*Source*: Richard Baxter (1696) *Reliquiae Baxterianae* edited by Matthew Sylvester, from pp. 41, 50–1, 53.]

When I was at Gloucester [in 1642] I saw the first contentions between the ministers and Anabaptists that ever I was acquainted with; for these were the first Anabaptists that ever I had seen in any country, and I heard but of a few more in those parts of England . . .

But this was the beginning of the miseries of Gloucester; for the Anabaptists somewhat increasing on one side, before I came away, a good man, called Mr Hart, came out of Herefordshire with Mr Vaughan, a gentleman, and they drew many to separation on another side; and after them in the wars came one Mr Bacon, a preacher of the army, and drew them to Antinomianism on another side, which together so distracted the good people, and ate out the heart of religion and charity (the ministers of the place being not so able and quick as they should have been in confuting them, and preserving the people) that the city which had before as great advantages for the prosperity of religion among them, as any in the land in the civility, tractableness, and piety of the people, became as low and poor as others, and the city of more happy places, while these tares did dwindle and wither away the solid piety of the place . . .

Naseby being not far from Coventry where I was, and the noise of the victory being loud in our ears, and I having two or three that of old had been my intimate friends in Cromwell's army, whom I had not seen of above two years, I was desirous to go see whether they were dead or alive; and so to Naseby Field I went two days after the fight, and thence by the army's quarters before Leicester to seek my acquaintance. When I found them I stayed with them a night, and I understood the state of the army much better than ever I had done before. We that lived quietly in Coventry did keep to our old principles, and thought all others had done so too, except a few very inconsiderable persons: we were unfeignedly for King and Parliament: we believed that the war was only to save the Parliament and Kingdom from papists and delinquents, and to remove the dividers, that the King might again return to his Parliament; and that no changes might be made in religion, but by the laws which had his free consent. We took the true happiness of King and people, church and state, to be our end, and so we understood the Covenant,[1] engaging both against papists and schismatics. And when the court news-book told the world of the swarms of Anabaptists in our armies, we thought it had been a mere lie, because it was not so with us, nor in any of the garrison or county forces about us. But when I came to the army among Cromwell's soldiers, I found a new face of things which I never dreamt of: I heard the plotting heads very hot upon that which intimated their intention to subvert both Church and State. Independency and Anabaptistry were most prevalent; Antinomianism and Arminianism were equally distributed; and Thomas Moor's followers (a weaver of Wisbech and Lynn, of excellent parts) had made some shifts to join these two extremes together.

Abundance of the common troopers, and many of the officers, I found to be honest, sober, orthodox men, and others tractable, ready to hear the truth, and of upright intentions; but a few proud, self-conceited, hot-headed sectaries had got into the highest places, and were Cromwell's chief favourites, and by their heat and activity bore down the rest, or carried them along with them, and were the soul of the army, though much fewer in number than the rest (being indeed not one to twenty throughout the army; their strength being in the General's and Whalley's and Rich's regiments of horse, and in the new placed officers in many of the rest . . .)

I found that many honest men of weak judgements and little acquaintance with such matters, had been seduced into a disputing vein, and made it too much of their religion to talk for this opinion and for that; sometimes for State democracy, and sometimes for Church democracy.

Note

1 'the Covenant': the Solemn League and Covenant, see p. 104, Note 1.

Plans for a State Church

66 The Propositions of Newcastle

[*Source*: S.R. Gardiner (1906, Third edition) *Constitutional Documents of the Puritan Revolution*, pp. 291–3.]

[From the proposals for a settlement, presented by Parliament to the King, July 1646.]

. . .

2 That His Majesty, according to the laudable example of his royal father of happy memory, may be pleased to swear and sign the late solemn League and Covenant;[1] and that an Act of Parliament be passed in both kingdoms respectively, for enjoining the taking thereof by all the subjects of the three kingdoms; and the Ordinances concerning the manner of taking the same in both kingdoms be confirmed by Acts of Parliament respectively, with such penalties as, by mutual advice of both kingdoms, shall be agreed upon.

3 That a Bill be passed for the utter abolishing and taking away of all Archbishops, Bishops, their Chancellors and Commissaries, Deans and Sub-deans, Deans and Chapters, Archdeacons . . .

4 That the Ordinances concerning the calling and sitting of the Assembly of Divines be confirmed by Act of Parliament.

5 That reformation of religion, according to the Covenant, be settled by Act of Parliament, in such manner as both Houses have agreed, or shall agree upon, after consultation had with the Assembly of Divines.

6 Forasmuch as both kingdoms are mutually obliged by the same Covenant, to endeavour the nearest conjunction and uniformity in matters of religion, according to the Covenant, as after consultation had with the Divines of both kingdoms assembled, is or shall be jointly agreed upon by both Houses of Parliament of England, and by the Church and kingdom of Scotland, be confirmed by Acts of Parliament of both kingdoms respectively.

7 That for the more effectual disabling Jesuits, Priests, Papists and Popish recusants from disturbing the State and deluding the laws, and for the better discovering and speedy conviction of recusants, an oath be established by Act of Parliament, to be administered to them, wherein they shall abjure and renounce the Pope's supremacy, the doctrine of transubstantiation, purgatory, worshipping of the consecrated host, crucifixes and images, and all other Popish superstitions and errors; and refusing the said oath, being tendered in such manner as shall be appointed by the said Act, to be a sufficient conviction of recusancy.

8 An Act of Parliament for education of the children of Papists by

Protestants in the Protestant religion.

9 An Act for the true levying of the penalties against them, which penalties to be levied and disposed in such manner as both Houses shall agree on, wherein to be provided that His Majesty shall have no loss.

10 That an Act be passed in Parliament, whereby the practices of Papists against the State may be prevented, and the laws against them duly executed, and a stricter course taken to prevent the saying or hearing of Mass in the Court or any other part of this kingdom.

11 The like for the kingdom of Scotland . . .

12 That the King do give his royal assent to an Act for the due observance of the Lord's Day;

And to the Bill for the suppression of innovations in churches and chapels, in and about the worship of God, . . .

And for the better advancement of the preaching of God's Holy Word in all parts of this kingdom;

And to the Bill against the enjoying of pluralities of benefices by spiritual persons, and non-residency.

Note

1 'solemn League and Covenant': see p. 104, Note 1.

67 The Heads of Proposals

[*Source*: Gardiner (1906) *Constitutional Documents*, p. 321.]

[From the draft constitution of the senior army officers, published 1 August 1647.]

. . .

XI An Act to be passed to take away all coercive power, authority, and jurisdiction of Bishops and all other Ecclesiastical Officers whatsoever, extending to any civil penalties upon any: and to repeal all laws whereby the civil magistracy hath been, or is bound, upon any ecclesiastical censure to proceed (*ex officio*) unto any civil penalties against any persons so censured.

XII That there be a repeal of all Acts or clauses in any Act enjoining the use of the Book of Common Prayer, and imposing any penalties for neglect thereof; as also of all Acts or clauses of any Act, imposing any penalty for not coming to church, or for meetings elsewhere for prayer or other religious duties, exercises or ordinances, and some other provision to be made for discovering of Papists and Popish recusants, and for disabling of them, and of all Jesuits or priests from disturbing the State.

XIII That the taking of the Covenant[1] be not enforced upon any, nor any penalties imposed on the refusers, whereby men might be restrained to take it against their judgments or consciences; but all Orders and Ordinances tending to that purpose to be repealed.

Note

1 'the Covenant': see p. 104, Note 1.

68 The Instrument of Government

[*Source*: C.H. Firth and R.S. Rait, editors (1911) *Acts and Ordinances of the Interregnum* volume two, pp. 821–2.]

[From the Constitution of December 1653, under which Cromwell became Lord Protector.]

. . .

xxxv That the Christian religion, as contained in the Scriptures, be held forth and recommended as the public profession of these nations; and that, as soon as may be, a provision, less subject to scruple and contention, and more certain than the present, be made for the encouragement and maintenance of able and painful teachers, for instructing the people, and for discovery and confutation of error, heresy and whatever is contrary to sound doctrine. And that until such provision be made, the present maintenance shall not be taken away nor impeached.

xxxvi That to the public profession held forth none shall be compelled by penalties or otherwise; but that endeavours be used to win them by sound doctrine, and the example of a good conversation.

xxxvii That such as profess faith in God by Jesus Christ (though differing in judgement from the doctrine, worship or discipline publicly held forth) shall not be restrained from, but shall be protected in, the profession of the faith, and exercise of their religion; so as they abuse not this liberty to the civil injury of others, and to the actual disturbance of the public peace on their parts. Provided this liberty be not extended to popery nor prelacy, nor to such as under the profession of Christ, hold forth and practise licentiousness.

xxxviii That all laws, statutes and ordinances, and clauses in any law, statute or ordinance to the contrary of the aforesaid liberty shall be esteemed as null and void.

The Debate on the Ministry

69 George Herbert: The Country Parson, a Pre-Civil War Ideal

[*Source*: R.A. Willmott, editor (1885) *The Works of George Herbert in Prose and Verse*, pp. 222 and 245–6.]

The country parson is full of all knowledge. They say, it is an ill mason that refuseth any stone; and there is no knowledge, but, in a skilful hand, serves either positively as it is, or else to illustrate some other knowledge. He condescends even to the knowledge of tillage, and pasturage, and makes great use of them in teaching, because people, by what they understand, are best led to what they understand not. But the chief and top of his knowledge consists in the book of books, the storehouse and magazine of life and comfort, the Holy Scriptures. There he sucks, and lives . . .

The country parson hath a special care of his church, that all things there be decent, and befitting his name, by which it is called. Therefore first, he takes orders that all things be in good repair; as walls plastered, windows glazed, floor paved, seats whole, firm and uniform, especially that the pulpit and desk, and communion table, and font be as they ought, for those great duties that are performed in them. Secondly, that the church be swept, and kept clean without dust, or cobwebs, and at great festivals strewed and stuck with boughs, and perfumed with incense. Thirdly, that there be fit and proper texts of scripture everywhere painted, and that all the painting be grave, and reverend, not with light colours or foolish antics. Fourthly, that all the books appointed by authority be there, and those not torn or fouled, but whole and clean, and well bound; and that there be a fitting and sightly communion cloth of fine linen, with a handsome, and seemly carpet of good and costly stuff, or cloth, and all kept sweet and clean, in a strong and decent chest, with a chalice, and cover, and a stoup or flagon, and a basin for alms and offerings; besides which, he hath a poor man's box conveniently seated, to receive the charity of well minded people, and to lay up treasure for the sick and needy. And all this he doth, not as out of necessity, or as putting a holiness in the things, but as desiring to keep the middle way between superstition and slovenliness, and as following the Apostle's two great and admirable rules in things of this nature: the first whereof is, 'Let all things be done decently and in order'; the second, 'Let all things be done to edification' (1 Cor 14).

70 William Walwyn

[*Source*: William Walwyn (1644) *The Compassionate Samaritane*, from pp. 23–5 and 31–2. Also printed in Haller, editor, *Tracts on Liberty*.]

They would not have us to think that a minister comes to be so, as another man comes to be a merchant, bookseller, tailor, &c, either by disposal of him by friends in his education, or by his own making choice to be of such a trade: no, there must be something spiritual in the business, a *Iure Divino* [Divine Right] must be brought in, and a succession from the Apostles, . . . as some would have us think kings to be anointed of God, because the Israelite kings were by his command, . . . If the people did not believe so, they would examine all that was said, and not take things upon trust from the ministers, as if whatsoever they spake, God spake in them. They would then try all things, and what they found to be truth, they would embrace as from God, for God is the author of truth; what they found to be otherwise, they would reject, and then, for the most part, they might spare their notings and repetitions too, unless the more to discover the groundlessness of the doctrine, and the giddiness of the divinity which they generally hear. They would then handle their ministers familiarly, as they do one another, shaking off that timorousness and awe which they have of the Divines, with which they are ignorantly brought up . . .

They have . . . made it a difficult thing to be a minister, and so have engrossed the trade to themselves, and left all other men by reason of their other professions in an incapacity of being such . . . If any do take upon them their profession without university breeding and skill in the arts and languages, (how knowing a man soever he be otherwise) they have fastened such an odium in the hearts of most of the people against him, that a thief or murderer cannot be more out of their favour than he . . . They, being furnished with these arts and languages, have a mighty advantage over all such as have them not, and are admirers thereof, as most men are, so that hereby they become masters of all discourses, and can presently stop the people's mouths, that put them too hard to it, by telling them that it is not for laymen to be too confident, being no scholars and ignorant of the original; that the original hath it otherwise than our translations. And thus they keep all in a mystery, that they only may be the oracles.

71 Thomas Hall

[*Source*: Thomas Hall (1651) *The Pulpit Guarded with Twenty Arguments*, pp. 12–13 and 25.]

The Pulpit Guarded

With XX

ARGUMENTS

PROVING

The Unlawfulness, Sinfulness and Danger of suffering Private persons to take upon them Publike Preaching, and expounding the Scriptures without a Call; as being contrary to the Word of God, contrary to the practice of all Reformed Churches, contrary to the Three and twentieth Article of Religion, contrary to two Ordinances of Parliament, and contrary to the Judgement of a whole Jury of learned, judicious, pious Divines, both Forraign and Domestick.

Occasioned by a Dispute at *Henly in Arden* in *Warwick*-shire, *Aug*. 20. 1650.

Against { *Lawrence Williams*, a Nailer-Publike-Preacher.
Tho. Palmer, a Baker-Preacher.
Tho. Hinde, a Plough-Wright-Publike-Preacher.
Sergeant *Oakes*, a Weaver-Preacher.
Hum. Rogers (lately) a Bakers boy-Publike-Preacher.

Here you have all their Arguments (never yet compiled in one Tract) refelled and answered many Texts of Scripture cleared the Quintessence and Marrow of most of our Modern Authors (in reference to this Controversie) collected, with References to such Authors as clear any Doubt more fully; many incident Cases resolved, the utmost extent of Lay-mens using their Gifts in Eleven Particulars demonstrated, and above Thirty Objections answered.

The Third Edition, with addition of Arguments, Answers, Quotations, Scriptures, and many useful enlargements; together with the correcting of those Errata which escaped in the former Editions.

In the close are added six Arguments, to prove our Ministers free from Antichristianism.

2 Tim. 3. 9. *They shall proceed no further: for their folly shall be manifest unto all men.*
Gen. 49. 6. *O my soul, come not thou unto their secret: unto their assembly, mine honor, be not thou united.*
Psal. 27. 3. *Though an host encamp against me, in this will I be confident.*

Veritas impugnata magis elucet. *Bern.*

Composed and compiled by a friend to Truth and Peace.

London, Printed by *J. Cottrel*, for *E. Blackmore*, at the Angel in *Pauls* Church-yard. 1651.

Title page from Thomas Hall *The Pulpit Guarded with XX Arguments* (1651) (Bodleian Library)

Briefly, there are two things that must concur to the making of a minister.

First, gifts, abilities, and qualifications both of life and learning, fit for so high and holy a calling . . . There are more gifts required in a minister than the world dreams of, as arts, sciences, Latin, Greek, Hebrew, reading, meditation, conference, utterance, memory etc, besides temperance, humility, piety, gravity, mortification, self-denial in many lawful liberties which others may take etc.

Secondly, he must have power and authority given him from the Presbytery to exercise those gifts. He must not run before he is sent but must have an outward call as well as an inward . . .

Let the nailer keep to his hammer, the husbandman his plough, the tailor to his shears, the baker to his kneading trough, the miller to his toll, the tanner to his hides and the soldier to his arms etc. They must not leap from the shop to the pulpit, from the army to the ministry, from the blue apron to the black gown etc. But if ever men would have comfort, let them keep the bounds and limits of their particular callings. God hath set every calling its bounds which none may pass. Superiors must govern, inferiors obey, and be governed. Ministers must study and preach, people must hear and obey.

72 William Hartley

[*Source*: William Hartley (1651) *The Prerogative Priest's Passing Bell, or Amen to the Rigid Clergy*, epistle, pp. 1 and 6–7.]

Your animosity is against laymen's preachings. Sure you are from Rome for your speech betrays you. In the commonwealth of Saints there is no such distinction of laity and clergy, but all are one, or alike, in Jesus Christ . . .

One main argument wherewith you deceive the people is drawn, as you say, from God's eternal decree who, as you argue, hath appointed every man a calling, viz. some carpenters, fishermen, tent makers, etc, others to be set apart for the ministry . . .

We answer that persons are qualified by God (the wise disposer of all things) with abilities in the management of the arts, mysteries and sciences for the benefit of the creation, but that persons, so qualified, are prohibited the ministerial function, viz. preaching of the Gospel, that I utterly deny . . .

Peter was a catcher of fish by nets, and men by preaching, and both allowable by Jesus Christ. Therefore trading and preaching is legitimate in the self same person.

As for that you call humane learning, we judge it good in its sphere, but that learning which truly qualifies a person to the preaching of the

Gospel is love, meekness, temperance, patience etc, and where Christ dwells in this nature, these things will be preached and exhorted to. Be it granted, that humane learning, rightly sanctified, may help the sight, yet in itself it gives no more light than spectacles to a blind man.

That we burn all books save the bible, that's your say-so. We are not of so fiery a temper, but those writings, wherein we find no resentment, may be reserved for officious uses.

73 Thomas Collier

[*Source*: Thomas Collier (1651) *The Pulpit Guard Routed*, p. 20.]

The mission you say, implies three things: election by the churches, probation and examination by the Presbytery, separation by ordination of the Presbytery. First, election by the church, but by what church? Not your parochial, provincial or national church: the New Testament never knew such a church, nor Christ in the New Testament never did, never will own such a church: a company of ignorant, prophane, carnal creatures, both priest and people, yet have gotten the name of a church and ministry, blessing themselves in that name, and yet are ignorant what it is; for a Church of Christ to whom election belongs, are a company of believers, Saints gathered out of the world by the power of the Lord in the ministry of the Gospel. (1 Cor. 1.2; Acts 2.47, 4.32) But you are enemies to this church; rail, reproach, persecute: they are the object of your scorn and malice. I grant that, where such a church is, election belongs to them, yet I say, a man may be sent to preach, though not elected by the church. (Acts 8.1–4) The whole church being scattered, preached, and I suppose none dare say that all of them were elected and ordained. For I said before, there is preaching by way of gift and office, and preaching by gift only, and it's the church's joy to see her members gifted and exercised in this way. But, as for yourselves, as your Church is no true church nor your ministry no true ministry so you fail likewise in your election by that church; for you are in your way first ordained, and then you are sent to your churches, parishes, whether they will or no, and you take them by violence if you have a mind to their tithes; you will be their minister, though never elected by them; and afterward, if you have a call to another place for your advantage, you will leave them again, and embrace the second, and the third too, it may be. Yet you dare be so bold as to tell of your electing by the church, whereas, first, it is no church, but a parish consisting for the most part of ignorant, carnal, souls; and secondly, you press yourselves upon them whether they will or no for the most part. Where, then, is your election by the church of Christ? Thus you fail in the first part of your mission, non-election by a church of Christ, and then, I pray, who sent you?

74 Richard Baxter

[*Source*: Richard Baxter (1656) *Gildas Salvianus: The First Part, i.e. The Reformed Pastor*, pp. 464–6.]

It is most desirable that the minister should be of parts above the people so far as to be able to teach them, and awe them, and manifest their weaknesses to themselves or to all. The truth is, for it cannot be hid, it is much long of [owing to] the ministers that our poor people are run into so many factions; and particularly, the weakness of too many is not the least cause, when a proud seducer shall have a nimble tongue, and a minister be dull or ignorant, so that such a one can baffle him or play upon him in the ears of others; it brings him into contempt, and overthrows the weak. For they commonly judge him to have the best cause that hath the most confident, plausible, triumphant tongue. But when a minister is able to open their shame to all, it mightily preserveth the church from the infection . . .

[From Baxter's advice to ministers.]

See that you preach to such auditors as these, some higher points, that stall their understandings, and feed them not all with milk, but sometime with stronger meat. For it exceedingly puffs them up with pride when they hear nothing from ministers but what they know already, or can say themselves. This makes them think themselves as wise as you, and as fit to be teachers, for they think you know no more than you preach. And this hath set so many of them on preaching, because they hear nothing from others but what they can say themselves, and ministers do not set them such patterns as may humble them and deter them from that work. Not that I would have you neglect the great fundamental verities, or wrong the weak and ignorant people, while you are dealing with such as these; but only when the main part of your sermon is as plain as you can speak, let some one small part be such as shall puzzle these self-conceited men.

75 Immanuel Bourne

[*Source*: I Bourne (1659) *A Defence and Justification of Ministers' Maintenance by Tithes*, pp. 73 and 81.]

Tithes were not appointed to teach men anything, but for the maintenance and livelihood of them that are teachers, the faithful preachers of the Gospel and ministers of Christ. Therefore tithes are not ceremonies, as the ceremonious Quakers would have them; but the just temporal, outward gain and reward for their labour, which the faithful ministers of Christ may lawfully seek by every man for his labour in his place . . .

I desire that men would enquire into the book of conscience, which one day shall be opened, and be fully resolved whether to take away tithes from their proper use, for which God and good men did give them, be not horrid sacrilege, that dreadful sin which subjects men to the wrath and curse of God.

* * * * * * * * * * *

76 Thomas Hall: A Looking-Glass for Anabaptists

[*Source*: Hall (1651) *The Pulpit Guarded.* The epistle to the lay-preachers.]

Their first tenent [tenet]is, that infant-baptism is a childish, needless thing; and that none must be baptized till he come to a perfect age, and can make a confession of his faith; that infant-baptism came from the Pope and the Devil.

2 That all gifted persons may preach without ordination.

3 That God reveals his will, not only by the written word, but also by dreams and visions; which they believe more than the word . . .

4 That the Saints in this life are pure, without spot, and need not use that petition, 'Forgive us our sins.'

5 No man can with a good conscience exercise the office of Magistrate under the New Testament.

6 They are rigid separatists; they separate themselves from all Reformed Churches.

7 They are tumultuous: they raised tumults in Germany, and filled it with the fire of sedition, . . .

8 They deny original sin to be in infants, that so they might overthrow baptism.

9 They hold free-will by nature in all spiritual things.

10 That a man may have more wives than one.

11 That clothes discover sin; therefore they being as perfect and pure as Adam in his innocency, they ought to go naked.

12 That Christ died intentionally for all.

13 No Christian ought with a safe conscience take an oath, nor by oath promise fidelity to a Magistrate.

14 That a Christian cannot with a safe conscience possess anything proper to himself; but he must let all be common.

15 That wives of contrary religion may be put away, and then 'tis lawful to take others.
16 Universities, humane arts and learning, they cry down as needless; they burnt all books save the Bible.
17 That 'tis unlawful to go to law.
18 Wars are unuseful, or any use of the sword.
19 [They deny] That preaching, praying, sacraments, singing of psalms, and all ordinances, are legal. The Spirit is all.
20 The Magistrate must compel none in matters of religion; but must tolerate all.
21 That the Father, Son, and Holy Ghost are not three distinct persons, and in essence one God.
22 That the soul sleeps when it parts from the body, and neither goes to Heaven or Hell till the day of judgement; and that the souls of men are but terrestrial vapours, like the life of beasts, perishing with the body.
23 That Christ hath removed the Law, and now the pure Gospel is our only rule.
24 The Old Testament is abrogate and useless; and at least, they prefer their new lights before the Gospel.
25 That the Saints are freed by Christ from all laws, covenants, vows, paying of tithes, or debts.
26 After rebaptization they cannot sin.
27 We may dissemble our Religion, deny Christ before men, so we keep the truth in our hearts. God delights not in our blood, nor requires that we die for the truth.
28 The Scripture is to be turned into allegories.
29 Heaven and Hell are nowhere but within a man.
30 They give a supreme and independent power, in all ecclesiastical causes and censures, to their single congregations.

The Quakers and their Opponents

77 James Nayler

[*Source*: James Nayler (1653) *A Caution to all who shall be found Persecutors* in George Whitehead, editor (1716). *A Collection of Sundry Books, Epistles and Papers* by James Nayler, pp. 85 and 89–90 (marginal references omitted).]

a.

Did ever any strive against God and prosper? He will break you with a rod of iron and dash you in pieces like a potter's vessel. Be wise, take heed, fear and tremble before the Lord, lest his wrath kindle against you, and you be consumed in his anger. Woe to him that striveth with his maker; let the potsherds strive with the potsherds of the earth; shall the clay question the work of the potter? . . .

. . . Take heed, you that tread the poor and helpless under your feet. Repent, repent, your day is coming on apace wherein the Lord will avenge the poor in him that is too strong for him. And how canst thou stand at that day when thou shalt become as weak as another man and no false pretences will be accepted? Thou must be judged according to thy works, good or evil. Oh! that you had hearts to humble yourselves before the Lord that ye might find mercy at that day, for why will you perish through your own will?

[*Source*: James Nayler (1656 edition) *The Power and Glory of the Lord Shining out of the North*, pp. 2 and 12–13 (marginal references omitted).]

b.

All your hirelings are strangers to Christ, and he knows them not: for though they may prophesy in his name, and in his name cast out devils, yet if they be workers of iniquity, Christ knows them not and such know not Christ. For he that sayeth I know him and keeps not his commandments is a liar. Now all people, cease from your strange guides and outside lights and return to the Light of Christ in you, that which shows you sin and evil and the deeds of darkness. For whatever makes manifest is Light; and this is that Light which shines into the conscience, which tells you that lying, swearing, pride, envy, coveteousness, backbiting and dissembling leads to condemnation. And this light checks you for sin and would have you to do to all men as you would be done to. And this light is not a chapter without you, in a book, but it is that light that revealed that to the Saints, in their several measures, which they spoke forth and which thou readest in the Chapter. And this light being minded will lead to the perfect day which declares all things as they are. . . .

. . . For your tithes, augmentations and set benefits, when did ever God require any such thing from any magistrates under the Gospel? And doth it serve for any other end but to hold up an idle loitering ministry, one pulling another out of places and setting themselves in their stead that they may heap up riches and live in their lusts . . . And do you fear that the hand of God is shortened that he will not raise up such as will go on his message unless you provide them wages? Did ever any that he sent complain to the world for want? . . . Those who are sent by Christ take little care for such earthly things, having a better reward in durable riches. And can you ever keep the ministers of Antichrist out of places (who will conform to anything for gain) so long as they can have you to feed them with money? And will not you be found guilty of keeping up the hirelings, that the woe is to, and them that hold them up and whom Christ is come to discover and cast out, and so you be found fighters against him? And when you leave all that say they are Christ's ministers to Christ's maintenance, set down in the Gospel, then it will appear who have run unsent and have not profited the people.

78 George Fox

[*Source*: George Fox (1659) *The Great Mistery of the Great Whore Unfolded*, the epistle to the reader.]

We found this light to be a sufficient teacher, to lead us to Christ, from whence this light came, and thereby it gave us to receive Christ, and to witness him to dwell in us, and through it the new covenant we came to enter into, to be made heirs of life and salvation; and in all things we found the light which we were enlightened withal, and all mankind (which is Christ) to be alone and only sufficient to bring to life and eternal salvation; and that all who did own the light in them which Christ hath enlightened every man withal, they needed no man to teach them, but the Lord was their teacher, by his light in their own consciences, and they received the holy anointing.

And so we ceased from the teachings of all men and their words, and their worships, and their temples, and all their baptisms, and churches, and we ceased from our own words, and professions, and practices in religion, in times before zealously performed by us, through divers forms, and we became fools for Christ's sake, that we might become truly wise, and by this light of Christ in us we were led out of all false ways and false preachings, and false ministers, and we met together often, and waited upon the Lord in pure silence, from our own words, and all men's words, and hearkened to the voice of the Lord.

79 Immanuel Bourne

[*Source*: Immanuel Bourne (1656) *A Defence of the Scriptures*, from the dedication to the Judges of England and to Major General Whalley, no pagination.]

We cannot but acknowledge that the Lord hath done great things in these nations, and we do enjoy peace and plenty, and many mercies, which we have not prized nor improved as we ought to the best advantage for God's glory and our own good. Under his Highness' protection, and the present government, through the grace of God, every man may sit quietly under his own vine and fig tree, without fear of plundering, a happiness which in a few years past we did not enjoy. Yes, we have good laws, and honourable, religious judges and magistrates, to see justice executed, and right done between man and man; and we enjoy our comfortable liberty of preaching and hearing the gospel of Christ. Yet can we not say, there is no complaining, nor cause of complaint in our streets. The church and people of God have met with enemies in all ages: 'As is the lily amongst the thorns, so is my beloved among the daughters' [Song of Solomon, 2.2], and as it was of old, so it is in these our days: the church and people of God, especially God's faithful ministers, suffer persecution by two sorts of people. The first, prophane Ranters, atheistical men, drunkards, gamesters, and ignorant, blind souls, such as neglect public ordinances in these times of liberty, and have no right principle of grace and goodness in them. These make it a delight to exercise their malice against the ministers of Christ. These would rob and spoil them to the uttermost if it were in their power; and this we can witness we have found true by troublesome experience.

Again, there is another sort of people which travel up and down the nation, under the name of Quakers, as the Jesuits and seminary priests have used to do secretly, so these now openly, disuading and seducing our people all they can from coming to our churches or meeting houses, calling our churches idol's temples. All our services to God in prayer, preaching of the word and other Christian exercises, ordinary and extraordinary, when we seek the face of God for the peace and welfare of the nation, for the prosperity of our navy and armies, both by sea and land, or our praising God for his mercies we do enjoy – all these, say the Quakers, are but idol-worship, and beastly services; and all the faithful and godly ministers of Christ, without exception, are thieves; our maintenance by tithes, anti-Christian and unlawful. Yea, they call us conjurors, Antichrists, witches, devils, liars, a viperous and serpentine generation, blasphemers, scarlet coloured beasts, Babylon's merchants, whited walls, painted sepulchres; and whatsoever the true prophets of God, or Christ our saviour, did justly call the false prophets, wicked priests, and scribes and pharisees, those names do these railing and reviling Quakers give to the godly, painful, learned and faithful ministers of Christ in the nation, disuading our people from hearing us or giving heed to anything we preach, disturbing us in our public ministry. And what can we call this but a persecution, like that of those wicked men against the good prophet Jeremiah.

80 Richard Baxter

[*Source*: Richard Baxter (1696) *Reliquiae Baxterianae*, edited Matthew Sylvester, p. 77.]

. . . The Quakers who were but the Ranters turned from horrid prophaneness and blasphemy to a life of extreme austerity on the other side. Their doctrines were mostly the same with the Ranters': they make the light which every man hath within him to be his sufficient rule, and consequently the scripture and ministry are set light by. They speak much for the dwelling and working of the spirit in us, but little of justification and the pardon of sin, and our reconciliation with God through Jesus Christ. They pretend their dependence on the spirit's conduct against set times of prayer, and against sacraments, and against their due esteem of scripture and ministry. They will not have the scripture called the word of God; their principal zeal lieth in railing at the ministers as hirelings, deceivers, false prophets, etc., and in refusing to swear before a magistrate, or to put off their hat to any, or to say 'You' instead of 'Thou' or 'Thee' which are their words to all. At first they did use to fall into tremblings and sometime vomitings in their meetings, and pretended to be violently acted by the spirit, but now that is ceased; they only meet, and he that pretendeth to be moved by the spirit speaketh, and sometime they say nothing, but sit an hour or more in silence and then depart. One while divers of them went naked through divers chief towns and cities of the land, as a prophetical act; some of them have famished and drowned themselves in melancholy, and others undertaken by the power of the spirit to raise them, as Susan Pearson did at Claines near Worcester, where they took a man out of his grave that had so made away with himself, and commanded him to arise and live, but to their shame. Their chief leader, James Nayler, acted the part of Christ at Bristol, according to much of the history of the Gospel, and was long laid in Bridewell for it, and his tongue bored as a blasphemer by the Parliament. Many Franciscan friars and other papists have been proved to be disguised speakers in their assemblies and to be among them, and it's like are the very soul of all these horrible delusions. But of late one William Penn is become their leader[1], and would reform the sect, and set up a kind of ministry among them.

Note

1 'William Penn . . .': Penn (1644–1718) was a dominant figure in the Quakers by the 1680s when he founded the colony of Pennsylvania and supported James II's Declaration of Indulgence. Baxter's editor believed this section of the *Reliquiae* had been written in 1664, but the comment on Penn must have been added some ten years later.

Spiritual Quests

81 John Rogers

[*Source*: John Rogers (1653) *Ohel or Beth-Shemesh: A Tabernacle for the Sun*, pp. 391, 419–21, 423–4, 428–35, and 438.]

We have sufficiently, I suppose, proved the assertion of the use of experiences declared in the Church, being much for the honour and glory of God . . . Now we all concur, school-men, ministers and all, that where there is true grace, experienced saints know it sweeter than the drops from the honey comb . . . So the Saints do tell by experience, how Jehovah hath helped them, and blessed them, even with spiritual blessings in heavenly places . . .

[The] testimony to the truth or further experience of John Rogers, preacher of the Gospel, and given in to two Churches in England and Ireland.

To give a formal account from year to year of my life, would make me too tedious, to you and myself; and I fear somewhat offensive to such as are to follow, though I may safely say in every year since I can remember, I have been enriched with so many and such remarkable experiences; as might make some of you rather admire than believe . . . And first when I was a school-boy at Malden in Essex, I began to be roused up by two men, viz. Mr Fenner, and Mr Marshall.[1] The first of these about the tenth year of mine age, as I take it, (for what I was before I know not, a mere – I know not what) although I was kept continually in good order, as to read every day, and be catechised and the like, yet then hearing Mr William Fenner full of zeal, stirring about, and thundering and beating the pulpit; I was amazed, and thought he was mad; I wondered what he meant, and whilst I was gazing upon him, I was struck, and saw it was we that were mad which made him so; O says he! you knotty! rugged! proud piece of flesh! you stony, rocky, flinty, hard-heart! What wilt thou do when thou art roaring in Hell amongst the damned! etc. This made me at first amazed, which run often in my mind after, and I began now to be troubled, being scared and frighted, and out of fear of Hell, I fell to duties, hear sermons, read the scriptures, (though I knew not what I had read, but only thought the bare reading was enough) morning and evening, and learn'd to pray (at first out of books, and all the graces (so called) that I could get) and besides family prayers, I was afraid every night lest the devil should carry me away to Hell, if I did not first to myself (whilst my brother my bed-fellow was fast asleep) say my prayers, and my 'Our Father', and 'I believe in God', etc. and the ten commandments, and my little catechism (Dr Hall's)[2] which I had learnt; and this I did every night duly before I durst sleep; and I made as much of them as of a charm to keep me well that night; . . .

I lived under a desperate fear; but for all this, Mr Marshall a while after in the same pulpit took me napping; whilst I was, I know not how, bewitched to nod, and began to sleep, but his powerful voice thundering against such as are drowsy, and sleep, and slumber away their salvation, was at that time picked out for me, and very prevalent; I started up with an aching heart, and was frighted at his words . . .O! I was sufficiently wounded, and fell a weeping; I could not hold, and after sermon I went home, where I boarded, and sat alone! crying and complaining that I had lost my time; and at that time I took up a purpose never to sleep at Church more, and made a covenant with it; which I think, to this day, I observed ever since . . .

But after all this, there is another remarkable passage that I must never forget, which I met with, or rather met with me to the purpose: about 1637 (as I take it) at Messing in Essex, I was playing with children (my fittest companions then) and running round about the house we lived in, through two or three little gates, in sport and idleness; as I was running with the rest, (I know not how, nor upon what occasion) I threw out vain words, and crying, O Lord! (which we were not suffered to do) my heart was suddenly smitten upon it, and I was suddenly set a running as if I had been possessed . . .until I was (headlong) carried through a little gate-way, where . . . there was set a naked sword, glistening with a fearful edge (I thought) and which took up the whole space of the gate from one post to another, with a broad blade most keen and cruel . . . I stood as one amazed, or rather as one that knew not whether he were alive or dead . . . What it was I know not, yet it left a lasting impression upon me, and the scar is yet to be seen in my heart, though the wound be healed. But, alas! how long and lamentable I lay afflicted and in continual fears after this! . . . At length I was tempted not to pray, read, hear, or do any duties at all: for I thought it not possible after all to be saved; and so I was sometimes tempted to deny all; sometimes I was also tempted to think there was no God, but all things come by nature . . . to require a sign and seek a proof . . . For as the distracted fits did much abate me, they did turn more to inward malady and melancholy . . .

This sad condition day and night lasted upon me, until I was persuaded that there was a God! and that this God was righteous, and that he would hear prayers if I continued but knocking with importunity and gave not over . . . I threw myself upon the bed, whilst my eyes were glazed with tears! and there I lay, in a sudden sleep which seized upon me . . . When I awakened, I was so much changed that I was amazed at myself, at the suddenness of it; for I dreamt I was comforted, and my heart filled with joy, and when I awaked it was so indeed . . . So I was persuaded that the righteousness of Christ was mine, . . . And after that I began plainly to see myself (and so by myself others) why I despaired, and was so long and so lamentably lost, that it was because I sought in the wrong place for justification, and therefore a wrong way for salvation . . . For after I had solemnized and celebrated my new life . . . yet Satan (my continual and never ceasing enemy) now began to muster up afresh more troubles against me, and to follow me with a host of afflictions and temptations . . .

I was looked upon as disobedient for keeping company with such as were godly Puritans, and accounted then Round-heads, and for praying and holding communion with them . . .

But after many dangers and troubles I footed it as far as Cambridge, where I sought from College to College to be but a sizar or poor scholar, my little stock of money being all gone . . . but I could have no place, and I had no money, and I wanted bread, and that so long that all others failed to do any thing for me, insomuch as I was forced for life to try all things, and eat leather, and drink water, and eat old quills and pens, where I could pick them up out of the dust or dunghills, roasted in a few coals, which were left in the chamber where I was, and I assayed sometimes to eat grass, and did it; yea, I grew to that height of penury and famine, that I sometimes tried to eat my own fingers, biting them till I could endure it no longer; then tearing my hair, and crying, I had to recourse to prayer . . . I could see no ways to evade death, for I had been beholding to all the scholars I could find any courtesy in, to bring me scraps, or skins of salt-fish, or something or other in their handkerchiefs or pockets, which kept me alive a while, till at last they were all weary, and I wasted almost to death, and ashamed to beg openly about . . . I drew my knife, whetted it sharp, opened my doublet and shirt, and in the midst of the room where I was alone, kneel'd down to prayer, to surrender my soul up into the hands of God; my knife lying by me prepared, and I prepared for the act, when behold a door which I thought was bolted all the night before, was but shut to, which a scholar opens, and with the screeching of it made me start up and throw my knife into the chimney in haste (as ashamed of what I was doing) and in comes the scholar to tell me of a place in Huntingdonshire to teach gentlemen's children at my Lord Brudenel's house,[3] and how one of our college was sent to, but refused it; by which means I was recovered out of that eminent danger . . .

At this time I came to be convinced of the Parliament's proceedings and cause, to be more regular and in order to the great work that God hath to do in nations than the kings, by comparing them together, and bringing them to the Word; and then I saw clearly, by the Word, that God would do what he hath to be done, by them and for them, and for the Commonwealth; it was not long after this that I was by a godly people in Toseland [Huntingdonshire] earnestly importuned, and at last prevailed with to preach the Gospel; and I was soon known in the country, and after sent for into Essex, where I settled (passing twice through the [Westminster] Assembly [of Divines] on examination and approbation) . . . And since that, I have been sent forth, as a Pastor and public teacher by the Church, and I know my ministerial commission and authority to be free from the Lord.

Notes

1 'Mr Fenner and Mr Marshall'; William Fenner (d. 1640), Puritan minister of

Rochford, Essex; Stephen Marshall (d. 1655), minister of Finchingfield, Essex, before the civil war and a leading Presbyterian in the 1640s.

2 'Dr Hall's' catechism: no such work is recorded in the standard catalogue of printed books; Rogers perhaps meant the very popular *A Short Catechisme* by John Ball (1585–1640), a non-conforming Puritan.

3 Thomas, Lord Brudenel, was a Huntingdonshire royalist.

82 Thomas Patient

[*Source*: Thomas Patient (1654) *The Doctrine of Baptism*. Epistle to the Reader.]

Beloved Reader, I know the world is filled with many books stuffed with very much of man's wisdom, which, though the Apostle saith is enmity against God; yet we find such discourses most pleasing to the carnal hearts of men in our age. Therefore if that be the thing that thy itching ears do thirst after, thou mayest spare thyself that labour, for thou wilt find that with as much simplicity and plainness as possibly I could, I have herein given out by clear Scripture – evidence, what the Lord hath made known to me . . .

For after it pleased God to reveal his Son in me, and to work a change in my heart, the great and weighty thing that God presented to me was, to make my calling and election sure, which I found to be a work filled with many difficulties, considering how far hypocrites might attain in the profession of godliness, and that they might come to have the counterfeit of all the grace in the Child of God . . .

But presently being convinced of the unwarrantableness of the government of the lordly prelates, and the liturgy in the Church of England, and the mixed communions in the parish asssemblies, I was resolved, God willing, to examine all religion, as well in worship, and the order of God's house, as I had done in other points. But I, at this time, being by the divine power of God, converted from the Church of England, though with a great deal of difficulty, being well furnished with arguments from pulpit and print, and divers able disputants for the defence of that false way . . . At this time many godly Christians going to New England, and being come up in my judgement to the way of New England in faith and order, went over thither, being not convinced of my error and great darkness in sprinkling the carnal seed of believers . . . And so I constantly resorted to the meetings of the people in New England, desiring to have good satisfaction in them, and their doctrine and practice, before I joined in Communion . . . I began to examine the grounds thereof, and the weight of their arguments . . . finding as I conceived, the foundation argument by them urged, so exceeding contrary to several foundations of religion, which both they and I did believe . . .

Notwithstanding, I found further objections in my heart, that though it was not men of parts, and outward learning, but babes and sucklings, having their hearts bowed to obedience, and to the holy fear of God, that God would teach; yet I was sensible of so much evil in my heart, that I questioned whether I might not be misled; upon which I was put upon humble and fervent prayers to the Lord to guide and teach me, and to reveal his mind to me . . . Upon which this temptation came in afresh upon me: what need I trouble myself in a point so disputable, for if by my search and trial in that matter, I should come to see grounds swaying in conscience against children's baptism, that then I should be generally despised, and slighted of all the godly in that country; and not only be frustrated of communion and fellowship with them, but must expect to suffer imprisonment, confiscation of goods, and banishment at least, which would be my ruin, not knowing where to go, but in the woods amongst Indians, and wild beasts?. . .

At the last it pleased the Lord to reveal his mind to me, so that I was enlightened in my understanding to see answers to whatsoever I had heard, the Lord breaking in with, not only a clear light in me, as to the matter in question [the baptizing of children], but three days one after another, coming into my soul with sealing manifestations of his love, and that with Scriptures so pertinent and suitable to my condition. There being a warrant at this time issued out to apprehend and bring me before the General Court in New England which was no trouble to me, being filled with unspeakable joy, as I walked up and down in the woods in that wilderness, about my business.

83 Laurence Clarkson

[*Source*: Laurence Clarkson (1660) *The Lost Sheep Found*, pp. 6–13, 15–16, 19–21, 23–9 and 32–4.]

Now if then you had asked me what I thought God was, the Devil was, what the Angels' nature was, what Heaven and Hell was, and what would become of my soul after death? My answer had plainly been this: that my God was a grave, ancient, holy, old man, as I supposed sat in Heaven in a chair of gold, but as for his nature I knew no more than a child; and as for the Devil, I really believed was some deformed person out of man, and that he could where, when and how, in what shape appear he pleased; and therefore the devil was a great scarecrow in so much that every black thing I saw in the night, I thought was the devil; but as for the Angels, I knew nothing at all; and for Heaven, I thought was a glorious place, with variety of rooms suitable for Himself, and his Son Christ, and the Holy Ghost; and Hell, where it was I knew not, but judged it a local place, all dark, fire and brimstone, which the devils did torment the wicked in, and that for ever; but for the soul at the hour of death, I believed was either by an Angel or a Devil fetched immediately to Heaven or Hell. This was the height of my knowledge under the Bishops' Government, and I am persuaded was the height of all Episcopal ministers then living . . .

After this I travelled into the Church of the Presbyterians . . . for herein consisted the difference of the Presbyterian and Episcopal, only in a few superstitious rites and ceremonies, as also their doctrine was more lively than the Episcopal, for they would thunder the pulpit with an unknown God, which then I thought was true, and sharply reprove sin, though since I saw we were the greatest sinners . . . The Presbyterians began to be a great people, and in high esteem, and at that time there was a great slaughter of the Protestants in Ireland [October 1641] that London was thronged with their ministers and people, and several collections were gathered for them; but this I observed, that as the Presbyterians got power, so their pride and cruelty increased against such as was contrary to them, so that thirdly I left them, and travelled to the Church of the Independents; for this I observed, as wars increased, so variety of judgements increased . . .

But I must return to the time then under Doctor Crisp's doctrine,[1] in which I did endeavour to become one of those that God saw no sin, and in some measure I began to be comforted therewith; but how, or which way to continue in the same I could not tell, having as yet but little understanding in the Scripture I was silent, only still enquiring after the highest pitch of light then held forth in London . . . Fourthly, take notice in this Sect I continued a certain time, for Church it was none, in that it was but part form, and part none . . .

Now after I had continued half a year, more or less [as a preacher in Norfolk] the Ministers began to envy me for my doctrine, it being free grace,[2] so contrary to theirs, and that the more [as] their people came from their own parish to hear me . . . Now I knowing no other but those sayings 'Go ye teach all Nations, baptizing them, and lo I am with you to the end of the world' [from Matthew 28: 19–20]; that continuance to the end of the world, was the load-stone that brought me to believe that the baptism of the Apostles was as much in force now, as in their days, and that command did as really belong to me as to them; so being convinced, for London I went to be further satisfied, so that after a little discourse with Patience,[3] I was by him baptized in the water that runneth about the Tower . . .

I continued preaching the Gospel and very zealous I was for obedience to the commands of Christ Jesus; which doctrine of mine converted many of my former friends and others to be baptized, and so into a Church-fellowship was gathered to officiate the order of the Apostles, so that really I thought if ever I was in a true happy condition, then I was . . . Now dipping being a command of Christ, I judged them rebels that did profess the name of Christ, and not submit their bodies to the ordinance of Christ, and that Christ requires obedience from none but such as was capable of being taught, and therefore no children, but men and women, ought to receive the ordinance of baptism . . .

[In January 1645 Clarkson was questioned about adult baptism by the parliamentary committee at Bury St Edmonds and kept under house arrest.] Then said Sir John Rouse [one of the Committee] we are informed you dipped six sisters one night naked. [Clarkson] That is nothing to me what you are informed, for I never did such a thing. Nay further, it is reported, that which of them you liked best, you lay with her in the water? Surely your experience teacheth you the contrary, that nature hath small desire to copulation in water, at which they laughed; but, said I, you have more cause to weep for the unclean thoughts of your heart . . .

[The committee challenged the legality of Clarkson's marriage, which had been contracted by mutual consent before his congregation.]

I being vexed at their folly, answered, marriage is no other, but a free consent in love each to the other before God, and who was sufficient to publish the contract as myself? . . .

After I had lain there [at Bury St Edmonds under arrest] a long time, Mr Sedgewick and Mr Erbury[4] came to visit me, with whom I had great discourse, and after they were gone, I had a great conceit in my mind, as touching the succession of baptism, which I could not see but in the death of the Apostles, there was never since no true administrator[5] . . . So . . . I was minded to travel into the wilderness; so seeing the vanity of the Baptists, I renounced them and had my freedom [July 1645].

Then, sixthly, I took my journey into the society of those people called Seekers, who worshipped God only by prayer and preaching . . . As all along in this my travel I was subject to that sin, and yet as saint-like, as though sin were a burden to me . . . I concluded there was none could live without sin in this world; for notwithstanding I had great knowledge in the things of God, yet I found my heart was not right to what I pretended, but full of lust and vain-glory of this world . . .

Now after this I return'd to my wife in Suffolk, and wholly bent my mind to travel up and down the country, preaching for moneys . . . There was few of the clergy able to reach me in doctrine or prayer; yet notwithstanding, not being a University man, I was very often turned out of employment, that truly I speak it, I think there was not any poor soul so tossed in judgement, and for a poor livelihood, as then I was . . .

[As a 'teacher' in the Army] I quartered in a private-house, who was a former friend of mine, asked me if I had heard not of a people called 'My one flesh' [The Ranters]? I said no, what was their opinion and how should I speak with any of them? Then she directed me to Giles Calvert.[6] So that now friends, I am travelling further into the wilderness . . . Seventhly, I took my progress into the wilderness . . . with many more words I affirmed that there was no sin, but as man esteemed it sin, and therefore none can be free from sin, till in purity it can be acted as no sin, for I judged that pure to me, which to dark understandings was impure, for to the pure all things, yea all acts were pure . . .

Now Copp[7] was by himself with a company ranting and swearing, which I was seldom addicted to, only proving by Scripture the truth of what I acted; and indeed Solomon's writings was the original of my filthy lust, supposing I might take the same liberty as he did, not then understanding his writings was no Scripture, that I was moved to write to the world what my principle was, so brought to public view a book called *The Single Eye* [October 1650] so that men and women came from many parts to see my face, and hear my knowledge in these things, being restless till they were made free, as then we called it. Now I being as they said, Captain of the Rant, I had most of the principal women came to my lodging for knowledge, which then was called The Headquarters. Now in the height of this ranting, I was made still careful for moneys for my wife, only my body was given to other women: so our company increasing, I wanted for nothing that heart could desire, but at last it became a trade so common, that all the froth and scum broke forth into the height of this wickedness, yea began to be a public reproach, that I broke up my quarters, and went into the country to my wife, where I had by the way disciples plenty . . .

The ground of this my judgement was, God had made all things good, so nothing evil but as man judged it; for I apprehended there was no such thing as theft, cheat, or a lie, but as man made it so: for if the creature had brought this world into no propriety, as Mine and Thine, there had been no such title as theft, cheat, or a lie; for the prevention hereof Everard and Gerrard Winstanley[8] did dig up the commons, that so all might have to live of themselves, then there had been no need of defrauding, but unity one with another . . .

But now to return to my progress, I came for London again, to visit my old society; which then Mary Midleton of Chelsford, and Mrs Star was deeply in love with me, so having parted with Mrs Midleton, Mrs Star and I went up and down the countries as man and wife, spending our time in feasting and drinking, so that taverns I called the house of God; and the drawers, messengers; and sack, divinity; reading in Solomon's writings it must be so, in that it made glad the heart of God; which before, and at that time we had several meetings of great company, and that some, no mean ones neither, where then, and at that time, they improved their liberty, where Doctor Paget's maid stripped herself naked, and skipped among them, but being in a cook's shop, there was no hunger, so that I kept myself to Mrs Star, pleading the lawfulness of our doings as aforesaid, concluding with Solomon all was vanity . . .

Now in the interim I attempted the art of astrology and physick, which in a short time I gained and therewith travelled up and down Cambridgeshire and Essex . . . improving my skill to the utmost, that I had clients many, yet could not be therewith contended [contented?] but aspired to the art of magic . . . I improved my genius to fetch goods back that were stolen, yea to raise spirits, and fetch treasure out of the earth, with many such diabolical actions . . . At that time I looked upon all was good, and God the author of all, and therefore have several times attempted to raise the devil, that so I might see what he was, but all in vain, so that I judged all was a lie, and that there was no devil at all, nor indeed no God but only nature; for when I have perused the Scriptures I have found so much contradiction as then I conceived, that I had no faith in it at all . . . I neither believed that Adam was the first creature, but that there was a creation before him . . . I really believed no Moses, Prophets, Christ, or Apostles, nor no resurrection at all; for I understood that which was life in man, went into that infinite bulk and bigness, so called God, as a drop into the ocean, and the body rotted in the grave, and for ever so to remain.

In the interim came forth a people called Quakers, with whom I had some discourse, from whence I discerned that they were no further than burning brick in Egypt [Exodus 5], though in a more purer way than their fathers before them . . .

[*c*. 1658] Then for London I went, and going to visit Chetwood my former acquaintance, she, with the wife of Midleton, related to me the two witnesses; so having some conference with Reeve the prophet,[9] and reading his writings, I was in a trembling condition . . . Now being at my journey's end as in point of notional worship, I came to see the vast difference of Faith from Reason, which before I conclude, you shall hear; and how that from Faith's royal prerogative all its seed in Adam was saved, and all Reason in the fallen Angel was damned, from whence I came to know my election and pardon of all my former transgressions; after which my revelation growing, moved me to publish to the world, what my Father was, where he liveth, and the glory of his house, as is confirmed by my writings now in public; so that now I can say, of all my formal righteousness, and professed wickedness, I am stripped naked, and in room thereof clothed with innocency of life, perfect assurance, and seed of discerning with the spirit of revelation.

Notes

1 Dr Crisp: Tobias Crisp, an Antinomian minister who preached in London in 1642–43.

2 'free grace': grace which does not have to be earned by works.

3 'Patience': Thomas Patient, see biographical index p. 387.

4 'Mr Sedgwick and Mr Erbury': William Sedgwick and William Erbury who were both ministers in the Isle of Ely at this time. They were identified with the 'Seekers', both rejecting church organization and stressing the importance of God's spirit within the individual before the Scriptures.

5 'no true administrator': Clarkson came to believe that all baptism was wrong because only the Apostles had been given the power to baptize by the Holy Ghost.

6 'Giles Calvert': a radical printer. He often acted as a link between the various sectaries whose works he published.

7 'Copp': Abiezer Coppe, the Ranter.

8 'Everard and Gerrard Winstanley': the Diggers. See p. 187 for Winstanley, and extracts from his writings.

9 'Reeve the prophet': John Reeve who founded the Muggletonian sect with Lodowick Muggleton. Reeve and Muggleton believed themselves to be the 'two witnesses' (Revelation 11) who were to declare a new system of faith and had the authority to decide the eternal fate of individuals. Reeve saw faith as the divine element in man, reason as the element that came from Satan. Clarkson was apparently a Muggletonian until his death.

SECTION ELEVEN: THE LEVELLERS

[The Levellers – 'the first democratic political movement in modern history'[1] developed from 1646 among the radical London craftsmen and small traders. The later 1640s were a time of severe economic problems and widespread disillusion with Parliament, whose victory in the war had meant little improvement in most people's lives. Indeed, as Richard Overton vividly argued in his *Remonstrance* (extract 85) Parliament could be quite as oppressive as Charles I had been. We have concentrated on Overton's pamphlets in this section because his clear, dramatic prose is among the most attractive produced by the Levellers. Overton's earliest publications were directed against the bishops (extracts 31 and 32 above) and he was equally opposed to Presbyterian authoritarianism (extract 84); but his later works were more secular in tone. Other Levellers first became active in opposition to religious orthodoxy: John Lilburne, whose sufferings at the hands of Parliament made him a focus for the London radicals in 1646–47 (extracts 85 and 86), became prominent in 1638 when he was punished in Star Chamber for distributing 'seditious' religious literature; William Walwyn had written in defence of religious freedom (extract 70 above). The Levellers argued for greater political democracy, although they disagreed on how far it should extend; they did not favour economic equality. But here too there were differences, and Walwyn was among the most concerned with social and economic reform. *Walwyns Wiles* (extract 90) is a highly exaggerated account of his views, however; it was written by a group of London Baptists and Congregationalists, strongly opposed to Walwyn on political and theological grounds.

The Levellers' links with the unrest in the New Model Army made them an important political force in 1647.[2] Parliament's proposals of spring 1647 to reduce the army and send much of it to Ireland without dealing with the soldier's practical grievances – such as pay arrears, or the lack of any indemnity for actions committed during the war – propelled the rank and file into political action which went far beyond their immediate demands. Section Ten gave examples of conservative alarm at the radicalism of the army (extracts 64 and 65) and here too the wider aspirations of some of the soldiers are illustrated. Amongst the grievances presented by two regiments to Parliament's negotiators in May 1647 was the lack of religious liberty (extract 87). The Levellers' political programme was outlined in the *Case of the Army* and the *Agreement of the People* (extracts 88 and 89). Both were ostensibly written by the 'agitators' or representatives of the army regiments, but it is likely that the London Leveller leaders were at least partly responsible. The climax of this political upheaval was the meeting of the General Council of the Army at Putney in late October 1647 when fundamental political principles were debated by officers, ordinary soldiers and Leveller leaders. The *Agreement* occupied much of the discussion with the attack on it led by Commissary General Henry Ireton, Cromwell's son-in-law.

Notes

1 G.E. Aylmer, *The Levellers in the English Revolution* (1975), p. 9.

2 These developments are considered in more detail in a cassette of the Putney debates, produced by the Open University as part of its A203 Course, or see Aylmer, *The Levellers*; A.S.P. Woodhouse, editor *Puritanism and Liberty* (paperback edition 1974).]

84 Richard Overton: The Arraignment of Mr Persecution

[*Source*: Richard Overton (1645) *The Arraignment of Mr Persecution*, pp. 9–13, 25–6, 33–4 and 46. Also printed in William Haller, editor, *Tracts on Liberty in the Puritan Revolution* (1934, reprinted 1965).]

[The trial of Mr Persecution is taking place; Mr God's Vengeance leads for the prosecution. He is addressing the Judge, Lord Parliament.]

God's Vengeance:

My Lord, I have from the beginning diligently observed the nature and inclinations of this prisoner ever to have been so averse to God and all goodness, that his action in all nations, kingdoms and states, amongst societies and people, have been in direct enmity to the end of Christ's coming: For he came not to destroy men's lives, but to save them (Luke 9. 56, John 3. 17). But this fellow Persecution destroyeth both life temporal and spiritual: he wasteth men's estates; the more godly and upright they are, the more cruel, raging and hateful he is against them; he bringeth misery, poverty and beggary on their wives and children. Yea, my Lord, this savage, blood-thirsty wretch hangeth, burneth, stoneth, tortureth, saweth asunder, casteth into the fiery furnace, into the lions' den, teareth in pieces with wild horses, plucketh out the eyes, roasteth quick, burieth alive, plucketh out the tongues, imprisoneth, scourgeth, revileth, curseth-yea, with bell, book and candle, belyeth, cutteth the ears, slitteth the nose, manacles the hands, gaggeth the mouthes, whippeth, pillorieth, banisheth into remote islands, makes them fly by whole shipfuls into wild deserts, stigmatiseth some, and sometimes maketh such, so stigmatised, when the wind turns, to stigmatise their friends with reproaches, calumnies, oppression of conscience etc.; deprives them of the communication of their friends, of all relief, of pen, ink and paper, separates man and wife, deprives parents of their children and children of their parents, imprisoneth men only for the discharge of a good conscience, stoppeth presses, whereby men cannot make their just defence; suffers nothing to be licensed, printed, preached or otherwise published, but what himself alloweth; and having thus bound the hands and stopped the mouthes of all good men, then he comes forth in print against them like an armed man, and furiously assaults them, exults and exalts himself over them; feigneth arguments for them, and then like a valiant champion, gives them a conquering answer, and thus puts them to flight, and pursues them with revilings, scandals, forgeries, and opprobrious nick-names, as Antinomians, Anabaptists, Brownists,[1] Independents, schismatics, heretics, etc. Thus he dealeth with the Godly party: yea, he forceth millions to make shipwreck of a good conscience, who for fear of such humanity deny the Lord that brought them, to their final condemnation. Oh! therefore, my Lord, if there be any bowels of mercy, any tender compassion in you! pity the destitute, the afflicted, the tormented, who wander about in sheepskins and in goatskins, in deserts and in mountains, in dens and in caves of the earth, of whom the world is not worthy.

Secondly, my Lord, he maketh a nation guilty of all the righteous blood spilt upon the earth, from the blood of Abel to the blood of Zacharias, and of all that are slain upon the earth, for it is all innocent blood that is shed in that case, purchased by the blood of Jesus Christ, who came not to destroy but to save men's lives; and therefore would have all taught in all nations, that all might be persuaded to the obedience of the truth, that all might be saved. Therefore to kill the unbeliever, as Turk, Pagan, Jew etc. is to slay such as Christ would have to live to repent, which must needs be murder in the highest nature: and cursed is he that shall slay an innocent person, and all the people shall say, Amen; the land that sheddeth innocent blood, innocent blood shall be upon it; and innocent blood the Lord will not pardon (Deuteronomy 27.25, 19.10; 2 Kings 24.4).

Thirdly, my Lord, he occasioneth treasons, conspiracies, rebellions, wars, foreign and domestic, in all nations and kingdoms in the earth; he divideth prince against prince, kingdom against kingdom, and kingdoms in themselves, breedeth and begetteth a national hatred betwixt prince and people, and amongst themselves; he setteth neighbour against neighbour, yea, father against son, and son against father; he breaketh the bonds of peace and friendship, national and domestic, enrageth and filleth the whole earth with blood and violence: for what at this day is the reason the Protestants seek the blood of the Papists, but because the Papists seek theirs? They hate and persecute the Papists because the Papists hate and persecute them: they would extirpate and root out the Papists because the Papists would do the like to them. And on the other side, the Papists plot and conspire against the Protestants because the Protestants will not suffer them to live amongst them, but banish, imprison, hang, draw, quarter and set up the limbs of some of them, in open defiance to the God of heaven and earth, upon the gates of the city, who though unhappily they be found traitors to the public peace and politic government, yet nature might teach them to bury their limbs, an eye for an eye, a tooth for a tooth, blood for blood, saith God; but now blood cannot satisfy inhuman cruelties: if this be canonical, let me have old Tobit's Apocrypha, who hazarded his life to bury the dead.[2]

Where two stand at enmity, there must needs be mastery, or else no safety: when one knoweth the other is his mortal enemy, he will use all the means, strength and policy that he can to subdue him. This enrageth to all manner of tyranny and bloodshed, setteth one kingdom against another, because each knoweth and taketh each other for his deadly enemy: their faith being built upon this rotten and devouring principle of forcing the consciences one of another. But if the Papist knew the Protestant, the Protestant the Papist to love another, and would not molest or in the least injure one another for their conscience, but live peaceably and quietly one by another, bearing one with another, and so of all religions, what man would lift up his hand against his neighbour? This could not but conduce to a general true settled peace, to the whole world. And in a short time, the enmity of heart between the Papist and Protestant etc. would be quite worn out. Why should we hate and destroy one another? Are we not all the creatures of one God, redeemed by one Lord Jesus Christ? This should provoke us to love and peace one towards another. If God have revealed more light of the Gospel to one than to another, shall the more knowing trample the ignorant under his feet? We should carry ourselves loving and meek one towards another, with patience persuading and exhorting the contrary minded, proving if at any time, God will turn their hearts, by this means the great incendiary of the world, an enforced, enraged conscience, would be at rest. What is more near and dear than our consciences? If that be enraged, who can appease it? If that be satisfied, what content, joy or peace like unto it, or what more mild, more gentle or loving? Therefore, how tender ought we to be in cases of conscience? It is a lion if enraged, a lamb if appeased; it is all honey, or all gall; enraged, it is like the wild boar of the forest; pleased, it is like the dove from the ark, no greater friend, no greater foe.

It is better therefore for kingdoms to set the conscience free as in Holland, Poland, Transylvania etc. and be at peace in themselves, than to bind and enforce it, and be rent in themselves with emulations, heart-burnings, conspiracies, rebellions, etc. If this fiery spirit were allayed, this ignorant zeal of forcing all to believe as we believe, extinct, national fears, jealousies and hatred would cease betwixt nation and nation, people and people; for as this violent implacable spirit suggesteth fears and jealousies betwixt one conscience-forcing king and another, kingdom and kingdom, nation and nation, so it forceth them to draw their swords, and stand in continual defiance and defence for fear of mutual invasion. Yea, under a false opinion of advancing God's glory by forcing others to their faith, they invade, assault and murder one another, and yet both, deluded by this seducer, think they do God good service, when alas it is all innocent blood that is shed. What was the main cause so many nations have been rent and divided in themselves, and one against another, and in their divisions devoured one another of late days? What occasioned the revolt of the German Princes from the House of Austria, of the Netherlanders from the King of Spain, the bloody massacry in France?[3] And amongst ourselves, what occasioned the rising of the Scots, the rebellion in Ireland, and those bloody divisions in England, but this devilish spirit of binding the conscience? One would compel the other to their faith and force them from their own, and that will not be borne: they had rather die than deny their faith; and therefore is it, that a considerable party rebelleth, and in that rebellion wallow in one another's blood, burn and destroy all before them, and yet both, as they suppose, fight the Lord's battle, while indeed the devil beareth the greatest share, whose servants they are in that quarrel one as well as the other. Does not the Holy Ghost make it a special mark of Antichrist to force all, both great and small, etc. and is it not the cause of the Woman's flight into the wilderness from the presence of the Dragon; the scattering of the church into deserts and secret places; the death of the two witnesses, and wearing out of the Saints of the most High? How cometh the Woman on the scarlet coloured beast, drunk with the blood of the Saints, and with the blood of the martyrs of Jesus, and all the blood of the earth to be found in her, but by this devilish spirit, even the spirit of devils, which goeth forth unto the kings of the earth and of the whole world to provoke them to war against the Saints [from Revelation, especially chapters 11–13, 17–8]; I mean, this binding of conscience, and forcing conformity, though never so much against knowledge and persuasion of heart, which at this day is so hotly endeavoured, preached and pleaded for by the proud prelatical Presbytery of this land, who by their subtle insinuations and secret delusions endeavour the infusion thereof into the hearts of their rulers, and to beget it as a principle of faith in the multitude. Should they possess a Parliament and Kingdom with this spirit, that Parliament and Kingdom cannot expect peace and safety to continue; the fire may be smothered for a time, but it will break out at last, as this Kingdom hath already found by woeful experience, the blood of its nobles and commons etc., whereof, my Lord, this infernal fiend (here arraigned before your Honour, a traitor to his Majesty's crown and dignity, the privileges of Parliament, rights and lib[erties] of the subject) is the cause. Yea, my Lord, he is Iakee [mischievous fellow] on both sides; it was he that occasioned the fears and jealousies betwixt his Majesty and the two Houses of Parliament, and unhappily drew them into the field of blood; neither party would be oppressed in conscience, or deprived of their religion; this was one half of the quarrel, and publicly professed the main, though it may be monarchy was the other half; and, my Lord, he seduced the King into the north, and provoked your Lordship unto arms, and hath continued to this day firmly on both sides, so that fall which side it will, he concludes to be conqueror, and be established absolute monarch, for so he deports himself betwixt you both, that both may persecute, and hitherto he hath too much prevailed with your Lordship. Therefore my Lord, if this vile incendiary, here happily detected and arraigned, be not cut off from betwixt you, there is no hopes of peace, till the sword, and it may be famine and pestilence too, wrestle it out to a conquest on one side; and when all is done, yet peace will not, nor can possibly, long endure, for where persecution is, there will be heart burnings, envyings, emulations, and murmurings, which at length will break out into commotions, conspiracies, insurrections and rebellions. And thus my Lord, I give place to what shall be further evidenced by the witnesses . . .

[Mr God's Vengeance calls Gaffer Christian, Gaffer Martyr and Gaffer Liberty of Conscience as his witnesses.]

Prisoner [Mr Persecution]
My Lord, I beseech you hear me after this tedious accusation, it is false and malicious, as by sound reason, and personages of honour I shall clearly evidence. First, my Lord, as for God's Vengeance my prosecutor, both the Juries, with divers others, together with the witnesses, enforced him to prosecute me, and I know not by what pretence they procured God's Vengeance against me; for, my Lord, I am innocent, and ever have been from my cradle from such and so heinous accusation, as is laid to my charge. And for that fellow [Gaffer Christian] that pretends he hath known me since the coming of Christ, he is a man of no reputation, without habitation, a beggarly fellow, a runagate [renegade], a loose fellow, he stays in no place, keeps no hospitality, blasphemeth that most divine, Levitical ever to [be] adored Ordinance for Tithes,[4] and counteth it as an unholy thing, pays none where he lives, but sharks here and there, where he can shuffle in his head, runs from house to house, to delude simple women, who are ever learning, and never learned; and, whereas he sayeth his name is Christian, his name is not Christian, neither is he of the generation of Christianity, but a most factious dissembling Anabaptist, a tub-preacher, and no Christian, as Sir Symon, Sir John, and divers other reverend, and honourable persons here present can witness. As for Gaffer Martyrs, he is as a sounding brass and tinkling cymbal, who though he giveth up his body to be burned, himself is but a castaway, and this I am able to make good unto your Honour, by the most grave and solid judgement of all the reverend divines, the clergy of Christendom. Therefore my Lord, it much mattereth not, what his evidence is, it being but the malice of a heretic; and as for Liberty-of-Conscience, Sir Symon, and that blessed babe, his son Sir John (sanctified from his mother's womb, the synodian whore of Babylon) hath informed your Honour of the unworthiness of his witness. My Lord, I desire Sir Symon may speak in my defence.

Sir Symon: [the counsel for the defence, Sir Symon Synod]
My Lord, this gentleman here arraigned is altogether innocent from this accusation. I have had ancient familiarity with him, a daily society hath passed betwixt us, and I never could find any such thing in him, and my Lord here is Mr Pontifical Revenue, Mr Ecclesiastical Supremacy, Mr National Conformity, Mr Rude Multitude, Mr Scotch Government, and my only son, Sir John Presbyter, all to witness his innocency from this accusation: and if your Lordship make any scruple hereof, that learned gentlemen, Justice Conformity, Of Lincoln's Inn Esq.[5] can thoroughly resolve you, both by scripture texts, precedents of all sorts, and the constant interrupted practices, examples, of the most eminent emperors, princes, councils, parliaments, etc.

Liberty-of-Conscience:
My Lord, the defendant smells of a fat benefice; see, see, his pockets are full of Presbyterian steeples, the spires stick under his girdle: ha, ha, hah; instead of weather-cocks, every spire hath got a black box upon it,

and in it the pure and immaculate Ordinance for Tithes, Oblations, etc. Sure shortly, instead of Moses and Aaron, and the Two Tables,[6] we shall have Sir Symon, and Sir John holding the late Solemn League and Covenant,[7] and that demure, spotless, pretty, lovely, sacred, divine, devout, and holy Ordinance for Tithes (the Two Tables of our new Presbyterian Gospel) painted upon all the churches in England. Oh brave Sir Symon, the bells in your pocket chime 'all in' while ours chime 'all-out'. I pray you give us a funeral homily for your friend here before he depart, here's twenty shillings for your pains, you know 'tis sacrilege to bring down the price, As it was in the beginning, is now and ever shall be, world without end. Amen.

Crier:
Make way there for the Jury.

The Jury withdraw, and thus fall into debate about their verdict . . . [The prisoner is found guilty and the Judge, Lord Parliament, asks him if he wishes to make a statement as to why the death sentence should not be passed on him.]

Persecution:
My Lord, the jury have not dealt honestly in their verdict, wherefore I appeal from them to the Assembly of Divines, for a trial of their honesty in this verdict.

Judge:
Persecution, indeed thou standest need of a long cloak to cover thy knavery; but there is no appeal from this Court, they are no sanctuary of refuge in this case, neither can I conceive such worthy gentlemen should perjure themselves, yet if thou hast anything else to say, to award the sentence of death, speak for thyself.

Persecution:
I thank your Honour. My Lord, I am so terrified in myself at the apprehension of death that I am not in case to speak for myself: I beseech your Lordship, that Sir Symon may speak in my behalf.

Sir Symon:
My Lord, the enemies of our peace in this matter have dealt very subtly, and most traitorously against the reverend assembly of the faithful, the clergy, to divide them from your Lordship's protection, to destroy and hinder the work of reformation, etc. For my Lord, this man here indicated by the name of Persecution, is none of the man; for here is Mr National Conformity, Mr Pontifical Revenue, Mr Ecclesiastical Supremacy, personages of honour and eminency throughout whole Christendom, to testify with me, that this prisoner hath ever endeavoured to purge the Church of God from heresy, schism and all manner of irregular exorbitant courses, and laboured for the peace of the Church, that we may lead a lazy and an easy life without God, and the people in the fear of the clergy. Indeed my Lord, he was once of the Church of Rome, and thereupon generally branded by the name of

Persecution; but my Lord, for this hundred years and upward he hath been of the true Protestant religion, even from the time of Luther, and at this present endeavoureth with us the good of the Church in its restitution to prelatical Presbytery. And upon his separation from Rome with Luther, he utterly renounced the nickname of Persecution, and though unhappily through Jesuitical suggestions and delusions he was too frequent in the Spanish Inquisition, and of late by episcopal sophistications enticed to officiate in the High Commission; yet, my Lord, he was ever in himself an honest reformer, and indeed his true name is Present Reformation, he was born not long after the primitive times, but his nature and inclinations by evil instruments have been so much abused, that he had even lost his name, and being nicknamed when he was young, and through long continuance of time, forgot his name, that indeed he answered a long time to the name of Persecution, but his true and proper name is Present Reformation, which by interpretation, is, Presbyterian government. Wherefore my Lord, I beseech you consider the subtlety of this malignant heretical faction, who have procured the apprehension and indictment of this Present Reformation under the odious name of Persecution, thereby at once to make your Honour both ruin yourself, and the Presbytery of the kingdom. Therefore my Lord, whether the jury have dealt honestly in their verdict, your Honour by this may easily discern.

Judge:
Persecution, what sayest thou to this? Is thy name Present Reformation?

Persecution:
Yes my Lord, and my name is according to my natural disposition.

Judge:
Who gave you that name?

Justice Reason:
My Lord, his god-fathers and god-mothers in his baptism, wherein he was made a member of the assembly, and an inheritor of the kingdom of Antichrist.

Judge:
His God-fathers, and god-mothers? Who are your god-fathers, and your god-mothers?

Persecution:
My Lord, Mr Ecclesiastical Supremacy, and Mr Scotch Government are my god-fathers, Mr State Ambition, and Mr Church Revenue are my god-mothers, and I was sprinkled into the Assembly of Divines at the taking of the late Solemn League and Covenant.

Justice Reason:
My Lord, he is at this time primate and metropolitan over all the

ecclesiastical courts of tyranny in the world, the Spanish Inquisition, the High Commission, and now our divines have sprinkled his federal holiness into their assembly, and hereupon changed his name from Persecution, and anabaptis'd him Present Reformation . . .

Judge:
Therefore the sentence of this Court is that thou shalt return to the place from whence thou camest, to wit, the noisome and filthy cage of every unclean and hateful bird, the clergy of Christendom, there to be fast bound with inquisition, synodical, classical, priest bitter-all chains until the appearing of that great and terrible judge of the whole earth who shall take thee alive with Sir Symon and his son, Sir John, and cast thee with them and their confederates into the lake of fire and brimstone, where the beast and the false prophet are [Revelation 19.20], there to be tormented day and night for ever and ever.

Notes
1 'Brownists': see p. 130, Note 1.
2 For Tobit see the Apocrypha, Tobit, 1. 17–20, 2. 7–8.
3 'bloody massacry in France': the massacre of the Protestant Huguenots by the Catholics on St Bartholomew's Day, 1572.
4 'Ordinance for Tithes': Parliament passed an ordinance enforcing the payment of tithes, 8 November 1644.
5 'Justice Conformity . . .': William Prynne, the Laudian martyr of the 1630s, a determined opponent of religious toleration.
6 'the Two Tables': the Ten Commandments.
7 'Solemn League and Covenant': see p. 104, Note 1.

85 Richard Overton: A Remonstrance of Many Thousand Citizens

[*Source*: Richard Overton (1646) *A Remonstrance of Many Thousand Citizens and other Freeborn People of England to their own House of Commons*.
Also printed in Haller, editor, *Tracts on Liberty*, and in D.M. Wolfe, editor, *Leveller Manifestos of the Puritan Revolution* (1944).]

We are well assured, yet cannot forget, that the cause of our choosing you to be Parliament-men, was to deliver us from all kind of bondage, and to preserve the commonwealth in peace and happiness. For effecting whereof, we possessed you with the same power that was in ourselves, to have done the same; for we might justly have done it ourselves without you, if we had thought it convenient, choosing you, as persons whom we thought fitly qualified and faithful, for avoiding some inconveniences.

But ye are to remember, this was only of us but a power of trust, which is ever revocable and cannot be otherwise, and to be employed to no other end than our own well being. Nor did we choose you to continue our trusts longer than the known established constitution of this commonly-wealth will justly permit, and that could be but for one year at the most: for by our law, a Parliament is to be called once every year, and oftener, if need be, as ye well know. We are your principals, and you our agents; it is a truth which you cannot but acknowledge. For if you or any other shall assume or exercise any power, that is not derived from our trust and choice thereunto, that power is no less than usurpation and an oppression, from which we expect to be freed, in whomsoever we find it; it being altogether inconsistent with the nature of just freedom, which ye also very well understand.

The history of our forefathers since they were conquered by the Normans, doth manifest that this nation hath been held in bondage all along ever since by the policies and force of the officers of trust in the commonwealth, amongst whom we always esteemed kings the chiefest; and what, in much of the former time, was done by war, and by impoverishing of the people, to make them slaves and to hold them in bondage, our latter princes have endeavoured to effect by giving ease and wealth unto the people, but withall corrupting their understanding, by infusing false principles concerning kings and government, and parliaments and freedoms; and also using all means to corrupt and vitiate the manners of the youth, and strongest prop and support of the people, the gentry . . .

But in conclusion, longer they would not bear, and then ye were chosen to work our deliverance, and to estate us in natural and just liberty agreeable to Reason, and common equity, for whatever our forefathers were, or whatever they did or suffered, or were enforced to yield unto, we are the men of the present age and ought to be absolutely free from all kinds of exorbitancies, molestations or arbitrary power, and you we chose to free us from all without exception or limitation, either in respect of persons, officers, degrees or things; and we were full of confidence, that ye also would have dealt impartially on our behalf, and made us the most absolute free people in the world.

But how ye have dealt with us, we shall now let you know, and let the righteous God judge between you and us; the continual oppressors of the nation have been kings, which is so evident that you cannot deny it; and ye yourselves have told the King, whom yet you own, that his whole 16 years' reign was one continued act of the breach of the law . . .

Ye have experience, that none but a king could do so great intolerable mischiefs; the very name of king proving a sufficient charm to delude many of our brethren in Wales, Ireland, England and Scotland too, so far as to fight against their own liberties, which you know, no man under heaven could ever have done.

And yet, as if you were of counsel with him, and were resolved to hold up his reputation, thereby to enable him to go on in mischief, you maintain, 'The King can do no wrong'; and apply all his oppressions to 'evil counsellors', begging and entreating him in such submissive language, to return to his kingly office and Parliament, as if you were resolved to make us believe he were a God, without whose presence all must fall to ruin, or as if it were impossible for any nation to be happy without a king.

You cannot fight for our liberties, but it must be in the name of King and Parliament; he that speaks of his cruelties must be thrust out of your House and society; your preachers must pray for him, as if he had not deserved to be excommunicated all Christian society; or as if ye or they thought God were a respecter of the persons of kings in judgement.

By this and other your like dealings, your frequent treating and tampering to maintain his honour, we that have trusted you to deliver us from his oppressions and to preserve us from his cruelties, are wasted and consumed in multitudes to manifold miseries, whilst you lie ready with open arms to receive him, and to make him a great and glorious king . . .

It is high time we be plain with you: we are not, nor shall not be so contented; we do expect, according to reason, that ye should, in the first place, declare and set forth King Charles his wickedness openly before the world, and withal, to show the intolerable inconveniences of having a kingly government, from the constant evil practices of those of this nation; and so to declare King Charles an enemy, and to publish your resolution never to have any more, but to acquit us of so great a charge and trouble for ever, and to convert the great revenue of the crown to the public treasure, to make good the injuries and injustices done heretofore, and of late, by those that have possessed the same; and this we expected long since at your hand, and until this be done, we shall not think ourselves well dealt withal in this original of all oppressions, to wit kings.

Ye must also deal better with us concerning the Lords, than you have done. Ye only are chosen by us the People, and therefore in you only is the power of binding the whole nation, by making, altering or abolishing of laws . . . What is this [i.e. the power of the House of Lords] but to blind our eyes, that we should not know where our power is lodged, nor to whom to apply ourselves for the use thereof; but if we want a law, we must await till the King and Lords assent; if an ordinance, then we must wait till the Lords assent; yet, ye knowing their assent to be merely formal (as having no root in the choice of the people from whom the power that is just must be derived) do frequently importune their assent, which implies a most gross absurdity . . .

We desire you to free us from these abuses, and their [i.e. the Lords'] negative voices, or else tell us, that it is reasonable we should be slaves; this being a perpetual prejudice in our government, neither consisting with freedom nor safety; with freedom it cannot, for in this way of voting in all affairs of the commonwealth, being not chosen thereunto by the people, they are therein masters and lords of the people, which necessarily implies the people to be their servants and vassals, and they have used many of us accordingly, by committing divers to prison upon their own authority, namely William Larner,[1] Lieutenant Colonel John Lilburne, and other worthy sufferers, who upon appeal unto you have not been relieved.

We must therefore pray you to make a law against all kinds of arbitrary government, as the highest capital offence against the commonwealth, and to reduce all conditions of men to a certainty, that none henceforward may presume or plead anything in way of excuse, and that ye will leave no favour or scruple of tyrannical power over us in any whatsoever . . .

We must deal plainly with you, ye have long time acted more like the House of Peers than the House of Commons: we can scarcely approach your door with a request or motion, though by way of petition, but ye hold long debates, whether we break not your privileges; the King's or the Lords' pretended prerogatives never made a greater noise, nor was made more dreadful than the name of privilege of the House of Commons.

Your members in all impositions must not be taxed in the places where they live, like other men; your servants have their privileges too. To accuse or prosecute any of you is become dangerous to the prosecutors. You have imprisonments as frequent for either witnesses or prosecutors as ever the Star Chamber had, and ye are furnished with new devised arguments to prove that ye only may justly do those gross injustices, which the Star Chamber, High Commission, and Council Board [i.e. the Privy Council] might not do.

And for doing whereof, whilst ye were untainted, ye abolished them, for ye now frequently commit men's persons to prison without showing cause; ye examine men upon interrogatories and questions against themselves, and imprison them for refusing to answer; and ye have officious, servile men, that write and publish sophistical arguments to justify your so doing, for which they are rewarded and countenanced, as the Star Chamber and High Commission beagles lately were.

Whilst those that ventured their lives for your establishment, are many of them vexed and molested and impoverished by them; ye have entertained to be your committees' servants, those very prowling varlets that were employed by those unjust courts who took pleasure to torment honest conscionable people; yea, vex and molest honest men for matters of religion, and difference with you and your Synod [i.e. the Westminster Assembly of Divines] in judgement, and take upon you to determine of doctrine and discipline approving this, and reproaching that, just like unto former ignorant, politic and superstitious Parliaments and Convocations; and thereby have divided honest people amongst themselves, by countenancing only those of the Presbytery, and discountenancing all the separation, Anabaptists and Independents.

And though it resteth in you to acquiet all differences in affection, though not in judgement, by permitting everyone to be fully persuaded in their own minds, commanding all reproach to cease; yet; as [if] ye also had admitted Machiavelli's maxim, '*Divide et impera*', divide and prevail, ye countenance only one, open the printing press only unto one, and that to the Presbytery, and suffer them to rail and abuse and domineer over all the rest, as if also ye had discovered and digested that, without a powerful compulsive Presbytery in the church, a compulsive mastership, or aristocratical government, over the people in the state, could never long be maintained.

Whereas truly we are well assured, neither you, nor none else, can have any into power at all to conclude the people in matters that concern the worship of God, for therein everyone of us ought to be fully assured in our own minds, and to be sure to worship him according to our consciences . . .

Ye know, the laws of this nation are unworthy a free people, and deserve from first to last to be considered and seriously debated, and reduced to an agreement with common equity and right reason, which ought to be the form and life of every government.

Magna Carta itself being but a beggarly thing, containing many marks of intolerable bondage, and the laws that have been made since by Parliaments have in very many particulars made our government much more oppressive and intolerable . . .

Ye know also, imprisonment for debt is not from the beginning; yet ye think not of these many thousand persons and families that are destroyed thereby; ye are rich, and abound in goods, and have need of nothing, but the afflictions of the poor, your hunger-starved brethren, ye have no compassion of . . .

We intreat you to consider what difference there is between binding a man to an oar, as a galley-slave in Turkey or Algiers, and pressing of men to serve in your war: to surprise a man on the sudden, force him from his calling where he lived comfortably, from a good trade, from his dear parents, wife or children, against inclination, disposition, to fight for a cause he understands not, and in company of such as he hath no comfort to be withal, for pay that will scarce give him sustenance; and if he live, to return to a lost trade or beggary, or not much better . . .

Ye are extremely altered in demeanour towards us: in the beginning ye seemed to know what freedom was, made a distinction of honest men, whether rich or poor, all were welcome to you, and ye would mix yourselves with us in a loving familiar way, void of courtly observance or behaviour . . .

What a multitude of precious lives have been lost? What a mass of moneys have been raised? What one way was proposed to advance moneys that was refused by you, though never so prejudicial to the people, allowing your committees to force men to pay or lend, or else to swear that they were not worth so or so: the most destructive course to tradesmen that could be devised; fifty entire subsidies to be lent throughout London, if not procured, yet authorised by you; never the like heard of, and the Excise, that being once settled, [it was promised that] all other assessments should cease.

Notwithstanding, in few months comes forth ordinance upon ordinance for more moneys; and for the customs, they were thought an oppression in the beginning, and, being so high, a hindrance to trade and extremely prejudicial to the nation; nevertheless is now confirmed, with many augmentations, insomuch as men of inferior trading find great trouble to provide moneys for customs, and have so many officers to please that it is a very slavery to have anything to do with them, and no remedy; the first commissioners being more harsh and ingenious than the late farmers,[2] and the last worse than the former.

Truly it is a sad thing, but too true, a plain, quiet-minded man in any place in England is just like a harmless sheep in a thicket: [he] can hardly move or stir but he shall be stretch'd and lose his wool; such committees have ye made in all cities and counties, and none are so ill used as honest, Godly men.

Ye have now sat full five years, which is four years longer than we intended, for we could choose you but for, at most, one year; and now we wish ye would publish to all the world the good that you have done for us, the liberty ye have brought us unto. If ye could excuse yourselves, as ye use to do, by saying it hath been a time of war, that will not do; for when [i.e. because] the war might in the beginning have been prevented if ye had drawn a little more blood from the right vein and might often, ere this, have been ended . . .

We have some hopes ye will, for amongst you there have been always faithful and worthy men, whose abundant grief it hath been to observe the strange progress of the chosen men of the commonwealth, and [who] have strove exceedingly on all occasions to produce better effects, and [have] some Christians of late produced to their praise.

Others there are, that have been only misled by the policies and strategems of politic men, and these, after this our serious advice, will make you more seriously study the common interest of this nation; others there are, and those a great number, that are newly chosen into your house, and we trust are such as will exceedingly strengthen the good part that hitherto hath been too weak to steer an even course amidst so many oppositions and cross waves . . .

Forsake and utterly renounce all crafty and subtle intentions; hide not your thoughts from us, and give us encouragement to be open-breasted unto you. Proclaim aforehand what ye determine to do, in establishing anything for continuance, and hear all things that can be spoken with or against the same; and, to that intent, let the imprisoned presses at liberty, that all men's understandings may be more conveniently informed and convinced, as far as is possible, by the equity of your proceedings.

We cannot but expect to be delivered from the Norman bondage whereof we now, as well as our predecessors, have felt the smart by these bloody wars; and from all unreasonable laws made ever since that unhappy conquest; as we have encouragement, we shall inform you further, and guide you, as we observe your doings.

The work, ye must note, is ours, and not your own, though ye are to be partakers with us in the well or ill doing thereof, and therefore ye must expect to hear more frequently from us than ye have done; nor will it be your wisdom to take these admonitions and cautions in evil part . . .

Ye are not to reckon that ye have any longer time to effect the great work we have entrusted unto you, for we must not lose our free choice of a Parliament once every year, fresh and fresh for a continual Parliament . . .

Our advice is, that ye order a meeting of the chosen [i.e. for the choosing] of Parliament-men, to be expressly upon one certain day in November, yearly throughout the land in the places accustomed, and to be by you expressed, there to make choice of whom they think good, according to law; and all men that have a right, to be there, not to fail upon a great penalty . . .

And that a Parliament so chosen in November, succeeding year by year, may come instead of the preceding Parliament, and proceed with the affairs of the commonwealth; nor would we have it in the power of our Parliament to remove any member from his place or service of the House, without the consent had of those counties, cities and boroughs respectively that chose him, great inconveniences depending thereon, whereof we have seen and felt too much.

Now, if ye shall conscionably perform your trust the year ensuing, and order the Parliaments to succeed as aforesaid, then we shall not doubt to be made absolute freemen in time, and become a just, plenteous and powerful nation; all that is past will be forgotten, and we shall yet have cause to rejoice in your wisdom and fidelity.

Notes

1 William Larner: a radical London bookseller, imprisoned by the Parliament in March 1646.

2 'the late farmers': the merchants who 'farmed' or leased the customs under Charles I; the 'commissioners' administered the customs for the Parliament.

86 Thomas Edwards: The Levellers

[*Source:* Thomas Edwards (1646) *Gangraena*, the third part, pp. 148–9, 153–6 and 158.]

There is one Richard Overton, a desperate sectary, one of Lilburne's breed and followers, who hath printed many scandalous things against the House of Peers, and notice being given of him, there was an order granted for the taking of him and seizing of his press (a press that had printed many wicked pamphlets, that have come out of late, against the King, the Lords, the Presbyterial government, the City [of London]; and for a toleration, and liberty, destructive to all religion, laws and government, yea overthrowing by the principles laid down in them the power of the House of Commons, whilst they seem to cry up and invest that House with the monopoly of all the power of the Kingdom); who, being apprehended by the messengers sent out for him, was brought before a committee of the House of Lords, where he refused to answer any questions, and carried himself with a great deal of contempt and scorn, both in words and gesture; and after this being brought before the House of Lords, he refused to answer any questions propounded by the Speaker as in the name of the House, and to that question, whether he were a printer or no, he would not answer, but told them he was resolved not to make answer to any interrogatories that should infringe his property, right or freedom in particular, or the rights, freedoms and properties of the nation in general. Besides, he gave saucy and peremptory words to the House of Lords; and appealed from the House of Lords to the House of Commons; whereupon the Lords committed him to Newgate, as he most justly deserved [on August 11 1646]. Now since his commitment to Newgate, there are some wicked railing pamphlets come out in his name, and sold openly; pamphlets venting a company of cursed principles, both against religion and civil government, tending to nothing else but the overthrow of the fundamental constitution of this Kingdom in King, Lords and Commons, and setting up the body of the common people, as the sovereign lord and king; denying King and Lords any power, and the House of Commons any further than the people's deputies, and at the pleasure and will of the people; and to the ruin of religion, by pleading against the ordinance for punishing blasphemies and heresies[1]. . .

There is one John Lilburne, an arch sectary, the great darling of the sectaries, highly extolled and magnified by them in many pamphlets[2] called, 'The Defender of the Faith', 'A Pearl in a Dung-hill', 'That worthy sufferer for his country's liberty', 'This worthy man', (a precious jewel indeed) of whom I had thought to have given a full relation in this book, and to have laid him open in all his colours, by following him from place to place, and showing how time after time he hath behaved himself since he came out of his apprenticeship: as by declaring what set him first on work to print books against the bishops; how he carried himself in the Fleet whilst he was prisoner there, [after his punishment in Star Chamber in 1638 for distributing forbidden religious literature]; how since this Parliament both before the wars began and since the wars, how whilst he was a prisoner in Oxford [in the winter of 1642–43], how in the Earl of Manchester's army, how in the City at many meetings about petitions since he left the wars, how before the Committee of Examinations [of the House of Commons], how the first time he was in Newgate by order of the House of Commons [August–October 1645 after an attack on the Commons' Speaker William Lenthall]; how be behaved himself before the House of Lords, and how the second time of his imprisonment in Newgate [in June 1646 for his opposition to the Earl of Manchester] and how since his last commitment to the Tower [from August 1646]; but because this narration alone will take up some sheets, there being many remarkable things to be written of him, of his insolent ungodly practices, and of his anarchical principles, destructive to all civil government whatsoever, and I have already filled up that number of sheets I at first intended when I resolved to write this third part (though I have many things yet to put in this third part); therefore I must defer it till a fourth part, and shall then, by the help of God, do it so largely and fully that I shall make his folly and wickedness known to all men, and vindicate the honour and power of the House of Peers from his, and all the sectaries' wicked libels; showing the weakness of those principles, that all power in government is founded upon the immediate free election of all those that are to be governed; and of a necessity, that all who are to be subject and obey must be represented; and that all who have power in government must be representers; which I shall do for the vindication of the just legal power of the King, the House of Lords, yea, and of the Commons; undertaking to make it good, that according to the sectarian principles now vented in so many books daily, and so much countenanced by too many, the power and privilege of the House of Commons would be overthrown and cut short as well as the King and Lords . . .

Many . . . instances I could give of those who have by the laws of England and other kingdoms, power of government, and that most justly, without any immediate election of the people, and persons to be governed by them; so that we must look for some other foundations and grounds of giving one man, or more, power in government over all, besides this immediate election and representation, which will be found firm and strong, and which indeed give the force to election and which in several cases, without any immediate election of the present persons to be governed, binds them before God and men to obedience and subjection in all lawful things . . .

The reader may observe what difference there is between the same sectaries in the year 1645 and the year 1646, such new light hath the success of the New Model, and the recruit of the House of Commons brought to the sectaries[3] . . .

Notes

1 Overton's best known pamphlet of this period was *An Arrow Against All Tyrants* which was published on 12 October 1646 and included the views criticized by Edwards. An Ordinance to prevent the spread of blasphemy and heresy was read twice in the House of Commons on 2 September, although it was 1648 before such a measure became law.

2 'many pamphlets . . .': Edwards is quoting from the titles and title pages of some of the many pamphlets published in Lilburne's support after his imprisonment by the House of Lords in June 1646. Overton's *Remonstrance* (see p. 169) was part of this series: 'that worthy sufferer . . .' is taken from its title page.

3 'The recruit of the House of Commons': the election of new members to replace those expelled as royalists.

87 The Religious Grievances of the Army, May 1647

[*Source*: A.S.P. Woodhouse, editor (1938) *Puritanism and Liberty* (J.M. Dent and Sons), p.399.]

That such rigour is already exercised that we are denied the liberty which Christ hath purchased for us, and abridged of our freedom to serve God according to our proportion of faith, and like to be imprisoned, yea, beaten and persecuted, to enforce us to a human conformity never enjoined by Christ.

That notwithstanding we have engaged our lives for you, ourselves, [and] posterity, that we might be free from the yoke of episcopal tyranny, yet we fear that the consciences of men shall be pressed beyond the light they have received from the rule of the Word in things appertaining to the worship of God, a thing wholly contrary to the Word of God [and] the best Reformed Churches.

That the ministers in their public labour by all means do make us odious to the kingdom, that they might take off their affections from us lest the world should think too well of us, and not only so but have printed many scandalous books against us, as Mr Edwards's *Gangraena* and Mr Love's *Sermons*.[1]

Note

1 For Thomas Edwards see biographical index p. 383, and for extracts from *Gangraena* pp. 131 and 176. Mr Love: Christopher Love, a Presbyterian minister executed in 1651 for plotting against the public.

88 The Case of the Army

[*Source: The Case of the Armie Truly Stated* (October 1647), pp. 15–16. Also printed in Wolfe, editor, *Leveller Manifestos*, and William Haller and Godfrey Davies, editors, *The Leveller Tracts* (1944).]

Whereas Parliaments rightly constituted are the foundation of the hopes of right and freedom to this people, and whereas the people have been prevented of Parliaments, though many positive laws have been made for a constant succession of Parliaments, that therefore it be positively and resolvedly insisted upon, that a law paramount be made, enacting it to be unalterable by Parliaments, that the people shall of course meet, without any warrants or writs, once in every two years, upon an appointed day in their respective countries, for the election of their representors in Parliament; and that all the freeborn at the age of 21 years and upwards be the electors, excepting those that have or shall deprive themselves of their freedom, either for some years or wholly, by delinquency; and that the Parliament so elected and called, may have a certain period of time set, wherein they shall of course determine, and that before the same period they may not be adjournable and dissolvable by the King, or any other except themselves.

Whereas all power is originally and essentially in the whole body of the people of this Nation, and whereas their free choice or consent by their representors is the only original or foundation of all just government; and the reason and end of the choice of all just governors whatsoever is their apprehension of safety and good by them, that it be insisted upon positively. That the supreme power of the people's representors, or Commons assembled in Parliament, be forthwith clearly declared as their power to make laws, or repeal laws (which are not, or ought not to be unalterable) as also their power to call to an account all officers in this Nation whatsoever, for their neglect or treacheries in their trust for the people's good, and to continue or displace and remove them from their offices, dignities or trust, according to their demerits, by their faithfulness or treachery in the business or matters wherewith they are entrusted. And further, that this power to constitute any kind of governors or officers that they shall judge to be for the people's good, be declared, and that upon the aforesaid considerations it be insisted upon, that all obstructions to the freedom and equality of the people's choice of their representors, either by patents, charters or usurpations by pretended customs be removed by these present Commons in Parliament, and that such a freedom of choice be provided for, as the people may be equally represented. This power of Commons in Parliament is the thing against which the King hath contended, and the people have defended with their lives, and therefore ought now to be demanded as the price of their blood.

89 The Agreement of the People

[*Source*: S.R. Gardiner (1906, third edition) *Constitutional Documents of the Puritan Revolution*, pp. 333–5.]

[The *Agreement* was drafted by 29 October 1647, when it was discussed at the Putney debates.]

An Agreement of the People for a firm and present peace upon grounds of common right.

Having by our late labours and hazards made it appear to the world at how high a rate we value our just freedom, and God having so far owned our cause as to deliver the enemies thereof into our hands, we do now hold ourselves bound in mutual duty to each other to take the best care we can for the future to avoid both the danger of returning into a slavish condition and the chargeable remedy of another war; for, as it cannot be imagined that so many of our countrymen would have opposed us in this quarrel if they had understood their own good, so may we safely promise to ourselves that, when our common rights and liberties shall be cleared, their endeavours will be disappointed that seek to make themselves our masters. Since, therefore, our former oppressions and scarce-yet-ended troubles have been occasioned, either by want of frequent national meetings in Council, or by rendering those meetings ineffectual, we are fully agreed and resolved to provide that hereafter our representatives be neither left to an uncertainty for the time nor made useless to the ends for which they are intended. In order whereunto we declare:

That the people of England, being at this day very unequally distributed by Counties, Cities, and Boroughs for the election of their deputies in Parliament, ought to be more indifferently proportioned according to the number of the inhabitants; the circumstances whereof for number, place, and manner are to be set down before the end of this present Parliament.

II

That, to prevent the many inconveniences apparently arising from the long continuance of the same persons in authority, this present Parliament be dissolved upon the last day of September which shall be in the year of our Lord 1648.

III

That the people do, of course, choose themselves a Parliament once in two years, viz. upon the first Thursday in every 2nd March, after the manner as shall be prescribed before the end of this Parliament, to begin to sit upon the first Thursday in April following, at Westminster or such other place as shall be appointed from time to time by the preceding Representatives, and to continue till the last day of September then next ensuing, and no longer.

IV

That the power of this, and all future Representatives of this Nation, is inferior only to theirs who choose them, and doth extend, without the consent or concurrence of any other person or persons, to the enacting, altering, and repealing of laws, to the erecting and abolishing of offices and courts, to the appointing, removing, and calling to account magistrates and officers of all degrees, to the making war and peace, to the treating with foreign States, and, generally, to whatsoever is not expressly or impliedly reserved by the represented to themselves:

Which are as followeth.

1 That matters of religion and the ways of God's worship are not at all entrusted by us to any human power, because therein we cannot remit or exceed a title of what our consciences dictate to be the mind of God without wilful sin: nevertheless the public way of instructing the nation (so it be not compulsive) is referred to their discretion.

2 That the matter of impressing and constraining any of us to serve in the wars is against our freedom; and therefore we do not allow it in our Representatives; the rather, because money (the sinews of war),

being always at their disposal, they can never want numbers of men apt enough to engage in any just cause.

3 That after the dissolution of this present Parliament, no person be at any time questioned for anything said or done in reference to the late public differences, otherwise than in execution of the judgments of the present Representatives or House of Commons.

4 That in all laws made or to be made every person may be bound alike, and that no tenure, estate, charter, degree, birth, or place do confer any exemption from the ordinary course of legal proceedings whereunto others are subjected.

5 That as the laws ought to be equal, so they must be good, and not evidently destructive to the safety and well-being of the people.

These things we declare to be our native rights, and therefore are agreed and resolved to maintain them with our utmost possibilities against all opposition whatsoever; being compelled thereunto not only by the examples of our ancestors, whose blood was often spent in vain for the recovery of their freedoms, suffering themselves through fraudulent accommodations to be still deluded of the fruit of their victories, but also by our own woeful experience, who, having long expected and dearly earned the establishment of these certain rules of government, are yet made to depend for the settlement of our peace and freedom upon him that intended our bondage and brought a cruel war upon us.

90 Walwyn's Wiles

[*Source*: William Kiffin and others (1649) *Walwyns Wiles* pp. 16–17. Also printed in Haller and Davies, editors, *Leveller Tracts*.]

This Mr Walwyn,[1] to work upon the indigent and poorer sort of people, and to raise up their spirits in discontents and clamours, etc did one time profess, he could wish with all his heart that there was neither pale, hedge nor ditch in the whole nation, and that it was an unconscionable thing that one man should have ten thousand pounds, and another more deserving and useful to the commonwealth, should not be worth two pence . . .

At another time, discoursing of the inequality and disproportion of the estates and conditions of men in the world, [he] had words to this purpose, that it was a sad and miserable thing that it should so continue, and that it would never be well until all things were common; and it being replied, will that be ever? – answered, we must endeavour it. It being said, that this would destroy all government; answered, that then there would be less need of government, for then there would be no thieves, no covetous persons, no deceiving and abusing of one another, and so no need of government, etc; but if in such a case they have a form and rule of government to determine cases as may fall out, yet there will be no need of standing officers in a commonwealth, no need of judges etc; but if any difference do fall out, or any criminal fact be committed, take a cobbler from his seat, or a butcher from his shop, or any other tradesman that is an honest and just man, and let him hear the case, and determine the same, and then betake himself to his work again.

Note

1 For Walwyn see biographical index p. 389.

SECTION TWELVE: THE ARMY LEADERSHIP AND THE KING, NOVEMBER 1648

[The second civil war united the army in the determination to bring Charles I to account for the blood he had shed. Cromwell, absent with the army in the north, took time to become convinced of the correct course, but by late November 1648 he was arguing that God's providences justified the army's actions (extract 92). The leading role was taken by Ireton who drafted the *Remonstrance* calling for a more representative Parliament and for the trial of the King (extract 91). The *Remonstrance* was adopted by the Council of the Army on 18 November 1648, presented to Parliament on 20 November, and decisively rejected by the Commons on 30 November, by which time the army was marching on London to prevent Parliament's treaty with the King. Ireton planned to dissolve Parliament, but the army's allies in the Commons persuaded him to agree to a purge only, which duly occurred on 6 December. The trial and execution of the king followed in January.[1] As Cromwell hinted, the army officers and the Levellers were reluctant allies during these weeks of crisis, but the cooperation was shortlived. The army officers presented a compromise *Agreement of the People* to the Rump in January 1649, but in March four Leveller leaders (Lilburne, Overton, Walwyn and a London tradesman Thomas Prince) were imprisoned, and in May a Leveller-influenced mutiny was suppressed by the army leadership at Burford.

Note

1 For the King's trial see the Open University cassette issued as part of the A203 course, or C.V. Wedgwood, *The Trial of Charles I* (1964).]

91 Oliver Cromwell to his cousin Colonel Robert Hammond, 25 November 1648

[*Source*: W.C. Abbott, editor (1937) *The Writings and Speeches of Oliver Cromwell* volume one, pp. 696–9.]

[Hammond was in charge of the forces guarding Charles I on the Isle of Wight. He did not acquiesce in the King's trial, and was arrested at the end of November.]

Dear Robin, thou and I were never worthy to be door-keepers in this service. If thou wilt seek, seek to know the mind of God in all that chain of Providence, whereby God brought thee thither, and that person [Charles I] to thee; how, before and since, God has ordered him, and affairs concerning him: and then tell me, whether there be not some glorious and high meaning in all this, above what thou has yet attained? And, laying aside thy fleshly reason, seek of the Lord to teach thee what that is; and He will do it. I dare be positive to say, it is not that the wicked should be exalted, that God should so appear as indeed He hath done. For there is no peace to them. No, it is set upon the hearts of such as fear the Lord, and we have witness upon witness, That it shall go ill with them and their partakers. I say again, seek that spirit to teach thee; which is the spirit of knowledge and understanding, the spirit of counsel and might, of wisdom and of the fear of the Lord. That spirit will close thine eyes and stop thine ears, so that thou shalt not judge by them, but thou shalt judge for the meek of the earth, and thou shalt be made able to do accordingly. The Lord direct thee to that which is well pleasing in His eyesight . . .

You say: God hath appointed authorities among the nations, to which active or passive obedience is to be yielded. This resides in England in the Parliament. Therefore active or passive etc.

Authorities and powers are the ordinance of God. This or that species is of human institution, and limited, some with larger, others with stricter bands, each one according to its constitution. I do not therefore think the authorities may do anything, and yet such obedience [be] due, but all agree there are cases in which it is lawful to resist. If so, your ground fails, and so likewise the interference. Indeed, dear Robin, not to multiply words, the query is, Whether ours be such a case? This ingenuously is the true question.

To this I shall say nothing, though I could say very much; but only desire thee to see what thou findest in thy own heart as to two or three plain considerations. First, whether *Salus Populi* be a sound position?[1] Secondly, whether in the way in hand,[2] really and before the Lord, before whom conscience must stand, this be provided for, or the whole fruit of the war like to be frustrated, and all most like to turn to what it was, and worse? And this, contrary to engagements, declarations, implicit covenants with those who ventured their lives upon those covenants and engagements, without whom perhaps, in equity, relaxation ought not to be? Thirdly, Whether this Army be not a lawful power, called by God to oppose and fight against the King upon some stated grounds; and being in power to such ends, may not oppose one name of authority, for those ends, as well as another, the outward authority that called them, not by their power making the quarrel lawful, but it being so in itself? If so it may be acting will be justified *in foro humano* [in human affairs]. But truly these kinds of reasonings may be but fleshly, either with or against: only it is good to try what truth may be in them. And the Lord teach us.

My dear friend, let us look into providences; surely they mean somewhat. They hang so together; have been so constant, so clear and unclouded. Malice, swoln malice against God's people, now called Saints, to root out their name; and yet they, by providence, having arms, and therein blessed with defence and more. I desire, he that is for a principle of suffering would not too much slight this. I slight not him who is so minded: but let us beware lest fleshly reasoning see more safety in making use of this principle than in acting. Who acts, and resolves not through God to be willing to part with all? Our hearts are very deceitful, on the right and on the left.

What think you of Providence disposing the hearts of so many of God's people this way, especially in this poor Army, wherein the great God has vouchsafed to appear. I know not one officer among us but is on the increasing hand. And let me say it is here in the North, after much patience, we trust the same Lord who hath framed our minds in our actings, is with us in this also. . . .

Dost thou not think this fear of the Levellers (of whom there is no fear) that they would destroy nobility, had caused some to rake up corruption; to find it lawful to make this ruining hypocritical agreement, on one part? Hath not this biased even some good men? I will not say, their fear will come upon them; but if it do, they will themselves bring it upon themselves. Have not some of our friends, by their passive principle (which I judge not, only I think it liable to temptation as well as the active, and neither good but as we are led into them by God, – neither to be reasoned into, because the heart is deceitful), been occasioned to overlook what is just and honest, and [to] think the people of God may have as much or more good the one way than the other? Good by this Man, against whom the Lord hath witnessed; and whom thou knowest. Is this so in their hearts; or is it reasoned, forced in?

Robin, I have done. Ask we our hearts, whether we think that, after all, these dispensations, the like to which many generations cannot afford, should end in so corrupt reasonings of good men, and should so hit the designings of bad? Thinkest thou, in thy heart, that the glorious dispensations of God point out to this? Or to teach His people to trust in Him, and to wait for better things, when, it may be, better are sealed to many of their spirits? And as a poor looker-on, I had rather live in the hope of that spirit, and take my share with them, expecting a good issue, than be led away with the other.

This trouble I have been at, because my soul loves thee, and I would not have thee swerve, nor lose any glorious opportunity the Lord puts into thy hand. The Lord be thy counsellor. Dear Robin, I rest thine.

Notes
1 'whether *Salus Populi* . . .': whether the safety of the people should be the supreme law.
2 'the way in hand': Parliament's negotiations with the King.

92 The Army's Judgment on the King

[*Source*: *A Remonstrance of his Excellency Thomas, Lord Fairfax, Lord Generall of the Parliaments Forces, and of the Generall Councell of Officers Held at St Albans, the 16 of November 1648*, pp. 21–2.]

Where a person trusted with a limited power to rule according to laws, and by his trust, with express covenant and oath also, obliged to preserve and protect the rights and liberties of the people, for, and by whom he is entrusted, shall not only pervert that trust, and abuse that power to the hurt and prejudice of the generality, and to the oppression, if not destruction of many of them; but also, by the advantage of the trust and power he hath, shall rise to the assuming of hurtful powers which he never had committed to him, and indeed to take away all those foundations of right and liberty, and of redress or remedy too, which the people had reserved from him, and to swallow up all into his own absolute will and power; to impose or take away, yea to destroy at pleasure; and declining all appeal herein to the established equal judgement, agreed upon as it were betwixt him and his people in all emergent matters of difference betwixt them, or to any judgement of men at all, shall fly to the way of force upon his trusting people, and attempt by it to uphold and establish himself in that absolute tyrannical power so assumed over them, and in the exercise thereof at pleasure; such a person, in so doing, does forfeit all that trust and power he had; and, absolving the people from the bonds of covenant and peace betwixt him and them, does set them free to take their best advantage, and, if he fall within their power, to proceed in judgement against him, even for that alone, if there were no more.

SECTION THIRTEEN: GERRARD WINSTANLEY, 1609–1676

[Gerrard Winstanley, by birth a Lancastrian, was apprenticed in London and became a freeman of the Merchant Taylors' Company in 1637. His trade failed in the difficult economic circumstances of the civil war, and by 1643 he was working as a labourer in Surrey. Winstanley's first publications, early in 1648, were radical religious tracts, and in the same year he became convinced that the earth should be 'a common treasury . . . to whole mankind' (extract 94). As a first step towards the achievement of a communist society, Winstanley led a group that began to cultivate the wasteland at St George's Hill, Walton-on-Thames on 1 April 1649 – the Diggers. Winstanley issued a manifesto to encourage others to follow this example (extract 93). The Diggers described themselves as 'True Levellers': Winstanley did not share the Levellers' belief in private property, arguing rather that political freedom was impossible without economic equality. Other 'digger' colonies were established in the midlands and the home counties, but all suffered from harassment by local landholders. The Walton group was forced to move to Cobham and was finally dispersed in April 1650.

This experience led Winstanley to modify some of his ideas. *The Law of Freedom* is his most detailed description of the kind of society he wanted; to achieve it, he looked not to the direct action of ordinary people, but to the goodwill of the powerful Commander in Chief of the Army, Oliver Cromwell, the hope of many radicals before 1653 (extract 97). In 1648–49 Winstanley had hoped that society would be rapidly transformed by the rising up of Christ (which he saw as the development of true reason) in individuals. In the *Law of Freedom* this inner transformation was seen as a more gradual process and laws were necessary in the Commonwealth to encourage the development of reason.

After 1651, as radical hopes withered, Winstanley withdrew from political activism. By the late 1650s he was established, with the help of his father-in-law, as a minor landed gentleman in Surrey. In the 1660s he returned to London, becoming a corn-chandler. He died there in 1676, as a follower of the Quakers. These extracts show the originality and power of Winstanley's social and political thought; they also reveal his vivid and colloquial prose style.]

93 The Diggers

[*Source*: Christopher Hill, editor (1973) *Winstanley: The Law of Freedom and Other Writings*, pp. 77–8.]

[From the *True Levellers' Standard Advanced*, written and published April 1649.]

In the beginning of time, the great creator Reason made the earth to be a common treasury, to preserve beasts, birds, fishes and man, the lord that was to govern this creation; for man had domination given to him, over the beasts, birds and fishes; but not one word was spoken in the beginning, that one branch of mankind should rule over another.

And the reason is this, every single man, male and female, is a perfect creature of himself; and the same spirit that made the globe dwells in man to govern the globe; so that the flesh of man being subject to reason, his maker, hath him to be his teacher and ruler within himself, therefore needs not run abroad after any teacher and ruler without him; for he needs not that any man should teach him, for the same anointing that ruled in the Son of Man teacheth him all things.

But since human flesh (that king of beasts) began to delight himself in the objects of the creation, more than in the spirit reason and righteousness, who manifests himself to be the indweller in the five senses of hearing, seeing, tasting, smelling, feeling; then he fell into blindness of mind and weakness of heart, and runs abroad for a teacher and ruler. And so selfish imagination, taking possession of the five senses and ruling as king in the room of reason therein, and working with covetousness, did set up one man to teach and rule over another; and thereby the spirit was killed and man was brought into bondage, and became a greater slave to such of his own kind, than the beasts of the field were to him.

And hereupon the earth (which was made to be a common treasury of relief for all, both beasts and men) was hedged into enclosures by the teachers and rulers, and the others were made servants and slaves: and that earth, that is within this creation made a common storehouse for all, is bought and sold and kept in the hands of a few, whereby the great creator is mightly dishonoured, as if he were a respecter of persons, delighting in the comfortable livelihood of some, and rejoicing in the miserable poverty and straits of others. From the beginning it was not so.

94 From A Watchword to the City of London and the Army, completed August 1649

[*Source*: Hill, editor (1973) *The Law of Freedom*, pp. 127–8.]

Thou City of London, I am one of thy sons by freedom, and I do truly love thy peace; while I had an estate in thee, I was free to offer my mite into thy public treasury, Guildhall, for a preservation to thee and the whole land; but by thy cheating sons in the thieving art of buying and selling, and by the burdens of and for the soldiery in the beginning of the war, I was beaten out both of estate and trade, and forced to accept the good will of friends crediting of me, to live a country life; and there likewise by the burden of taxes and much free-quarter, my weak back found the burden heavier than I could bear. Yet in all the passages of these eight years' troubles I have been willing to lay out what my talent was, to procure England's peace inward and outward, and yet all along I have found such as in words have professed the same cause to be enemies to me. Not a full year since, being quiet at my work, my heart was filled with sweet thoughts, and many things were revealed to me which I never read in books, nor heard from the mouth of any flesh, and when I began to speak of them, some people could not bear my words, and amongst those revelations this was one: that the earth shall be made a common treasury of livelihood to whole mankind, without respect of persons; and I was made to write a little book called *The new Law of righteousness* [completed January 1649], and therein I declared it; yet my mind was not at rest, because nothing was acted, and thoughts run in me that words and writings were all nothing and must die, for action is the life of all, and if thou dost not act, thou dost nothing.

95 From the Preface to Several Pieces Gathered into One Volume (1650)

[*Source*: Hill, editor (1973) *The Law of Freedom*, pp. 155–6.]

[The Preface to a reprint of Winstanley's five earliest pamphlets, completed in December 1649.]

Sometimes my heart hath been full of deadness and uncomfortableness, wading like a man in the dark and slabby [slushy] weather; and within a little time I have been filled with such peace, light, life and fulness, that if I had had two pair of hands, I had matter enough revealed to have kept them writing a long time; . . .

Then I took the opportunity of the spirit and writ, and the power of self at such over-flowing times was so prevalent in me, that I forsook my ordinary food whole days together; and if my household-friends would persuade me to come to meat, I have been forced with that inward fulness of the power of life to rise up from the table and leave them to God, to write. Thus I have been called in from my ordinary labour, and the society of friends sometimes hath been a burden to me, and best I was when I was alone. I was so filled with that love and delight in the life within that I have sat writing whole winter days from morning till night and the cold never offended me, though when I have risen I was so stark with cold that I was forced to rise by degrees and hold by the table, till strength and heat came into my legs, and I have been secretly sorry when night came, which forced me to rise. The joy of that sweet anointing was so precious and satisfactory within my spirit that I could truly say, *O that I had a tabernacle builded here, that I might never know or seek any other frame of spirit!*

96 From Fire in the Bush, published March 1650

[*Source*: Hill, editor (1973) *The Law of Freedom*, pp. 230–1.]

'Then thou seest the treachery of men beset thee, poverty threatening thee, thy body weak, thy mind distempered with fear and care what to do and how to live. Some laughs at thee, others cheats thee, yea, such as seem to profess the same spirit thou strivest for, are most bitter against thee; and they look after objects more than the inward life, for who more covetous and hard than they? And wilt thou be alone? Yea, thou art alone, where is any one that owns or tenders thee.'

'Well', saith the soul, 'this is an evil time'; and then saith imaginary fear, filling the soul with sorrow, 'O that this body had never been born. I would I had died in the womb; if this be the happiness of a man, I would I had been a bird, a beast or some other creature. While I had no care of doing rightly, I could live, I had friends, I had peace; but since I began to do as I would be done by, friends now stands afar off; everybody hates me, and I am open to all misery. Does righteousness bring thee to this, O miserable wretch?'

* * * * * * * * * * *

97 The Epistle to Oliver Cromwell from The Law of Freedom in a Platform

[*Source*: Hill, editor (1973) *The Law of Freedom*, pp. 275–90.]

[From Winstanley's last known work, completed November 1651 and published 1652.]

Sir,

God hath honoured you with the highest honour of any man since Moses's time, to be the head of a people who have cast out an oppressing Pharaoh. For when the Norman power had conquered our forefathers, he took the free use of our English ground from them, and made them his servants. And God hath made you a successful instrument to cast out that conqueror, and to recover our land and liberties again, by your victories, out of that Norman hand.

That which is yet wanting on your part to be done is this, to see the oppressor's power to be cast out with his person; and to see that the free possession of the land and liberties be put into the hands of the oppressed commoners of England.

For the crown of honour cannot be yours, neither can those victories be called victories on your part, till the land and freedoms won be possessed by them who adventured person and purse for them.

Now you know, Sir, that the kingly conqueror was not beaten by you only as you are a single man, nor by the officers of the Army joined to you; but by the hand and assistance of the commoners, whereof some came in person and adventured their lives with you; others stayed at home and planted the earth and payed taxes and free-quarter to maintain you that went to war.

So that whatsoever is recovered from the conqueror is recovered by a joint consent of the commoners: therefore it is all equity, that all the commoners who assisted you should be set free from the conqueror's power with you: as David's law was, *The spoil shall be divided between them who went to war, and them who stayed at home.*

And now you have the power of the land in your hand, you must do one of these two things: first, either set the land free to the oppressed commoners who assisted you and paid the Army their wages; and then you will fulfil the Scriptures and your own engagements, and so take possession of your deserved honour:

Or secondly, you must only remove the conqueror's power out of the King's hand into other men's, maintaining the old laws still; and then your wisdom and honour is blasted for ever, and you will either lose yourself, or lay the foundation of greater slavery to posterity than you ever knew.

You know that while the King was in the height of his oppressing power, the people only whispered in private chambers against him: but afterwards it was preached upon the house-tops that he was a tyrant and a traitor to England's peace; and he had his overturn.

The righteous power in the creation is the same still. If you and those in power with you should be found walking in the King's steps, can you secure yourselves or posterities from an overturn? Surely no.

The spirit of the whole creation (who is God) is about the reformation of the world, and he will go forward in his work. For if he would not spare kings who have sat so long at his right hand governing the world, neither will he regard you, unless your ways be found more righteous than the King's.

You have the eyes of the people all the land over, nay I think I may say all neighbouring nations over, waiting to see what you will do. And the eyes of your oppressed friends who lie yet under kingly power are waiting to have the possession given them of that freedom in the land which was promised by you, if in case you prevailed. Lose not your crown; take it up and wear it. But know that it is no crown of honour, till promises and engagements made by you be performed to your friends. *He that continues to the end shall receive the crown.* Now you do not see the end of your work unless the kingly law and power be removed as well as his person.

Jonah's gourd is a remembrancer to men in high places. [Jonah 4. 6–10]

The worm in the earth gnawed the root and the gourd died, and Jonah was offended.

Sir, I pray bear with me; my spirit is upon such a lock that I must speak plain to you, lest it tell me another day, 'If thou hadst spoke plain, things might have been amended'.

The earth wherein your gourd grows is the commoners of England.

The gourd is that power which covers you, which will be established to you by giving the people their true freedoms, and not otherwise.

The root of your gourd is the heart of the people, groaning under kingly bondage and desiring a commonwealth's freedom in their English earth.

The worm in the earth, now gnawing at the root of your gourd, is discontents, because engagements and promises made to them by such as have power are not kept.

And this worm hath three heads. The first is a spirit waiting opportunities till a blasting wind arise to cause your gourd to wither; and yet pretends fair to you, etc.

Another spirit shelters under your gourd for a livelihood, and will say as you say in all things; and these are called honest, yet no good friends to you nor the commonwealth, but to their own bellies.

There is a third spirit, which is faithful indeed and plain-dealing, and many times for speaking truth plainly he is cashiered, imprisoned and crushed: and the oppressions laid upon this spirit kindles the fire which the two former waits to warm themselves at.

Would you have your gourd stand for ever? Then cherish the root in the earth, that is the heart of your friends, the oppressed commoners of England, by killing the worm. And nothing will kill this worm but performance of professions, words and promises, that they may be made free men from tyranny.

It may be you will say to me, 'What shall I do?' I answer, 'You are in place and power to see all burdens taken off from your friends, the commoners of England.' You will say, 'What are those burdens?'

I will instance in some, both which I know in my own experience and which I hear the people daily complaining of and groaning under, looking upon you and waiting for deliverance.

Most people cry, 'We have paid taxes, given free-quarter, wasted our estates and lost our friends in the wars, and the task-masters multiply over us more then formerly.' I have asked divers this question, 'Why do you say so?'

Some have answered me that promises, oaths and engagements have been made as a motive to draw us to assist in the wars; that privileges of Parliament and liberties of subjects should be preserved, and that all popery and episcopacy and tyranny should be rooted out; and these promises are not performed. Now there is an opportunity to perform them.

For first, say they, 'The current of succeeding Parliaments is stopped, which is one of the great privileges (and people's liberties) for safety and peace; and if that continue stopped, we shall be more offended by an hereditary Parliament than we were oppressed by an hereditary king'.

And for the commoners, who were called subjects while the kingly conqueror was in power, have not as yet their liberties granted them: I will instance them in order, according as the common whisperings are among the people.

For, they say, the burdens of the clergy remains still upon us, in a threefold nature.

First, if any man declare his judgment in the things of God contrary to the clergy's report or the mind of some high officers, they are cashiered, imprisoned, crushed and undone, and made sinners for a word, as they were in the pope's and bishops' days; so that though their names be cast out, yet their High Commission Court's power remains still, persecuting men for conscience' sake when their actions are unblameable.

Secondly, in many parishes there are old formal ignorant episcopal priests established; and some ministers who are bitter enemies to commonwealth's freedom and friends to monarchy are established preachers, and are continually buzzing their subtle principles into the minds of the people, to undermine the peace of our declared commonwealth, causing a disaffection of spirit among neighbours, who otherwise would live in peace.

Thirdly, the burden of tithes remains still upon our estates, which was taken from us by the kings and given to the clergy to maintain them by our labours; so that though their preaching fill the minds of many with madness, contention and unsatisfied doubting, because their imaginary and ungrounded doctrines cannot be understood by them, yet we must pay them large tithes for so doing. This is oppression.

Fourthly, if we go to the lawyer, we find him to sit in the conqueror's chair though the kings be removed, maintaining the kings' power to the height; for in many courts and cases of law the will of a judge and lawyer rules above the letter of the law, and many cases and suits are lengthened to the great vexation of the clients and to the lodging of their estates in the purse of the unbounded lawyer. So that we see, though other men be under a sharp law, yet many of the great lawyers are not, but still do act their will as the conqueror did; as I have heard some belonging to the law say, 'What cannot we do?'

Fifthly, say they, if we look upon the customs of the law itself, it is the same it was in the kings' days, only the name is altered; as if the commoners of England had paid their taxes, free-quarter and shed their blood not to reform but to baptize the law into a new name, from kingly law to state law; by reason whereof the spirit of discontent is strengthened, to increase more suits of law than formerly was known to be. And so, as the sword pulls down kingly power with one hand, the kings' old law builds up monarchy again with the other.

And indeed the main work of reformation lies in this, to reform the clergy, lawyers and law; for all the complaints of the land are wrapped up within them three, not in the person of a king.

Shall men of other nations say that notwithstanding all those rare wits in the Parliament and Army of England, yet they could not reform the clergy, lawyer and law, but must needs establish all as the kings left them?

Will not this blast all our honour, and make all monarchical members laugh in their sleeves, to see the government of our commonwealth to be built upon the kingly laws and principles?

I have asked divers soldiers what they fought for; they answered, they could not tell; and it is very true, they cannot tell indeed, if the monarchical law be established without reformation. But I wait to see what will be done; and I doubt not but to see our commonwealth's government to be built upon his own foundation.

Sixthly, if we look into parishes, the burdens there are many.

First, for the power of lords of manors remains still over their brethren, requiring fines and heriots; beating them off the free use of the common land, unless their brethren will pay them rent; exacting obedience as much as they did, and more, when the King was in power.

Now saith the people, 'By what power do these maintain their title over us!' Formerly they held title from the King, as he was the conqueror's successor. But have not the commoners cast out the King, and broke the bond of that conquest? Therefore in equity they are free from the slavery of that lordly power.

Secondly, in parishes where commons lie, the rich Norman freeholders, or the new (more covetous) gentry, over-stock the commons with sheep and cattle; so that inferior tenants and poor labourers can hardly keep a cow, but half starve her. So that the poor are kept poor still, and the common freedom of the earth is kept from them, and the poor have no more relief than they had when the king (or conqueror) was in power.

Thirdly, in many parishes two or three of the great ones bears all the sway in making assessments, over-awing constables and other officers; and when time was to quarter soldiers, they would have a hand in that, to ease themselves and over-burden the weaker sort; and many times make large sums of money over and above the justice's warrant in assessments, and would give no account why, neither durst the inferior people demand an account, for he that spake should be sure to be crushed the next opportunity; and if any have complained to committees or justices, they have been either wearied out by delays and waiting, or else the offence hath been by them smothered up; so that we see one great man favoured another, and the poor oppressed have no relief.

Fourthly, there is another grievance which the people are much troubled at, and that is this: country people cannot sell any corn or other fruits of the earth in a market town but they must either pay toll or be turned out of town. Now say they, 'This is a most shameful thing, that we must part with our estates in taxes and free-quarter to purchase the freedom of the land and the freedom of the towns, and yet this freedom must be still given from us into the hands of a covetous Norman toll-taker, according to the kings' old burdensome laws, and contrary to the liberty of a free commonwealth.'

'Now,' saith the whisperings of the people, 'the inferior tenants and labourers bears all the burdens, in labouring the earth, in paying taxes and free-quarter beyond their strength, and in furnishing the armies with soldiers, who bear the greatest burden of the war; and yet the gentry, who oppress them and that live idle upon their labours, carry away all the comfortable livelihood of the earth.'

For is not this a common speech among the people? 'We have parted with our estates, we have lost our friends in the wars, which we willingly gave up, because freedom was promised us; and now in the end we have new task-masters and our old burdens increased: and though all sorts of people have taken an Engagement to cast out kingly power, yet kingly power remains in power still in the hands of those who have no more right to the earth than ourselves.'

'For,' say the people, 'if the lords of manors and our task-masters hold title to the earth over us from the old kingly power, behold that power is beaten and cast out.'

'And two acts of Parliament are made: the one to cast out kingly power, backed by the Engagement against King and House of Lords, the other to make England a free commonwealth.'[1]

'And if lords of manors lay claim to the earth over us from the Army's victories over the King, then we have as much right to the land as they, because our labours and blood and death of friends were the purchasers of the earth's freedom as well as theirs.'

'And is not this a slavery,' say the people, 'that though there be land enough in England to maintain ten times as many people as are in it, yet some must beg of their brethren, or work in hard drudgery for day wages for them, or starve or steal and so be hanged out of the way, as men not fit to live in the earth, before they must be suffered to plant the waste land for their livelihood, unless they will pay rent to their brethren for it?' Well, this is a burden the creation groans under; and the subjects (so called) have not their birthright freedoms granted them from their brethren, who hold it from them by club law, but not by righteousness.

'And who now must we be subject to, seeing the conqueror is gone?'

I answer, we must either be subject to a law, or to men's wills. If to a law, then all men in England are subjects, or ought to be, thereunto: but what law that is to which every one ought to be subject is not yet established in execution. If any say the old kings' laws are the rule, then it may be answered that those laws are so full of confusion that few knows when they obey and when not, because they were the laws of a conqueror to hold the people in subjection to the will of the conqueror; therefore that cannot be the rule for everyone. Besides, we daily see many actions done by state officers, which they have no law to justify them in but their prerogative will.

And again if we must be subject to men, then what men must we be subject to, seeing one man hath as much right to the earth as another, for no man now stands as a conqueror over his brethren by the law of righteousness?

You will say, 'We must be subject to the ruler'. It is true, but not to suffer the rulers to call the earth theirs and not ours, for by so doing they betray their trust and run into the line of tyranny; and we lose our freedom and from thence enmity and wars arise.

A ruler is worthy double honour when he rules well, that is, when he himself is subject to the law, and requires all others to be subject thereunto, and makes it his work to see the laws obeyed and not his own will; and such rulers are faithful, and they are to be subjected unto us therein, for all commonwealth's rulers are servants to, not lords and kings over, the people. But you will say, 'Is not the land your brother's? And you cannot take away another man's right by claiming a share therein with him.'

I answer, it is his either by creation right, or by right of conquest. If by creation right he call the earth his and not mine, then it is mine as well as his; for the spirit of the whole creation, who made us both, is no respecter of persons.

And if by conquest he call the earth his and not mine, it must be either by the conquest of the kings over the commoners, or by the conquest of the commoners over the kings.

If he claim the earth to be his from the kings' conquest, the kings are beaten and cast out, and that title is undone.

If he claim title to the earth to be his from the conquest of the commoners over the kings, then I have right to the land as well as my brother, for my brother without me, nor I without my brother, did not cast out the kings; but both together assisting with person and purse we prevailed, so that I have by this victory as equal a share in the earth which is now redeemed as my brother by the law of righteousness.

If my brother still say he will be landlord (through his covetous ambition) and I must pay him rent, or else I shall not live in the land, then does he take my right from me, which I have purchased by my money in taxes, free-quarter and blood. And O thou spirit of the whole creation, who hath this title to be called King of righteousness and Prince of Peace: judge thou between my brother and me, whether this be righteous, etc.

'And now', say the people, 'is not this a grievous thing that our brethren that will be landlords, right or wrong, will make laws and call for a law to be made to imprison, crush, nay put to death, any that denies God, Christ and Scripture; and yet they will not practise that golden rule, *Do to another as thou wouldst have another do to thee*, which God, Christ and Scriptures hath enacted for a law? Are not these men guilty of death by their own law, which is the words of their own mouth? Is it not a flat denial of God and Scripture?'

O the confusion and thick darkness that hath over-spread our brethren is very great. I have no power to remove it, but lament it in the secrets of my heart. When I see prayers, sermons, fasts, thanksgiving, directed to this God in words and shows, and when I come to look for actions of obedience to the righteous law, suitable to such a profession, I find them men of another nation, saying and not doing; like an old courtier saying 'Your servant', when he was an enemy. I will say no more, but groan and wait for a restoration.

Thus, Sir, I have reckoned up some of those burdens which the people groan under.

And I being sensible hereof was moved in my self to present this platform of commonwealth's government unto you, wherein I have declared a full commonwealth's freedom, according to the rule of righteousness, which is God's Word. It was intended for your view above two years ago, but the disorder of the times caused me to lay it aside, with a thought never to bring it to light, etc. Likewise I hearing that Mr Peters[2] and some others propounded this request, that the Word of God might be consulted with to find out a healing government, which I liked well and waited to see such a rule come forth, for there are good rules in the Scripture if they were obeyed and practised. Thereupon

I laid aside this in silence, and said I would not make it public; but this word was like fire in my bones ever and anon, *Thou shalt not bury thy talent in the earth*; therefore I was stirred up to give it a resurrection, and to pick together as many of my scattered papers as I could find, and to compile them into this method, which I do here present to you, and do quiet my own spirit.

And now I have set the candle at your door, for you have power in your hand, in this other added opportunity, to act for common freedom if you will: I have no power.

It may be here are some things inserted which you may not like, yet other things you may like, therefore I pray you read it, and be as the industrious bee, suck out the honey and cast away the weeds.

Though this platform be like a piece of timber rough hewed, yet the discreet workmen may take it and frame a handsome building out of it.

It is like a poor man that comes clothed to your door in a torn country garment, who is unacquainted with the learned citizens' unsettled forms and fashions; take off the clownish language, for under that you may see beauty.

It may be you will say, 'If tithes be taken from the priests and impropriators, and copyhold services from lords of manors, how shall they be provided for again; for is it not unrighteous to take their estates from them?'

I answer, when tithes were first enacted, and lordly power drawn over the backs of the oppressed, the kings and conquerors made no scruple of conscience to take it, though the people lived in sore bondage of poverty for want of it; and can there be scruple of conscience to make restitution of this which hath been so long stolen goods? It is no scruple arising from the righteous law, but from covetousness, who goes away sorrowful to hear he must part with all to follow righteousness and peace.

But though you do take away tithes and the power of lords of manors, yet there will be no want to them, for they have the freedom of the common stock, they may send to the store-houses for what they want, and live more free than now they do; for now they are in care and vexation by servants, by casualties, by being cheated in buying and selling and many other encumbrances, but then they will be free from all, for the common store-houses is every man's riches, not any one's.

'Is it not buying and selling a righteous law?' No, it is the law of the conqueror, but not the righteous law of creation: how can that be righteous which is a cheat? For is not this a common practice, when he hath a bad horse or cow, or any bad commodity, he will send it to the market, to cheat some simple plain-hearted man or other; and when he comes home will laugh at his neighbour's hurt, and much more etc.

When mankind began to buy and sell, then did he fall from his innocence; for then they began to oppress and cozen one another of their creation birthright. As for example: if the land belong to three persons, and two of them buy and sell the earth and the third give no consent, his right is taken from him, and his posterity is engaged in a war.

When the earth was first bought and sold, many gave no consent: as when our crown lands and bishops' lands were sold, some foolish soldiers yielded, and covetous officers were active in it, to advance themselves above their brethren;[3] but many who paid taxes and free-quarter for the purchase of it gave no consent but declared against it as an unrighteous thing, depriving posterity of their birthrights and freedoms.

Therefore this buying and selling did bring in, and still doth bring in, discontent and wars, which have plagued mankind sufficiently for so doing. And the nations of the world will never learn to beat their swords into ploughshares, and their spears into pruning hooks, and leave off warring, until this cheating device of buying and selling be cast out among the rubbish of kingly power.

'But shall not one man be richer than another?'

There is no need of that; for riches make men vain-glorious, proud, and to oppress their brethren; and are the occasion of wars.

No man can be rich, but he must be rich either by his own labours, or by the labours of other men helping him. If a man have no help from his neighbour, he shall never gather an estate of hundreds and thousands a year. If other men help him to work, then are those riches his neighbours' as well as his; for they may be the fruit of other men's labours as well as his own.

But all rich men live at ease, feeding and clothing themselves by the labours of other men, not by their own; which is their shame, and not their nobility; for it is a more blessed thing to give than to receive. But rich men receive all they have from the labourer's hand, and what they give, they give away other men's labours, not their own. Therefore they are not righteous actors in the earth.

'But shall not one man have more titles of honour than another?'

Yes. As a man goes through offices, he rises to titles of honour till he comes to the highest nobility, to be a faithful commonwealth's man in a Parliament House. Likewise he who finds out any secret in nature shall have a title of honour given him, though he be a young man. But no man shall have any title of honour till he win it by industry, or come to it by age or office-bearing. Every man that is above sixty years of age shall have respect as a man of honour by all others that are younger, as is shewed hereafter.

'Shall every man count his neighbour's house as his own, and live together as one family?'

No. Though the earth and storehouses be common to every family, yet every family shall live apart as they do; and every man's house, wife, children and furniture for ornament of his house, or anything which he hath fetched in from the store-houses, or provided for the necessary use of his family, is all a property to that family, for the peace thereof. And if any man offer to take away a man's wife, children or furniture of his house, without his consent, or disturb the peace of his dwelling, he shall suffer punishment as an enemy to the commonwealth's government, as is mentioned in the platform following.

'Shall we have no lawyers?'

There is no need of them, for there is to be no buying and selling; neither any need to expound laws, for the bare letter of the law shall be both judge and lawyer, trying every man's actions. And seeing we shall have successive Parliaments every year, there will be rules made for every action a man can do.

But there is to be officers chosen yearly in every parish, to see the laws executed according to the letter of the laws; so that there will be no long work in trying of offences, as it is under kingly government, to get the lawyers money and to enslave the commoners to the conqueror's prerogative law or will. The sons of contention, Simeon and Levi,[4] must not bear rule in a free commonwealth.

At the first view you may say, 'This is a strange government'. But I pray judge nothing before trial. Lay this platform of commonwealth's government in one scale, and lay monarchy or kingly government in the other scale, and see which give true weight to righteous freedom and peace. There is no middle path between these two, for a man must either be a free and true commonwealth's man, or a monarchical tyrannical royalist.

If any say, 'This will bring poverty'; surely they mistake. For there will be plenty of all earthly commodities, with less labour and trouble than now it is under monarchy. There will be no want, for every man may keep as plentiful a house as he will, and never run into debt, for common stock pays for all.

If you say, 'Some will live idle': I answer, No. It will make idle persons to become workers, as is declared in the platform: there shall be neither beggar nor idle person.

If you say, 'This will make men quarrel and fight':

I answer, No. It will turn swords into ploughshares, and settle such a peace in the earth, as nations shall learn war no more. Indeed the government of kings is a breeder of wars, because men being put into the straits of poverty are moved to fight for liberty, and to take one another's estates from them, and to obtain mastery. Look into all armies, and see what they do more, but make some poor, some rich; put some into freedom, and others into bondage. And is not this a plague among mankind?

Well, I question not but what objections can be raised against this commonwealth's government, they shall find an answer in this platform following. I have been something large, because I could not contract my self into a lesser volume, having so many things to speak of.

I do not say, nor desire, that every one shall be compelled to practise this commonwealth's government; for the spirits of some will be enemies at first, though afterwards will prove the most cordial and true friends thereunto.

Yet I desire that the commonwealth's land, which is the ancient commons and waste land; and the lands newly got in by the Army's victories out of the oppressors' hands, as parks, forests, chases and the like, may be set free to all that have lent assistance, either of person or purse, to obtain it; and to all that are willing to come in to the practice of this government and be obedient to the laws thereof. And for others who are not willing, let them stay in the way of buying and selling, which is the law of the conqueror, till they be willing.

And so I leave this in your hand, humbly prostrating my self and it before you; and remain

A true lover of commonwealth's government, peace and freedom,
Gerrard Winstanley.

Notes

1 'two acts of Parliament': the monarchy was abolished by an Act of 17 March 1649; England became a commonwealth (or republic) by an Act of 19 May 1649; for the Engagement see p. 126, Note 22.

2 'Mr Peters': Winstanley probably refers to *Good Work for a Good Magistrate*, by the radical minister Hugh Peter, published in June 1651.

3 'when our crown lands . . .': under the Act for the sale of crown lands (July 1649) soldiers were given land equal to the value of their pay arrears. Bishops' lands were put up for sale under an Ordinance of November 1646; here no special priority was given to military purchasers.

4 'Simeon and Levi': the sons of Jacob, see Genesis 49. 5–7.

SECTION FOURTEEN: POLITICAL SETTLEMENTS IN THE 1650s

[In this section we examine some of the political changes between the army's forcible ejection of the Rump in April 1653, and the peak of Oliver Cromwell's power in 1657. Some of these changes are symbolized by different aspects of Cromwell's personality. In his speech to the 'Barebones' Parliament we see the Cromwell who was convinced he was God's instrument, welcoming the rule of the 'Saints' (extract 98). The Barebones Parliament, nominated by the senior army officers, met in July 1653, but it offended too many vested interests, and in December of the same year the Instrument of Government (extract 68 above) established the constitution under which Cromwell became Lord Protector. When Cromwell addressed his first Parliament, he spoke as a conservative country gentleman, anxious for the 'settling' of the nation (extracts 99 and 100). Cromwell was, however, unable to effect a reconciliation between the conservative gentry, and the army on which his power ultimately rested. Royalist unrest in 1655 led to a period of overt military supremacy when the Major Generals supervised all aspects of local government. The work of the Major Generals is revealed through their letters to Cromwell and to John Thurloe, the Secretary of State who supervised all intelligence matters (extracts 101–104). We also include a republican critique of military rule (extract 105). The first session of Cromwell's second Parliament (1656–57) marked a decisive shift back to the moderate gentry. In May 1657 the 'Humble Petition and Advice' gave Cromwell the power to nominate a second parliamentary chamber, and to choose his own successor. Besides these extracts dealing with actual political developments, we present part of the radical programme of the Fifth Monarchists who adopted the widespread millenial ideas of the 1650s in a particularly concrete form (extract 105). They believed in the imminence of the 'fifth monarchy' when Christ and his Saints would rule on earth, and derived their general programme from the Bible although many of their specific aims were shared by other radicals.]

98 Cromwell to the 'Barebones' or Nominated Parliament, 4 July 1653

[*Source*: W.C. Abbott, editor (1945) *The Writings and Speeches of Oliver Cromwell*, volume three, pp.53–5, 60–1 and 63–5.]

. . . What the several successes and issues have been, is not fit to mention at this time neither; though I confess I thought to have enlarged myself upon that subject; forasmuch as considering the works of God, and the operations of His hands, is a principal part of our duty; and a great encouragement to the strengthening of our hands and of our faith, for that which is behind those marvellous dispensations which have been given us. Among other ends that's a principal end, which ought to be minded by us . . .

I shall now begin a little to remember to you the passages that have been transacted since Worcester.[1] From whence, coming with the rest of my fellow officers and soldiers, we expected, and had some reasonable confidence that our expectations should not be frustrated, that, having such an history to look back unto, such a God, so eminently visible, even our enemies confessing that God Himself was certainly engaged against them, else they should never have been disappointed in every engagement. For that may be said (by the way) had we miscarried but once, where had we been? I say we did think, and had some reasonable confidence that coming up then, the mercies God had shown, and the expectations which were upon our hearts, and the hearts of all good men, would have prompted those who were in authority [the Rump] to have done those good things which might, by honest men, have been judged fit for such a God, and worthy of such mercies; and indeed a discharge of duty from those for whom all these mercies had been shown, for the true interest of this nation. If I should now labour to be particular in enumerating how some businesses that have been transacted from that time to the dissolution of the late Parliament [20 April 1653], indeed I should be upon a theme which would be troublesome to myself. For I think I may say for myself and my fellow officers, that we have rather desired and studied healing and prospiciency, that to rake into sores and to look backward,– to render things in those colours that would not be very pleasing to any good eye to look upon. Only this we shall say for our own vindication, and as thereby laying some foundation for the making evident the necessity and duty that was incumbent upon us, to make this last great change – I think it will not be amiss to offer a word or two to that. As I said before, we are loath to rake into businesses, were there not a necessity so to do.

Indeed we may say without commending ourselves that, ever since the coming-up of myself and those gentlemen who have been engaged in the military part, it hath been full in our hearts and thoughts, to desire and use all the fair and lawful means we could have had the nation reap the fruit of all the blood and treasure that had been spent in this cause: and we have had many desires, and thirstings in our spirits, to find out ways and means wherein we might be anywise instrumental to help it forward . . .

Having done that that we have done upon this ground of necessity which we have declared, which was not a feigned necessity but real, to the end that the government might not be at a loss; to the end that we might manifest to the world the singleness of our hearts and our integrity, who did these things, not to grasp after the power ourselves, to keep it in military hands, no not for a day; but, as far as God enabled us with strength and ability, to put it into the hands of those that might be called from the several parts of the nation. This necessity, I say, and I hope we may say for ourselves, this integrity of labouring to divest the sword of the power and authority in the civil administration, hath moved us to conclude this course,[2] and having done this, truly we think we cannot, with the discharge of our own consciences, but offer somewhat to you, as I said before, for our own exoneration. . . . .

Truly God hath called you to this work by, I think, as wonderful providences as ever passed upon the sons of men in so short a time. And truly I think, taking the argument of necessity, for the government must not fall; taking the appearance of the hand of God in this thing, I am sure you would have been loath it should have been resigned into the hands of wicked men and enemies. I am sure God would not have it so. It comes, therefore, to you by the way of necessity, by the way of the wise Providence of God, though through weak hands. . . .

I confess I never looked to see such a day as this, – it may be nor you neither, – when Jesus Christ should be so owned as He is, at this day, and in this work. Jesus Christ is owned this day by your call; and you own Him by your willingness to appear for Him; and you manifest this, as far as poor creatures can, to be the day of the power of Christ. . . .

I say, you are called with a high call. And why should we be afraid to say or think, that this may be the door to usher in the things that God has promised; which have been prophesied of; which He has set the hearts of His people to wait for and expect? We know who they are that shall war with the lamb,[3] against his enemies; they shall be a people called, and chosen and faithful. And God hath, in a military way – we may speak it without flattering ourselves, and I believe you know it – He hath appeared with them and for them; and now in these civil powers and authorities does not He appear? These are not ill prognostications of that good we wait for. Indeed I do think something is at the door: we are at the threshold; and therefore it becomes us to lift up our heads, and encourage ourselves in the Lord. . . .

As I have said elsewhere, if I were to choose any servant, the meanest officer for the Army or the Commonwealth, I would choose a godly man that hath principles, especially where a trust is to be committed, because I know where to have a man that hath principles. I believe if any man of you should choose a servant, you would do so. And I would all our magistrates were so chosen:– this may be done; there may be good effects of this! . . .

Notes

1 'Worcester': the battle of Worcester, 3 September 1651, at which Cromwell commanded the army that defeated Charles II and his Scottish forces.
2 'this course': of summoning this Parliament.
3 'war with the lamb': an echo of Revelation 17. 14.

99 Cromwell to the First Parliament of the Protectorate, 4 September 1654

[*Source*: Abbott, editor (1945) *Writings and Speeches* volume three, pp.434–42.]

Gentlemen,

You are met here on the greatest occasion that, I believe, England ever saw, having upon your shoulders the interest of three great nations, with the territories belonging to them. And truly, I believe I may say it without an hyperbole, you have upon your shoulders the interest of all the Christian people in the world . . .

That which I judge to be the end of your meeting, the great end, which was likewise remembered to you this day, to wit, healing and settling. And the remembering transactions too particularly, perhaps instead of healing (at least in the hearts of many of you) may set the wound fresh a-bleeding.

I must profess this to you (whatever thoughts pass upon me) that if this day, that is this meeting, prove not healing, what shall we do? But as I said before, seeing (I trust) it is in the minds of you all, and much more in the mind of God, which must cause healing, – it must be first in his mind, and he being pleased to put it into yours it will be a day indeed, and such a day as generations to come will bless you for, – I say for this and the other reasons, have I forborne to make a particular remembrance and enumeration of things, and of the manner of the Lord's bringing us through so many changes and turnings, as have passed upon us.

Howbeit, I think it will be more than necessary to let you know (at the least so well as I may) in what condition this, nay these nations were, when this government was undertaken.

For order sake, it's very natural for us to consider, what our condition was in civils, in spirituals. What was our condition? Every man's hand (almost) was against his brother, at least his heart, little regarding anything that should cement and might have a tendency in it to cause us to grow into one. All the dispensations of God, his terrible ones, he having met us in the way of his judgment in a ten years' civil war, a very sharp one, his merciful dispensations, they did not, they did not work upon us, but we had our humours[1] and interests; and indeed I fear our humours were more than our interests. And certainly as it fell out, in such cases, our passions were more than our judgments.

Was not everything (almost) grown arbitrary? Who knew where, or how to have right, without some obstruction or other intervening? Indeed, we were almost grown arbitrary in everything.

What was the face that was upon our affairs as to the interest of the nation? to the authority of the nation? to the magistracy? to the ranks and orders of men, whereby England hath been known for hundreds of years? A nobleman, a gentleman, a yeoman? (That is a good interest of the nation and a great one.) The magistracy of the nation, was it not almost trampled under foot, under despite and contempt by men of Levelling principles?

I beseech you, for the orders of men and ranks of men, did not that Levelling principle tend to the reducing all to an equality? Did it think to do so, or did it practise towards it for propriety [property] and interest? What was the design, but to make the tenant as liberal a fortune as the landlord? Which I think, if obtained, would not have lasted long! The men of that principle, after they had served their own turns, would have cried up interest and property then fast enough. . . .

Such considerations and pretensions of liberty, liberty of conscience and liberty of subjects, two as glorious things to be contended for as any God hath given us, yet both these also abused for the patronizing of villanies, insomuch as that it hath been an ordinary thing to say and in dispute to affirm, that it was not in the magistrate's power, he had nothing to do with it, not so much as the printing a Bible to the nation for the use of the people, lest it be imposed upon the consciences of men; for they must receive the same traditionally and implicitly from the power of the magistrate, if thus received.

The aforementioned abominations did thus swell to this height amongst us.

The axe was laid to the root of the Ministry; it was Antichristian, it was Babylonish. It suffered under such a judgment, that the truth of it is, as the extremity was great on that, I wish it prove not so on this hand. The extremity was, that no man having a good testimony, having received gifts from Christ, might preach if not ordained. So now, many are [affirm] on the other hand, that he who is ordained, hath a nullity or Antichristianism stamped upon his calling, so that he ought not to preach or not be heard.

I wish it may not too justly be said that there was severity and sharpness, yea, too much of an imposing spirit in matter of conscience, a spirit unchristian enough in any times, most unfit for these, – denying liberty to those who have earned it with their blood, who have gained civil liberty, and religious also, for those who would thus impose upon them.

We may reckon among these, our spiritual evils, an evil that hath more refinedness in it, and more colour for it, and hath deceived more people of integrity than the rest have done. For few have been catched with the former mistakes, but such as have apostatized from their holy profession, such as being corrupt in their consciences, have been forsaken by God and left to such noisome opinions. But, I say, there are others more refined, many honest people, whose hearts are sincere, many of them belonging to God, and that is the mistaken notion of the Fifth Monarchy. A thing pretending more spirituality than anything else. A notion I hope we all honour, wait, and hope for, that Jesus Christ will have a time to set up his reign in our hearts, by subduing those corruptions and lusts and evils that are there, which reign now more in the world than, I hope, in due time they shall do. And when more fullness of the Spirit is poured forth to subdue iniquity and bring in everlasting righteousness, then will the approach of that glory be. The carnal divisions and contentions amongst Christians, so common, are not the symptoms of that kingdom.

But for men to entitle themselves, upon this principle, that they are the only men to rule kingdoms, govern nations, and give laws to people; to determine of property and liberty and everything else, upon such a pretence as this is: truly, they had need give clear manifestations of God's presence with them, before wise men will receive or submit to their conclusions. . . .

If, . . . they were but notions, they were to be let alone. Notions will hurt none but them that have them. But when they come to such practices, as to tell us that liberty and property are not the badges of the kingdom of Christ, and tell us that instead of regulating laws, laws are to be abrogated, indeed subverted, and perhaps would bring in the Judaical law instead of our known laws settled amongst us, – this is worthy of every magistrate's consideration, especially where every stone is turned to bring confusion. I think, I say, this will be worthy of the magistrate's consideration.

Whilst these things were in the midst of us, and the nation rent and torn in spirit and principle from one end to another after this sort and manner I have now told you, – family against family, husband against wife, parents against children, and nothing in the hearts and minds of men but overturning, overturning, overturning, (a Scripture very much abused and applied to justify unpeaceable practices by all men of discontented spirits,) the common adversary in the meantime he sleeps not . . .

We know very well that emissaries of the Jesuits never came in these swarms, as they have done since these things were set on foot. . . .

In the meantime all endeavours possible were used to hinder the work in Ireland, and the progress of the work of God in Scotland . . .

Persons were stirred up and encouraged from these divisions and discomposure of affairs, to do all they could to encourage and foment the war in both those places.

To add yet to our misery, whilst we were in this condition, we were in war, deeply engaged in a war with the Portugal [Portuguese], whereby our trade ceased; and the evil consequences by that war were manifest and very considerable.

And not only this, but we had a war with Holland, consuming our treasure, occasioning a vast burden upon the people; a war that cost this nation full as much as the taxes came unto. . . .

At the same time we had a war with France. And besides the sufferings in respect of the trade of the nation, it's most evident, that the purse of the nation had not been possibly able longer to bear it, by reason of the advantages taken by other States to improve their own and spoil our manufacture of cloth and hinder the vent thereof, which is the great staple commodity of this nation.

This was our condition; spoiled in our trade, and we at this vast expense, thus dissettled at home, and having these engagements abroad.

These things being thus, (as I am persuaded it is not hard to convince every person here, they were thus,) what a heap of confusions were upon these poor nations! And either things must have been left to have sunk into the miseries these premises would suppose, or a remedy must be applied.

A remedy hath been applied; that hath been this government; a thing I shall say little unto. The thing is open and visible, to be seen and read by all men, and therefore let it speak for itself. . . .

It hath had some things in desire, and it hath done some things actually. It hath desired to reform the laws, to reform them; and for that end, it hath called together persons (without reflection) of as great ability and as great integrity as are in these nations, to consider how the laws might be made plain and short, and less chargeable to the people, how to lessen expense for the good of the nation. . . .

The Chancery hath been reformed, – and I hope to the just satisfaction of all good men . . .

It hath endeavoured to put a stop to that heady way (touched of likewise this day) of every man making himself a Minister and a preacher. It hath endeavoured to settle a way for the approbation of men of piety and ability for the discharge of that work.[2] And I think I may say, it hath committed that work to the trust of persons, both of the Presbyterian and Independent judgments, men of as known ability, piety, and integrity, as I believe any this nation hath. And I believe also that in that care they have taken, they have laboured to approve themselves to Christ, the nation, and their own consciences. . . .

One thing more this government hath done. It hath been instrumental to call a free Parliament, which, blessed be God, we see here this day. I say a free Parliament; and that it may continue so, I hope is in the heart and spirit of every good man in England, save such discontented persons as I have formerly mentioned. It is that which, as I have desired above my life, I shall desire to keep it so above my life. . . .

[In April 1654 the war with the Dutch ended, and a commercial treaty was signed with Sweden. Similar treaties with Portugal and Denmark followed in July and September.]

You have now (though it be not the first in time) peace with Sweden, an honourable peace . . .

You have a peace with the Dane, a State that lay contiguous to that part of this Island which hath given us the most trouble . . . satisfaction for your merchants' ships, not only to their content, but to their rejoicing . . .

You have a peace with the Dutch . . . And I think it was as desirable and as acceptable to the spirit of this nation, as any one thing that lay before us. And as I believe nothing so much gratified our enemies as to see us at odds, so I persuade myself, nothing is of more terror nor trouble to them, than to see us thus reconciled.

As a peace with the Protestant States hath much security in it, so it hath as much of honour and of assurance to the Protestant interest abroad, without which no assistance can be given thereunto. I wish it may be written upon our hearts to be zealous for that interest, for if ever it were like to come under a condition of suffering, it is now . . .

You have a peace likewise with . . . Portugal, . . . a peace that your merchants make us believe is of good concernment to their trade, their assurance being greater, and so their profit in trade thither, than to other places. And this hath been obtained in that treaty, (which never was since the Inquisition was set up there,) that our people which trade thither have liberty of conscience.

Indeed peace is, as you were well told to-day, desirable with all men, as far as it may be had with conscience and honour.

We are upon a treaty with France. . . . And I dare say that there is not a nation in Europe, but they are very willing to ask a good understanding with you . . .

As I said before, when this government was undertaken, we were in the midst of these divisions, and animosities, and scatterings; also thus engaged with these enemies round about us, at such a vast charge, six score thousand pounds a month for the very fleet, (which was the very utmost penny of your assessments.) Aye, and then all your treasure was exhausted and spent, when this government was undertaken; all accidental ways of bringing in treasure, to a very inconsiderable sum consumed. That is to say, the lands are sold, the treasures spent, rents, fee-farms, king's, queen's, princes', bishops', dean and chapters', delinquents' lands sold. These were spent when this government was undertaken.

I think it is my duty to let you know so much. And that's the reason why the taxes do lie so heavy upon the people, of which we have abated thirty thousand pounds a month for the next three months. . . .

We are thus far through the mercy of God. We have cause to take notice of it, that we are not brought into misery; but, as I said before, a door of hope [is] open.

It's one of the great ends of calling this Parliament, that this ship of the Commonwealth may be brought into a safe harbour, which I assure you it will not well be without your counsel and advice. . . .

Notes

1 'humours': capricious mood (from the humours as the four chief fluids of the body, believed to determine an individual's physical and mental disposition).

2 'a way for the approbation...': Cromwell established Commissioners for the Approbation of Public Preachers (the 'Triers') by an Ordinance of March 1654.

100 Cromwell to the First Parliament of the Protectorate, 12 September 1654

[*Source*: Abbott, editor (1945) *Writings and Speeches* volume three, pp.452 and 454–62.]

[Cromwell is replying to Parliament's attempts to revise the Instrument of Government so that Parliament had more power.]

... I called not myself to this place. I say again, I called not myself to this place; of that, God is witness. And I have many witnesses who, I do believe, could readily lay down their lives to bear witness to the truth of that, that is to say, that I called not myself to this place. And being in it, I bear not witness to myself; but God and the people of these nations have borne testimony to it also ...

I was by birth a gentleman, living neither in any considerable height, nor yet in obscurity. I have been called to several employments in the nation ... and ... I did endeavour to discharge the duty of an honest man in those services, to God and his people's interest, and of the Commonwealth ...

[Cromwell then gave an account of the political developments between 1651 and 1653 which had brought him to power.]

[The 'Barebones' Parliament not] succeeding, as I have formerly said to you, and giving such a disappointment to our hopes, I shall not now make any repetition thereof. Only the effect was, that they came and brought to me a parchment, signed by very much the major part of them, expressing their resigning and re-delivery of the power and authority that was committed to them back again into my hands. And I can say it in the presence of divers persons here, that do know whether I lie in that, that I did not know one tittle of that resignation, until they all came and brought it, and delivered it into my hands; of this there are also in this presence many witnesses ...

My power again by this resignation was as boundless and unlimited as before; all things being subjected to arbitrariness, and [myself] a person having power over the three nations boundlessly and unlimited, and upon the matter, all government dissolved, all civil administration at an end, as will presently be made [to] appear ...

When they had finished their model [the Instrument of Government] in some measure ... they told me that except I would undertake the government, they thought things would hardly come to a composure and settlement, but blood and confusion would break in upon us. I denied it again and again, as God and those persons know, not complimentingly as they also know and as God knows . . .

I had the approbation of the officers of the army in the three nations of England, Scotland, and Ireland; I say, of the officers. I had that by their Remonstrances, and under signature. There was went along with that explicit consent, an implicit consent of persons that had somewhat to do in the world, that had been instrumental by God to fight down the enemies of God and His people in the three nations. And truly, until my hands were bound, and I limited, (wherein I took full contentment, as many can bear me witness,) when I had in my hands so great a power and arbitrariness, the soldiery were a very considerable part of the nations, especially all government being dissolved. I say, when all government was thus dissolved, and nothing to keep things in order but the sword; and yet they, (which many histories will not parallel,) even they were desirous that things might come to a consistency, and arbitrariness might be taken away, and the government put into a person (limited and bounded as in the Act of Settlement) whom they distrusted the least, and loved not the worst. This was another evidence.

I would not forget the honourable and civil entertainment, with the approbation I found in the great City of London . . .

I had not only this witness, but I have had . . . from the county of York, and City of York, and other counties and places, assembled in their public and general assizes; the Grand Jury in the name of the noblemen, gentlemen, yeomen, and inhabitants of that county, giving very great thanks to me for undertaking this heavy burden at such a time, and giving very great approbation and encouragement to me to go through with it. These are plain; I have them to shew, and by these in some measure it will appear, I do not bear witness to myself.

This is not all. The Judges, (and truly I had almost forgotten it,) they thinking that there was a dissolution of government, met and consulted, and did declare one to another that they could not administer justice to the satisfaction of their consciences, until they had received commissions from me . . .

And I shall now make you my last witnesses, and ask you whether you came not hither by my writs, directed to the several sheriffs . . . with proviso that the persons so chosen shall not have power to alter the government as it is now settled in one single person and a Parliament. . . .

Yea surely, and this being so, though I told you in my last speech that you were a free Parliament, yet I thought it was understood that I was the Protector, and the authority that called you, and that I was in possession of the government by a good right from God and men . . .

There are some things in the Establishment that are fundamental, and some things are not so, but are circumstantial . . .

The government by a single person and a Parliament is a fundamental; it is the *esse* [being], it is constitutive . . .

That Parliaments should not make themselves perpetual is a fundamental . . .

Is not liberty of conscience in religion a fundamental? . . . Every sect saith, Oh! Give me liberty. But give him it, and to his power he will not yield it to anybody else. Where is our ingenuity? Truly, that's a thing ought to be very reciprocal. The magistrate hath his supremacy, and he may settle religion according to his conscience. And I may say it to you, I can say it: all the money of this nation would not have tempted men to fight upon such an account as they have engaged, if they had not had hopes of liberty, better than they had from Episcopacy, or than would have been afforded them from a Scottish Presbytery, or an English either, if it had made such steps or been as sharp and rigid as it threatened when it was first set up.

This I say is a fundamental. It ought to be so: it is for us, and the generations to come. And if there be an absoluteness in the imposer, without fitting allowances and exceptions from the rule, we shall have our people driven into wildernesses, as they were when those poor and afflicted people, that forsook their estates and inheritances here, where they lived plentifully and comfortably, for the enjoyment of their liberty, and were necessitated to go into a vast howling wilderness in New England . . .

Another, which I had forgotten, is the Militia; that's judged a fundamental, if anything be so. That it should be well and equally placed, is very necessary. For put the absolute power of the Militia into one without a check, what doth it? . . . they or he hath power to make what they please of all the rest . . .

Necessities, imaginary necessities, are the greatest cozenage that men can put upon the providence of God, and make pretences to break known rules by. But it is as legal and as carnal and as stupid, to think that there are no necessities that are manifest necessities, because necessities may be abused or feigned . . .

I say that the wilful throwings away of this government, such as it is, so owned by God, so approved by men, so testified to in the fundamentals of it, as is before mentioned, and that in relation to the good of these nations and posterity; I can sooner be willing to be rolled into my grave, and buried with infamy, than I can give my consent unto . . .

Seeing the authority calling you is so little valued and so much slighted, till some such assurance be given and made known, that the fundamental interest of the government be settled and approved, according to the proviso contained in the Return, and such a consent testified, as will make it appear that the same is accepted, I have caused a stop to be put to your entrance into the Parliament House.

I am sorry, I am sorry, and I could be sorry to the death, that there is cause for this. But there is cause. And if things be not satisfied, that are reasonably demanded, I for my part shall do that that becomes me, seeking my counsel from God . . .

[The M.P.s were then asked to sign a 'recognition' that the government was settled in 'one single person and a Parliament' as a condition of their continued sitting. Most did sign, but with reluctance.]

The Major Generals
Letters

101 Major General Hezekiah Haynes to Secretary Thurloe, from Bury St Edmunds, 19 November 1655

[*Source*: Thomas Birch, editor (1742) *A Collection of the State Papers of John Thurloe* volume four, pp. 216–17.]

[Hezekiah Haynes (1619–1693), Ralph Josselin's friend (see p. 117) was the son of an Essex gentleman who became the first Governor of Connecticut. Hezekiah served in the Eastern Association army and later in the New Model. As a Major General he was deputy to Charles Fleetwood and responsible for Norfolk, Suffolk, Essex, Cambridgeshire, Ely, Oxfordshire and Buckinghamshire. Haynes supported the army in 1659–60, and was under arrest until the end of 1661.]

I have nothing to plead as excuse, that I wrote not to you since the 8th instant, save that I was constantly attending the commissioners in Norfolk, who have sat *de die in diem* [from day to day] for the carrying on the service desired of them; and I am confident none in England will appear to be more forward. As also was I desirous to see such progress in the work, especially in the tax,[1] as that the whole might be perfected in time. Indeed, such acceptance had this affair in the hearts of all, that it carried its conviction with it, honest men encouraging one another in the action, and the delinquent not one word to say why aught should be remitted him; that every tongue must confess it was of the Lord, who is a righteous God in the execution of his judgements; and when his hand is lifted up, he shall not only make them, though most unwilling, to see, but also make them ashamed for their envy to his people. The commissioners did the most of them meet every day for ten days together till Friday last; and the greatest part of the most necessary work being done, they have now adjourned themselves to every Thursday and Friday in the week, until they shall have perfected the whole, or so much as they may take a further liberty for their meeting without prejudice to the service. They have given summons to almost all [who] will be qualified to bear any part of the charge; and the greatest part of them have they assessed, and that with the greatest care they could possibly, exceeding in their assessing the books of sequestration.[2] That which remains there to be done will not be found to be much; so that I fear in that county there will not be enough by a great deal raised to pay the three troops therein, unless his Highness and Council shall judge those of Yarmouth, that withstood our forces in

48,[3] and such as were sequestered for going beyond the seas (who are yet as malignant as any) to be liable to the general charge, for of the last are the principal persons of estate in that county, who made friends after their sequestration, and return home to free their estates from composition, and so consequently are better able to bear this tax. These things are more fully represented by the commissioners in their letter to my Lord President,[4] which they pray may be communicated to his Highness and Council, and therefore desired these for their covert [covering] to your hands. You will also find by their own letters, that they have considered and acted upon the second head of his Highness and Council's orders[5] in the apprehending and securing of Mr Cleveland, a most desperate enemy to God and good men, and one Mr Sherman, a most malignant episcopal minister, who, though of a sober life, yet of most destructive principles to the government and good people, and professedly owned and held forth by him most seditiously in a sermon preached before the authority of that city.[6] Indeed he is the more dangerous by how much the government of the city is so bad, being in the hands of persons notoriously disaffected upon the worst principles, and he one that artificially draws them after him. But I shall not trouble you further as to these particular persons, referring you to the commissioners' certificates in that behalf; only by how much mention hath been made of the government of the city, I would humbly entreat the consideration of charters may be timously taken up, and of this city as soon as any, being as bad as any other in England, as to persons in authority, the commonalty having by degrees (encouraged thereto by the malignant aldermen) for these three years last past rid their hands of the honest interest. Further, there being one Mr Boteman, formerly of Hull, and great with Colonel Overton,[7] and formerly zealous for the Parliament, who now hath changed his principles and fallen in with Mr Sherman aforesaid, and is thought to be the more active instrument to strengthen the malignant, and work disaffection upon every dissatisfied person. It's rumoured that there was an order from the Council three years since for his removing out of Hull. I could desire it might be found to help him out [of] here, he not so clearly falling under the commissioners' powers as Mr Sherman, yet no less dangerous to the peace of that place; and therefore, have some of the commissioners and myself treated [with] him, to try if we can get him to leave the place; and in case he will not otherwise go, it's the desire of the gentlemen, that an order of his Highness or Council may be obtained in that behalf. Pray, good Sir, help in this, and I do well hope to stop by that means the great growth of episcopacy and malignancy in that city, which is hardly to be believed, and yet most true. As yet we hear nothing of the Registrar's office[8] at London, to which so much of our work relates. One word to it: the post, that went from Colchester to Bury [St Edmunds] and so to Norwich, is exceedingly wanted to the great dissatisfaction of those places. I think it may be yet helped. The lists of sheriffs you sent will by no means hold proportion with those qualifications you intimate. There is but one of all the four counties I have relation to, who is like to answer expectation, and that is Mr Ward of Norfolk. Indeed, Sir, it's very difficult to find fit persons. I have travelled in my own thoughts, and privately discoursed [with] friends more knowing of men than myself; and for these four counties I cannot find out any so fit as these in the enclosed lists; and I humbly apprehend, as they are named, so are they for fitness; but I should be most unwilling to put our friends upon it to contract expenses, unless some way might be found out to help them to bear the burden. I am now ashamed I have been so troublesome to you. This week I hope to set the wheels agoing in this county [Suffolk], and the next in Cambridgeshire; of all which you shall not, God willing, fail of an account from, Sir,

Your honour's truly humble servant . . . [Postscript] I most humbly thank your honour for the copies of the letters of my fellow labourers in this work. I hope you'll not judge me of neglect, because I have not communicated the instructions to the gentlemen of so many counties as they, rather judging it most for your service to perfect what possibly may be as I go.

Notes

1 'the tax': the decimation tax which took a tenth of the income of royalists; its proceeds financed the local militias commanded by the Major Generals.
2 'books of sequestration': the books that recorded the values of royalists' estates while they were confiscated in the 1640s.
3 'Yarmouth . . . 48': in July 1648 there was disorder in Yarmouth when the royalist fleet lay offshore.
4 'Lord President': the President of the Council of State was Henry Lawrence, an old friend and neighbour of Cromwell's.
5 'the second head . . .': the second order to the Major Generals was to disarm royalists and Catholics.
6 'that city': John Cleveland, the royalist poet, and Mark Sherman, a Suffolk minister ejected from his living, were seized at Norwich.
7 'Colonel Overton': Robert Overton rose to high command in the army but became a fifth monarchist in the 1650s and was arrested in December 1654 for plotting against the government.
8 'the Registrar's office': in October 1655 a registry was set up to record the names and movements of royalists and Catholics as reported by the Major Generals. The securities pledged by royalists for their good behaviour were also listed.

102 Major General Charles Worsley to the Protector, 24 December 1655

[*Source*: Birch, editor (1742) *State Papers of John Thurloe* volume four, pp. 340–1.]

[Worsley was born in Manchester in 1622 and rose to become a Lieutenant Colonel in Parliament's army by 1650. He was Major General for Cheshire, Lancashire and Staffordshire, and died in office in 1656.]

I hold it my duty to give your Highness an account of my proceedings upon those orders and instructions you gave me in charge. We have had meetings in the several counties, and have proceeded to the extraordinary tax upon divers of the delinquents of greatest estates, and have sent out our orders for the rest to appear before us to be proceeded against accordingly. I cannot but observe a visible hand of God going along with us in this work, as well as in raising up the hearts and spirits of good men to be active therein, as also the unexpected submission and subjection of them we have to deal with; so much that truly I have not heard of one man of them, that any way disputes or complains against the justice of those orders and instructions we act upon. We have in Staffordshire taxed as many as amounts to about thirteen or fourteen hundred pounds *per annum* and have discovered about one hundred pounds *per annum* in lands of Penruddock,[1] who was in arms at Salisbury, and after executed for his rebellion. In Cheshire we have taxed as many as amounted to one thousand, five hundred pounds *per annum* and in Lancashire about one thousand, one hundred pounds *per annum* and hope at our next meetings to go through with the greatest part of the tax; and in all the three counties we have put in execution the ordinance for ejecting scandalous ministers and schoolmasters; and the last Thursday sent orders for divers articles against and witnesses to appear at our next meeting in this county of Lancaster. Many of the delinquents in this county were papist-delinquents, and their estates quite sold by the state,[2] which will make us all much short of what we expected. We have found out a considerable estate, which we conceive is in John Wildman.[3] We have seized and secured the same to your Highness' use, and hope to find some more. I am now taking security from disaffected persons in the several counties. We are now proceeding against some considerable persons, which we conceive will fall under the first particular in your Highness's orders and instructions.[4] I find as many dangerous persons in these counties, whose estates fall short of one hundred pounds *per annum* as any of what quality soever; so if your Highness shall please but to order us to descend to estates of fifty pounds *per annum* in lands, and five hundred pounds in personal estate, we shall raise much more than else we can; for in these countries one hundred pounds *per annum* is a considerable estate, and many, that justly deserved to fall under the tax, might be fetched in at fifty pounds *per annum* whose estates reach not one hundred.[5] We are about to make some progress upon the rest of the particulars, especially upon that of wandering idle persons, some being already apprehended. Our greatest want will be for a convenient place, and a guard upon them. By the good help of God I doubt not but to give your Highness a good account of the rest of the particulars you gave me in charge. The Quakers abound much in these countries, to the great disturbance of the best people. I have done and shall what I can; but crave your Highness' further orders and instructions, how to deal with them. No more, but that I am,

Your Highness's faithful servant

Notes

1 'Penruddock': John Penruddock, leader of the royalist rising in Wiltshire, March 1655.
2 'papist-delinquents . . .': Catholics who had supported the king, along with the most prominent royalists, were not allowed to compound for their estates, which were sold under three Acts of 1651–52.
3 'John Wildman': a Leveller spokesman at the Putney debates, became an agent for the purchase of confiscated estates in the 1650s, usually buying as the trustee of royalist families. From February 1655 until June 1656 Wildman was under arrest because of his involvement in murky plots involving royalists and Levellers.
4 'the first particular': the first order to the Major Generals was to use the militia to suppress all internal unrest and any external threats.
5 The decimation tax (see p. 215, Note 1) did not apply to those worth less than £100 p.a.

103 Major General Edward Whalley to Thurloe, from Nottingham, 14 July 1656

[*Source*: Birch, editor (1742) *State Papers of John Thurloe* volume five, pp. 211–12.]

[Whalley was Major General of Nottinghamshire (his native county), Lincolnshire, Derbyshire, Leicestershire and Warwickshire. He had fought for Parliament from 1642, and was Commissary General of Horse in the 1650 Scottish campaign. Whalley was Cromwell's cousin and a staunch supporter of the Protectorate. As a regicide he was forced to flee the country in 1660, taking refuge in New England with his son-in-law William Goffe.]

I shall now only mind you of some things, which in my haste in my last made me forget. Horse stealers, robbers, and other condemned rogues lie in the gaols. To continue them there is a charge to the country; to give them liberty here, is to make more; and your this long forbearing them without sending them beyond the seas, I fear hath increased the number, to the dissatisfaction of the country. When you expect great things from them, you shall do well to gratify them with as many small things as you can. The clearing the gaols and countries of rogues would be very pleasing to them. Your last instructions[1] will be very difficult for us to put in execution, these countries, all but Lincolnshire, being the mediterranean of this nation, and few or no merchants in any part of Lincolnshire; we shall make the best inquiry we can; for the sending away, though but a few, would have a great influence upon the rest. There are many other things, that would be very acceptable to the country, which by the grand juries in these countries were desired. You have them in our propositions, and you may quickly do them; and I wish they were dispatched before the Assizes, for in vain it is for either the country or us to propose good things, if after they come to you, they shall be buried. That amongst other of weights and measures, the inequality of them was presented as a grievance by all the grand juries of these counties; and truly it would be thought very strange at these Assizes, that after complaint of such a grievance, nothing should be done in it. I confess I should be ashamed to appear in the face of the country; however I should have nothing to say, why it is not done. All that is desired, as you may see in our propositions, is that the Council would be pleased to issue out a proclamation throughout England to reduce weights and measures to one standard, to begin at a certain day prefixed; and commend the care of it to the Major Generals. I would see it done in these counties by a law already established; but should it be only here put in execution, I should be injurious to them. Sir, I have in the face of all my counties, on the behalf of his Highness and the Council (declared)[2] that they cannot be so forward to desire and propound anything for the good of the country but his Highness and the Council will be as forward to promote it; and I doubt not but it will be made good; and that they may do abundantly more, is the prayer of,

Sir, yours most affectionately to serve you.

Notes

1 'Your last instructions': presumably concerned clearing Whalley's counties of 'rogues' by deportation.

2 'declared': an addition by Birch, the eighteenth-century editor of Thurloe's papers.

104 Major General William Goffe to Thurloe, 9 September 1656

[*Source*: Birch, editor 1742) *State Papers of John Thurloe* volume five, pp. 396–7.]

[Goffe was Major General for Sussex, Hampshire and Berkshire. He was the son of a Sussex clergyman who had served in Parliament's armies since the start of the civil war, becoming a Colonel in 1650. Like Edward Whalley, whose daughter he married, he was a regicide and a consistent supporter of the Protectorate. He fled to New England with Whalley in 1660.]

On Monday last I spoke with Cole of Southampton, who I find to be a perfect Leveller, and so well known in Southampton, that he is called by the name of Common Freedom. He told me, he was where he was, and where the army was seven years ago, and pulled out of his pocket the Agreement of the People,[1] so called indeed by the officers of the army, but, as I told him, not consented to but rejected by the people. After a great deal of discourse, he not confessing or denying, but putting me upon the proof that he dispersed the pamphlet, I demanded of him what assurance he would give me for his peaceable demeanour. He told me, he would promise me not to disperse any of those books, and that it was his intention to live peaceably for that he knew a war was not so easily ended as begun. Whereupon with the best exhortation I could give him, I dismissed him for the present, apprehending if I should have done otherwise, they would have made their advantage of it. The post master is very honest, and one of the militia troop; so also is the postmaster of this town, to whom the letter was sent. Clem. Ireton was last week at Southampton, and remembered himself to me by Mr Cole; but I hear he expressed great dissatisfactions against my Lord Protector. He told Captain Dunch that his Highness would be forced in a few days to lay his hand upon some of the Saints, and other stuff of that nature, that bespeaks him a Fifth Monarchy Man. I fear he may be engaged amongst the hot spirited men in London. He is my old acquaintance and friend, but I doubt [fear] misled.

The design in this county worketh notable high, and I hope God will turn it to good; for I hope some are awaken'd that were asleep before, and I hope my Lord R. and Colonel Norton[2] will see a necessity to join their strength in a list that goeth industriously about the country. These are both left out as also Mr Major,[3] and all that have any relation to his Highness. Their list you may see in the margin,[4] but I hope, through God, we shall prevent them. His Highness' letters do come very seasonably. I find they are very well accepted by some honest men that I have communicated them to, who promise their prayers and utmost assistance, and with their lives to stand by his Highness and to pursue the things that make for peace. The common enemy's last and great design is now to divide between the Protector and Parliament, which speaks aloud our duty to seek an agreement; which that it may be accomplish'd shall be the fervent prayers and faithful endeavours of,

Your very affectionate friend and servant . . .

Notes

1 'The Agreement of the People': the Agreement drafted by senior army officers during their period of cooperation with the Levellers; it was presented to Parliament in January 1649.

2 'my Lord R. and Colonel Norton': Richard Cromwell, son of the Protector and Richard Norton, Governor of Portsmouth. Goffe hopes they will stand for election to Parliament.

3 'Mr Major': Richard Major, Richard Cromwell's father-in-law and a member of the Protector's Council.

4 'in the margin': the anti-Cromwellian candidates for Parliament listed in the margin were Mr [Robert] Wallop, Mr [Robert] Reynolds, Mr [Nicholas] Love, Mr [John] Bulkeley, Mr Rivett, Mr Tillney, Sir William Waller, Sir Henry Worsley, and Mr [Edward] Hooper. It is impossible to ascertain precisely the political affiliations of all these men but the group included both conservative 'Presbyterians' like Waller, the civil war parliamentary general imprisoned at Pride's Purge, and more radical republican opponents of the Protector like Love, Ludlow's companion in exile. The results of the election were mixed: of the anti-Cromwellians listed by Goffe, Wallop, Bulkeley and Hooper were elected; supporters of the regime who were chosen as MPs included Goffe himself, Richard Cromwell, Richard Norton, William Sydenham, the Governor of the Isle of Wight, and John Lisle, a legal officer under the Protectorate.

105 Ludlow: The Rule of the Major Generals

[*Source:* C.H. Firth editor (1894) *The Memoirs of Edmund Ludlow* volume one, pp. 405–6; volume two, pp. 3, 9–10 and 18–22.]

[The *Memoirs* of the republican Edmund Ludlow first appeared in 1698–99, part of a series of Whig publications covering the civil war and interregnum. A section of Ludlow's manuscript has recently been found, and it is now known that his work was cut (possibly by as much as three-quarters) and completely rewritten by his Whig editor. Ludlow's *Memoirs* are a contribution to the political controversies of the 1690s as well as an historical account of 1640–72: the account was intended as an implicit criticism of the regime of William III. The radical Whigs especially opposed William III's plan to retain a sizeable army after the 1697 peace treaty with France, holding that standing armies were incompatible with English liberties. The part of Ludlow's manuscript that deals with the Major Generals remains missing, and the following passsage, from the *Memoirs*, should be read critically: a scathing attack on military rule in the 1650s was of immediate relevance to readers of the late 1690s; and the editor may well have adjusted Ludlow's original account in order to highlight contemporary parallels.[1]

Note

1 Edmund Ludlow, *A Voyce from the Watch Tower* edited by A.B. Worden (Camden Society 1978), introduction.]

The usurper was not a little startled at this insurrection,[1] suspecting that so small a number would not have appeared without more considerable encouragement; and therefore though he had so lately meanly stooped to court the Cavalier party, and thereby highly provoked his ancient friends to a just jealousy and indignation, he resolved now to fall upon them, and to break through all their compositions, even the Act of Oblivion itself,[2] in the obtaining and passing of which he had so great a hand. To this end he commanded a tenth part of their estates to be levied, in order as he pretended to maintain those extraordinary forces which their turbulent and seditious practices obliged him to keep up.[3] In defence of which oppression I could never yet hear one argument offered that carried any weight, either with respect to justice or policy: for having by his treachery and usurpation disobliged those with whom he first engaged, he seemed to have no other way left to support himself, but by balancing his new with his old enemies, whom by this fresh act of injustice he rendered desperate and irreconcilable; they being not able to call anything their own, whilst by the same rule that he seized one tenth, he might also take away the other nine parts at his pleasure. And to put this detestable project in execution, he divided England into cantons, over each of which he placed a Bashaw[4] under the title of Major General, who was to have the inspection and government of inferior commissioners in every county, with orders to seize the persons, and distrain the estates of such as should be refractory, and to put in execution such further directions as they should receive from him [October 1655] . . .

The Major Generals carried things with unheard of insolence in their several precincts, decimating to extremity whom they pleased, and interrupting the proceedings at law upon petitions of those who pretended themselves aggrieved; threatening such as would not yield a ready submission to their orders with transportation to Jamaica or some other plantations in the West Indies; and suffering none to escape their persecution, but those that would betray their own party by discovering the persons that had acted with them or for them. And here I cannot omit to mention a farmer in Berkshire, who being demanded to pay his tenth, desired to know of the commissioners, in case he did so, what security he should have for the other nine parts; and answer being made that he should have Cromwell's order and theirs for the enjoyment of the rest, he replied that he had already an Act of Parliament for the whole which he could not but think to be as good security as they could give. 'But,' said he, 'if goodman such a one'and another whom he named of his neighbours, 'will give me their bond for it, I know what to say to such a proposal, for if they break their agreement, I know where to right myself, but these swordmen are too strong for me.' . . .

The usurper having governed as he thought long enough by virtue of the Instrument of Government,[5] which though drawn up by himself and his creatures, was now thought to lay too great a restraint upon his ambitious spirit; and resolving to rest satisfied with nothing less than the succession of his family to the crown, he attempted to make himself King. To this end he thought it necessary to call a Parliament [about June 1656]; and that he might engage the army to assist him in all parts to procure such men to be chosen as would be fit for his purpose, he pretended that this assembly was called only in order to raise money for the payment of the army and fleet, to confirm the authority of the Major Generals and that of the Instrument of Government. By this means he obtained his desires in great measure, especially in Scotland and Ireland, where all kinds of artifice, and in many places the most irregular courses, were taken to get such men returned as were proposed by the court. But knowing the people of England not to be of so mercenary a spirit and that, as they were better instructed in the principles of civil liberty, so they were not wanting in courage to assert it, he used his utmost endeavours to disable and incapacitate such men from being chosen, whom he thought most likely to obstruct his designs . . . .

[After the elections the Council of State scrutinized all the results and gave a certificate to those M.P.s they approved of. When Parliament opened, on 17 September 1656, a guard of soldiers turned away all MPs who lacked a certificate. About 100 were refused admittance, and some 50 more withdrew from Parliament to protest.]

[The remaining M.P.s] proceeded to prepare divers bills, which tended chiefly to gratify the soldiery and such persons as had received grants of land from Cromwell and his Council, which were confirmed to them. Yet for all this harmony there were sometimes bitter reflections cast upon the proceedings of the Major Generals by the lawyers and country gentlemen, who accused them to have done many things oppressive to the people in interrupting the course of the law and threatening such as would not submit to their arbitrary orders with transportation beyond the seas. On the other hand the Major Generals insisted vehemently with the Assembly to confirm the Instrument of Government, and to establish their authority in particular; and when it was proposed by some who were unwilling to settle such an arbitrary power by a law, that to compose these differences an Act of Indemnity should be granted for what was past, one of the Major Generals had the insolence to say, they would not thank them for that, for whilst they had their swords by their sides, they could protect and indemnify themselves. So confident was the soldiery grown, that they durst openly avow themselves to be our lords and masters. But the lawyers and others of the assembly, having privately received encouragement from those who were more powerful than the Major Generals,[6] desisted not from endeavouring the suppression of their authority, loading them with many heavy accusations, for which they had given but too just cause. Yet the Major Generals, confident of the strength of their party, moved for a day when the Instrument of Government and the confirmation of their power, should be debated; which having obtained and the time come, they moved that the whole Instrument might be confirmed at once; but that being rejected, it was debated in parts. When the power of the Major Generals came under consideration, all men were in great expectation concerning the issue of it. It was supposed that Cromwell, who had erected their authority, and engaged them in those actions for which they were now become odious, would support them against all attempts; because there appeared now no way so probable to maintain his own power, as by keeping the army firmly united to him. But ambition had corrupted his understanding to that degree, that he made no scruple to sacrifice these men who, to say no worse, had enlarged their consciences to an extraordinary size in the execution of his orders, to those who in requital of the favour had promised to make him king. Hitherto he had given good words to the Major Generals, but when their power came to be debated [on 7 January 1657], Mr Claypole his son-in-law first stood up, which was unusual for him to do at all, and told the House that he could but start the game, and must leave those who had more experience to follow the chase; and therefore should only say, that he had formerly thought it necessary in respect to the condition in which the nation had been, that the Major Generals should be entrusted with the authority which they had exercised, but in the present state of affairs he conceived it inconsistent with the laws of England, and liberties of the people, to continue their power any longer. This motion was a clear direction to the sycophants of the court, who being fully persuaded that Claypole had delivered the sense, if not the very words of Cromwell in this matter, joined as one man in opposing the Major Generals, and so their authority was abrogated . . . .

Those who were of the Major Generals' and soldiers' party, finding that Cromwell was abandoning them to espouse another interest, struck in with those who still retained some affection to the Commonwealth; and all together . . . [perceived] that these new measures had been advised by the craft of our old enemy, to make use of Cromwell's ambition as the only probable means to reduce us to our former servitude.

Notes

1 'this insurrection': Penruddock's rising.
2 'the Act of Oblivion', passed in February 1652, granted a pardon for most offences committed before 1651. Royalists were no longer liable to prosecution provided certain conditions were fulfilled.
3 'to this end . . .': Ludlow refers to the decimation tax, which supported the militias commanded by the Major Generals.
4 'Bashaw': an imperious military commander (a variant of Pasha, a Turkish military officer).
5 'The Instrument of Government': the constitutional settlement of December 1653, under which Cromwell became Lord Protector for life, with a Council and triennial parliaments to assist him (see p. 137 for an extract from the 'Instrument').
6 'more powerful than the Major Generals': Ludlow is referring to Cromwell's moderate advisers among whom were his son-in-law John Claypole and the Irish politician Lord Broghill, brother of Robert Boyle.

* * * * * * * * * *

106 A Fifth Monarchist Programme

[*Source*: William Medley *A Standard Set Up* (1657), pp. 12–22.]

[From the pamphlet that served as the manifesto for the fifth monarchist 'Venner plot' of 1657.]

1 . . . That all earthly governments, and worldly constitutions may be broken and removed by the first administration of the Kingdom of Christ, appointed unto him by the decree of the Father, and is the inheritance of the Saints, as joint heirs with him (Daniel 2.44, 7.26–7. Romans 8.17) . . .

6 That the supreme absolute legislative power and authority to make laws for the governing of the nations, and the good and well being

of mankind, is originally and essentially in the Lord Jesus Christ, by right, conquest, gift, election, and inheritance, who is the only absolute single person, whom the Father hath loved, decreed, sworn to, anointed, and given all power unto in heaven and in earth. (Isaiah 9. 6, 32.1, 33.22; Jeremiah 10.7; Psalms 2. 7–8; Acts 2.30; James 4.12).

7 That the scriptures, being given by inspiration of God with his holy spirit, are the revealed will and rule of this legislator, to be constantly owned and submitted unto in times of war and peace, as a constant standing rule, for the inward and outward man . . . For so they were to the commonwealth of Israel, the only type of the Lamb's government. (2 Timothy 3. 15–17) . . .

8 That a Sanhedrin, or Supreme Council (this interest now up once removed) – men of choicest light and spirit; indued with judgement, righteousness, wisdom, knowledge, understanding; able men, men of truth, and of known integrity, fearing God . . . be duly chosen and constituted upon and according to the principles of right and freedom. (Deuteronomy 1.13; Numbers 11.16; Exodus 18. 21–2; Isaiah 32.1, 33.5–6; 2 Samuel 23).

9 That such a Council, so constituted, shall be the Representative, for our Lord and King, of the whole body of the Saints, whose day this is, and people in the nations.

10 That the said Representative, as princes under Christ, from whom, with his people, their power is derived, shall rule in judgement or have the exercise of the chief-magistracy and the power of administering the laws residing in them: shall consult and provide for the safety and welfare of the state and people; shall determine and give judgement in all supreme matters of civil counsel, (not to prescribe forms of worship for their brethren, nor to take the power upon them given to the church) according to their present light; and shall rule and govern the people with just judgement; and that freely without respect of persons, or taking of gifts or bribes, and the poor with righteousness and equity; and shall save the children of the needy, with him that hath no helper. So that all just and honourable ends, for which they are entrusted, may be answered. (Isaiah 32.1; Deuteronomy 16, 18–19; Psalms 72).

11 That the power of ordering and disposing the militia, and forces of Zion at sea and land . . . be in this Representative . . .

17 That, it having been found by experience inconsistent with the good and well being of the governed, the supreme power actually in the great Council, as the Representees of the whole body of the Saints, be not perpetuated upon the persons of any during life, or any term of years, or longer than they shall be found fit for, or faithful in, and to their worthy service, and that great trust reposed in them by Christ, his followers, people and subjects. But that at the end of twelve months (to be accounted from the first day of their call and assembling together) the said power in course fall into the Body, at every one of the said periods of time.

18 That upon the last day of the said term successively, or sooner if it shall be determined, the Lord's freemen (i.e. those that have a right with Christ in and according to the new Covenant . . .) shall be assembled together, and shall then make their new elections of members . . .

19 That it be not in the power of the Supreme Council to violate, take away, give up or enervate any of the foundations of common right and freedom, which are, or shall be, agreed upon, save in case of a further convincing light; and such alterations may be according to law, and the good of the people.

20 That no person of what rank, degree, or quality soever be privileged from law and subjection, but all to own obedience to the righteous rule of the head of this government . . .

21 That in this blessed interest of our Lord Jesus, men, as they are men, shall be blessed, preserved and protected in their peaceable enjoyment of their estates, liberties and privileges under him . . .

First, as under the law of this commonwealth, they shall be freed from violence and oppression, and all tyrannical and Anti-Christian yokes upon the outward man: he shall break in pieces the oppressor. And:

1 That no man be committed, or detained in prison without the cause be legally expressed and known . . .

2 That there be no impressing, or enforcing of men for soldiers . . .

3 That there be no longer continuance of that wicked and unlawful oppression of excise, neither of customs upon the native inhabitants.

4 That there be no assessments or taxes levied upon and compelled from the people in times of peace, neither in time of war, but by their common consent and according to our law; but that the war, once raised, be principally carried on at the charge of those that are the occasioners thereof, the beast and false prophet, the wicked, bloody, Anti-Christian magistracy, ministry, lawyers etc. . .

5 That all oppressions and grievances in the tenures of lands, copyhold and customary,. . . be abrogated and clean removed.

6 That there be no place found for tithes, being judged as Anti-Christian, and altogether inconsistent with the gospel spirit; and that the glorious gospel of the kingdom be freely held forth, and preached to all; and to that end that ministers be sent forth of the church, according to the primitive institution and rule of the gospel, who are to be maintained as the gospel will warrant, either at the labour of their hands, or the free contributions of saints and churches . . .

Secondly, Man shall be blessed in this interest . . . in that he shall be restored by God unto right reason and wisdom . . . And great will be the peace of this day, when the beast, and the false prophet is taken in opposing the Lamb with their armies and cast alive into a lake of fire. (Revelation 19. 19–20.)

SECTION FIFTEEN: THE DEBATE OVER EDUCATION

[Those who rejected a State Church and an established ministry (see Section Ten) opposed the universities' role as 'the fountain of the ministry'. Such opposition was expressed strongly at the time of the 'Barebones' Parliament which raised the hopes of many radicals (extract 98 above). William Dell's writings (extract 107) are a good example of the radicals' criticisms; as our extract shows, Dell also had a positive programme for the reform of the whole education system. John Webster suggested an alternative curriculum for the universities (extract 108): he rejected the scholastic theories of Aristotle and proposed instead an approach based on practical experience and experimentation in science. Similar views found wide support after 1660 although they then lost their radical connotations (Section Twenty-one below). Finally, the scientists Seth Ward and John Wilkins, both important figures in the early Royal Society and, in the 1650s, moderate Puritans, represent a 'middle of the road' view of the functions of the universities (extracts 109 and 110).]

107 William Dell

[*Source*: William Dell (1653) *A Tryal of Spirits Both in Teachers and Hearers*, Appendix (a) p.2; (b) pp.26–30.]

a. 'A Testimony from the Word against Divinity Degrees in the University'
Thus doth the university, through power received from antichrist, give men, chiefly for money, divinity degrees: and through those degrees, it gives authority and privilege to Bachelors in Divinity to expound part of the Scriptures, and to Doctors to expound and profess all the Scriptures; and they that gain these degrees to themselves are, as there is good reason, the great men in account with the university, how destitute soever they be of the faith and spirit of the gospel . . .

I cannot choose but give in my testimony against this glorious and gainful privilege of the universities . . . creating them masters in that mystery which none can teach but God himself; and which none can learn but true believers, who are born of God and his true disciples . . . Degrees in divinity, for I meddle with none else, given by the universities to their children are plainly and grossly antichristian, being most manifestly contrary to the word of the Gospel and the light that shines in the New Testament.

b. 'The Right Reformation of Learning, School and Universities'.
I conceive it meet that the civil power or chief magistrates should take great care of the education of youth, as one of the greatest works that concerns them and as one of the worthiest things they can do in the world: inasmuch as what the youth now is, the whole commonwealth will shortly be.

To this end, it is meet that schools, if wanting, be erected through the whole nation, and that not only in cities and great towns, but also, as much as may be, in all lesser villages. And that the authority of the nation take great care that godly men especially have the charge of greater schools; and also that no women be permitted to teach little children in villages, but such as are the most sober and grave; and that the magistrate afford to all this work all suitable encouragement and assistance.

That in such schools they first teach them to read their native tongues, which they speak without teaching; and then presently as they understand, bring them to read the Holy Scriptures; which though for the present they understand not, yet they may, through the blessing of God, come to understand them afterwards.

That in cities and greater towns, where are the greater schools and the greater opportunities to send children to them, they teach them also the Latin and Greek tongues, and the Hebrew also, which is the easiest of them all, and ought to be in great account with us for the Old Testament's sake. And it is most heedfully to be regarded, that in teaching youth the tongues, to wit, the Greek and Latin, such heathenish authors be most carefully avoided, be their language never so good, those writings are full of the fables, vanities, filthiness, lasciviousness, idolatries, and wickedness of the heathen . . .

It may be convenient also, that there may be some universities or colleges, for the instructing of youth in the knowledge of the liberal arts, beyond grammar and rhetoric; as in logic, which as it is in divinity, as one calls it, *gladius diaboli*, the devil's sword, so in human things it may be of good use, if reason manage that art of reason; but the mathematics especially are to be had in good esteem in universities, as arithmetic, geometry, geography, and the like; which as they carry no wickedness in them, so are they besides very useful to human society, and the affairs of this present life.

There may be also in these universities or colleges allowed the study of physic, and of the law, according to that reformation which a wise and godly authority will cause them to pass under, both being now exceedingly corrupt and out of order, both for practice and fees.

But why these universities or colleges should be only at Cambridge and Oxford, I know no reason. Nay, if human learning be so necessary to the knowledge and teaching of the scriptures, as the universities pretend, they surely are without love to their brethren, who would have these studies thus confined to these places, and do swear men to read and teach them nowhere else: certainly it is most manifest, that these men love their own private gain more than the common good of the people . . . The universities usually have been places of great licentiousness and profaneness; whereby it often comes to pass, that parents sending them children far from them, young and hopeful, have for all their care and cost, after several years received them back again with their tongues and arts, proud, profane, wicked, abominable and incorrigible wretches. Wherefore doubtless it would be more suitable to a Commonwealth (if we become so in deed, and not in word only) and more advantageous to the good of all the people to have universities or colleges, one at least, in every great town or city in the nation, as in London, York, Bristol, Exeter, Norwich and the like; and for the state to allow to these colleges an honest and competent maintenance, for some godly and learned men to teach the tongues and arts, under a due reformation. And this the state may the better do, by provision out of every county or otherwise . . . The people having colleges in their own cities, near their own houses, may maintain their children at home whilst they learn in the schools, which would be indeed the greatest advantage to learning that can be thought of.

It should also be considered whether it be according to the word of God that youth should spend their time only in reading of books whilst they are well, strong and fit for business . . . To remedy which great evil . . . it may be so ordered that the youth . . . spend some part of the day in learning or study, and the other part of the day in some lawful calling; or one day in study and another in business, as necessity or occasion shall require . . .

And if this course were taken . . . twenty would learn then, where one learns now; and also by degrees, many men on whom God shall please to pour forth his spirit, may grow up to teach the people, whilst yet they live in an honest calling and employment, as the Apostles did . . . If the faithful shall desire anyone that is more apt to teach, and hath received a greater measure of the anointing than his brethren, to spend more of his time in the word and prayer than his calling will afford, at such times they ought to supply him; and the law of love in the hearts of the faithful will be law enough in this matter, without calling in the aid of the magistrate.

And by this means may the chargeable and burdensome maintenance of the ministers by degrees be taken away, and the church of Christ and the very nations themselves be supplied with a more faithful Christian and spiritual ministry than now it hath, at a far less rate.

Now for conclusion, I do conceive that none of the faithful and wise have any just cause to be offended for speaking of the use of human learning in this reformed way, which the gospel will permit; seeing by this means, these two errors of antichrist would be dissolved among us: the one making universities the fountain of the ministry, which one thing is, and will be more and more, as Christ's kingdom shall rise up and prevail in the world, a mill-stone about their necks; and the other, of making the clergy a distinct sect or order, or tribe, from other Christians, contrary to the simplicity of the gospel.

108 John Webster

[*Source*: John Webster (1653) *Academiarum Examen or the Examination of Academies*, pp.104–8; a facsimile of the whole work is included in A.G. Debus, editor (1970) *Science and Education in the Seventeenth Century: The Webster–Ward Debate*.]

Whether all the whole body of the Aristotelian philosophy should be eliminated and thrown away?

To which I answer, no: for there are many things in his *History of Animals*, and some things in his *Politics*, *Ethics*, *Logic*, *Metaphysics* and *Rhetoric* that are commodious and useful, yet do they all stand in need of reformation and amendment. But for his natural *Philosophy* and his *Astronomy* depending thereon, it admits of no reformation but eradication, that some better may be introduced in the place thereof . . .

1 It cannot be expected that physical science will arrive at any wished perfection unless the way and means so judiciously laid down by our learned countryman the Lord Bacon be observed, and introduced into exact practice. And therefore I shall humbly desire and earnestly press that his way and method may be embraced and set up for a rule and pattern: that no axioms may be received but what are evidently proved and made good by diligent observation, and luciferous [enlightening] experiments; that such may be recorded

in a general history of natural things, that so every age and generation, proceeding in the same way, and upon the same principles, may daily go on with the work, to the building up of a well-grounded and lasting fabric, which indeed is the only true way for the instauration and advance of learning and knowledge.[1]

2 How unfit and unsuitable is it, for people professing the Christian religion to adhere unto that philosophy which is altogether built upon ethnical principles, and indeed contrary and destructive to their tenents [tenets]? So that I shall offer as a most fit expedient that some physical learning might be introduced into the schools, that is grounded upon sensible, rational, experimental and scripture principles: and such a complete piece in the most particulars of all human learning (though many vainly and falsely imagine there is no such perfect work to be found) is the elaborate writings of that profoundly learned man Dr Fludd,[2] than which for all the particulars before mentioned (notwithstanding the ignorance and envy of all opposers) the world never had a more rare, experimental and perfect piece.

3 That the philosophy of Plato, revived and methodized by Francesco Patrizi, Marsilio Ficino and others; that of Democritus, cleared and in some measure demonstrated by Rene Descartes, Regius, Phocylides Holwarda, and some others; that of Epicurus, illustrated by Pierre Gassendi; that of Philolaus, Empedocles and Parmenides, resuscitated by Telesio, Campanella, and some besides; and that excellent magnetical philosophy found out by Dr Gilbert; that of Hermes, revived by the Paracelsian school, may be brought into examination and practice, that whatsoever in any of them, or others of what sort soever, may be found agreeable to truth and demonstration, may be embraced and received; for there are none of them but have excellent and profitable things, and few of them but may justly be equalised with Aristotle and the scholastic learning; nay, I am confident upon due and serious perusal and trial, would be found far to excel them.[3]

4 That youth may not be idly trained up in notions, speculations and verbal disputes, but may learn to inure their hands to labour, and put their fingers to the furnaces; that the mysteries discovered by pyrotechny [the use of fire], and the wonders brought to light by chemistry, may be rendered familiar unto them: that so they may not grow proud with the brood of their own brains, but truly to be taught by manual operation and ocular [visible] experiment, that so they may not be sayers, but doers, not idle speculators, but painful operators; that so they may not be sophisters and philosophers, but sophists indeed, true natural magicians, that walk not in the external circumference but in the centre of nature's hidden secrets, which can never come to pass, unless they have laboratories as well as libraries, and work in the fire, better than build castles in the air.[4]

5 That the Galenical way of the medicinal part of physic (a path that

> hath been long enough trodden to yield so little fruit) may not be the prison that all men must be enchained in; and ignorance, cheating and impostorage maintained by laws and charters; but that the more sure, clear and exquisite way of finding the true causes, and certain cures of diseases, brought to light by those two most eminent and laborious persons, Paracelsus and Helmont, may be entertained, prosecuted and promoted; that it may no longer be disputable whether medicine . . . be more helpful than hurtful, or kill more than it cures.[5]. . .

The next is metaphysics, to help which I shall only offer this expedient, that it might be reduced to some certain grounds and principles, from whence demonstrations might be drawn, that men might proceed with some certainty, and not wander in the dark they know not whither, and so that the most sure way of Rene Descartes[6] may be brought into use and exercise, who hath traced it unto the head of the spring, and shaken off the loose and superfluous questions, notions, and frivolous chimeras thereof. That so it might become useful and beneficial, which as it now stands and is used (or rather abused) serves for little else but only to amuse and amaze the understanding, to blow up the fantasy with airy and empty notions, and to make men vainly and fruitlessly waste their most precious time, which should be bestowed in things of more necessary use and of greater concernment.

As for ethical knowledge, I suppose it better taught by precedent and practice than by words and precepts, for seeing virtue doth consist in action, it must of necessity be far more laudable that men be brought up to live virtuously, than to talk and dispute of virtue . . .

Lastly, for rhetoric and poesy, I shall prescribe nothing, but leave every man to the freedom of his genius; only to add this, that emperors and kings can make and create dukes, marquesses and earls, but cannot make one orator or poet.

Notes

1 'the instauration . . .': these phrases are taken from Bacon.

2 'Dr Fludd': Robert Fludd (1574–1637) doctor and chemist, foremost English exponent of Paracelsian ideas, and a great opponent of Aristotelianism. Paracelsus (died 1541) was a Swiss alchemist and physician. He and his followers believed they were reviving the ancient 'Hermetic' ideas; they stressed the unity of God and nature, and believed the world was permeated by magical forces. They developed a macrocosm–microcosm model, whereby man was the mirror of the universe, and the creation was the reflection of God. The study of nature was therefore an act of true faith, and knowledge of nature came through mystical revelation but also through observation and experiments. Chemistry, esecially, was the means by which man could uncover the secrets of nature and participate in the natural magic of the world. Webster's fourth numbered paragraph outlines a Paracelsian programme.

3 In this paragraph Webster recommends the study of various classical philosophers and of the scholars of the fifteenth–seventeenth centuries who drew on their ideas. They represent various strands of thought, but all were overt opponents of Aristotle, or came from alternative classical traditions. All emphasized practical experimentation and observation rather than reliance on ancient authority.

4 see Note 2.

5 Paracelsians were especially interested in medicine, advocating chemical remedies in place of the traditional cures of Galen. Their ideas brought them into frequent conflict with the medical establishment. Jan van Helmont (?1577–?1644) was a Flemish physician and chemist who opposed much of Paracelsus' mysticism, but adopted many of his specific remedies.

6 Descartes (1596–1650) leading European philosopher and founder of the 'Cartesian' school. He developed the 'mechanical philosophy', explaining all natural phenomena through the motion of matter.

109 John Wilkins

[*Source*: [Set]h [War]d (1654) *Vindiciae Academiarum*, the epistle dedicatory by [Joh]n [Wilkin]s, pp.1–2. A facsimile of the whole work can be found in Debus, editor (1970) *Science and Education*.]

Two grand incapacities for such a work he [Webster] quickly discovers himself guilty of, that are not to be pardoned or excused in such an undertaker.

1 His ignorance of the present state of our universities which he pretends to reform.

2 His ignorance in the common grounds of those arts and sciences which he undertakes to advance and promote. In both which respects he must needs fall under that censure of folly and shame which Solomon doth ascribe unto those that will venture to judge of a matter before they understand it. (Proverbs 18.13)

1 For the present state of the universities, he supposes and takes it for granted that they are so tied up to the dictates of Aristotle, that whatsoever is taught either against or besides him by way of refutation or supply, they do by no means admit of, . . . but are wholly ignorant of it. Which is so notoriously false, that I should very much wonder with what confidence he could suppose it, if I did not find Mr Hobbes[1] likewise guilty of the same mistake. Whereas those that understand these places, do know that there is not to be wished a more general liberty in point of judgement or debate, than what is here allowed. So that there is scarce any hypothesis which hath been formerly or lately entertained by judicious men, and seems to have in it any clearness or consistency, but hath here its strenuous assertors, as the atomical and magnetical in philosophy, the Copernican in astronomy etc.[2]

And though we do very much honour Aristotle for his profound judgement and universal learning, yet are we so far from being tied up to his opinions, that persons of all conditions amongst us take liberty to dissent from him, and to declare against him, according as any contrary evidence doth engage them, being ready to follow the banner of truth by whomsoever it shall be lifted up.

Witness the public lectures of our Professors, the positions or questions maintained in the public exercises of the university for degrees and in the private exercises of colleges, besides the instructions and readings of many tutors, wherein the principal things which this author doth accuse us to be ignorant of, and enemies unto, are taught and owned, and I can assure him they are so well learnt, that for all his contempt of the universities, we have here many young boys, who have not yet attained to that 'very proud and vainglorious title of Bachelors of Art', as he is pleased to phrase it, that are able to reform this reformer in those things wherein he thinks us all so ignorant and himself so great a master.

Notes

1 'Mr Hobbes': Hobbes wrote in *Leviathan*, Chapter 46, that the Aristotelian philsosphy only was taught in the universities. (See also *Leviathan*, Chapters 1 and 30, for Hobbes on the universities.) For Hobbes on Aristotle, see extract 128 below.

2 'the atomical . . .': Wilkins refers to the ideas of the French scientist Pierre Gassendi (1592–1655) who revived classical atomist ideas, arguing that the world was made up of particles of matter in motion; to the work of William Gilbert on magnetism; and to the heliocentric astronomical theories of Copernicus. For Gilbert and Copernicus see also p. 344, Note 1 below.

110 Seth Ward

[*Source*: Ward (1654) *Vindiciae Academiarum*, p.50.]

Our academies are of a more general and comprehensive institution, and as there is a provision here made that whosoever will be excellent in any kind in any art, science or language, may here receive assistance, and be led by the hand till he come to be excellent; so is there a provision likewise, that men be not forced into particular ways, but may receive an institution variously answerable to their genius and design.

Of those very great numbers of youth, which come to our universities, how few are there whose design is to be absolute in natural philosophy? Which of the nobility or gentry desire when they send their sons hither, that they should be set to chemistry, or agriculture, or mechanics? Their removal is from hence commonly in two or three years to the Inns of Court, and the desire of their friends is not that they be engaged in those experimental things, but that their reason and fancy and carriage be improved by lighter institutions and exercises, that they may become rational and graceful speakers, and be of an acceptable behaviour in their countries [localities].

I am persuaded that of all those who come hither for institution, there is not one of many hundreds who, if they may have their option, will give themselves to be accomplished natural philosophers, (such as will, ought certainly to follow this course); the pain is great, the reward but slender, unless we reckon in the pleasure of contemplation; that indeed is great and high, but therefore to draw all men that way, by reason of the pleasure, were to present a feast all of custard or tart, and not to consult the variety of tastes, and tempers of our guests.

SECTION SIXTEEN: JAMES HARRINGTON: PROPERTY AND POLITICAL POWER

[James Harrington was born into a Northamptonshire gentry family in 1611 and had a conventional gentleman's education involving university, Inn of Court and extensive European travel. He took no part in the civil war but served as a personal attendant on Charles I from May 1647–January 1649. The meagre information available about Harrington's personal life does little to explain the development of his political ideas.

In the autumn of 1656 Harrington's first and major work *The Commonwealth of Oceana* was published – a product in part of the disquiet felt in army circles at Cromwell's betrayal of the republican ideals of the 'Good Old Cause'. In discussing the historical development of 'Oceana' (a thinly disguised England) Harrington argued that landed property was the basis of political power, and that changes in land ownership should therefore be accompanied by the transformation of the political structure. The present balance of property in Oceana was suited to a commonwealth or a republic, although this republic would only be secured by the passing of an agrarian law limiting incomes to £2000 p.a. (extract 111). Harrington put forward a precise framework for the foundation of the republic. It was to have both aristocratic and democratic elements: an elected senate – an aristocracy of wealth and wisdom – discussed and proposed legislation while a popular assembly decided on the senate's proposals. The franchise was extended to all except servants but those with incomes of over £100 p.a. were given more weight: only they could vote for the senate, for example. To ensure wide participation and prevent the development of a self-perpetuating oligarchy all offices were to be rotated and voting was by secret ballot.

Harrington's ideas were widely discussed in the period of upheaval between the death of Oliver Cromwell and the Restoration. Harrington issued a stream of pamphlets during these months, and, under the influence of his friend Henry Neville, a member of the restored Rump's Council of State, he presented the ideas of *Oceana* in a simpler way and began to write overtly about England. (Extract 112 from *The Art of Lawgiving* published early in 1659 is an example.) Harrington, Neville and the Leveller leader of the 1640s, John Wildman, were among the organizers of a republican club meeting in 1659–60, first at Bow Street and then as the famous 'Rota Club'. Until the autumn of 1659 Harrington believed that his commonwealth was an immediate possibility although he was alarmed by the oligarchical tendencies of many Rumpers and feared that confusion would lead many to turn again to monarchy.

Harrington published nothing, and wrote little, after March 1660. He suffered a mental and physical collapse during a period of imprisonment in 1661–62 and never fully recovered. He died in 1677, just as his ideas were again becoming influential. A modified 'Harringtonianism' was an element in the late seventeenth century 'country' opposition to increasing executive power while in the next century his theories contributed to the ideology of the American Revolution.

Twentieth-century historians first studied Harrington as an analyst of the economic determinants of political power and of the transition from feudalism to capitalism.[1] However, Harrington's most recent editor argues that he was not interested in economic developments as such; rather he followed Machiavelli in seeing the ability to bear arms as the foundation for individual participation in government, and was concerned to establish the forms of property ownership that made such an independent citizenry possible. On this view, Harrington's importance is as the foremost English exponent of the republican ideas of Machiavelli and the civic humanists.[2]

Notes

1 R.H. Tawney 'Harrington's Interpretation of his Age' *Proceedings of The British Academy* XXVII (1941); extracts from this lecture are included in Volume 2 of this Reader.

2 J.G.A. Pocock's introduction to *The Political Works of James Harrington* (1977).]

111 From The Commonwealth of Oceana, 1656

[*Source:* J.G.A. Pocock, editor (1977) *The political Works of James Harrington*, pp. 163–5.]

[The extract is from 'The Preliminaries, showing the principles of government'.]

Empire is of two kinds, domestic and national, or foreign and provincial.

Domestic empire is founded upon dominion.

Dominion is property real or personal; that is to say in lands, or in money and goods.

Lands, or the parts and parcels of a territory, are held by the proprietor or proprietors, lord or lords of it, in some proportion; and such (except it be in a city that hath little or no land, and whose revenue is in trade) as is the proportion or balance of dominion or property in land, such is the nature of the empire.

If one man be sole landlord of a territory, or overbalance the people, for example, three parts in four, he is grand signor, for so the Turk is called from his property; and his empire is absolute monarchy.

If the few or a nobility, or a nobility with the clergy, be landlords, or overbalance the people unto the like proportion, it makes the Gothic balance (to be shown at large in the second part of this discourse) and the empire is mixed monarchy, as that of Spain, Poland, and late of Oceana.

And if the whole people be landlords, or hold the lands so divided among them, that no one man, or number of men, within the compass of the few or aristocracy, overbalance them, the empire (without the interposition of force) is a commonwealth.

If force be interposed in any of these three cases, it must either frame the government unto the foundation, or the foundation unto the government, or, holding the government not according unto the balance, it is not natural but violent; and therefore, if it be at the devotion of a prince, it is tyranny; if at the devotion of the few, oligarchy; or if in the power of the people, anarchy; each of which confusions, the balance standing otherwise, is but of short continuance, because against the nature of the balance which, not destroyed, destroyeth that which opposeth it.

But there be certain other confusions which, being rooted in the balance, are of longer continuance and of greater horror: as first, where a nobility holdeth half the property, or about that proportion, and the people the other half; in which case, without altering the balance, there is no remedy but the one must eat out the other, as the people did the nobility in Athens, and the nobility the people in Rome. Secondly, when a prince holdeth about half the dominion, and the people the other half – which was the case of the Roman emperors, planted partly upon their military colonies and partly upon the senate and the people – the government becometh a very shambles both of the princes and the people. Somewhat of this nature are certain governments at this day, which are said to subsist by confusion. In this case to fix the balance is to entail misery; but in the three former not to fix it is to lose the government. Wherefore, it being unlawful in Turkey that any should possess land but the grand signor, the balance is fixed by the law, and that empire firm. Nor, though the kings often fell, was the throne of Oceana known to shake, until the statute of alienations broke the pillars, by giving way unto the nobility to sell their estates. *Si terra recedat, Ionium Aegaeo frangat mare.*[1] Lacedaemon, while she held unto her division of land made by Lycurgus,[2] was immovable, but breaking that, could stand no longer. This kind of law fixing the balance in lands is called agrarian, and was first introduced by God himself, who divided the land of Canaan unto his people by lots, and is of such virtue that, wherever it hath held, that government hath not altered, except by consent; as in that unparalleled example of the people of Israel, when being in liberty they would needs choose a king. But without an agrarian, government, whether monarchical, aristocratical or popular, hath no long lease.

For dominion personal or in money, it may now and then stir up a Melius or a Manlius,[3] which, if the commonwealth be not provided with some kind of dictatorian power, may be dangerous, though it have been seldom or never successful; because unto property producing empire, it is required that it should have some certain root or foothold, which, except in land, it cannot have, being otherwise as it were upon the wing.

Neverthless, in such cities as subsist most by trade and have little or no land, as Holland and Genoa, the balance of treasure may be equal unto that of land in the cases mentioned.

But Leviathan, though he seems to skew at antiquity, following his furious master Carneades, hath caught hold of the public sword, unto which he reduceth all manner and matter of government; as where he affirms 'the opinion that any monarch receiveth his power by covenant, that is to say upon condition, to proceed from want of understanding this easy truth, that covenants, being but words and breath, have no force to oblige, contain, constrain or protect any man, but what they have from the public sword'.[4] But as he said of the law that without this sword it is but paper, so he might have thought of this sword that without an hand it is but cold iron. The hand which holdeth this sword is the militia of a nation; and the militia of a nation is either an army in the field, or ready for the field upon occasion. But an army is a beast that hath a great belly and must be fed; wherefore this will come unto what pastures you have, and what pastures you have will come unto the balance of property, without which the public sword is but a name or mere spitfrog.[5] Wherefore, to set that which Leviathan saith of arms and of contracts a little straighter: he that can graze this beast with the great belly, as the Turk doth his timariots [feudal vassals] may well deride him that imagines he received his power by covenant, or is obliged unto any such toy: it being in this case only that covenants are but words and breath. But if the property of the nobility stocked with their tenants and retainers be the pasture of that beast, the ox knows his master's crib; and it is impossible for a king in such a constitution to reign otherwise than by covenant; or if he break it, it is words that come to blows.

Notes

1 'Si terra . . .': 'If the land recedes, the Ionian Sea will break into the Aegean'. (From *Pharsalia*, the Latin epic by Lucan, lines 102–3.)
2 'Lacedaemon . . . Lycurgus': the Greek city state of Sparta, and her legendary legislator.
3 'Melius . . . Manlius': Romans who sought imperial power.
4 'Leviathan . . .': T. Hobbes's *Leviathan* Part 2, Chapter 18.
'Carneades': a sceptical Greek philosopher of the second century B.C.
5 'spit frog': a contemptuous term for a sword.

112 From The Art of Lawgiving, 1659

[*Source*: Pocock, editor (1977) *Political Works of James Harrington*, pp. 606–10.]

CHAPTER II

SHOWING THE VARIATION OF THE ENGLISH BALANCE

The lands in the hold of the nobility and clergy of England, till Henry the Seventh, cannot be esteemed to have over-balanced those in the hold of the people less than four to one. Whereas in our days, the clergy being destroyed, the lands in hold of the people over-balance those in the hold of the nobility, at the least nine in ten. In showing how this change came about, some would have it that I assume unto myself more than my share; albeit they find not me delivering that which must rely upon authority, and not vouching my authors. But Henry the Seventh, being conscious of infirmity in his title, yet finding with what strength and vigour he was brought in by the nobility, conceived jealousies of like power in case of decay or change of affections. *Nondum orbis adoraverat Romam.*[1] The lords yet led country lives; their houses were open to retainers, men experienced in military affairs, and capable of leading; their hospitality was the delight of their tenants, by their tenures or dependence obliged to follow their lords in arms. So that this being the militia of the nation, a few noblemen discontented could at any time levy a great army, the effect whereof, both in the Barons' Wars and those of York and Lancaster, had been well known unto diverse kings. This state of affairs was that at which Henry the Seventh made advantage of troubled times, and frequent unruliness of retainers, to take his aim; while, under pretence of curbing riots, he obtained the passing of such laws as cut off retainers, in which the nobility lost their officers. Then, whereas the dependence of the people upon their lords was of a strict tie or nature, he found means to loosen this also, by laws which he obtained upon as fair a pretence, even that of population. Thus:

> Farms were so brought unto a standard that, the houses being kept up, each of them did of necessity enforce a dweller; and the proportion of land laid unto each house did of necessity enforce that dweller not to be a beggar or cottager, but a man able to keep servants, and set the plough on going. By which means a great part of the lands of this nation came in effect to be amortised [alienated] unto the hold of the yeomanry or middle people,[2]

whereof consisted the main body of the militia, hereby incredibly advanced, and which henceforth, like cleaner underwood less choked by their staddles [roots of felled trees], began to grow exceedingly. But the nobility, who by the former laws had lost their officers, by this lost their soldiery. Yet remained unto them their estates till, the same prince introducing the statutes for alienations, these also became loose; and the lords, less taken (for the reasons shown) with their country lives, where their trains were clipped, by degrees became courtiers – where greater pomp and expense, by the statutes of alienations, began to plume them of their estates. The court was yet at Bridewell, nor reached London any farther than Temple Bar. The latter growth of this city, and in that the declining of the balance unto popularity, deriveth from the decay of the nobility and of the clergy. In the reign of the succeeding king were abbeys (than which nothing more dwarfs a people) demolished. I did not, I do not attribute the effects of these things thus far unto my own particular observation, but always did and do attribute a sense thereof unto the reign of Queen Elizabeth, and the wisdom of her council. There is yet living testimony that the ruin of the English monarchy, through the causes mentioned, was frequently attributed unto Henry VII by Sir Henry Wotton;[3] which tradition is not unlike to have descended upon him from the Queen's council. But there is difference between having a sense of a thing, and making a right use of that sense. Let a man read Plutarch in the lives of Agis and of the Gracchi; there can be no plainer demonstration of the Lacedaemonian [Spartan] or Roman balance; yet read his discourse of government in his *Morals*, and he hath forgotten it; he maketh no use, no mention at all of any such thing. Who could have been plainer upon this point than Sir Walter Ralegh where, to prove that the kings of Egypt were not elective but hereditary, he allegeth that if the kings of Egypt had been elective, 'the children of Pharaoh must have been more mighty than the king, as landlords of all Egypt and the king himself their tenant'?[4] Yet when he cometh to speak of government, he hath no regard unto, no remembrance of, any such principle. In Mr Selden's *Titles of Honour*, he hath demonstrated the English balance of the peerage, without making any application of it, or indeed perceiving it, there or in times when the defect of the same came to give so full a sense of it.[5] The like might be made apparent in Aristotle, in Machiavel, in my Lord Verulam, in all, in any politician; there is not one of them in whom may not be found as right a sense of this principle as in this present narrative, or in whom may be found a righter use of it than was made by any of the parties thus far concerned in this story, or by Queen Elizabeth and her council.

> If a prince (saith a great author), to reform a government, were obliged to depose himself, he might, in neglecting of it, be capable of some excuse, but, reformation of government being that with which a principality may stand, he deserveth no excuse at all. [Machiavelli, *Discourses* 1, 10]

It is indeed not observed by this author that where, through declination of the balance unto popularity, the state requireth reformation in the superstructures, there the prince cannot rightly reform unless from sovereign power he descend unto a principality in a commonwealth; nevertheless upon like occasions this faileth not to be found so in nature and experience. The growth of the people of England, since the ruins mentioned of the nobility and the clergy, came in the reign of Queen Elizabeth to more than stood with the interest, or indeed the nature of well-founded or durable monarchy; as was prudently perceived, but withal temporised, by her council who (if the truth of her government be rightly weighed) seem rather to have put her upon the exercise of principality in a commonwealth, than of sovereign power in a monarchy. Certain it is that she courted not her nobility, nor gave her mind, as monarchs seated upon the like order, to balance her great men, or reflect upon their power now inconsiderable, but ruled wholly (with an art she had unto high perfection) by humouring and blessing her people. For this but shadow of a commonwealth is she yet famous, and shall ever be; though had she introduced the full perfection of the orders requisite unto popular government, first, it had established such principality unto her successors as they might have held. Secondly, this principality (the commonwealth, as Rome of Romulus, being born of such a parent) might have retained the royal dignity and revenue to the full, improved and discharged of all envy.[6] Thirdly, it had saved all the blood and confusion which, through this neglect in her and her successors, hath ensued. Fourthly, it had bequeathed unto the people a light not so naturally by them to be discovered, which is pity;

> For even as the many through the difference of opinions that must needs abound among them, are not apt to introduce a government, as not understanding the good of it, so the many, having by trial or

experience once attained unto this understanding, agree not to quit such a government. [Machiavelli, *Discourses* 1, 9]

And lastly, it had estated this nation in that full facility [possibly felicity] which, so far as concerneth mere prudence, is in the capacity of human nature. To this queen succeeded King James, who likewise regardless of this point (in which nevertheless he was so seen, as not seldom to prophesy sad things unto his successors), neither his new peerage (which in abundance he created) nor the old availed him against that dread wherein, more freely than prudently, he discovered himself to stand of parliaments, as now mere popular councils and running unto popularity of government like a bowl down the hill; not so much (I may say) of malice prepensed, as of natural instinct, whereof the Petition of Right,[7] well heeded, is sufficient testimony. All persuasion of court eloquence, all patience for such as but looked that way, was now lost. There remained nothing unto the destruction of a monarchy retaining but the name, more than a prince who by striving should make the people to feel those advantages which they could not see. And this happened in the next king who, too secure in that undoubted right whereby he was advanced unto a throne which had no foundation, dared to put this unto unseasonable trial; on whom therefore fell the tower in Siloam.[8] Nor may we think that they upon whom this tower fell were sinners above all men; but that we, unless we repent and look better unto foundations, must likewise perish. We have had latter princes, latter parliaments; in what have they excelled, or where are they? The balance not heeded, no effectual work can be made as to settlement; and heeded, as it now stands in England, requireth unto settlement no less than the superstructures natural unto popular government; and the superstructures natural unto popular government require no less than the highest skill or art that is in political architecture. The sum of which particulars amounteth unto this: that the safety of the people of England is now plainly cast upon skill or sufficiency in political architecture. It is not enough that there are honest men addicted unto all the good ends of a commonwealth, unless there be skill also in the formation of those proper means whereby such ends may be attained unto. Which is as sad as a true account; this being in all experience, and in the judgement of all politicians, that whereof the many are incapable. And though the meanest citizen, not informing the commonwealth of what he knoweth or conceiveth to concern her safety, commit an heinous crime against God and his country; such is the temper of later times that a man, having offered any aid at this loss, hath scaped well if he be scorned and not ruined.

But to proceed: if the balance or state of property in a nation be the efficient cause of government, and, the balance being not fixed, the government (as by the present narrative is evinced) must remain inconstant or floating, then the process in formation of a government must be first by fixation of the balance, and next by erecting such superstructures as the nature thereof are necessary.

CHAPTER III

OF FIXATION OF THE BALANCE, OR OF AGRARIAN LAWS

Fixation of the balance of property is not to be provided for but by laws; and the laws whereby such provision is made are commonly called agrarian laws. Now as governments through the diverse balance of property are of diverse or contrary natures, that is monarchical or popular; so are such laws. Monarchy requires of the standard of property that it be vast or great; and of agrarian laws that they bar recess or diminution, at least insomuch as is thereby entailed upon the honour. But popular government requires that her standard be moderate, and that her agrarian bar accumulation. In a territory not exceeding England in revenue, if the balance be in more hands than three hundred,[9] it is upon swaying from monarchy; and if it be in fewer than five thousand hands, it is swaying from a commonwealth; which as to this point may suffice at present.

Notes

1 '*Nondum orbis . . .*': Not yet was Rome adored by the world.
2 A rough quotation from *Oceana*, 'The Second Part of the Preliminaries'; both passages are closely based on Francis Bacon, *History of King Henry VII* (first published 1622).
3 'Sir Henry Wotton': (1568–1639) diplomat and author.
4 'Sir Walter Ralegh . . .': Ralegh, *History of the World* (first published 1614) Book II, Chapter 2, Section 3.
5 John Selden's *Titles of Honour*, first published in 1614, was Harrington's main source for English feudal history.
6 Harrington here noted in the margin: 'The great council of Venice hath the sovereign power, and the Duke the sovereign dignity'.
7 'The Petition of Right': see pp. 35–36.
8 'The tower in Siloam': Luke 13.4.
9 Harrington's marginal note: 'It is at present in more hands, but without fixation may come into fewer.'

113 Aphorisms Political

[*Source*: Pocock, editor (1977) *Political Works of James Harrington*, pp. 762–3 and 770.]

[The first edition was published 25 August 1659 and a second appeared on 12 September. These extracts, from the second edition, reveal Harrington's concern with the immediate political situation.]

I

The errors and sufferings of the people are from their governors.

II

When the foundation of a government cometh to be changed, and the governors change not the superstructures accordingly, the people become miserable.

III

The monarchy of England was not a government by arms, but a government by laws, though imperfect or ineffectual laws.

IV

The latter governments in England have been governments by arms.

V

The people cannot see, but they can feel.

VI

The people, having felt the difference between a government by laws and a government by arms, will always desire the government by laws and abhor that of arms.

VII

Where the spirit of the people is impatient of a government by arms and desirous of a government by laws, there the spirit of the people is not unfit to be trusted with their liberty.

VIII

The spirit of the people of England, not trusted with their liberty, driveth at the restitution of monarchy by blood and violence.

IX

The spirit of the people of England, trusted with their liberty, if the form be sufficient, can never set up a king; and if the form be insufficient (as a parliament with a council in the intervals, or two assemblies co-ordinate), will set up a king without blood or violence.

X

To light upon a good man may be in chance; but to be sure of an assembly of good men is not in prudence.

XI

Where the security is no more than personal, there may be a good monarch, but can be no good commonwealth.

XII

The necessary action or life of each thing is from the nature of the form.

XIII

Where the security is in the persons, the government maketh good men evil; where the security is in the form, the government maketh evil men good.

XIV

Assemblies legitimately elected by the people are that only party which can govern without an army.

XV

Not the party which cannot govern without an army, but the party which can govern without an army, is the refined party, as to this intent and purpose truly refined; that is by popular election, according to the precept of Moses and the rule of Scripture: *Take ye wise men, and understanding, and known among your tribes, and I will make them rulers over you.* [Deuteronomy 1.13]. . . .

LXI

If Sir George Booth[1] had prevailed, he must either have introduced a commonwealth or have restored a king.

LXII

If a king were restored, he must either govern by an army or by parliaments.

LXIII

A king, governing now in England by an army, would for the same causes find the same effects with the late Protector.

LXIV

A king, governing now in England by parliaments, would find the nobility of no effect at all.

LXV

A parliament where the nobility is of no effect at all is a mere popular council.

LXVI

A mere popular council will never receive law from a king.

LXVII

A mere popular council, giving law unto a king, becometh thereby a democracy or equal commonwealth; or the difference is no greater than in the imperfection of the form.

LXVIII

A commonwealth or democracy, to be perfect in the form, must consist especially of such an assembly, the result whereof can go upon no interest whatsoever but that only which is the common interest of the whole people.

LXIX

An assembly consisting of a few may go upon the interest of one man, as a king; or upon the interest of one party, as that of divines, lawyers and the like; or the interest of themselves, and the perpetuation of their government. . . .

Note

1 'Sir George Booth': Cheshire gentleman who led an abortive Presbyterian–royalist uprising in July 1659.

SECTION SEVENTEEN: THE RESTORATION

[The death of Oliver Cromwell in September 1658 was followed by eighteen months of confusion during which Cromwellians, civilian republicans and the military leaders quarrelled among themselves, radicals briefly re-emerged into activity, and conservatives reunited. The intervention of General George Monck, commander of the army in Scotland, ensured the victory of conservatives. Monck and his forces began to march on London in January 1660. At first Monck simply demanded the admission of the excluded members to the restored Rump, but ultimately he secured a new Parliament and the return of the Stuarts. The Convention met on 25 April 1660; Charles II was proclaimed on 8 May, and he entered London on his thirtieth birthday, 29 May. This section shows some of the reactions to the upheavals of these months: the early forebodings of a republican friend of Milton (extract 114); the skilfully drafted declaration of the exiled King (115); a suggestion of the mood in the Convention as the members awaited Charles II (116); the death of a man who did not believe the Good Old Cause was defeated (117); and the determination of the resurgent conservatives who formed Charles II's 'Cavalier Parliament' to prevent a repetition of the events of 1641 (118). (See also Ralph Josselin's comments on the approach of the Restoration p. 125 above.)]

114 Moses Wall to John Milton, 26 May 1659

[*Source*: David Masson (1877) *The Life of John Milton* volume five, p. 602.]

You complain of the non-progressency of the nation, and of its retrograde motion of late, in liberty and spiritual truths. It is much to be bewailed; but yet, let us pity human frailty. When those who had made deep protestations of their zeal for our liberty, both spiritual and civil, and made the fairest offers to be the asserters thereof, and whom we thereupon trusted, – when these, being instated in power, shall betray the good thing committed to them, and lead us back to Egypt, and by that force which we gave them to win us liberty, hold us fast in chains, – what can poor people do? You know who they were that watched our Saviour's sepulchre to keep him from rising.[1] Besides, whilst people are not free, but straitened in accommodations for life, their spirits will be dejected and servile . . . There should be an improving of our native commodities, as our manufactures, our fishery, our fens, forests and commons, and our trade at sea, etc.: which would give the body of the nation a comfortable subsistence. And the breaking that cursed yoke of tithes would much help thereto. Also another thing I cannot but mention, which is that the Norman conquest and tyranny is continued upon the nation without any thought of removing it: I mean the tenure of land by copyhold, and holding for life under a lord, or rather tyrant, of a manor; whereby people care not to improve their land by cost upon it, not knowing how soon themselves or theirs may be outed it, nor what the house is in which they live, for the same reason; and they are far more enslaved to the lord of the manor than the rest of the nation is to a king or supreme magistrate.

We have waited for liberty, but it must be God's work and not man's; who thinks it sweet to maintain his pride and worldly interest to the gratifying of the flesh, whatever becomes of the precious liberty of mankind. But let us not despond, but do our duty; God will carry on that blessed work, in despite of all opposites, and to their ruin if they persist therein.

Note

1 'who they were that watched . . .': soldiers, see Matthew 27. 64–6; 28. 11–15.

115 The Declaration of Breda

[*Source*: J.P. Kenyon (1966) *The Stuart Constitution 1603–1688: Documents and Commentary*, pp.357–8.]

[Issued by Charles II at his court in Breda, Holland, 4 April 1660, published in England 1 May.]

Charles, by the Grace of God, King of England, Scotland, France and Ireland, Defender of the Faith, etc., to all our loving subjects, of what degree or quality soever, greeting. If the general distraction and confusion which is spread over the whole kingdom doth not awaken all men to a desire and longing that those wounds which have so many years together been kept bleeding may be bound up, all we can say will be to no purpose. However, after this long silence we have thought it our duty to declare how much we desire to contribute thereunto, and that, as we can never give over the hope in good time to obtain the possession of that right which God and Nature hath made our due, so we do make it our daily suit to the Divine Providence that he will, in compassion to us and our subjects, after so long misery and sufferings, remit and put us into a quiet and peaceable possession of that our right, with as little blood and damage to our people as is possible. Nor do we desire more to enjoy what is ours, than that all our subjects may enjoy what by law is theirs, by a full and entire administration of justice throughout the land, and by extending our mercy where it is wanted and deserved.

And to the end that the fear of punishment may not engage any, conscious to themselves of what is passed, to a perseverance in guilt for the future, by opposing the quiet and happiness of their country in the restoration both of king, peers and people to their just, ancient and fundamental rights, we do by these presents declare, that we do grant a free and general pardon, which we are ready upon demand to pass under our Great Seal of England, to all our subjects, of what degree or quality soever, who within forty days after the publishing hereof shall lay hold upon this our grace and favour, and shall by any public act declare their doing so, and that they return to the loyalty and obedience of good subjects (excepting only such persons as shall hereafter be excepted by Parliament). Those only excepted, let all our loving subjects, how faulty soever, rely upon the word of a king, solemnly given by this present Declaration, that no crime whatsoever committed against us or our royal father before the publication of this shall ever rise in judgement or be brought in question against any of them, to the least endamagement of them either in their lives, liberties or estates, or (as far forth as lies in our power) so much as to the prejudice of their reputations by any reproach or term of distinction from the rest of our best subjects, we desiring and ordaining that henceforward all notes of discord, separation and difference of parties be utterly abolished among all our subjects, whom we invite and conjure to a perfect union among themselves, under our protection, for the resettlement of our just rights and theirs in a free Parliament, by which, upon the word of a king, we will be advised.

And because the passion and uncharitableness of the times have produced several opinions in religion, by which men are engaged in parties and animosities against each other, which, when they shall hereafter unite in a freedom of conversation, will be composed and better understood, we do declare a liberty to tender consciences, and that no man shall be disquieted or called in question for differences of opinion in matter of religion which do not disturb the peace of the kingdom; and that we shall be ready to consent to such an act of parliament as, upon mature deliberation, shall be offered to us, for the full granting that indulgence.

And because, in the continued distractions of so many years and so many and great revolutions, many grants and purchases of estates have been made, to and by many officers, soldiers and others, who are now possessed of the same, and who may be liable to actions at law upon several titles, we are likewise willing that all such differences, and all things relating to such grants, sales and purchases, shall be determined in Parliament, which can best provide for the just satisfaction of all men who are concerned.

And we do further declare, that we will be ready to consent to any Act or Acts of parliament to the purposes aforesaid, and for the full satisfaction of all arrears due to the officers and soldiers of the army under the command of General Monck, and that they shall be received into our service upon as good pay and conditions as they now enjoy.

116 Richard Baxter

[*Source*: Richard Baxter (1660) *A Sermon of Repentance*, pp.42–4.]

[An extract from Baxter's *Sermon of Repentance* preached before the House of Commons 30 April 1660, at a fast 'for the settling of these nations'. The text was Ezekiel 36. 31: 'Then shall ye remember your own evil ways, and your doings that were not good, and shall lothe yourselves in your own sight for your iniquities and for your abominations.']

O that the Lord would yet show so much mercy to a sinful nation, as to put it into your hearts to promote but the practice of those Christian principles which we are all agreed in. I hope there is no controversy among us whether God should be obeyed and hell avoided, and heaven first sought, and Scripture be the rule and test of our religion, and sin abhorred and cast out. O that you would but further the practice of this with all your might. We crave not of you any lordship or dominion, nor riches, nor interest in your temporal affairs: we had rather see a law to exclude all ecclesiastics from all power of force. The God of heaven that will judge you and us, will be a righteous judge betwixt us, whether we crave anything unreasonable at your hands. These are the sum of our requests: 1. that holiness may be encouraged, and the overspreading prophaneness of this nation effectually kept down; 2. that an able, diligent ministry may be encouraged, and not corrupted by temporal power; 3. that discipline may be seriously promoted, and ministers no more hindered by magistrates in the exercise of their office, than physicians and schoolmasters are in theirs; seeing it is but a government like theirs, consisting in the liberty of conscionable managing the works of our own office that we expect. Give us but leave to labour in Christ's vineyard with such encouragement as the necessity of obstinate souls requireth, and we will ask no more. . . The anti-disciplinarian magistrate I could as resolutely suffer under as the superstitious; it being worse to cast out discipline than to err in the circumstances of it. The question is not, whether bishops or no, but whether discipline or none, and whether enow to use it? 4. We earnestly request that Scripture sufficiency as the test of our religion, and only universal law of Christ may be maintained; and that nothing unnecessary may be imposed as necessary, nor the Church's unity laid on that which will not bear it nor ever did. O that we might but have leave to serve God only as Christ hath commanded us, and to go to heaven in the same way as the Apostles did! These are our desires, and whether they are reasonable God will judge.

Give first to God the things that are God's, and then give Caesar the things that are Caesar's. Let your wisdom be first pure, and then peaceable. Not but that we are resolved to be loyal to sovereignty, though you deny us all these: whatever malicious men pretend, that is not nor shall not be our difference. I have proved more publicly when it was more dangerous to publish it, that the generality of the orthodox, sober ministers and godly people of this nation did never consent to king killing and resisting sovereign power, nor to the change of the ancient government of this land; but abhorred the pride and ambition that attempted it.

117 The Death of Major General Harrison, October 1660

[*Source*: Edmund Ludlow (1978) *A Voyce from the Watch Tower* edited by A.B. Worden, pp.214–16.]

[When Ludlow's editor revised his manuscript for publication in the 1690s, he removed most of the intense, millenarian religious passages to suit the more sedate atmosphere of the late seventeenth century. The changes are clearly seen in the accounts of the deaths of the regicides. In the published *Memoirs*, the regicides die like Roman heroes, in the manuscript they die like 'early Christian martyrs'.[1]

Ludlow's original description of the death of Thomas Harrison provides an example. Harrison rose to high rank in the army, played an important part in the King's trial and was a major inspiration behind the calling of the 'Nominated Parliament' of 1653. His Fifth Monarchist sympathies led him to oppose Cromwell's assumption of personal power, and he was frequently imprisoned in the later 1650s.]

As he was coming forth of the dungeon to suffer . . . said he, 'I do find so much of the power of the Lord coming in, that I am carried far above the fear of death, being going to receive that glorious and incorruptible crown that fades not away, which Christ hath prepared for me.' He assisted the Sergeant to tie the rope about his shoulders and back, desiring his friends to take notice that God had given him power to receive it with thanksgiving. And to a friend, who came weeping to take his leave of him, he said, 'Hinder me not, for I am going about a work for my master'; and looking about him said, 'Sirs, it is easy to follow God when he makes a hedge about us, and liberal provision for us, but it's hard for most to follow him in such a dispensation as this; yet my master and Lord is as sweet and glorious to me now, as he was in the time of my greatest prosperity.' He also said, that according to the light God had given him, he had served him and his country with integrity and uprightness of heart, not willingly nor wittingly wronging any. He professed that death was not terrible to him, having learned to die long ago; and was often heard to say, 'Shall not the Lord do with his own as he pleaseth?' And as he was drawn on the sledge, he was often heard to say with a loud voice, 'Next to the sufferings of Christ, I go to suffer in the most glorious cause that ever was in the world.' And one, as he passed by, asking him in derision where the good old cause was, he with a cheerful smile clapped his hands on his breast and said, 'Here it is, and I go to seal it with my blood.'

In his speech on the ladder, he highly justified the cause wherein he was engaged, and the action for which he suffered; blessing the Lord from his heart that he had accounted him worthy to be instrumental in so glorious a work; professing that his aim in all his proceedings was the glory of God, the good of the people, and the welfare of the Commonwealth; and would have suffered more than this, rather than have fallen in with those who, having been eminent in the work, did wickedly turn aside . . . Then desired all to take notice, that for being instrumental in the cause and interest of the Son of God, which hath been pleaded amongst us, and which God had witnessed to, by appeals and wonderful victories, he was brought to that place to suffer death that day; and if he had ten thousand lives, he could freely and cheerfully lay them down all, to witness to this cause; professing that though he had gone joyfully and willingly many a time to lay down his life upon the account of Christ, yet never with so much joy and freedom as at this time, not laying it down by constraint but willingly . . .

Then, having prayed to himself with tears, he desired the people of God not to have hard thoughts of the good ways of the Lord for all this, for that he, having been for several years in a suffering state, had found the way of God to be a perfect way, his word a perfect word, and he a buckler to those that trust in him; assuring them, that though the people of God might suffer hard things, yet the end would be for his glory, and his people's good; and therefore encouraged them to be cheerful in the Lord, and to hold fast that which they had, and not to be afraid of sufferings, for God would make bitter things sweet, and hard things easy, to those that trusted in him; and that notwithstanding the cloud that was now upon them, the sun would shine, and God would give a testimony to what he had been doing in a short time. And then committing his concernments into the hands of the Lord, and his saviour Jesus Christ, he breathed forth his soul into his bosom, where it rests, singing perpetual hallelujahs.

Note

1 *A Voyce from the Watch Tower*, edited Worden, p. 6; see p. 220 for further discussion of Ludlow's *Memoirs*.

118 The Act Against Tumultuous Petitioning, 1661

[*Source*: C.G. Robertson, editor (First edition 1904; here taken from seventh edition 1942) *Select Statutes, Cases and Documents*, p.26.]

An Act against tumults and disorders, upon pretence of preparing or presenting public petitions, or other addresses to his Majesty or the parliament.

Whereas it hath been found by sad experience, that tumultuous and other disorderly soliciting and procuring of hands by private persons to petitions, complaints, remonstrances and declarations, and other addresses to the King, or to both or either houses of parliament, for alteration of matters established by law, redress of pretended grievances in church or state, or other public concernments, have been made use of to serve the ends of factious and seditious persons gotten into power, to the violation of the public peace, and have been a great means of the late unhappy wars, confusion and calamities in this nation; for preventing the like mischief for the future.

II Be it enacted . . . That no person or persons whatsoever shall from and after the first of August, one thousand six hundred and sixty one, solicit labour or procure the getting of hands, or other consent of any persons above the number of twenty or more, to any petition, complaint, remonstrance, declaration, or other address to the King, or both or either houses of parliament, for alteration of matters established by law in church or state, unless the matter thereof have been first consented unto and ordered by three or more justices of that county, or by the major part of the grand jury of the county . . .

And that no person or persons whatsoever shall repair to his Majesty, or both or either of the houses of parliament, upon pretence of delivering or delivering any petition . . . accompanied with excessive number of people, nor at any one time with above the number of ten persons; upon pain of incurring a penalty not exceeding the sum of one hundred pounds in money, and three months imprisonment . . .

Provided always, That this act, . . . shall not . . . extend to debar or hinder any person or persons, not exceeding the number of ten aforesaid, to present any public or private grievance or complaint to any member or members of parliament after his election . . . or to the King's majesty, for any remedy to be thereupon had; nor to extend to any address whatsoever to his Majesty, by all or any of the members of both or either houses of parliament, during the sitting of parliament, but that they may enjoy their freedom of access to his Majesty, as heretofore hath been used.

SECTION EIGHTEEN: POLITICS AND RELIGION AFTER 1660

[The religious movements that flourished in the freer atmosphere of the 1640s and 1650s (Section Ten above) could not be eliminated by the conservative reaction at the Restoration. Indeed, 1660 marks the start of the permanent division in England between Anglican and Dissenter; the rift between church and chapel that has been an important factor in intellectual, social and political life until very recent times. In 1660–61 one possibility was a policy of comprehension: the broadening of the Church of England so that moderate Presbyterians, at least, could be accommodated within it. In 1661 Charles II summoned an equal number of 'Anglican' and 'Presbyterian' divines to consult at the Savoy Conference about changes in the liturgy and the Prayer Book: Richard Baxter, a participant, describes the failure of this attempt at comprehension (extract 119). An alternative policy – that of toleration for non-conformists outside the Church of England – had been promised by the King in the Declaration of Breda (extract 115 above) but the Cavalier Parliament rejected toleration and embarked instead on the programme of repressive legislation that has become known as the 'Clarendon Code' (although the initiative does not seem to have come from the Lord Chancellor). The Corporation Act (extract 120) sought to exclude dissenters from political power while the Act of Uniformity led to some 1,000 non-conformist ministers losing their livings in 1662, in addition to those who had been forced out after 1660 by the return of ministers removed in the 1640s and 1650s. The Acts against Conventicles made life difficult for inveterate meeting holders like Hanserd Knollys (extract 122). Temporary respite came with the lifting of this legislation by successive royal Declarations of Indulgence in 1662, 1672 (extract 123), 1687 (extract 124), and 1688. However, the Declarations were discredited by their association with the absolutist policies of the Stuart kings, particularly their claim that the royal prerogative included the power to suspend statute law. Toleration won Charles and James little long-term support from dissenters for it was clear that their main aim was the relief of Roman Catholics. Parliament forced the withdrawal of the 1662 Declaration within three months while the Declaration of 1672 lasted just under a year. James II's Declarations hastened the Revolution of 1688. In 1689 a limited and grudging toleration was granted Protestant non-conformists, but it was not until the nineteenth century that religious dissenters were freed of political and educational disabilities.]

119 Richard Baxter: The Savoy Conference

[*Source*: Richard Baxter (1696) *Reliquiae Baxterianae*, edited by Matthew Sylvester, pp.305–7, 333–6, 340, 344–6, 363–5, 369 and 373.]

[The Conference lasted from 5 April until 23 July 1661.]

A meeting was appointed, and the Savoy (the Bishop of London's lodgings) named by them for the place . . . The Archbishop of York[1] (a peaceable man) spake first, and told us that he knew nothing of the business, but perhaps the Bishop of London[2] knew more of the king's mind in it, and therefore was fitter to speak in it than he. The Bishop of London told us that it was not they, but we that had been the seekers of this conference, and that desired alterations in the liturgy; and therefore they had nothing to say or do till we brought in all that we had to say against it in writing, and all the additional forms and alterations which we desired. Our brethren were very much against this motion, and urged the king's commission, which requireth us to meet together, advise and consult . . . But the Bishop of London resolutely insisted on it, not to do anything, till we brought in all our exceptions, alterations and additions at once. In this I confess . . . I was wholly of his mind, and prevailed with my brethren to consent, but I conjecture, upon contrary reasons . . . I told the bishops that we accepted of the task which they imposed on us; yet so as to bring all our exceptions at one time, and all our additions at another time, which they granted.

When we were withdrawn, it pleased our brethren presently to divide the undertaken work: the drawing up of exceptions against the Common Prayer they undertook themselves; . . . the drawing up of the additions or new forms they imposed upon me alone, because I had been guilty of that design from the beginning, and of engaging them in that piece of service (and some of them thought it would prove odious to the Independents, and others who are against a liturgy as such). Hereupon I departed from them, and came among them no more till I had finished my task (which was a fortnight's time). My leisure was too short for the doing of it with that accurateness which a business of that nature doth require . . . and at the fortnight's end I brought it to the other commissioners . . .

When I brought my draft to the brethren I found them but entering on their work of exceptions against the Common Prayer . . . and what passages soever seemed to make the Common Prayer Book odious, or savour of spleen and passion they did reject whoever offered them. My principal business was to keep out such accusations as would not bear weight, and to repress the opinions of one of the brethren . . . who was absolutely against all parts of the Common Prayer, because they had been used by papists to idolatry. And I drew up such faults as in perusing the Common Prayer Book itself did occur to me; and which were they which I most disliked in the forms . . . I always took the faults of the Common Prayer to be chiefly disorder and defectiveness; and so that it was a true worship, though imperfect . . .

When the exceptions against the liturgy were finished, the brethren oft read over the reformed liturgy which I offered them. At first they would have had no rubric or directory, but bare prayers, because they thought our commission allowed it not. That at last they yielded to the reasons which I gave them, and resolved to take them in . . . At this time was the Convocation[3] chosen; for till now it was deferred. Had it been called when the king came in, the inferior clergy would have been against the diocesan and imposing way; but afterwards many hundreds were turned out that all the old sequestered ministers might come in. And the opinion of reordination being set afoot, all those ministers that for twenty years together, while bishops were laid aside, had been ordained without diocesans, were in many countries [areas] denied any voices in the election of clerks for the Convocation: by all which means and by the scruples of abundance of ministers, who thought it unlawful to have anything to do in the choosing of such a kind of assembly, the diocesan party wholly carried it in the choice . . .

When the brethren came to examine the reformed liturgy, and had oft read it over, they passed it at last . . . And because I foresaw what was like to be the end of our conference, I desired the brethren that we might draw up a plain and earnest petition to the bishops, to yield to such terms of peace and concord as they themselves did confess to be lawful to be yielded to . . . We might this way have that opportunity to produce our reasons for peace, which else we were not like to have . . .

When we met with the bishops to deliver in those papers, I was required to deliver them; and if it were possible, to get audience for the petition before all the company. I told them that though we were equals in the present work, and our appointed business was to treat, yet we were conscious of our place and duty, and had drawn up a petition to them which, though somewhat long, I humbly craved their consent that I might read it to them. Some were against it, and so they would have been generally if they had known what was in it but at last they yielded to it. But their patience was never so put to it by us, as in hearing so long and ungrateful a petition . . .

I have reason to think that the generality of the bishops and doctors present never knew what we offered them in the reformed liturgy, nor in this reply, nor in any of our papers, save those few which we read openly to them. For they were put up and carried away, and I conjecture scarce any but the writers of their confutations would be at the labour of reading them over . . . Yea, the chief of them confessed when they bid me read it, that they knew no such thing; so that it seems before they knew what was in them, they resolved to reject our papers, right or wrong, and to deliver them up to their contradictors.

When we came to our debates, I first craved of them their animadversions on our additions and alterations of the liturgy, which we had put in long before; and that they would tell us what they allowed or disallowed in them, that we might have the use of them according to the words in the king's declaration and commission. But they would not by any importunity be entreated at all to debate that, nor to give any of their opinions about those papers . . . [We could] never prevail with them to say anything about them in word or writing . . .

When they had cast out that part of our desired conference, our next business was to desire them by friendly conference to go over the particulars which we excepted against, and to tell us how much they could abate, and what alterations they could yield to. This Bishop Reynolds[4] oft pressed them to, and so did all the rest of us that spake. But they resolutely insisted on it, that they had nothing to do till we had proved that there was any necessity of alteration, which we had not yet done; and that they were there ready to answer to our proofs. We urged them again and again with the very words of the king's declaration and commission . . .

But the bishops would have that to be our task or none; to prove by disputation that any alteration was necessary to be made; while they confuted our proofs . . . And here we were left in a very great strait: if we should enter upon dispute with them, we gave up the end and hope of our endeavours; if we refused it we knew that they would boast that when it came to the setting to, we would not so much as attempt to prove anything unlawful in the liturgy, nor durst dispute it with them . . . But we spoke to the deaf; they had other ends and were other men and had the art to suit the means unto their ends. For my part, when we saw that they would do nothing else, I persuaded our brethren to yield to a disputation with them, and let them understand that we were far from fearing it, seeing they would give us no hopes of concord; but withal, first to profess to them, that the guilt of disappointing his majesty and the kingdom lay not upon us, who desired to obey the king's commission, but on them. And so we yielded to spend the little time remaining in disputing with them, rather than go home and do nothing, and leave them to tell the court that we durst not dispute with them when they so provoked us, nor were able to prove our accusations of the liturgy . . .

When I told them that if they cast out all the Non-conformists, there would not be tolerable ministers enow to supply the congregations, Bishop Morley[5] answered that so it was in the late times, and that some places had no ministers at all, through all those times of usurpation . . . So had these men rather one thousand eight hundred godly faithful ministers were silenced at once and a hundred thousand godly Christians kept out of the Church's communion and persecuted, than one ceremony should be cast out of the church, or left indifferent, or one line reformed in their Common Prayer . . .

This speech they were offended at, and said that I sought to make them odious, by representing them as cruel, and persecutors, as if they intended to silence and cast out so many. And it was one of the greatest matters of offence against me, that I foreknew and foretold them what they were about to do. They said, that this was but to stir up the fears of the people, and cause them to disaffect the government, by talking of silencing us, and casting out the people from communion . . . Our dispute at the Savoy ended, and with it our endeavours for reconciliation upon the warrant of the King's commission . . .

When this work was over, the rest of our brethren met again, and resolved to draw up an account of our endeavours, and present it to his majesty, with our petition for his promised help yet for those alterations and abatements which we could not procure of the bishops; and that first we should acquaint the Lord Chancellor[6] withal, and consult with him about it. Which we did; and as soon as we came to him, according to my expectation, I found him most offended at me, and that I had taken off the distaste and blame from all the rest . . .

When we showed our paper to the Lord Chancellor (which the brethren had desired me to draw up, and had consented to without any alteration) he was not pleased with some passages in it, which he thought too pungent or pressing: but would not bid us put them out . . .

And in the conclusion of this business, seeing we could prevail with these prelates and prelatical men (after so many calamities by divisions, and when they pretended desires of unity) to make no considerable alterations at all; the reason of it seeming unsearchable to some, was by others confidently conjectured to be these:

1 They extremely prejudiced the persons that sought this peace, and therefore were glad of means to cast them out and ruin them.
2 The effects of the Parliament's conquest had exasperated them to the height.
3 They would not have any reformation or change to occasion men to think that ever they were in an error, or that their adversaries had reasonably desired, or had procured a reformation.
4 Some confidently thought that a secret resolution to unite with the papists . . . was the greatest cause of all; and that they would never have lost so great a party, as they did but gain a greater (at home and abroad together) . . .

And now our calamities began to be much greater than before: we were called all by the name of Presbyterians (the odious name), though we never put up one petition for Presbytery, but pleaded for primitive episcopacy. We were represented in the common talk of those who thought it their interest to be our adversaries, as the most seditious people, unworthy to be used like men, or to enjoy our common liberty among them. We could not go abroad but we met with daily reproaches and false stories of us: either we were feigned to be plotting, or to be disaffecting the people.

Notes

1 'The Archbishop of York': Accepted Frewen, son of a Puritan minister.
2 'The Bishop of London': Gilbert Sheldon, Archbishop of Canterbury from 1663 until his death in 1677.

3 'the Convocation': the representative body of the English Church (equivalent to a Parliament).
4 'Bishop Reynolds': Edward Reynolds, Bishop of Norwich, a moderate who sided with the Presbyterians.
5 'Bishop Morley': George Morley, Bishop of Worcester 1660, Bishop of Winchester from 1662.
6 'the Lord Chancellor': Edward Hyde, Earl of Clarendon, see biographical index p. 385.

120 The Corporation Act, 1661

[*Source*: J.P. Kenyon (1966) *The Stuart Constitution 1603–1688 Documents and Commentary*, pp.376–8.]

Whereas questions are likely to arise concerning the validity of elections of magistrates and other officers and members in corporations, as well in respect of removing some as placing others during the late Troubles, contrary to the true intent and meaning of their charters and liberties, and to the end that the succession in such corporations may be most probably perpetuated in the hands of persons well affected to his Majesty and the established government, it being too well known that notwithstanding all his Majesty's endeavours and unparalleled indulgence in pardoning all that is past nevertheless many evil spirits are still working, wherefore for prevention of the like mischief for the time to come and for preservation of the public peace both in Church and State, be it enacted . . .

III . . . that all persons who upon 24 December, 1661, shall be mayors, aldermen, recorders, bailiffs, town clerks, common councilmen and other persons then bearing any office or offices of magistracy, or places or trusts or other employment relating to or concerning the government of the said respective cities, corporations and boroughs and cinque ports and their members, and other port towns, shall at any time before 25 March 1663, when they shall be thereunto required by the said respective commissioners [appointed to enforce the Act] or any three of them, take the Oaths of Allegiance and Supremacy and this oath following:

> I, A.B., do declare and believe that it is not lawful upon any pretence whatsoever to take arms against the King, and that I do abhor the traitorous position of taking arms by his authority against his person or against those that are commissioned by him. So help me God.

And also at the same time shall publicly subscribe before the said commissioners or any three of them the following declaration:

> I, A.B., do declare that I hold that there lies no obligation upon me or any other person from the oath commonly called the Solemn League

and Covenant, and that the same was in itself an unlawful oath and imposed upon the subjects of this realm against the known laws and liberties of the kingdom.

IV And that all such of the said mayors and other the persons aforesaid . . . who shall refuse to take and subscribe the same within the time and in manner aforesaid shall from and immediately after such refusal be by authority of this Act (*ipso facto*) removed and displaced of and from the said offices and places respectively; and the said offices and places from and immediately after such refusal shall . . . be void to all intents and purposes as if the said respective persons so refusing were naturally dead.

V And nevertheless be it enacted . . . that the said commissioners or any five or more of them shall have full power by virtue of this Act by order and warrant under their hands and seals to displace or remove any of the persons aforesaid from the said respective offices . . . if the said commissioners or the major part of them then present shall deem it expedient for the public safety, although such persons shall have taken and subscribed or be willing to take and subscribe the said oaths and declaration.

VI And be it also enacted that the said respective commissioners or any five or more of them as aforesaid shall have power to restore such person or persons as have been illegally or unduly removed into the places out of which he or they were removed, and also to put and place into the offices and places which by any of the ways aforesaid shall be void respectively some other person or persons then being or which have been members or inhabitants of the said respective cities . . .[etc.], and that the said persons, from and after the taking of the said oaths and subscribing the said declaration shall hold and enjoy and be vested in the said offices and places as if they had been duly elected and chosen according to the charters and former usages of the said respective cities . . .

IX Provided also . . . that from and after the expiration of the said commissions no person or persons shall for ever hereafter be placed, elected or chosen in or to any the offices or places aforesaid that shall not have within one year next before such election or choice taken the Sacrament of the Lord's Supper according to the rites of the Church of England, . . . and in default hereof every such placing, election and choice is hereby enacted and declared to be void.

[The Commissioners' powers were to expire on 25 March 1663 and hereafter the oaths were to be administered by the persons empowered under corporation charters to take the normal oaths of office holders, or else by two county JPs.]

121 The Act of Uniformity, 1662

[*Source*: Kenyon (1966) *The Stuart Constitution*, pp.378–81.]

Whereas in the first year of the late Queen Elizabeth there was one uniform Order of Common Service and Prayer and of the administration of Sacraments, Rites and Ceremonies in the Church of England (agreeable to the Word of God and usage of the Primitive Church) compiled by the reverend bishops and clergy, set forth in one book, entitled 'The Book of Common Prayer and Administration of Sacraments and other Rites and Ceremonies in the Church of England', and enjoined to be used by Act of Parliament [1559] . . . very comfortable to all good people desirous to live in Christian conversation and most profitable to the estate of this realm, . . . and yet, this notwithstanding, a great number of people in divers parts of this realm, following their own sensuality and living without knowledge and due fear of God, do wilfully and schismatically abstain and refuse to come to their parish churches, . . . and whereas by the great and scandalous neglect of ministers in using the said order or liturgy so set forth and enjoined as aforesaid great mischiefs and inconveniences during the times of the late unhappy troubles have arisen and grown, and many people have been led into factions and schisms, to the great decay and scandal of the reformed religion of the Church of England, and to the hazard of many souls; for prevention whereof in time to come, for settling the peace of the Church, and for allaying the present distempers which the indisposition of the time hath contracted, the King's Majesty, according to his Declaration of 25 October, 1660, granted his commission under the Great Seal of England to several bishops and other divines to review the Book of Common Prayer . . . Since when time, upon full and mature deliberation, they . . . have accordingly reviewed the said books, and have made some alterations . . . and presented the same unto his Majesty in writing in one book, entitled 'The Book of Common Prayer and Administration of the Sacraments and other Rites and Ceremonies of the Church according to the use of the Church of England, . . .'

Now in regard that nothing conduceth more to the settling of the peace of this nation (which is desired by all good men) nor to the honour of our religion and the propagation thereof than a universal agreement in the public worship of Almighty God, and to the intent that every person within this realm may certainly know the rule to which he is to conform in public worship . . . be it enacted . . . that all and singular ministers in any cathedral, collegiate or parish church or chapel or other place of public worship within this realm . . . shall be bound to say and use the Morning Prayer, Evening Prayer, celebration and administration of both the Sacraments, and all other the public and common prayer in such order and form as is mentioned in the said Book annexed and joined to this present Act . . .

II And to the end that uniformity in the public worship of God (which is so much desired) may be speedily effected, be it further enacted . . . that every parson, vicar or other minister whatsoever who now hath and enjoyeth any ecclesiastical benefice or promotion within this realm of England or places aforesaid shall in the church, chapel or place of public worship belonging to his said benefice or promotion upon some Lord's day before the Feast of St Bartholomew [24 August], 1662, openly, publicly and solemnly read the Morning and Evening Prayer appointed to be read by and according to the said Book of Common Prayer at the times thereby appointed, and after such reading thereof shall openly and publicly before the congregation there assembled declare . . . in these words and no other:

> I, A.B. do declare my unfeigned assent and consent to all and every thing contained and prescribed in and by the book entitled the Book of Common Prayer . . .

III And that all and every such person who shall . . . neglect or refuse to do the same within the time aforesaid . . . shall *ipso facto* be deprived of all his spiritual promotions, and that from henceforth it shall be lawful to and for all patrons and donors of all and singular the said spiritual promotions or any of them according to their respective rights and titles to present or collate to the same as though the person or persons so offending or neglecting were dead . . .

[IV Henceforward any new incumbent was obliged to make this declaration within two months of entering upon his benefice, under pain of deprivation as above.] . . .

VI And be it further enacted . . . that every dean, canon and prebendary of every cathedral or collegiate church, and all masters and other heads, fellows, chaplains and tutors of or in any college, hall, house of learning or hospital, and every public professor and reader in either of the universities and in every college elsewhere, and every parson, vicar, curate,lecturer and every other person in holy orders, and every schoolmaster keeping any public or private schools, and every person instructing or teaching any youth in any house or private family as a tutor or schoolaster, . . . shall before the Feast Day of St Bartholomew, 1662, or at or before his or their respective admission to be incumbent or have possession aforesaid subscribe the Declaration or Acknowledgement following:

> I, A.B., do declare that it is not lawful upon any pretence whatsoever to take arms against the King, and that I do abhor that traitorous position of taking arms by his authority against his person or against those that are commissioned by him, and that I will conform to the liturgy of the Church of England as it is now by law established. *And I do declare that I do hold there lies no obligation upon me or on any other person from the oath commonly called the Solemn League and Covenant*[1] *to endeavour*

any change or alteration of government either in Church or State. And that the same was in itself an unlawful oath and imposed upon the subjects of this realm against the known laws and liberties of this kingdom.

[This oath was to be subscribed before the Vice-chancellors of the universities, archbishops, bishops or other officials, who would give the incumbent a certificate to read to his parishioners, under pain of deprivation, as in III above.]

Note

1 'the Solemn League and Covenant': see p. 104, Note 1.

122 The Life of Hanserd Knollys

[*Source*: *The Life and Death of . . . Mr Hanserd Knollys* (1692), pp.23–5, 32.]

I was . . . Pastor to a Church which I had gathered two or three years before, in the year 1645, with whom I have walked ever since, except that I was absent from the Church sometimes upon just occasions, and with their leave, or forced from them by violent persecution; my chiefest means of livelihood hath been by teaching school . . . I received from the Church always according to their ability, most of the members of the Church being poor; but I coveted no man's gold nor silver, but chose rather to labour, knowing it is more blessed to give than to receive . . . And during twenty five years now past, the Church hath continued in the Apostles' doctrine, fellowship, and in breaking of bread, and in prayer, without division and separation of any part thereof, or party therein; though some particular members being led away by some error in their judgement, have forsaken the assembling of themselves with the Church, as the manner of some is, and was in the Apostles' time. In the year 1660 upon Venner's Rising[1] . . . myself and many other godly and peaceable persons, were taken out of their own dwelling houses, and brought to Woodstreet Compter [prison], and many to Newgate, and other prisons, though we were innocent and knew not of their design; at which time I suffered imprisonment 18 weeks, till we were delivered by an Act of Pardon upon the King's Coronation, unto all offenders, except murderers. We were above four hundred prisoners kept all this time in Newgate, because we refused to take the Oaths of Allegiance and Supremacy. After I was set at liberty out of prison, I went to Holland . . . [After his return to London] By virtue of the Acts of Parliament touching private meetings and conventicles, commencing May the 10th 1670,[2] I was taken at a meeting in George-yard, and the then Lord Mayor committed me to the compter in Bishopsgate for preaching there, but having favour in the eyes of the keepers, I had liberty to preach to the prisoners there, twice every day of the week, in the common hall, where most of the prisoners came and heard me, and some of them blessed God, that ever I came to that prison. Soon after I was set at liberty.

Notes

1 'Venner's Rising': the fifth monarchist plot of January 1661, led by Thomas Venner.
2 'The Acts of Parliament . . . 1670': the Conventicle Act of 1670 imposed fines on those who attended nonconformist religious assemblies. It replaced an Act of 1664, which had expired in 1668.

123 The Declaration of Indulgence, 15 March 1672

[*Source*: Kenyon (1966) *The Stuart Constitution*, pp.407–8.]

Our care and endeavours for the preservation of the rights and interests of the church have been sufficiently manifested to the world by the whole course of our government since our happy restoration, and by the many and frequent ways of coercion that we have used for reducing all erring or dissenting persons, and for composing the unhappy differences in matters of religion which we found among our subjects upon our return. But it being evident by the sad experience of twelve years that there is very little fruit of all those forcible courses, we think ourself obliged to make use of that supreme power in ecclesiastical matters which is not only inherent in us but hath been declared and recognised to be so by several statutes and acts of Parliament; and therefore we do now accordingly issue this our Declaration, as well for the quieting the minds of our good subjects in these points, for inviting strangers in this conjuncture to come and live under us, and for the better encouragement of all to a cheerful following of their trade and callings, from whence we hope by the blessing of God to have many good and happy advantages to our government; as also for preventing for the future the danger that might otherwise arise from private meetings and seditious conventicles.

And in the first place we declare our express resolution, meaning and intention to be, that the Church of England be preserved and remain entire in its doctrine, discipline and government, as now it stands established by law; and that this be taken to be, as it is, the basis, rule and standard of the general and public worship of God, and that the orthodox, conformable clergy do receive and enjoy the revenues belonging thereunto; and that no person, though of a different opinion and persuasion, shall be exempt from paying his tithes or other dues whatsoever. And further, we declare that no person shall be capable of holding any benefice or preferment of any kind in this our kingdom of England who is not exactly conformable.

We do in the next place declare our will and pleasure to be, that the execution of all and all manner of penal laws in matters ecclesiastical, against whatsoever sort of nonconformists or recusants, be immediately suspended; and all judges, judges of assize and gaol-delivery, sheriffs, justices of the peace, mayors, bailiffs and other officers whatsoever, whether ecclesiastical or civil, are to take notice of it, and pay due obedience thereunto.

And that there may be no pretence for any of our subjects to continue their illegal meetings and conventicles, we do declare that we shall from time to time allow a sufficient number of places, as they shall be desired, in all parts of this our kingdom, for the use of such as do not conform to the Church of England, to meet and assemble in in order to their public worship and devotion, which places shall be open and free to all persons.

But to prevent such disorders and inconveniences as may happen by this our indulgence, if not duly regulated, and that they may be the better protected by the civil magistrate, our express will and pleasure is that none of our subjects do presume to meet in any place until such place be allowed, and the teacher of that congregation be approved by us.

And lest any should apprehend that this restriction should make our said allowance and approbation difficult to be obtained, we do further declare that this our indulgence, as to the allowance of the public places of worship and approbation of the teachers, shall extend to all sorts of nonconformists and recusants, except the recusants of the Roman Catholic religion, to whom we shall in no way allow public places of worship, but only indulge them their share in the common exemption from the execution of the penal laws, and the exercise of their worship in their private houses only.

And if after this our clemency and indulgence any of our subjects shall presume to abuse this liberty and shall preach seditiously, or to the derogation of the doctrine, discipline or government of the Established Church, or shall meet in places not allowed by us, we do hereby give them warning, and declare, that we will proceed against them with all imaginable severity; and we will let them see we can be as severe to punish such offenders, when so justly provoked, as we are indulgent to truly tender consciences.

124 The Declaration of Indulgence, 4 April 1687

[*Source*: Kenyon (1966) *The Stuart Constitution*, pp.410–13.]

It having pleased Almighty God not only to bring us to the imperial crown of these kingdoms through the greatest difficulties, but to preserve us by a more than ordinary providence upon the throne of our royal ancestors, there is nothing now that we so earnestly desire as to establish our government on such a foundation as may make our subjects happy, and unite them to us by inclination as well as duty. Which we think can be done by no means so effectually as by granting to them the free exercise of their religion for the time to come, and add that to the perfect enjoyment of their property, which has never been in any case invaded by us since our coming to the crown. Which being the two things men value most, shall ever be preserved in these kingdoms during our reign over them, as the truest methods of their peace and our glory.

We cannot but heartily wish, as it will easily be believed, that all the people of our dominions were members of the Catholic Church, yet we humbly thank Almighty God it is and hath of long time been our constant sense and opinion (which upon divers occasions we have declared), that conscience ought not to be constrained, nor people forced in matters of mere religion. It has ever been directly contrary to our inclination, as we think it is to the interest of government, which it destroys by spoiling trade, depopulating countries and discouraging strangers; and finally, that it never obtained the end for which it was employed. And in this we are the more confirmed by the reflections we have made upon the conduct of the four last reigns. For after all the frequent and pressing endeavours that were used in each of them to reduce this kingdom to an exact conformity in religion, it is visible the success has not answered the design, and that the difficulty is invincible. We therefore, out of our princely care and affection unto all our loving subjects, that they may live at ease and quiet, and for the increase of trade and encouragement of strangers, have thought fit by virtue of our royal prerogative to issue forth this our Declaration of Indulgence, making no doubt of the concurrence of our two houses of Parliament when we shall think it convenient for them to meet.

In the first place we do declare, that we will protect and maintain our archbishops, bishops and clergy, and all other our subjects of the Church of England in the free exercise of their religion as by law established, and in the quiet and full enjoyment of all their possessions, without any molestation or disturbance whatsoever.

We do likewise declare, that it is our royal will and pleasure that from henceforth the execution of all and all manner of penal laws in matters ecclesiastical, for not coming to church, or not receiving the sacrament, or for any other nonconformity to the religion established, or for or by reason of the exercise of religion in any manner whatsoever, be immediately suspended; and the further execution of the said penal laws and every of them is hereby suspended.

And to the end that by the liberty hereby granted the peace and security of the government in the practice thereof may not be endangered, we have thought fit, and do hereby straitly charge and command all our loving subjects, that as we do freely give them leave to meet and serve God after their own way and manner, be it in private houses or places purposely hired or built for that use, so that they take especial care, that nothing be preached or taught amongst them which may any ways tend to alienate the hearts of our people from us or our government, and that their meetings and assemblies be peaceably, openly and publicly held, and all persons freely admitted to them, and that they do signify and make known to some one or more of the next justices of the peace, what place or places they set apart for their uses.

And that all our subjects may enjoy such their religious assemblies with greater assurance and protection, we have thought it requisite, and do hereby command, that no disturbance of any kind be made or given unto them, under pain of our displeasure, and to be further proceeded against with the utmost severity.

And forasmuch as we are desirous to have the benefit of the service of all our loving subjects, which by the law of nature is inseparably annexed to and inherent in our royal person; and that none of our subjects may for the future be under any discouragement or disability (who are otherwise well inclined and fit to serve us) by reason of some oaths or tests that have been usually administered on such occasions, we do hereby further declare, that it is our royal will and pleasure that the oaths commonly called 'the oaths of supremacy and allegiance', and also the several tests and declarations mentioned in the Acts of Parliament made in the 25th and 30th years of the reign of our late royal brother, King Charles II,[1] shall not at any time hereafter be required to be taken, declared or subscribed by any person or persons whatsoever who is or shall be employed in any office or place of trust either civil or military under us, or in our government. And we do further declare it to be our pleasure and intention from time to time hereafter to grant our royal dispensations under our Great Seal to all our loving subjects so to be employed, who shall not take the said oaths, or subscribe or declare the said tests or declarations in the above-mentioned Acts and every of them. . .

[James granted a free pardon to all those who had suffered penalties for religious non-conformity.]

And although the freedom and assurance we have hereby given in relation to religion and property might be sufficient to remove from the minds of our loving subjects all fears and jealousies in relation to either, yet we have thought fit further to declare, that we will maintain them in all their properties and possessions, as well of church and abbey lands as in any other their lands and properties whatsoever.

Note

1 'the several tests and declarations . . .': the 'Test Acts' of 1673 and 1678, here suspended by James. The first Act barred Catholics from holding public office by imposing stringent oaths on all office holders; the second disabled Catholics from sitting in Parliament.

SECTION NINETEEN: SOME EXAMPLES OF ENGLISH PROSE

[Many of the extracts in this volume have been selected for their 'style' as well as for their 'content': they are illustrations of the changes in the use of the English language during the seventeenth century as well as documents with some general historical significance. The passages from Bacon (extract 4), Bastwick (24), Overton (31 and 32; 84 and 85), Winstanley (93–97), Clarendon (12, 19, 22, 26, 28, 30, 37, 43–46, 57, 62), Sprat (139) and Dryden (135) should especially be mentioned in this context.

Many passages were chosen primarily as examples of seventeenth-century prose style (this is not intended to undervalue their content). The sermons of Andrewes and Donne (extracts 125 and 126) are from the 'witty' or 'metaphysical' style of preaching, popular at court in the early part of our period. Extract 127 is one of the best illustrations of Browne's exotic and elaborate prose; while the interest in self-analysis and the discussion of personality, characteristic of the century, is shown in several of the other extracts (128, 129 and 131). In their different ways, the talents of Pepys for observation and vivid description, and Halifax's elegant and ironic political commentaries both bear out Sprat's discussion of prose style in the later seventeenth century, characterized as it was by a 'native easiness' (extracts 129–131; for Sprat see extract 139 below).]

125 Lancelot Andrewes: from Sermon 11 of the Nativity

[*Source*: G.M. Story, editor (1967) Lancelot Andrewes, *Sermons*, pp. 57–8.]

[Preached before the King at Whitehall, Christmas Day 1616; on Psalm 85. 10–11: 'Mercy and truth are met together; righteousness and peace have kissed each other.

Truth shall spring out of the earth; and righteousness shall look down from heaven.']

As for Peace, she went between both,[1] to see, if she could make them meet again in better terms. For, without such a meeting, no good to be done for us.

For, meet they must, and that in other terms, or it will go wrong with us; our salvation lies a bleeding, all this while. The plea hangs, and we stand, as the prisoner at the bar, and know not what shall become of us. For, though two be for us, there are two against us,[2] as strong and more stiff than they. So that, much depends upon this second meeting; upon the composing or taking up this difference. For, these must be at peace between themselves, before they at peace with us, or we with God. And this is sure: we shall never meet in heaven, if they meet no more.

And, many means were made for this meeting, many times; but, it would not be. Where stayed it? It was not long of [owing to] Mercy, she would easily be entreated, to give a new meeting: (no question of her). Oft did she look up to heaven, but Righteousness would not look down: not look? not that? Small hope, she would be got to meet, that would not look that wayward [way].

Indeed, all the question is of her. It is Truth, and she, that holds off: but specially she. Upon the birth (you see) here is no mention of any in particular, but of her; as much to say as, the rest might be dealt with; she only it was, that stood out. And yet, she must be got to meet, or else no meeting.

All the hope is, that she does not refuse simply, never to meet more: but, stands upon satisfaction: else Righteousness should not be righteous. Being satisfied; then, she will: remaining unsatisfied; so, she will not meet.

All stands then on her satisfying; how to devise, to give her satisfaction to her mind, that so she may be content, once more (not to meet and argue, as ere-while, but) to meet, and kiss; meet in a joint concurrence to save us, and set us free.

And (indeed) *hoc opus* [that is the work], there lies all: how to set a song of these four parts, in good harmony; how to make these meet, at a love-day; how to satisfy Justice, upon whom all the stay is.

And this (say I) no Religion in the world doth, or can do, but the

Christian. No queer [choir] sing this psalm, but ours: none make Justice meet, but it. Consequently, none quiet the conscience soundly, but it: consequently, no Religion but it.

Notes
1 'both': Righteousness and Mercy.
2 'though two be for us . . .': Mercy and Peace are for our salvation, Righteousness and Truth, against.

126 John Donne

[*Source*: John Donne (1640) *LXXX Sermons*: (a) pp.776–7; (b) pp.665–6.]

a From a Sermon Preached to the Earl of Carlisle at Sion House

[(?) Autumn 1622, on the text, 'he that believeth not shall be damned' (Mark 16. 16). Sion House, London, belonged to Carlisle's father in law, the Earl of Northumberland.]

When all is done, the hell of hells, the torment of torments is the everlasting absence of God, and the everlasting impossibility of returning to his presence; '*Horrendum est*', says the Apostle, 'It is a fearful thing to fall into the hands of the living God'. Yet there was a case, in which David found an ease, to fall into the hands of God, to 'scape the hands of men: '*Horrendum est*', when God's hand is bent to strike, 'it is a fearful thing, to fall into the hands of the living God'; but to fall out of the hands of the living God, is a horror beyond our expression, beyond our imagination.

That God should let my soul fall out of his hand into a bottomless pit, and roll an unremoveable stone upon it, and leave it to that which it finds there (and it shall find that there which it never imagined, till it came thither) and never think more of that soul, never have more to do with it. That of that providence of God, that studies the life and preservation of every weed, and worm, and ant, and spider, and toad, and viper, there should never, never any beam flow out upon me; that that God, who looked upon me, when I was nothing, and called me when I was not, as though I had been, out of the womb and depth of darkness, will not look upon me now, when, though a miserable, and a banished, and a damned creature, yet I am his creature still, and contribute something to his glory, even in my damnation; that that God, who hath often looked upon me in my foulest uncleanness, and when I had shut out the eye of the day, the sun, and the eye of the night, the taper, and the eyes of all the world, with curtains and windows and doors, did yet see me, and see me in mercy, by making me see that he saw me, and sometimes brought me to a present remorse, and (for that time) to a forbearing of that sin, should so turn himself from me, to his glorious Saints and Angels, as that no Saint nor Angel, nor Christ Jesus himself, should ever pray him to look towards me, never remember him, that such a soul there is; that that God, who hath so often said to my soul, '*Quare morieris*?' Why wilt thou die? and so often sworn to my soul, '*Vivit Dominus*,' as the Lord liveth, I would not have thee die, but live, will neither let me die, nor let me live, but die an everlasting life, and live an everlasting death; that that God, who, when he could not get into me by standing and knocking, by his ordinary means of entering, by his Word, his mercies, hath applied his judgements, and hath shaked the house, this body, with agues and palsies, and set this house on fire, with fevers and calentures, and frighted the master of the house, my soul, with horrors, and heavy apprehensions, and so made an entrance into me; that that God should frustrate all his own purposes and practices upon me, and leave me, and cast me away, as though I had cost him nothing, that this God at last, should let this soul go away, as a smoke, as a vapour, as a bubble, and that then this soul cannot be a smoke, a vapour, nor a bubble, but must lie in darkness, as long as the Lord of light is light itself, and never a spark of that light reach to my soul; what Tophet[1] is not paradise, what brimstone is not amber, what gnashing is not a comfort, what gnawing of the worm is not a tickling, what torment is not a marriage bed to this damnation, to be secluded eternally, eternally, eternally from the sight of God? Especially to us, for as the perpetual loss of that is most heavy, with which we have been best acquainted, and to which we have been most accustomed; so shall this damnation, which consists in the loss of the sight and presence of God, be heavier to us than others, because God hath so graciously, and so evidently, and so diversely appeared to us, in his pillar of fire, in the light of prosperity, and in the pillar of the cloud, in hiding himself for a while from us; we that have seen him in all the parts of this commission, in his word, in his sacraments, and in good example, and not believed, shall be further removed from his sight, in the next world, than they to whom he never appeared in this. But *Vincenti & credenti*, to him that believes aright, and overcome all tentations [temptations] to a wrong belief, God shall give the accomplishment of fulness, and fulness of joy, and joy rooted in glory, and glory established in eternity, and this eternity is God; to him that believes and overcomes, God shall give himself in an everlasting presence and fruition, *Amen*.

Note

1 'Tophet': a high place in Jerusalem where the Jews sacrificed their children to Moloch (Jeremiah 7. 31–2; Isaiah 30. 33).

b From the Second Prebend Sermon

[Preached at St Paul's, 29 January 1626, on the text, 'Because thou hast been my help, therefore in the shadow of thy wings will I rejoice.' (Psalm 63. 7)]

Let me wither and wear out mine age in a discomfortable, in an unwholesome, in a penurious prison, and so pay my debts with my bones, and recompense the wastefulness of my youth with the beggary of mine age; let me wither in a spital[1] under sharp, and foul, and infamous diseases, and so recompense the wantonness of my youth, with that loathsomeness in mine age; yet, if God withdraw not his spiritual blessings, his grace, his patience; if I can call my suffering his doing, my passion his action, all this that is temporal, is but a caterpillar got into one corner of my garden, but a mildew fallen upon one acre of my corn; the body of all, the substance of all is safe, as long as the soul is safe. But when I shall trust to that, which we call a good spirit, and God shall deject, and impoverish, and evacuate that spirit; when I shall rely upon a moral constancy, and God shall shake, and enfeeble, and enervate, destroy and demolish that constancy; when I shall think to refresh myself in the serenity and sweet air of a good conscience, and God shall call up the damps and vapours of hell itself, and spread a cloud of diffidence, and an impenetrable crust of desperation upon my conscience; when health shall fly from me, and I shall lay hold upon riches to succour me, and comfort me in my sickness, and riches shall fly from me, and I shall snatch after favour, and good opinion, to comfort me in my poverty; when even this good opinion shall leave me, and calumnies and misinformations shall prevail against me; when I shall need peace, because there is none but thou, O Lord, that should stand for me, and then shall find, that all the wounds that I have, come from thy hand, all the arrows that stick in me, from thy quiver; when I shall see, that because I have given myself to my corrupt nature, thou hast changed thine; and because I am all evil towards thee, therefore thou hast given over being good towards me; when it comes to this height, that the fever is not in the humours [i.e. the body], but in the spirits; that mine enemy is not an imaginary enemy, fortune, nor a transitory enemy, malice in great persons, but a real, and an irresistible, and an inexorable, and an everlasting enemy, the Lord of Hosts himself, the Almighty God himself; the Almighty God himself only knows the weight of this affliction, and except he put in that *pondus gloriae*, that exceeding weight of an eternal glory, with his own hand into the other scale, we are weighed down, we are swallowed up, irreparably, irrevocably, irrecoverably, irremediably.

Note

1 'spital': a charitable foundation for the reception of the poor and sick.

127 Sir Thomas Browne: Hydriotaphia

[*Source*: R.H.A. Robbins, editor (1972) *Sir Thomas Browne, Religio Medici, Hydriotaphia and the Garden of Cyrus*, pp.126–33.]

[An extract from a meditation on death occasioned by the discovery of Roman burial urns in Norfolk, first published 1658. Notes followed by *B* are Browne's own.]

Now since these dead bones have already outlasted the living ones of Methuselah,[1] and, in a yard under ground and thin walls of clay, outworn all the strong and specious buildings above it, and quietly rested under the drums and tramplings of three conquests[2] – what prince can promise such diuturnity [longlastingness] unto his relics, or might not gladly say,

Sic ego componi versus in ossa velim.[3]

Time, which antiquates antiquities, and hath an art to make dust of all things, hath yet spared these minor monuments. In vain we hope to be known by open and visible conservatories, when to be unknown was the means of their continuation, and obscurity their protection. If they died by violent hands, and were thrust into their urns, these bones become considerable; and some old philosophers would honour them, whose souls they conceived most pure which were thus snatched from their bodies, and to retain a stronger propension [attachment] unto them; whereas they weariedly left a languishing corpse, and with faint desires of reunion. If they fell by long and aged decay, yet, wrapped up in the bundle of time, they fall into indistinction, and make but one blot with infants. If we begin to die when we live, and long life be but a prolongation of death, our life is a sad composition: we live with death, and die not in a moment. How many pulses made up the life of Methuselah were work for Archimedes:[4] common counters sum up the life of Moses[5] his man. Our days become considerable, like petty sums, by minute accumulations; where numerous fractions make up but small round numbers, and our days of a span long make not one little finger.[6]

If the nearness of our last necessity brought a nearer conformity unto it, there were a happiness in hoary hairs, and no calamity in half senses. But the long habit of living indisposeth us for dying, when avarice makes us the sport of death; when even David grew politicly cruel [2 Samuel 8.2], and Solomon could hardly be said to be the wisest of men [1 Kings 11. 1–8].But many are too early old, and before the date of age: adversity stretcheth our days, misery makes Alcmena's nights,[7] and time hath no wings unto it. But the most tedious being is that which can unwish itself, content to be nothing, or never to have been; which was beyond the malcontent of Job, who cursed, not the day of his life, but his nativity [Job 3. 1–16]: content to have so far been as to have a title to future being, although he had lived here but in an hidden state of life, and, as it were, an abortion.

What song the sirens sang, or what name Achilles assumed when he hid himself among women, though puzzling questions,[8] are not beyond all conjecture. What time the persons of these ossuaries entered the famous nations of the dead,[9] and slept with princes and counsellors [Job 3. 13–15, *B*], might admit a wide solution. But who were the proprietaries of these bones, or what bodies these ashes made up, were a question above antiquarism, not to be resolved by man – nor easily perhaps by spirits, except we consult the provincial guardians, or tutelary observators.[10] Had they made as good provision for their names as they have done for their relics, they had not so grossly erred in the art of perpetuation; but to subsist in bones, and be but pyramidally[11] extant, is a fallacy in duration. Vain ashes, which, in the oblivion of names, persons, times, and sexes, have found unto themselves a fruitless continuation, and only arise unto late posterity as emblems of mortal vanities, antidotes against pride, vainglory, and madding vices! Pagan vainglories which thought the world might last for ever had encouragement for ambition, and, finding no Atropos[12] unto the immortality of their names, were never damped with the necessity of oblivion. Even old ambitions had the advantage of ours in the attempts of their vainglories, who, acting early, and before the probable meridian of time,[13] have by this time found great accomplishment of their designs, whereby the ancient heroes have already outlasted their monuments and mechanical [artificial] preservations. But in this latter scene of time we cannot expect such mummies unto our memories, when ambition may fear the prophecy of Elias,[14] and Charles V[15] can never hope to live within two Methuselahs of Hector.[16]

And, therefore, restless inquietude for the diuturnity of our memories, unto present considerations, seems a vanity almost out of date, and superannuated piece of folly. We cannot hope to live so long in our names as some have done in their persons; one face of Janus[17] holds no proportion unto the other. 'Tis too late to be ambitious: the great mutations of the world are acted, or time may be too short for our designs. To extend our memories by monuments, whose death we daily pray for[18] (and whose duration we cannot hope without injury to our expectations) in the advent of the last day, were a contradiction to our beliefs. We whose generations are ordained in this settling part of time are providentially taken off from such imaginations; and, being necessitated to eye the remaining particle of futurity, are naturally constituted unto thoughts of the next world, and cannot excusably decline the consideration of that duration which maketh pyramids pillars of snow, and all that's past a moment. . .

But the iniquity of oblivion blindly scattereth her poppy, and deals with the memory of men without distinction to merit of perpetuity. Who can but pity the founder of the pyramids? Herostratus lives, that burnt the temple of Diana:[19] he is almost lost that built it. Time hath spared the epitaph of Adrian's horse,[20] confounded that of himself. In vain we compute our felicities by the advantage of our good names, since bad have equal durations, and Thersites is like to live as long as Agamemnon.[21] Who knows whether the best of men be known, or whether there be not more remarkable persons forgot than any that stand remembered in the known account of time? Without the favour of the everlasting register, the first man had been as unknown as the last, and Methuselah's long life had been his only chronicle.

Oblivion is not to be hired: the greater part must be content to be as though they had not been, to be found in the register of God, not in the record of man. Twenty-seven names make up the first story [before the flood-*B*], and the recorded names ever since contain not one living century. The number of the dead long exceedeth all that shall live; the night of time far surpasseth the day – and who knows when was the equinox? Every hour adds unto that current arithmetic, which scarce stands one moment. And since death must be the Lucina[22] of life, and even pagans[23] could doubt whether thus to live were to die; since our longest sun sets at right descensions, and makes but winter arches,[24] and therefore it cannot be long before we lie down in darkness, and have our light in ashes;[25] since the brother of death [sleep] daily haunts us with dying mementoes, and time, that grows old itself, bids us hope no long duration – diuturnity is a dream and folly of expectation . . .

Life is a pure flame, and we live by an invisible sun within us. A small fire sufficeth for life: great flames seemed too little after death, while men vainly affected precious pyres, and to burn like Sardanapalus.[26] But the wisdom of funeral laws[27] found the folly of prodigal blazes, and reduced undoing fires unto the rule of sober obsequies, wherein few could be so mean as not to provide wood, pitch, a mourner, and an urn.[28] . . .

Pyramids, arches, obelisks, were but the irregularities of vainglory, and wild enormities of ancient magnanimity. But the most magnanimous resolution rests in the Christian religion, which trampleth upon pride, and sets on the neck of ambition, humbly pursuing that infallible perpetuity unto which all others must diminish their diameters, and be poorly seen in angles of contingency.[29]

Pious spirits who passed their days in raptures of futurity made little more of this world than the world that was before it – while they lay obscure in the chaos of preordination, and night of their fore-beings. And if any have been so happy as truly to understand Christian annihilation, extasis [ecstasy], exolution,[30] liquefaction, transformation, the kiss of the Spouse [God], gustation of God, and ingression into the divine shadow – they have already had an handsome anticipation of heaven: the glory of the world is surely over, and the earth in ashes unto them.

To subsist in lasting monuments; to live in their productions; to exist in their names, and predicament of chimeras,[31] was large satisfaction unto old expectations, and made one part of their Elysiums. But all this is nothing in the metaphysics of true belief. To live indeed is to be again ourselves, which being not only an hope but an evidence in noble believers, 'tis all one to lie in St Innocent's Churchyard[32] as in the sands of Egypt: ready to be anything, in the ecstasy of being ever, and as content with six foot as the moles of Adrianus.[33]

Lucan:[34]
. . . Tabesne cadavera solvat
An rogus haud refert . . .

Notes

1 'Methuselah': who lived 969 years – Genesis 5.27.
2 'thre conquests': Anglo-Saxon, Danish and Norman.
3 '*Sic ego . . .*': Thus let me be placed when I am turned to bones, Tibullus, 3.2.26–*B.*
4 'Archimedes': who calculated the number of grains of sand in the universe.
5 'Moses': of the Psalm of Moses, Psalms 90.10–*B.*
6 'one little finger': according to the ancient arithmetic of the hand wherein the little finger of the right hand, contracted, signified an hundred–*B.*
7 'Alcmena's nights': one night made as long as three by Zeus for his pleasures with Hercules's mother.
8 'puzzling questions': of Tiberius unto grammarians–*B.*
9 'nations of the dead': *Odyssey* 10.526–*B.*
10 'provincial . . . observators': guardian angels of provinces or persons.
11 'pyramidally': as a merely physical relic.
12 'Atropos': the Fate who cut the thread of life.
13 'meridian of time': 1000 B.C., assuming the world to have been created in 4000 B.C, and to last 6000 years.
14 'prophecy of Elias': that the world may last but 6000 years–*B.*
15 'Charles V': the Habsburg Emperor, born in 1500, with only 500 years left before the supposed end of the world.
16 'Hector': Hector's fame lasting above two lives of Methuselah before that famous prince [Charles V] was extant–*B.* Hector was the leading Trojan warrior, killed by Achilles.
17 'Janus': the Roman god with two faces, regarding time past and time to come.
18 'daily pray for': in the Lord's Prayer–'Thy kingdom come'.
19 'Herostratus': who fired the temple to immortalize himself, by coincidence on the night in 356 B.C. when Alexander the Great was born.
20 'Adrian's horse': it is recorded that the Emperor Hadrian had an epitaph inscribed for his horse; one of dubious authenticity was published in the sixteenth century.
21 'Thersites . . . Agamemnon': Thersites was a deformed and scurrilous soldier in the Greek army that besieged Troy; Agamemnon, King of Argos, commanded the same army.
22 'Lucina': Roman goddess of childbirth, and thus of birth itself.
23 'pagans': e.g. Euripides, quoted by Plato, *Gorgias* 492e–*B.*
24 'winter arches': our longest possible life is but as a winter's day.
25 'light in ashes': according to the custom of the Jews, who place a lighted wax candle in a pot of ashes by the corpse–*B.*
26 'Sardanapalus': King of Assyria, who, hopelessly besieged, burnt himself with all his treasures, concubines, and wives.
27 'funeral laws': Cicero, *Laws*, 2.23 (59).
28 'an urn': according to the epitaph of Rufus and Beronica in Gruter, *Inscriptiones Antiquae* (1603, p.xiv. 8): No more was found of their goods than sufficed to buy a pyre, and pitch with which the bodies might be burnt, and a woman hired to weep at the head of the cortege, and an urn bought–*B.*
29 'angles of contingency': the least of angles–*B.*
30 'exolution': release of the soul.
31 'predicament of chimeras': a state of existing only in name or legend.
32 'St Innocent's Churchyard': in Paris, where bodies soon consume–*B.*
33 'moles of Adrianus': a stately mausoleum or sepulchral pile built by Hadrian in Rome, where now standeth the Castle of St Angelo–*B.*
34 'Lucan': *Pharsalia*, 7.809–10: Whether corruption dissolves corpses or a pyre does not matter.

128 John Aubrey: Thomas Hobbes, 1588–1679

[*Source*: Oliver Lawson Dick, editor (1978 Penguin edition) *Aubrey's Brief Lives*: (a) pp.310–11; (b) pp.316–17; (c) pp.317–18.]

a The Writing of the Leviathan

After he began to reflect on the interest of the king of England as touching his affairs between him and parliament, for ten years together his thoughts were much, or almost altogether, unhinged from the mathematics; which was a great putback to his mathematical improvement; for in ten years, or better, discontinuance of that study, especially, one's mathematics will become very rusty.

When the parliament sat that began in April 1640 and was dissolved in May following, and in which many points of the regal power, which were necessary for the peace of the kingdom and safety of his Majesty's person, were disputed and denied, Mr Hobbes wrote a little treatise in English, wherein he did set forth and demonstrate, that the said powers and rights were inseparably annexed to the sovereignty, which sovereignty they did not then deny to be in the king; but it seems understood not, or would not understand, that inseparability. Of this treatise, though not printed, many gentlemen had copies, which occasioned much talk of the author; and had not his Majesty dissolved the Parliament, it had brought him in danger of his life.

Bishop Manwaring (of St David's)[1] preached his doctrine; for which, among others, he was sent prisoner to the Tower. Then thought Mr Hobbes, 'tis time now for me to shift for myself, and so withdrew into France, and resided at Paris. This little MS treatise grew to be his book *De Cive* [published 1642], and at last grew there to be the so formidable LEVIATHAN; the manner of writing of which book (he told me) was thus. He said that he sometimes would set his thoughts upon researching and contemplating always with this rule that he very much and deeply considered one thing at a time (*scilicet*, a week or sometimes a fortnight). He walked much and contemplated, and he had in the head of his staff a pen and ink-horn, carried always a notebook in his pocket, and as soon as a notion darted, he presently entered it into his book, or else he should perhaps have lost it. He had drawn the design of the book into chapters, etc., so he knew whereabout it would come in. Thus that book was made.

He wrote and published the *Leviathan* [in 1651] far from the intention either of disadvantage to his Majesty [Charles II], or to flatter Oliver (who was not made Protector till three or four years after) on purpose to facilitate his return; for there is scarce a page in it that he does not upbraid him.

Note
1 'Bishop Manwaring': Dr Roger Manwaring–see extract 14.

b Hobbes and Religion

Mr Edmund Waller[1] said to me, when I desired him to write some verses in praise of him, that he was afraid of the churchmen: that, what was chiefly to be taken notice of in his eulogy was that he, being but one, and a private person, pulled down all their churches, dispelled the mists of ignorance, and laid open their priest-craft.

There was a report, and surely true, that in Parliament, not long after the King was settled, some of the Bishops made a motion to have the good old gentleman burnt for a heretic. Which, he hearing, feared that his papers might be searched by their order, and he told me he had burnt part of them; among other things, a poem, in Latin hexameter and pentameter, of the encroachment of the clergy (both Roman and Reformed) on the civil power.

That he was a Christian 'tis clear, for he received the sacrament of Dr Pearson, and in his confession to Dr John Cosin,[2] on his (as he thought) death-bed, declared that he liked the religion of the Church of England best of all other.

Notes
1 'Edmund Waller': royalist poet.
2 'Dr Pearson . . . Dr John Cosin': John Pearson, scholar and cleric, Bishop of Chester from 1673 until his death in 1686; Cosin (1594–1672) leading Laudian clergyman before the civil war, and Bishop of Durham from 1660.

c Hobbes and his Contemporaries

Mr Benjamin Jonson, poet laureate, was his loving and familiar friend and acquaintance.

His nephew Francis pretty well resembled his uncle Thomas, especially about the eye; and probably had he had good education might have been ingenious; but he drowned his wit in ale.

When he was at Florence, he contracted a friendship with the famous Galileo Galilei, whom he extremely venerated and magnified; and not only as he was a prodigious wit, but for his sweetness of nature and manners. They pretty well resembled one another as to their countenances, as by their pictures doth appear; both were cheerful and melancholic-sanguine; and had both a consimility [similarity] of fate, to be hated and persecuted by the ecclesiastics.

Mr Robert Hooke loved him, but was never but once in his company.

William Harvey, Dr of Physic and Surgery, inventor of the circulation of the blood, left in his will ten pounds, as a token of his love.

Mr John Dryden, poet laureate, is his great admirer, and oftentimes makes use of his doctrine in his plays – from Mr Dryden himself.

Sir Jonas Moore, mathematician, Surveyor of his Majesty's Ordnance who had a great veneration for Mr Hobbes, and was wont much to lament he fell to the study of the mathematics so late.

Lucius Carey, Lord Falkland was his great friend and admirer, and so was Sir William Petty; both which I have here enrolled amongst those friends I have heard him speak of, but Dr Blackburne[1] left 'em both out, to my admiration [amazement]. I asked him why he had done so. He answered because they were both ignote [unknown] to foreigners.

Descartes and he were acquainted and mutually respected one another. He would say that had he kept himself to geometry he had been the best geometer in the world but that his head did not lie for philosophy.

I have heard him say that Aristotle was the worst teacher that ever was, the worst politician and ethic – a country fellow that could live in the world would be as good: but his *Rhetoric* and *Discourse of Animals* was rare.

He had a high esteem for the Royal Society, having said that natural philosophy was removed from the universities to Gresham College, meaning that Royal Society that meets there; and the Royal Society (generally) had the like for him: and he would long since have been ascribed a member there, but for the sake of one or two persons, whom he took to be his enemies: viz. Dr Wallis (surely their mercuries are in opposition) and Mr Boyle. I might add Sir Paul Neile, who disobliges everybody.[2]

Notes

1 'Dr Blackburne': Richard Blackburne published a Latin biography of Hobbes based largely on Aubrey's material.

2 Of the individuals mentioned by Aubrey, further information on Jonson, Hooke, Wallis, and Boyle will be found in the Biographical Index; for Dryden see Section Twenty below; for Galileo and Harvey see p. 344, Note 1; for Petty p. 332, Note 3; Neile p. 332, Note 5. Lord Falkland: moderate royalist killed during the civil war, close friend of Clarendon; Rene Descartes (1596–1650) French philosopher, mathematician and scientist.

129 Samuel Pepys's Diary, 2 September 1666

[*Source*: Robert Latham and William Matthews, editors (1972) *The Diary of Samuel Pepys* volume seven, pp.267–72.]

[Pepys here describes the start of the Great Fire of London which raged for four days and nights. Some 100,000 people were left homeless, and only one-fifth of the City remained standing. No attempt has been made to note the individuals and places mentioned by Pepys.]

Lords day. Some of our maids sitting up late last night to get things ready against our feast today, Jane called us up, about 3 in the morning, to tell us of a great fire they saw in the City. So I rose, and slipped on my nightgown [dressing gown] and went to her window, and thought it to be on the back side of Mark Lane at the furthest; but being unused to such fires as followed, I thought it far enough off, and so went to bed again and to sleep. About 7 rose again to dress myself, and there looked out at the window and saw the fire not so much as it was, and further off. So to my closet to set things to rights after yesterday's cleaning. By and by Jane comes and tells me that she hears that above 300 houses have been burned down tonight by the fire we saw, and that it was now burning down all Fish Street by London Bridge. So I made myself ready presently, and walked to the Tower and there got up upon one of the high places, Sir J. Robinson's little son going up with me; and there I did see the houses at that end of the bridge all on fire, and an infinite great fire on this and the other side the end of the bridge – which, among other people, did trouble me for poor little Michell and our Sarah on the Bridge. So down, with my heart full of trouble, to the Lieutenant of the Tower, who tells me that it begun this morning in the King's baker's house in Pudding Lane, and that it hath burned down St Magnus Church and most part of Fish Street already. So I down to the water-side and there got a boat and through bridge, and there saw a lamentable fire. Poor Michell's house, as far as the Old Swan, already burned that way and the fire running further, that in a very little time it got as far as the Steelyard while I was there. Everybody endeavouring to remove their goods, and flinging into the river or bringing them into lighters that lay off. Poor people staying in their houses as long as till the very fire touched them, and then running into boats or clambering from one pair of stair by the water-side to another. And among other things, the poor pigeons I perceive were loath to leave their houses, but hovered about the windows and balconies till they were some of them burned, their wings, and fell down.

Having stayed, and in an hour's time seen the fire rage every way, and nobody to my sight endeavouring to quench it, but to remove their goods and leave all to the fire; and having seen it get as far as the Steelyard, and the wind mighty high and driving it into the city, and everything, after so long a drought, proving combustible, even the very stones of churches, and among other things, the poor steeple by which pretty Mrs [Horsley] lives, and whereof my old school-fellow Elborough is parson, taken fire in the very top and there burned till it fall down – I to Whitehall with a gentleman with me who desired to go off from the Tower to see the fire in my boat – to Whitehall, and there up to the King's closet in the chapel, where people came about me and I did give them an account dismayed them all; and word was carried in to the King, so I was called for and did tell the King and Duke of York what I saw, and that unless his Majesty did command houses to be pulled down, nothing could stop the fire. They seemed much troubled, and the King commanded me to go to my Lord Mayor from him and command him to spare no houses but to pull down before the fire every way. The Duke of York bid me to tell him that if he would have any more soldiers, he shall; and so did my Lord Arlington afterward, as a great secret. Here meeting with Captain Cocke, I in his coach, which he lent me, and Creed with me, to Paul's; and there walked along Watling Street as well as I could, every creature coming away loaden with goods to save – and here and there sick people carried away in beds. Extraordinary good goods carried in carts and on backs. At last met my Lord Mayor in Canning Street like a man spent, with a hankercher about his neck. To the King's message, he cried like a fainting woman, 'Lord, what can I do? I am spent! People will not obey me. I have been pull[ing] down houses. But the fire overtakes us faster than we can do it.' That he needed no more soldiers; and that for himself, he must go and refresh himself, having been up all night. So he left me, and I him, and walked home – seeing people all almost distracted and no manner of means used to quench the fire. The houses too, so very thick thereabouts, and full of matter for burning, as pitch and tar, in Thames Street – and warehouses of oil and wines and brandy and other things. Here I saw Mr Isaac Houblon, that handsome man – prettily dressed and dirty at his door at Dowgate, receiving some of his brother's things whose houses were on fire; and as he says, have been removed twice already, and he doubts (as it soon proved) that they must be in a little time removed from his house also – which was a sad consideration. And to see the churches all filling with goods, by people who themselves should have been quietly there at this time.

By this time it was about 12 a-clock, and so home and there find my guests, which was Mr Wood and his wife, Barbary Shelden, and also Mr Moone – she mighty fine, and her husband, for aught I see, a likely man. But Mr Moone's design and mine, which was to look over my closet and please him with the sight thereof, which he hath long desired, was wholly disappointed, for we were in great trouble and disturbance at this fire, not knowing what to think of it. However, we had an extraordinary good dinner, and as merry as at this time we could be.

While at dinner, Mrs Batelier came to enquire after Mr Woolfe and Stanes (who it seems are related to them), whose houses in Fish Street are all burned, and they in a sad condition. She would not stay in the fright.

As soon as dined, I and Moone away and walked through the City, the streets full of nothing but people and horses and carts laden with goods, ready to run over one another, and removing goods from one burned house to another – they now removing out of Canning Street (which received goods in the morning) into Lombard Street and further; and among others, I now saw my little goldsmith Stokes receiving some friend's goods, whose house itself was burned the day after. We parted at Paul's, he home and I to Paul's-Wharf, where I had appointed a boat to attend me; and took in Mr Carcasse and his brother, whom I met in the street, and carried them below and above bridge, to and again, to see the fire, which was now got further, both below and above, and no likelihood of stopping it. Met with the King and Duke of York in their barge, and with them to Queens-hithe and there called Sir R. Browne to them. Their order was only to pull down houses apace, and so below bridge at the water-side; but little was or could be done, the fire coming upon them so fast. Good hopes there was of stopping it at the Three Cranes above, and at Botolphs-Wharf below bridge, if care be used; but the wind carries it into the City, so as we know not by the water-side what it doth there. River full of lighter[s] and boats taking in goods, and good goods swimming in the water; and only, I observed that hardly one lighter or boat in three that had the goods of a house in, but there was a pair of virginals in it. Having seen as much as I could now, I away to Whitehall by appointment, and there walked to St James's Park, and there met my wife and Creed and Wood and his wife and walked to my boat, and there upon the water again, and to the fire up and down, it still increasing and the wind great. So near the fire as we could for smoke; and all over the Thames, with one's face in the wind you were almost burned with a shower of firedrops – this is very true – so as houses were burned by these drops and flakes of fire, three or four, nay five or six houses, one from another. When we could endure no more upon the water, we to a little alehouse on the Bankside over against the Three Cranes, and there stayed till it was dark almost and saw the fire grow; and as it grow darker, appeared more and more, and in corners and upon steeples and between churches and houses, as far as we could see up the hill of the City, in a most horrid malicious bloody flame, not like the fine flame of an ordinary fire. Barbary and her husband away before us. We stayed till, it being darkish, we saw the fire as only one entire arch of fire from this to the other side the bridge, and in a bow up the hill, for an arch of above a mile long. It made me weep to see it. The churches, houses, and all on fire and flaming at once, and a horrid noise the flames made, and the cracking of houses at their ruin. So home with a sad heart, and there find everybody discoursing and lamenting the fire; and poor Tom Hater came with some few of his goods saved out of his house, which is burned upon Fish Street hill. I invited him to lie at my house, and did receive his goods: but was deceived in his lying there, the noise coming every moment of the growth of the Fire, so as we were forced to begin to pack up our own goods and prepare for their removal. And did by moonshine (it being brave, dry, and moonshine and warm weather) carry much of my goods into the garden, and Mr Hater and I did remove my money and iron-chests into my cellar – as thinking that the safest place. And got my bags of gold into my office ready to carry away, and my chief papers of accounts also there, and my tallies into a box by themselves. So great was our fear, as Sir W. Batten had carts come out of the country to fetch away his goods this night. We did put Mr Hater, poor man, to bed a little; but he got but very little rest, so much noise being in my house, taking down of goods.

Halifax

130 The Character of a Trimmer

[*Source*: J.P. Kenyon, editor (1969) *Halifax, Complete Works*; 130: pp.63–4, 101–2; 131: pp 251–2, 255–7 and 265–7.]

[Halifax's 'Trimmer' was an advocate of compromise and moderation, opposed to factions and parties. Most contemporaries, however, applied the term to moderate Anglicans, and a group of 'Trimmers' in Halifax's sense never emerged. This work was circulating in manuscript by the end of 1684, and was first published in 1688. Halifax's authorship was not acknowledged until 1699.]

Our Government is like our climate. There are winds which are sometimes loud and unquiet, and yet with all the trouble they give us, we owe great part of our health unto them; they clear the air, which else would be like a standing pool, and instead of refreshment would be a disease unto us. There may be fresh gales of asserting liberty, without turning into such storms or hurricanes, as that the state should run any hazard of being cast away by them. These strugglings, which are natural to all mixed governments, while they are kept from growing into convulsions do by a mutual agitation from the several parts rather support and strengthen than weaken or maim the constitution; and the whole frame, instead of being torn or disjointed, cometh to be the better and closer knit by being thus exercised. But whatever faults our Government may have, or a discerning critic may find in it when he looketh upon it alone, let any other be set against it, and then it showeth its comparative beauty. Let us look upon the most glittering outside of unbounded authority, and upon a nearer enquiry we shall find nothing but poor and miserable deformity within. Let us imagine a Prince living in his kingdom as if in a great galley, his subjects tugging at the oar, laden with chains, and reduced to real rags, that they may gain him imaginary laurels; let us represent him grazing among his flatterers and receiving their false worship like a child never contradicted and therefore always cozened – or like a lady complimented only to be abused – condemned never to hear truth, and consequently never to do justice, wallowing in the soft bed of wanton and unbridled greatness, not less odious to the instruments themselves than to the objects of his tyranny, blown up into an ambitious dropsy, never to be satisfied by the conquest of other people, or by the oppression of his own. By aiming to be more than a man, he falleth lower than the meanest of them, a mistaken creature, swelled with panegyrics and flattered out of his senses, and not only an encumbrance but a common nuisance to mankind, a hardened and unrelenting soul. Like some creatures that grow fat with poisons, he groweth great by other men's miseries; an ambitious ape of the divine greatness, an unruly giant that would storm even Heaven itself, but that his scaling ladders are not long enough; in short, a wild and devouring creature in rich trappings, and with all his pride no more than a whip in God Almighty's hand, to be thrown into the fire when the world hath been sufficiently scourged with it. This picture, laid in right colours, would not incite men to wish for such a government, but rather to acknowledge the happiness of our own, under which we enjoy all the privilege reasonable men can desire, and avoid all the miseries many others are subject to; so that our Trimmer would fain keep it with all its faults, and doth as little forgive those who give the occasion of breaking it, as he doth those that take it. . .

Our Trimmer . . . dreads a general discontent, because he thinketh it differeth from a rebellion only as a spotted fever doth from the plague, the same species under a lower degree of malignity. It worketh several ways; sometimes like a slow poison that hath its effects at a great distance from the time it was given, sometimes like dry flax prepared to catch at the first fire, or like seed in the ground ready to sprout upon the first shower; in every shape it is fatal, and our Trimmer thinketh no pains or precaution can be too great to prevent it.

In short, he thinketh himself in the right, grounding his opinion upon that truth which equally hateth to be under the oppressions of wrangling sophistry on the one hand or the short dictates of mistaken authority on the other.

Our Trimmer adoreth the goddess Truth, though in all ages she hath been scurvily used, as well as those that worshipped her; it is of late become such a ruining virtue that mankind seemeth to be agreed to commend and avoid it. Yet the want of practice which repealeth the other laws hath no influence upon the Law of Truth, because it hath a root in Heaven, and an intrinsic value in itself that can never be impaired. She showeth her greatness in this, that her enemies even when they are successful are ashamed to own it; nothing but powerful Truth hath the prerogative of triumphing, not only after victories but in spite of them, and to put Conquest herself out of countenance; she may be kept under and suppressed, but her dignity still remaineth with her, even when she is in chains. Falsehood with all her impudence hath not enough to speak ill of her before her face; such majesty she carrieth about her that her most prosperous enemies are fain to whisper their treason. All the power upon earth can never extinguish her; she hath lived in all ages; and let the mistaken zeal of prevailing authority christen any opposition to it with what name they please, she maketh it not only an ugly and unmannerly, but a dangerous thing to persist. She hath lived very retired indeed, nay sometimes so buried that only some few of the discerning part of mankind could have a glimpse of her; with all that she hath eternity in her, she knoweth not how to die, and from the darkest clouds that shade and cover her she breaketh from time to time with triumph for her friends and terror to her enemies.

Our Trimmer, therefore, inspired by this divine virtue, thinketh fit to conclude with these assertions: That our climate is a Trimmer, between that part of the world where men are roasted, and the other where they are frozen; That our Church is a Trimmer between the frenzy of platonic visions and the lethargic ignorance of popish dreams; That our laws are Trimmers, between the excess of unbounded power and the extravagance of liberty not enough restrained; That true virtue hath ever been thought a Trimmer, and to have its dwelling in the middle between the two extremes; that even God Almighty himself is divided between his two great attributes, his mercy and his justice.

In such company, our Trimmer is not ashamed of his name, and willingly leaveth to the bold champions of either extreme the honour of contending with no less adversaries than Nature, Religion, Liberty, Prudence, Humanity and Commonsense.

131 A Character of Charles II

[Written probably in the early 1690s, and first published in 1750.]

His DISSIMULATION

One great objection made to him was the concealing himself, and disguising his thoughts. In this there ought to be a latitude given; it is a defect not to have it at all, and a fault to have it too much. Human nature will not allow the mean; like all other things, as soon as ever men get to do them well, they cannot easily hold from doing them too much. It is the case even in the least things, as singing, etc..

In France he was to dissemble injuries and neglects, from one reason; in England he was to dissemble too, though for other causes. A King upon the throne hath as great temptations (though of another kind) to dissemble as a King in exile. The King of France might have his times of dissembling as much with him, as he could have to do it with the King of France; so he was in a school.

No King can be so little inclined to dissemble but he must needs learn it from his subjects, who every day give him such lessons of it. Dissimulation is like most other qualities, it hath two sides; it is necessary, and yet it is dangerous too. To have none at all layeth a man open to contempt, to have too much exposeth him to suspicion, which is only the less dishonourable inconvenience. If a man doth not take very great precautions, he is never so much showed as when he endeavoureth to hide himself. One man cannot take more pains to hide himself than another will do to see into him, especially in the case of kings.

It is none of the exalted faculties of the mind, since there are chamber-maids will do it better than any prince in Christendom. Men given to dissembling are like rooks [card-sharpers] at play, they will cheat for shillings, they are so used to it. The vulgar definition of dissembling is downright lying; that kind of it which is less ill-bred cometh pretty near it. Only princes and persons of honour must have gentler words given to their faults than the nature of them may in themselves deserve.

Princes dissemble with too many not to have it discovered; no wonder then that he carried it so far that it was discovered. Men compared notes and got evidence, so that those whose morality would give them leave took it for an excuse for serving him ill. Those who knew his face fixed their eyes there and thought it of more importance to see than to hear what he said. His face was as little a blab as most men's, yet though it could not be called a prattling face it would sometimes tell tales to a good observer. When he thought fit to be angry he had a very peevish memory, there was hardly a blot that escaped him. At the same time that this showed the strength of his dissimulation it gave warning too; it fitted his present purpose, but it made a discovery that put men more upon their guard against him. Only self-flattery furnisheth perpetual arguments to trust again; the comfortable opinion men have of themselves keepeth up human society, which would be more than half destroyed without it. . .

HIS CONDUCT TO HIS MINISTERS

He lived with his ministers as he did with his mistresses; he used them, but he was not in love with them. He showed his judgment in this, that he cannot properly be said ever to have had a Favourite, though some might look so at a distance. The present use he might have of them made him throw favours upon them which might lead the lookers on into that mistake; but he tied himself no more to them than they did to him, which implied a sufficient liberty on either side.

Perhaps he made dear purchases. If he seldom gave profusely but where he expected some unreasonable thing, great rewards were material evidences against those who received them.

He was free of access to them, which was a very gaining quality. He had at least as good a memory for the faults of his ministers as for their services, and whenever they fell the whole inventory came out; there was not a slip omitted.

That some of his Ministers seemed to have a superiority did not spring from his resignation to them, but to his ease. He chose rather to be eclipsed than to be troubled.

His brother [later James II] was a minister, and he had his jealousies of him. At the same time that he raised him, he was not displeased to have him lessened. The cunning observers found this out, and at the same time that he reigned in the cabinet he was very familiarly used at the private supper.

A minister turned off is like a lady's waiting woman, that knoweth all her washes, and hath a shrewd guess at her strayings; so there is danger in turning them off as well as in keeping them.

He had back stairs to convey informations to him, as well as for other uses; and though such informations are sometimes dangerous (especially to a Prince that will not take the pains necessary to digest them), yet in the main that humour of hearing everybody against anybody kept those about him in more awe than they would have been without it. I do not believe that ever he trusted any man or any set of men so entirely as not to have some secrets in which they had no share; as this might make him less well served, so in some degree it might make him the less imposed upon.

You may reckon under this article his female ministry; for though he had ministers of the Council, Ministers of the Cabinet and Ministers of the Ruelle [a ladies' salon], the Ruelle was often the last appeal. Those who were not well there were used because they were necessary at the time, not because they were liked, so that their tenure was a little uncertain. His Ministers were to administer business to him as doctors do physic, wrap it up in something to make it less unpleasant; some skilful digressions were so far from being impertinent that they could not many times fix him to a fair audience without them. His aversion to formality made him dislike a serious discourse, if very long, except it was mixed with something to entertain him. Some, even of the graver sort too, used to carry this very far, and rather than fail, use the coarsest kind of youthful talk.

In general, he was upon pretty even terms with his ministers, and could as easily bear their being hanged as some of them could his being abused . . .

CONCLUSION

After all this, when some rough strokes of the pencil have made several parts of the picture look a little hard, it is justice that would be due to every man, much more to a Prince, to make some amends, and to reconcile men as much as may be to it by the last finishing.

He had as good a claim to a kind interpretation as most men. First as a Prince, living and dead, generous and well-bred men will be gentle to them; next as an unfortunate Prince in the beginning of his time, and a gentle one in the rest.

A Prince neither sharpened by his misfortunes whilst abroad nor by his power when restored is such a shining character that it is a reproach not to be so dazzled with it as not to be able to see a fault in its full light. It would be a scandal in this case to have an exact memory. And if all who are akin to his vices should mourn for him, never Prince would be better attended to his grave. He is under the protection of common frailty, that must engage men for their own sakes not to be too severe where they themselves have so much to answer.

What therefore an angry philosopher would call lewdness, let frailer men call a warmth and sweetness of the blood, that would not be confined in the communicating itself; an overflowing of good nature, of which he had such a stream that it would not be restrained within the banks of a crabbed and unsociable virtue.

If he had sometimes less firmness than might have been wished, let the kindest reason be given; and if that should be wanting, the best excuse. I would assign the cause of it to be his loving at any rate to be easy, and his deserving the more to be indulged in it by his desiring that everybody else should be so.

If he sometimes let a servant fall, let it be examined whether he did not weigh so much upon his master as to give him a fair excuse. That yieldingness, whatever foundations it might lay to the disadvantage of posterity, was a specific to preserve us in peace for his own time. If he loved too much to lie upon his own down bed of ease, his subjects had the pleasure during his reign of lolling and stretching upon theirs. As a sword is sooner broken upon a feather bed than upon a table, so his pliantness broke the blow of a present mischief much better than a more immediate resistance would perhaps have done.

Ruin saw this, and therefore removed him first to make way for further overturnings.

If he dissembled, let us remember first, that he was a King, and that dissimulation is a jewel of the crown; next, that it is very hard for a man not to do sometimes too much of that which he concludeth necessary for him to practice. Men should consider that as there would be no false dice if there were no true ones, so if dissembling is grown universal it ceaseth to be foul play, having an implied allowance by the general practice. He that was so often forced to dissemble in his own defence might the better have the privilege sometimes to be the aggressor, and to deal with men at their own weapon.

Subjects are apt to be as arbitrary in their censure as the most assuming Kings can be in their power. If there might be matter for objections, there is not less reason for excuses; the defects laid to his charge are such as may claim indulgence from mankind.

Should nobody throw a stone at his faults but those who are free from them, there would be but a slender shower.

What private man will throw stones at him because he loved? Or what Prince, because he dissembled?

If he either trusted or forgave his enemies, or in some cases neglected his friends more than could in strictness be allowed, let not those errors be so arraigned as take away the privilege that seemeth to be due to princely frailties. If Princes are under the misfortune of being accused to govern ill their subjects have the less right to fall hard upon them, since they generally so little deserve to be governed well.

The truth is, the calling of a King, with all its glittering, hath such an unreasonable weight upon it, that they may rather expect to be lamented than to be envied for being set upon a pinnacle, where they are exposed to censure if they do not do more to answer men's expectations than corrupted nature will allow.

It is but justice therefore to this Prince to give all due softenings to the less shining parts of his life; to offer flowers and leaves to hide, instead of using aggravations to expose them.

Let his royal ashes then lie soft upon him, and cover him from harsh and unkind censures; which though they should not be unjust can never clear themselves from being indecent.

SECTION TWENTY: JOHN DRYDEN

[John Dryden was born in 1631 into a strongly Puritan Northamptonshire gentry family. The Drydens were staunch Parliamentarians and John himself contributed to a volume of poems on Cromwell's death, published in 1659. However, he welcomed the Restoration of Charles II in verse (extract 132) and unlike other intellectuals of the period such as Locke and Newton, he remained a staunch supporter of absolute monarchy. Dryden became Poet Laureate in 1668 and Historiographer Royal in 1670, but in the years following his appointment he devoted himself to drama, rather than poetry. In 1668 he became a shareholder in the Theatre Royal, agreeing to provide three plays a year for the company. In fact he rarely produced more than one in each year, but twenty-one plays appeared between 1663 and 1685, with five more after 1688. Among the best of these are *The Conquest of Granada* (extract 133, 1670/1), *Marriage a la Mode* (1672) and *All for Love* (1677), Dryden's version of the story of Anthony and Cleopatra. In 1681 he published his most famous poem *Absalom and Achitophel* (extract 134) an 'official' satire on the Popish Plot and the Exclusion Crisis. In *Religio Laici* (1682) Dryden attempted to justify – to himself as much as to his audience – the Anglican Church. From 1685, however, he found permanent spiritual satisfaction within Roman Catholicism, and *The Hind and the Panther* (1687) was a verse apologia for that creed. He thus lost all his posts at the Revolution, being replaced by the Whigs' champion, Shadwell, whom he had satirized unmercifully in *MacFlecknoe* (written 1678, published 1684). Dryden's irretrievable loss of official favour led to financial problems while his writings from 1688 until his death in 1700 were less influenced by current events: he concentrated mainly on translation, although he also produced some original verse. Dryden was an immensely prolific and versatile author; he was a pioneering critic as well as a poet, a dramatist and a translator. Apart from the *Essay of Dramatic Poesy*, published separately in 1668, Dryden's critical prose is found in the prefaces to other works (extract 135, preface to extract 134). In the extracts that follow we do no more than suggest the range of Dryden's talents, and we have chosen to emphasize his involvement with the political controversies of his times.]

132 From Astraea Redux: A Poem on the Happy Restoration and Return of His Sacred Majesty Charles II (1660)

[*Source*: W.D. Christie, editor (1871) *Dryden*, pp. 17–19.]

['Astrea' was the classical goddess of justice who lived among men in the golden age, but abandoned the world during the Iron Age. Her return (and Charles's restoration) thus marked a renewal of the golden age.]

. . .
And welcome now, great Monarch, to your own!
Behold the approaching cliffs of Albion;
It is no longer motion cheats your view;
As you meet it, the land approacheth you.
The land returns, and in the white it wears
The marks of penitence and sorrow bears.
But you, whose goodness your descent doth show,
Your heavenly parentage and earthly too,
By that same mildness which your father's crown
Before did ravish, shall secure your own.
Not tied to rules of policy, you find
Revenge less sweet than a forgiving mind.
Thus, when the Almighty would to Moses give
A sight of all he could behold and live,
A voice before His entry did proclaim
Long-suffering, goodness, mercy, in His name.[1]
Your power to justice doth submit your cause,
Your goodness only is above the laws,
Whose rigid letter, while pronounced by you,
Is softer made. So winds, that tempests brew,
When through Arabian groves they take their flight,
Made wanton with rich odours, lose their spite.
And as those lees that trouble it refine
The agitated soul of generous wine,
So tears of joy, for your returning spilt,
Work out and expiate our former guilt.
Methinks I see those crowds on Dover's strand,
Who in their haste to welcome you to land
Choked up the beach with their still growing store
And made a wilder torrent on the shore:
While, spurred with eager thoughts of past delight,
Those who had seen you court a second sight,
Preventing still your steps and making haste

To meet you often wheresoe'er you past.
How shall I speak of that triumphant day,
When you renewed the expiring pomp of May!
A month that owns an interest in your name;
You and the flowers are its peculiar claim.[2]
That star, that at your birth shone out so bright[3]
It stained the duller sun's meridian light,
Did once again its potent fires renew,
Guiding our eyes to find and worship you.
  And now Time's whiter series is begun,[4]
Which in soft centuries shall smoothly run,
Those clouds that overcast your morn shall fly;
Dispelled to farthest corners of the sky.
Our nation, with united interest blest,
Not now content to poise, shall sway the rest.
Abroad your empire shall no limits know,
But, like the sea, in boundless circles flow;
Your much-loved fleet shall with a wide command
Besiege the petty monarchs of the land;
And as old Time his offspring swallowed down,
Our ocean in its depth all seas shall drown.
Their wealthy trade from pirates' rapine free,
Our merchants shall no more adventurers be;
Nor in the farthest East those dangers fear
Which humble Holland must dissemble here.
Spain to your gift alone her Indies owes,
For what the powerful takes not he bestows;
And France that did an exile's presence fear[5]
May justly apprehend you still too near.
At home the hateful names of parties cease,
And factious souls are wearied into peace.
The discontented now are only they
Whose crimes before did your just cause betray:
Of those your edicts some reclaim from sins,
But most your life and blest example wins.
Oh happy Prince, whom Heaven hath taught the way
By paying vows to have more vows to pay!
Oh happy age! Oh times like those alone
By fate reserved for great Augustus' throne,
When the joint growth of arms and arts foreshew
The world a Monarch, and that Monarch you!

Notes

1 Lines 262–5 are taken from Exodus 33.20–23, 34.6.
2 Lines 284–7: Charles II re-entered London on his 30th birthday, 29 May 1660.
3 Line 288, 'That star': a bright star was seen in the day time sky on the day of Charles's birth in 1630; an allusion to the star of Bethlehem is also intended.
4 Line 292, 'whiter': more fortunate.

5 Line 310: under the Anglo-French treaty of October 1655, France agreed not to harbour Charles and other leading royalists. Charles had left France in June 1654 when Mazarin began to move closer to Cromwell.

133 From The Conquest of Granada

[*Source*: First published 1672, under the title *Almanzor and Almahide or the Conquest of Granada by the Spaniards*; here taken from George Saintsbury, editor (1949) *John Dryden* volume one, pp. 44–50.]

[In his preface to the published version of *The Conquest of Granada*, Dryden defined the heroic play thus: 'an heroic play ought to be an imitation, in little, of an heroic poem; and consequently . . . love and valour ought to be the subject of it.' These extravagant dramas were very popular in the 1660s and 1670s, and Dryden's *Conquest of Granada* is one of the finest examples of the genre. Part One, from which our extract is taken, was first performed in December 1670; a second part followed in the next month. The scene is the besieged Moorish city of Granada, just before its fall to the army of the Christian kings of Spain. The passage describes one of the remarkable feats of the hero, Almanzor – his success in quelling the conflict between two factions among the Moors (the Zegrys and the Abencerrages) after the failure of the weak King, Mahomet Boabdelin.]

A confused noise within

Boabdelin: The alarm bell rings from our Alhambra walls,
And from the streets sounds drums and atabals.[1]

Within, a bell, drums and trumpets

Enter a Messenger

How now? from whence proceed these new alarms?
Mess: The two fierce factions are again in arms;
And changing into blood the day's delight,
The Zegrys with the Abencerrages fight;
On each side their allies and friends appear;
The Macas here, the Alabezes there:
The Gazuls with the Bencerrages join,
And, with the Zegrys, all great Gomel's line.
Boab: Draw up behind the Vivarambla place;
Double my guards – these factions I will face:
And try if all the fury they can bring,
Be proof against the presence of their king.

Exit Boab.

The Factions appear: At the head of the Abencerrages, OZMYN; *at the head of the Zegrys,* ZULEMA, HAMET, GOMEL, *and* SELIN: ABENAMAR *and* ABDELMELECH *joined with the Abencerrages.*

Zul: The faint Abercerrages quit their ground;
Press them; put home your thrusts to every wound.
Abdelm: Zegry, on manly force our line relies;
Thine poorly takes the advantage of surprise:
Unarmed and much out-numbered we retreat;
You gain no fame, when basely you defeat.
If thou art brave, seek nobler victory;
Save Moorish blood; and, while our bands stand by,
Let two and two an equal combat try.
Ham: 'Tis not for fear the combat we refuse,
But we our gained advantage will not lose.
Zul: In combating, but two of you will fall;
And we resolve we will despatch you all.
Ozm: We'll double yet the exchange before we die,
And each of ours two lives of yours shall buy.

ALMANZOR[7] *enters betwixt them, as they stand ready to engage*

Alm: I cannot stay to ask which cause is best;
But this is so to me, because opprest.

Goes to the Aben.

To them BOABDELIN *and his guards, going betwixt them*

Boab: On your allegiance, I command you stay;
Who passes here, through me must make his way;
My life's the Isthmus; through this narrow line
You first must cut, before those seas can join.
What fury, Zegrys, has possessed your minds?
What rage the brave Abencerrages blinds?
If of your courage you new proofs would show,
Without much travel you may find a foe.
Those foes are neither so remote nor few,
That you should need each other to pursue.
Lean times and foreign wars should minds unite;
When poor, men mutter, but they seldom fight.
O holy Allah! that I live to see
Thy Granadines assist their enemy!
You fight the Christians' battles; every life
You lavish thus, in this intestine strife,

Does from our weak foundations take one prop
Which helped to hold our sinking country up.
Ozm: 'Tis fit our private enmity should cease;
Though injured first, yet I will first seek peace.
Zul: No, murderer, no; I never will be won
To peace with him, whose hand has slain my son.
Ozm: Our prophet's curse
On me, and all the Abencerrages light,
If, unprovoked, I with your son did fight.
Abdelm: A band of Zegrys ran within the place,
Matched with a troop of thirty of our race.
Your son and Ozmyn the first squadrons led,
Which, ten by ten, like Parthians, charged and fled,
The ground was strowed with canes where we did meet,
Which crackled underneath our coursers' feet:
When Tarifa (I saw him ride apart)
Changed his blunt cane for a steel-pointed dart,
And, meeting Ozmyn next –
Who wanted time for treason to provide –
He basely threw it at him, undefied.
Ozm: (*showing his arms*) Witness this blood – which when by treason sought,
That followed, sir, which to myself I ought.
Zul: His hate to thee was grounded on a grudge,
Which all our generous Zegrys just did judge:
Thy villain-blood thou openly didst place
Above the purple of our kingly race.
Boab: From equal stems their blood both houses draw,
They from Morocco, you from Cordova.
Ham: Their mongrel race is mixed with Christian breed;
Hence 'tis that they those dogs in prisons feed.
Abdelm: Our holy prophet wills, that charity
Should even to birds and beasts extended be:
None knows what fate is for himself designed;
The thought of human chance should make us kind.
Gom: We waste that time we to revenge should give:
Fall on: let no Abencerrago live.
Advancing before the rest of his party.
ALMANZOR, *advancing on the other side, and describing a line with his sword.*
Almanz: Upon thy life pass not this middle space;
Sure death stands guarding the forbidden place.
Gom: To dare that death, I will approach yet nigher
Thus – wert thou compassed in with circling fire.

They fight.

Boab: Disarm them both; if they resist you, kill.
ALMANZOR, *in the midst of the guards, kills* GOMEL, *and then is disarmed.*

Almanz: Now you have but the leavings of my will.
Boab: Kill him! this insolent unknown shall fall,
And be the victim to atone you all.
Ozm: If he must die, not one of us will live:
That life he gave for us, for him we give.
Boab: It was a traitor's voice that spoke those words;
So are you all, who do not sheathe your swords.
Zul: Outrage unpunished, when a prince is by,
Forfeits to scorn the rights of majesty:
No subject his protection can expect,
Who what he owes himself does first neglect.
Aben: This stranger, sir, is he,
Who lately in the Vivarambla place
Did, with so loud applause, your triumphs grace.
Boab: The word which I have given, I'll not revoke;
If he be brave, he's ready for the stroke.
Almanz: No man has more contempt than I of breath
But whence hast thou the right to give me death?
Obeyed as sovereign by thy subjects be,
But know, that I alone am king of me.
I am as free as nature first made man,
Ere the base laws of servitude began,
When wild in woods the noble savage ran.
Boab: Since, then, no power above your own you know,
Mankind should use you like a common foe;
You should be hunted like a beast of prey:
By your own law I take your life away.
Almanz: My laws are made but only for my sake;
No king against himself a law can make.
If thou pretend'st to be a prince like me,
Blame not an act, which should thy pattern be.
I saw the oppressed, and thought it did belong
To a king's office to redress the wrong:
I brought that succour, which thou ought'st to bring,
And so, in nature, am thy subjects' king.
Boab: I do not want your counsel to direct,
Or aid to help me punish or protect.
Almanz: Thou want'st them both, or better thou wouldst know,
Than to let factions in thy kingdom grow.
Divided interests, while thou think'st to sway,
Draw, like two brooks, thy middle stream away:
For though they band and jar, yet both combine
To make their greatness by the fall of thine.
Thus, like a buckler, thou art held in sight,
While they behind thee with each other fight.
Boab: Away, and execute him instantly!

To his Guards.

Almanz: Stand off; I have not leisure yet to die.

To them, enter ABDALLA,
[the King's brother] *hastily*

Abdal: Hold, sir! for heaven's sake hold!
Defer this noble stranger's punishment,
Or your rash orders, you will soon repent.
Boab: Brother, you know not yet his insolence.
Abdal: Upon yourself you punish his offence:
If we treat gallant strangers in this sort,
Mankind will shun the inhospitable court:
And who, henceforth, to our defence will come,
If death must be the brave Almanzor's doom?
From Africa I drew him to your aid,
And for his succour have his life betrayed.
Boab: Is this the Almanzor whom at Fez you knew,
When first their swords the Xeriff brothers[3] drew?
Abdal: This, sir, is he, who for the elder fought,
And to the juster cause the conquest brought;
Till the proud Santo, seated on the throne,
Disdained the service he had done to own:
Then to the vanquished part his fate he led:
The vanquished triumphed, and the victor fled.
Vast is his courage, boundless is his mind,
Rough as a storm, and humorous as wind:
Honour's the only idol of his eyes;
The charms of beauty like a pest he flies;
And, raised by valour from a birth unknown,
Acknowledges no power above his own.
Boabdelin coming to Almanzor.
Boab: Impute your danger to our ignorance:
The bravest men are subject most to chance:
Granada much does to your kindness owe;
But towns, expecting sieges, cannot show
More honour, than to invite you to a foe.
Almanz: I do not doubt but I have been to blame:
But, to pursue the end for which I came,
Unite your subjects first; then let us go,
And pour their common rage upon the foe.
Boab: (*to the Factions*). Lay down your arms, and let me beg you cease
Your enmities.
Zul: We will not hear of peace,
Till we by force have first revenged our slain.
Abdelm: The action we have done we will maintain.
Selin: Then let the king depart, and we will try
Our cause by arms.
Zul: For us and victory.
Boab: A king entreats you.
Almanz: What subjects will precarious kings regard?

A beggar speaks too softly to be heard:
Lay down your arms! 'tis I command you now.
Do it – or, by our prophet's soul I vow,
My hands shall right your king on him I seize.
Now let me see whose look but disobeys.
All: Long live King Mahomet Boabdelin!
Almanz: No more; but hushed as midnight silence go:
He will not have your acclamations now.
Hence, you unthinking crowd! –
The Common People go off on both parties.
Empire, thou poor and despicable thing,
When such as these make or unmake a king!
Abdal: How much of virtue lies in one great soul,
Embracing him.
Whose single force can multitudes control!

Notes

1 'atabals': kettle drums.
2 Almanzor is modelled chiefly on the Greek hero Achilles.
3 'Xeriff brothers': of the royal family of Morocco.

134 Absalom and Achitophel: A Poem

[*Source*: Philip Roberts, editor (1973) *Absalom and Achitophel and other Poems*, pp. 22–53.]

[*Absalom and Achitophel* was published in November 1681, shortly before the Earl of Shaftesbury's trial for high treason. It was intended as support for Charles II's counter-attack against the Whigs after the royal tribulations of the Popish Plot and the Exclusion Crisis. The biblical story of David and Absalom, from which Dryden took only what was relevant to his purposes, is found in 2 Samuel. 13–19.]

Si propius stes
Te capiet magis.[1]

TO THE READER

It is not my intention to make an apology for my poem: some will think it needs no excuse, and others will receive none. The design, I am sure, is honest; but he who draws his pen for one party must expect to make enemies of the other. For wit and fool are consequents of Whig and Tory; and every man is a knave or an ass to the contrary side. There's a treasury of merits in the Fanatic Church, as well as in the Papist; and a pennyworth to be had of saintship, honesty, and poetry, for the lewd, the factious, and the blockheads; but the longest chapter in Deuteronomy has not curses enough for an anti-Bromingham [a Tory]. My comfort is, their manifest prejudice to my cause will render their judgment of less authority against me. Yet if a poem have a genius, it will force its own reception in the world; for there's a sweetness in good verse, which tickles even while it hurts, and no man can be heartily angry with him who pleases him against his will. The commendation of adversaries is the greatest triumph of a writer, because it never comes unless extorted. But I can be satisfied on more easy terms: if I happen to please the more moderate sort, I shall be sure of an honest party, and, in all probability, of the best judges; for the least concerned are commonly the least corrupt. And, I confess, I have laid in for those, by rebating the satire (where justice would allow it) from carrying too sharp an edge. They who can criticise so weakly, as to imagine I have done my worst, may be convinced, at their own cost, that I can write severely with more ease than I can gently. I have but laughed at some men's follies, when I could have declaimed against their vices; and other men's virtues I have commended, as freely as I have taxed their crimes. And now, if you are a malicious reader, I expect you should return upon me that I affect to be thought more impartial than I am. But if men are not to be judged by their professions, God forgive you Commonwealth's-men [republicans], for professing so plausibly for the government. You cannot be so unconscionable as to charge me for not subscribing of my name; for that would reflect too grossly upon your own party, who never dare, though they have the advantage of a jury to secure them. If you like not my poem, the fault may, possibly, be in my writing (though it is hard for an author to judge against himself); but, more probably, it is in your morals, which cannot bear the truth of it. The violent, on both sides, will condemn the character of Absalom, as either too favourably or too hardly drawn. But they are not the violent whom I desire to please. The fault on the right hand is to extenuate, palliate, and indulge; and, to confess freely, I have endeavoured to commit it. Besides the respect which I owe his birth, I have a greater for his heroic virtues; and David himself could not be more tender of the young man's life than I would be of his reputation. But since the most excellent natures are always the most easy, and, as being such, are the soonest perverted by ill counsels, especially when baited with fame and glory; it is no more a wonder that he withstood not the temptations of Achitophel, than it was for Adam not to have resisted the two devils, the serpent and the woman. The conclusion of the story I purposely forbore to prosecute, because I could not obtain from myself to show Absalom unfortunate. The frame of it was cut out but for a picture to the waist, and if the draught be so far true, it is as much as I designed.

Were I the inventor, who am only the historian, I should certainly conclude the piece with the reconcilement of Absalom to David. And who knows but this may come to pass? Things were not brought to an extremity where I left the story; there seems yet to be room left for a composure; hereafter there may only be for pity. I have not as much as an uncharitable wish against Achitophel, but am content to be accused of a good-natured error, and to hope with Origen,[2] that the Devil himself may at last be saved. For which reason, in this poem, he is neither brought to set his house in order, nor to dispose of his person afterwards as he in wisdom shall think fit. God is infinitely merciful; and his vicegerent is only not so, because he is not infinite.

The true end of satire is the amendment of vices by correction. And he who writes honestly is no more an enemy to the offender, than the physician to the patient, when he prescribes harsh remedies to an inveterate disease; for those are only in order to prevent the chirurgeon's work of an *ense rescindendum* [something that has to be cut off with the sword], which I wish not to my very enemies. To conclude all: if the body politic have any analogy to the natural, in my weak judgment, an act of oblivion were as necessary in a hot, distempered state, as an opiate would be in a raging fever.

[Notes
1 '*Si propius . . .*': from Horace *De Arte Poetica* – 'if you stand closer, you will find it more attractive.'
2 'Origen': Christian theologian of the first half of the third century.]

In pious times, ere priestcraft did begin,
Before polygamy was made a sin;
When man on many multiplied his kind,
Ere one to one was cursedly confined;
When nature prompted, and no law denied
Promiscuous use of concubine and bride;
Then Israel's monarch[1] after Heaven's own heart,
His vigorous warmth did variously impart
To wives and slaves; and, wide as his command,
Scattered his Maker's image through the land.
Michal,[2] of royal blood, the crown did wear;
A soil ungrateful to the tiller's care:
Not so the rest; for several mothers bore
To godlike David several sons before.
But since like slaves his bed they did ascend,
No true succession could their seed attend.
Of all this numerous progeny was none
So beautiful, so brave, as Absolon[3]
Whether, inspired by some diviner lust,
His father got him with a greater gust;
Or that his conscious destiny made way,
By manly beauty, to imperial sway.
Early in foreign fields he won renown,
With kings and states allied to Israel's crown:
In peace the thoughts of war he could remove,
And seemed as he were only born for love.
Whate'er he did, was done with so much ease,

In him alone 'twas natural to please:
His motions all accompanied with grace;
And Paradise was opened in his face.
With secret joy indulgent David viewed
His youthful image in his son renewed:
To all his wishes nothing he denied;
And made the charming Annabel[4] his bride.
What faults he had (for who from faults is free?)
His father could not, or he would not see.
Some warm excesses which the law forbore,
Were construed youth that purged by boiling o'er,
And Amnon's murder,[5] by a specious name,
Was called a just revenge for injured fame.
Thus praised and loved the noble youth remained,
While David, undisturbed, in Sion[6] reigned.
But life can never be sincerely blest;
Heaven punishes the bad, and proves[7] the best.
The Jews,[8] a headstrong, moody, murmuring race,
As ever tried th'extent and stretch of grace;
God's pampered people, whom, debauched with ease,
No king could govern, nor no God could please
(Gods they had tried of every shape and size,
That god-smiths could produce, or priests devise);
These Adam-wits,[9] too fortunately free,
Began to dream they wanted liberty;
And when no rule, no precedent was found,
Of men by laws less circumscribed and bound;
They led their wild desires to woods and caves,
And thought that all but savages were slaves.
They who, when Saul was dead, without a blow,
Made foolish Ishbosheth the crown forgo;[10]
Who banished David did from Hebron[11] bring,
And with a general shout proclaimed him king:
Those very Jews, who, at their very best,
Their humour[12] more than loyalty expressed,
Now wondered why so long they had obeyed
An idol monarch, which their hands had made;
Thought they might ruin him they could create,
Or melt him to that golden calf, a State.[13]
But these were random bolts; no formed design,
Nor interest made the factious crowd to join:
The sober part of Israel, free from stain,
Well knew the value of a peaceful reign,
And, looking backward with a wise affright,
Saw seams of wounds, dishonest[14] to the sight:
In contemplation of whose ugly scars
They cursed the memory of civil wars.
The moderate sort of men, thus qualified,

Inclined the balance to the better side;
And David's mildness managed it so well,
The bad found no occasion to rebel.
But when to sin our biased nature leans,
The careful Devil is still at hand with means;
And providently pimps for ill desires.
The Good Old Cause[15] revived, a plot requires:
Plots, true or false, are necessary things,
To raise up commonwealths, and ruin kings.
   Th' inhabitants of old Jerusalem[16]
Were Jebusites;[17] the town so called from them;
And theirs the native right –
But when the chosen people[18] grew more strong,
The rightful cause at length became the wrong;
And every loss the men of Jebus bore,
They still were thought God's enemies the more.
Thus worn and weakened, well or ill content,
Submit they must to David's government:
Impoverished and deprived of all command,
Their taxes doubled as they lost their land;
And, what was harder yet to flesh and blood,
Their gods disgraced, and burnt like common wood.
This set the heathen priesthood in a flame;
For priests of all religions are the same:
Of whatsoe'er descent their godhead be,
Stock, stone, or other homely pedigree,
In his defence his servants are as bold,
As if he had been born of beaten gold.
The Jewish rabbins, though their enemies,
In this conclude them honest men and wise:
For 'twas their duty, all the learned think,
T'espouse his cause, by whom they eat and drink.
From hence began that Plot,[19] the nation's curse,
Bad in itself, but represented worse;
Raised in extremes, and in extremes decried;
With oaths affirmed, with dying vows denied;
Not weighed or winnowed by the multitude;
But swallowed in the mass, unchewed and crude.
Some truth there was, but dashed and brewed with lies,
To please the fools, and puzzle all the wise.
Succeeding times did equal folly call,
Believing nothing, or believing all.
Th'Egyptian rites[20] the Jebusites embraced;
Where gods were recommended by their taste.
Such savoury deities must needs be good,
As served at once for worship and for food.[21]
By force they could not introduce these gods,
For ten to one in former days was odds;

So fraud was used (the sacrificer's[22] trade):
Fools are more hard to conquer than persuade.
Their busy teachers mingled with the Jews,
And raked for converts even the court and stews:[23]
Which Hebrew priests the more unkindly took,
Because the fleece[24] accompanies the flock.
Some thought they God's anointed meant to slay
By guns, invented since full many a day:
Our author swears it not; but who can know
How far the Devil and Jebusites may go?
This Plot, which failed for want of common sense,
Had yet a deep and dangerous consequence:
For, as when raging fevers boil the blood,
The standing lake soon floats into a flood,
And every hostile humour,[25] which before
Slept quiet in its channels, bubbles o'er;
So several factions from this first ferment
Work up to foam, and threat the government.
Some by their friends, more by themselves thought wise,
Opposed the power to which they could not rise.
Some had in courts been great, and thrown from thence,
Like fiends were hardened in impenitence.
Some, by their monarch's fatal mercy, grown
From pardoned rebels kinsmen to the throne,
Were raised in power and public office high;
Strong bands, if bands ungrateful men could tie.
  Of these the false Achitophel[26] was first;
A name to all succeeding ages cursed:
For close designs and crooked counsels fit;
Sagacious, bold, and turbulent of wit;
Restless, unfixed in principles and place;
In power unplèased, impatient of disgrace:
A fiery soul, which, working out its way,
Fretted the pigmy body to decay,
And o'er-informed the tenement of clay.
A daring pilot in extremity;
Pleased with the danger, when the waves went high,
He sought the storms; but, for a calm unfit,
Would steer too nigh the sands, to boast his wit.
Great wits are sure to madness near allied,
And thin partitions do their bounds divide;
Else why should he, with wealth and honour blest,
Refuse his age the needful hours of rest?
Punish a body which he could not please;
Bankrupt of life, yet prodigal of ease?
And all to leave what with his toil he won,
To that unfeathered two-legged thing, a son;
Got, while his soul did huddled notions try;

And born a shapeless lump, like anarchy.
In friendship false, implacable in hate;
Resolved to ruin or to rule the State.
To compass this the Triple Bond[27] he broke;
The pillars of the public safety shook;
And fitted Israel for a foreign yoke:[28]
Then seized with fear, yet still affecting fame,
Usurped a patriot's all-atoning name.
So easy still it proves in factious times,
With public zeal to cancel private crimes.
How safe is treason, and how sacred ill,
Where none can sin against the people's will!
Where crowds can wink, and no offence be known,
Since in another's guilt they find their own!
Yet fame deserved no enemy can grudge;
The statesman we abhor, but praise the judge.
In Israel's courts ne'er sat an Abbethdin[29]
With more discerning eyes, or hands more clean;
Unbribed, unsought, the wretched to redress;
Swift of dispatch, and easy of access.
O! had he been content to serve the crown,
With virtues only proper to the gown;
Or had the rankness of the soil been freed
From cockle, that oppressed the noble seed;
David for him his tuneful harp had strung,
And Heaven had wanted one immortal song.[30]
But wild Ambition loves to slide, not stand,
And Fortune's ice prefers to Virtue's land.
Achitophel, grown weary to possess
A lawful fame, and lazy happiness,
Disdained the golden fruit to gather free,
And lent the crowd his arm to shake the tree.
Now, manifest of crimes contrived long since,
He stood at bold defiance with his prince;
Held up the buckler of the people's cause
Against the crown, and skulked behind the laws.
The wished occasion of the Plot he takes;
Some circumstances finds, but more he makes.
By buzzing emissaries fills the ears
Of listening crowds with jealousies and fears
Of arbitrary counsels brought to light,
And proves the king himself a Jebusite.[31]
Weak arguments! which yet he knew full well
Were strong with people easy to rebel.
For, governed by the moon, the giddy Jews
Tread the same track when she the prime renews;
And once in twenty years, their scribes record,
By natural instinct they change their lord.

Achitophel still wants a chief, and none
Was found so fit as warlike Absalom:
Not that he wished his greatness to create
(For politicians neither love nor hate),
But, for he knew his title not allowed,
Would keep him still depending on the crowd:
That kingly power, thus ebbing out, might be
Drawn to the dregs of a democracy.[32]
Him he attempts with studied arts to please,
And sheds his venom in such words as these:
'Auspicious prince, at whose nativity
Some royal planet ruled the southern sky;
Thy longing country's darling and desire;
Their cloudy pillar and their guardian fire:
Their second Moses, whose extended wand
Divides the seas, and shows the promised land;
Whose dawning day in every distant age
Has exercised the sacred prophets' rage:
The people's prayer, the glad diviners' theme,
The young men's vision, and the old men's dream!
Thee, Saviour, thee, the nation's vows confess,
And, never satisfied with seeing, bless:
Swift unbespoken pomps thy steps proclaim,
And stammering babes are taught to lisp thy name.
How long wilt thou the general joy detain,
Starve and defraud the people of thy reign?
Content ingloriously to pass thy days
Like one of Virtue's fools that feeds on praise;
Till thy fresh glories, which now shine so bright,
Grow stale and tarnish with our daily sight.
Believe me, royal youth, thy fruit must be
Or gathered ripe, or rot upon the tree.[33]
Heaven has to all allotted, soon or late,
Some lucky revolution of their fate;
Whose motions if we watch and guide with skill
(For human good depends on human will),
Our Fortune rolls as from a smooth descent,
And from the first impression takes the bent:
But, if unseized, she glides away like wind,
And leaves repenting Folly far behind.
Now, now she meets you with a glorious prize,
And spreads her locks before her as she flies.
Had thus old David, from whose loins you spring,
Not dared, when Fortune called him, to be king,
At Gath[34] an exile he might still remain,
And Heaven's anointing oil had been in vain.
Let his successful youth your hopes engage;
But shun the example of declining age:

Behold him setting in his western skies,
The shadows length'ning as the vapours rise.
He is not now, as when on Jordan's sand[35]
The joyful people thronged to see him land,
Covering the beach, and blackening all the strand;
But, like the Prince of Angels, from his height
Comes tumbling downward with diminished light;
Betrayed by one poor plot to public scorn
(Our only blessing since his cursed return);
Those heaps of people which one sheaf did bind,
Blown off and scattered by a puff of wind.
What strength can he to your designs oppose,
Naked of friends, and round beset with foes?
If Pharaoh's[36] doubtful succour he should use,
A foreign aid would more incense the Jews:
Proud Egypt would dissembled friendship bring;
Foment the war, but not support the king:
Nor would the royal party e'er unite
With Pharaoh's arms t'assist the Jebusite;
Or if they should, their interest soon would break,
And with such odious aid make David weak.
All sorts of men by my successful arts,
Abhorring kings, estrange their altered hearts
From David's rule: and 'tis the general cry,
"Religion, commonwealth, and liberty."
If you, as champion of the public good,
Add to their arms a chief of royal blood,
What may not Israel hope, and what applause
Might such a general gain by such a cause?
Not barren praise alone, that gaudy flower
Fair only to the sight, but solid power;
And nobler is a limited command,
Given by love of all your native land,
Than a successive title, long and dark,
Drawn from the mouldy rolls of Noah's ark.'
  What cannot praise effect in mighty minds,
When flattery soothes, and when ambition blinds!
Desire of power, on earth a vicious weed,
Yet, sprung from high, is of celestial seed:
In God 'tis glory; and when men aspire,
'Tis but a spark too much of heavenly fire.
The ambitious youth, too covetous of fame,
Too full of angels' metal in his frame,
Unwarily was led from virtue's ways,
Made drunk with honour, and debauched with praise.
Half loth, and half consenting to the ill
(For loyal blood within him struggled still),
He thus replied: 'And what pretence have I

To take up arms for public liberty?
My father governs with unquestioned right;
The faith's defender, and mankind's delight;
Good, gracious, just, observant of the laws:
And Heaven by wonders has espoused his cause.
Whom has he wronged in all his peaceful reign?
Who sues for justice to his throne in vain?
What millions has he pardoned of his foes,
Whom just revenge did to his wrath expose?
Mild, easy, humble, studious of our good;
Inclined to mercy, and averse from blood;
If mildness ill with stubborn Israel suit,
His crime is God's beloved attribute.
What could he gain, his people to betray,
Or change his right for arbitrary sway?
Let haughty Pharaoh curse with such a reign
His fruitful Nile, and yoke a servile train.
If David's rule Jerusalem displease,
The Dog-star heats their brains to this disease.
Why then should I, encouraging the bad,
Turn rebel and run popularly mad?
Were he a tyrant, who, by lawless might
Oppressed the Jews, and raised the Jebusite,
Well might I mourn; but nature's holy bands
Would curb my spirits and restrain my hands:
The people might assert their liberty;
But what was right in them were crime in me.
His favour leaves me nothing to require,
Prevents[37] my wishes, and outruns desire.
What more can I expect while David lives?
All but his kingly diadem he gives:
And that' – But there he paused; then sighing, said –
'Is justly destined for a worthier head.
For when my father from his toils shall rest,
And late augment the number of the blessed,
His lawful issue shall the throne ascend,
Or the collateral line, where that shall end.
His brother,[38] though oppressed with vulgar spite,
Yet dauntless, and secure of native right,
Of every royal virtue stands possessed;
Still dear to all the bravest and the best.
His courage foes, his friends his truth proclaim;
His loyalty the king, the world his fame.
His mercy even th'offending crowd will find;
For sure he comes of a forgiving kind.
Why should I then repine at Heaven's decree,
Which gives me no pretence to royalty?
Yet O that fate, propitiously inclined,

Had raised my birth, or had debased my mind;
To my large soul not all her treasure lent,
And then betrayed it to a mean descent!
I find, I find my mounting spirits bold,
And David's part disdains my mother's mould.
Why am I scanted by a niggard birth?
My soul disclaims the kindred of her earth;
And, made for empire, whispers me within,
"Desire of greatness is a godlike sin." '
  Him staggering so when hell's dire agent found,
While fainting Virtue scarce maintained her ground,
He pours fresh forces in, and thus replies:
  'The eternal God, supremely good and wise,
Imparts not these prodigious gifts in vain:
What wonders are reserved to bless your reign!
Against your will, your arguments have shown,
Such virtue's only given to guide a throne.
Not that your father's mildness I contemn;
But manly force becomes the diadem.
'Tis true he grants hey crave;
And more, perhaps, than subjects ought to have:
For lavish grants suppose a monarch tame,
And more his goodness than his wit proclaim.
But when should people strive their bonds to break,
If not when kings are negligent or weak?
Let him give on till he can give no more,
The thrifty Sanhedrin[39] shall keep him poor;
And every shekel which he can receive,
Shall cost a limb of his prerogative.
To ply him with new plots shall be my care;
Or plunge him deep in some expensive war;
Which when his treasure can no more supply,
He must, with the remains of kingship, buy.
His faithful friends, our jealousies and fears
Call Jebusites, and Pharaoh's pensioners;
Whom when our fury from his aid has torn,
He shall be naked left to public scorn.
The next successor, whom I fear and hate,
My arts have made obnoxious to the State;
Turned all his virtues to his overthrow,
And gained our elders to pronounce a foe.
His right, for sums of necessary gold,
Shall first be pawned, and afterwards be sold;
Till time shall ever-wanting David draw,
To pass your doubtful title into law:
If not, the people have a right supreme
To make their kings; for kings are made for them.
All empire is no more than power in trust,

Which, when resumed, can be no longer just.
Succession, for the general good designed,
In its own wrong a nation cannot bind;
If altering that the people can relieve,
Better one suffer than a nation grieve.
The Jews well know their power: ere Saul they chose,
God was their king, and God they durst depose.[40]
Urge now your piety, your filial name,
A father's right, and fear of future fame;
The public good, that universal call,
To which even Heaven submitted, answers all.
Nor let his love enchant your generous mind;
'Tis Nature's trick to propagate her kind.
Our fond begetters, who would never die,
Love but themselves in their posterity.
Or let his kindness by th'effects be tried,
Or let him lay his vain pretence aside.
God said he loved your father; could he bring
A better proof, than to anoint him king?
It surely showed he loved the shepherd well,
Who gave so fair a flock as Israel.
Would David have you thought his darling son?
What means he then, to alienate the crown?
The name of godly he may blush to bear:
'Tis after God's own heart to cheat his heir.
He to his brother gives supreme command,
To you a legacy of barren land:
Perhaps th'old harp, on which he thrums his lays,
Or some dull Hebrew ballad in your praise.
Then the next heir, a prince severe and wise,
Already looks on you with jealous eyes;
Sees through the thin disguises of your arts,
And marks your progress in the people's hearts.
Though now his mighty soul its grief contains,
He meditates revenge who least complains;
And, like a lion, slumbering in the way,
Or sleep dissembling, while he waits his prey,
His fearless foes within his distance draws,
Constrains his roaring, and contracts his paws:
Till at the last, his time for fury found,
He shoots with sudden vengeance from the ground;
The prostrate vulgar[41] passes o'er and spares,
But with a lordly rage his hunter tears.
Your case no tame expedients will afford:
Resolve on death, or conquest by the sword,
Which for no less a stake than life you draw;
And self-defence is nature's eldest law.
Leave the warm people no considering time;

For then rebellion may be thought a crime.
Prevail[42] yourself of what occasion gives,
But try your title while your father lives;
And that your arms may have a fair pretence,
Proclaim you take them in the king's defence,
Whose sacred life each minute would expose
To plots, from seeming friends, and secret foes.
And who can sound the depth of David's soul?
Perhaps his fear his kindness may control.
He fears his brother, though he loves his son,
For plighted vows too late to be undone.
If so, by force he wishes to be gained;
Like women's lechery, to seem constrained.
Doubt not: but, when he most affects the frown,
Commit a pleasing rape upon the crown.
Secure his person to secure your cause:
They who possess the prince, possess the laws.'
He said, and this advice above the rest,
With Absalom's mild nature suited best:
Unblamed of life (ambition set aside),
Not stained with cruelty, nor puffed with pride;
How happy had he been, if destiny
Had higher placed his birth, or not so high!
His kingly virtues might have claimed a throne,
And blessed all other countries but his own.
But charming greatness since so few refuse,
'Tis juster to lament him than accuse.
Strong were his hopes a rival to remove,
With blandishments to gain the public love;
To head the faction while their zeal was hot,
And popularly prosecute the Plot.
To further this, Achitophel unites
The malcontents of all the Israelites;
Whose differing parties he could wisely join,
For several ends, to serve the same design:
The best (and of the princes some were such)
Who thought the power of monarchy too much;
Mistaken men, and patriots in their hearts;
Not wicked, but seduced by impious arts.
By these the springs of property were bent,
And wound so high, they cracked the government.
The next for interest sought to embroil the State,
To sell their duty at a dearer rate;
And make their Jewish markets of the throne,
Pretending public good, to serve their own.
Others thought kings an useless heavy load,
Who cost too much, and did too little good.
These were for laying honest David by,

On principles of pure good husbandry.
With them joined all the haranguers of the throng,
That thought to get preferment by the tongue.
Who follow next, a double danger bring,
Not only hating David, but the king:
The Solymæan rout,[43] well-versed of old
In godly faction, and in treason bold;
Cowering and quaking at a conqueror's sword;
But lofty to a lawful prince restored;
Saw with disdain an Ethnic plot[44] begun,
And scorned by Jebusites to be outdone.
Hot Levites headed these; who, pulled before
From th'ark, which in the Judges' days they bore,[45]
Resumed their cant, and with a zealous cry
Pursued their old beloved Theocracy:
Where Sanhedrin and priest enslaved the nation,
And justified their spoils by inspiration:
For who so fit for reign as Aaron's race,[46]
If once dominion they could found in grace.
These led the pack; though not of surest scent,
Yet deepest mouthed against the government.
A numerous host of dreaming saints succeed,
Of the true old enthusiastic breed:
'Gainst form and order they their power employ,
Nothing to build, and all things to destroy.
But far more numerous was the herd of such,
Who think too little, and who talk too much.
These, out of mere instinct, they knew not why,
Adored their fathers' God and property;
And, by the same blind benefit of fate,
The Devil and the Jebusite did hate:
Born to be saved, even in their own despite,
Because they could not help believing right.
Such were the tools; but a whole Hydra more
Remains, of sprouting heads too long to score.
  Some of their chiefs were princes of the land:
In the first rank of these did Zimri[47] stand;
A man so various, that he seemed to be
Not one, but all mankind's epitome:
Stiff in opinions, always in the wrong;
Was everything by starts, and nothing long;
But, in the course of one revolving moon,
Was chemist, fiddler, statesman, and buffoon:
Then all for women, painting, rhyming, drinking,
Besides ten thousand freaks that died in thinking.
Blest madman, who could every hour employ,
With something new to wish, or to enjoy!
Railing and praising were his usual themes;

And both (to show his judgment) in extremes:
So over-violent, or over-civil,
That every man, with him, was God or Devil.
In squandering wealth was his peculiar art:
Nothing went unrewarded but desert.
Beggared by fools, whom still he found too late,
He had his jest, and they had his estate.
He laughed himself from court; then sought relief
By forming parties, but could ne'er be chief;
For, spite of him, the weight of business fell
On Absalom and wise Achitophel:
Thus, wicked but in will, of means bereft,
He left not faction, but of that was left.
  Titles and names 'twere tedious to rehearse
Of lords, below the dignity of verse.
Wits, warriors, Commonwealth's-men,[48] were the best;
Kind husbands, and mere nobles, all the rest.
And therefore, in the name of dullness, be
The well-hung Balaam[49] and cold Caleb,[50] free;
And canting Nadab[51] let oblivion damn,
Who made new porridge for the Paschal Lamb.
Let friendship's holy band some names assure;
Some their own worth, and some let scorn secure.
Nor shall the rascal rabble here have place,
Whom kings no titles gave, and God no grace:
Not bull-faced Jonas,[52] who could statutes draw
To mean rebellion, and make treason law.
But he, though bad, is followed by a worse,
The wretch who Heaven's anointed dared to curse:
Shimei,[53] whose youth did early promise bring
Of zeal to God and hatred to his king,
Did wisely from expensive sins refrain,
And never broke the Sabbath, but for gain;
Nor ever was he known an oath to vent,
Or curse, unless against the government.
Thus heaping wealth, by the most ready way
Among the Jews, which was to cheat and pray,
The city, to reward his pious hate
Against his master, chose him magistrate.
His hand a vare[54] of justice did uphold;
His neck was loaded with a chain of gold.
During his office, treason was no crime;
The sons of Belial[55] had a glorious time;
For Shimei, though not prodigal of pelf,
Yet loved his wicked neighbour as himself.
When two or three were gathered to declaim
Against the monarch of Jerusalem,
Shimei was always in the midst of them;

And if they cursed the king when he was by,
Would rather curse than break good company.
If any durst his factious friends accuse,
He packed a jury of dissenting Jews;
Whose fellow-feeling in the godly cause
Would free the suffering saint from human laws.
For laws are only made to punish those
Who serve the king, and to protect his foes.
If any leisure time he had from power
(Because 'tis sin to misemploy an hour),
His business was, by writing, to persuade
That kings were useless, and a clog to trade;
And, that his noble style he might refine,
No Rechabite[56] more shunned the fumes of wine.
Chaste were his cellars, and his shrieval board
The grossness of a city feast abhorred:
His cooks, with long disuse, their trade forgot;
Cool was his kitchen, though his brains were hot.
Such frugal virtue malice may accuse,
But sure 'twas necessary to the Jews;
For towns once burnt such magistrates require
As dare not tempt God's providence by fire.
With spiritual food he fed his servants well,
But free from flesh that made the Jews rebel;
And Moses' laws he held in more account,
For forty days of fasting in the mount.
To speak the rest, who better are forgot,
Would tire a well-breathed witness of the Plot.
Yet, Corah,[57] thou shalt from oblivion pass:
Erect thyself, thou monumental brass,
High as the serpent of thy metal made,
While nations stand secure beneath thy shade.[58]
What though his birth were base, yet comets rise
From earthy vapours, ere they shine in skies.
Prodigious actions may as well be done
By weaver's issue as by prince's son.
This arch-attestor for the public good
By that one deed ennobles all his blood.
Who ever asked the witnesses' high race,
Whose oath with martyrdom did Stephen grace?
Ours was a Levite,[59] and as times went then,
His tribe were God Almighty's gentlemen.
Sunk were his eyes, his voice was harsh and loud,
Sure signs he neither choleric was nor proud:
His long chin proved his wit; his saintlike grace
A church vermilion, and a Moses' face.[60]
His memory, miraculously great,
Could plots exceeding man's belief, repeat;

Which therefore cannot be accounted lies,
For human wit could never such devise.
Some future truths are mingled in his book;
But where the witness failed, the prophet spoke:
Some things like visionary flights appear;
The spirit caught him up, the Lord knows where;
And gave him his rabbinical degree,
Unknown to foreign university.[61]
His judgment yet his memory did excel;
Which pieced his wondrous evidence so well,
And suited to the temper of the times,
Then groaning under Jebusitic crimes.
Let Israel's foes suspect his heavenly call,
And rashly judge his writ apocryphal;
Our laws for such affronts have forfeits made:
He takes his life, who takes away his trade.
Were I myself in witness Corah's place,
The wretch who did me such a dire disgrace,
Should whet my memory, though once forgot,
To make him an appendix of my plot.
His zeal to Heaven made him his prince despise,
And load his person with indignities;
But zeal peculiar privilege affords,
Indulging latitude to deeds and words;
And Corah might for Agag's murder[62] call,
In terms as coarse as Samuel used to Saul.
What others in his evidence did join
(The best that could be had for love or coin),
In Corah's own predicament will fall;
For *witness* is a common name to all.
  Surrounded thus with friends of every sort,
Deluded Absalom forsakes the court;
Impatient of high hopes, urged with renown,
And fired with near possession of a crown.
Th'admiring crowd are dazzled with surprise,
And on his goodly person feed their eyes.
His joy concealed, he sets himself to show,
On each side bowing popularly low;
His looks, his gestures, and his words he frames,
And with familiar ease repeats their names.
Thus formed by nature, furnished out with arts,
He glides unfelt into their secret hearts.
Then, with a kind compassionating look,
And sighs, bespeaking pity ere he spoke,
Few words he said; but easy those and fit,
More slow than Hybla-drops,[63] and far more sweet.
  'I mourn, my countrymen, your lost estate;
Though far unable to prevent your fate:

Behold a banished man, for your dear cause
Exposed a prey to arbitrary laws!
Yet O! that I alone could be undone,
Cut off from empire, and no more a son!
Now all your liberties a spoil are made;
Egypt and Tyrus[64] intercept your trade,
And Jebusites your sacred rites invade.
My father, whom with reverence yet I name,
Charmed into ease, is careless of his fame;
And, bribed with petty sums of foreign gold,
Is grown in Bathsheba's[65] embraces old;
Exalts his enemies, his friends destroys;
And all his power against himself employs.
He gives, and let him give, my right away;
But why should he his own and yours betray?
He, only he, can make the nation bleed,
And he alone from my revenge is freed.
Take then my tears (with that he wiped his eyes),
'Tis all the aid my present power supplies:
No court-informer can these arms accuse;
These arms may sons against their fathers use:
And 'tis my wish, the next successor's reign
May make no other Israelite complain.'
   Youth, beauty, graceful action seldom fail;
But common interest always will prevail;
And pity never ceases to be shown
To him who makes the people's wrongs his own.
The crowd, that still believe their kings oppress,
With lifted hands their young Messiah bless:
Who now begins his progress to ordain
With chariots, horsemen, and a numerous train;[66]
From east to west his glories he displays,
And, like the sun, the promised land surveys.
Fame runs before him as the morning star,
And shouts of joy salute him from afar:
Each house receives him as a guardian god,
And consecrates the place of his abode.
But hospitable treats did most commend
Wise Issachar,[67] his wealthy western friend.
This moving court, that caught the people's eyes,
And seemed but pomp, did other ends disguise:
Achitophel had formed it, with intent
To sound the depths, and fathom, where it went,
The people's hearts; distinguish friends from foes,
And try their strength, before they came to blows.
Yet all was coloured with a smooth pretence
Of specious love, and duty to their prince.
Religion, and redress of grievances,

Two names that always cheat and always please,
Are often urged; and good King David's life
Endangered by a brother and a wife.[68]
Thus in a pageant show a plot is made,
And peace itself is war in masquerade.
O foolish Israel! never warned by ill!
Still the same bait, and circumvented still!
Did ever men forsake their present ease,
In midst of health imagine a disease;
Take pains contingent mischiefs to foresee,
Make heirs for monarchs, and for God decree?
What shall we think! Can people give away,
Both for themselves and sons, their native sway?
Then they are left defenceless to the sword
Of each unbounded, arbitrary lord:
And laws are vain, by which we right enjoy,
If kings unquestioned can those laws destroy.
Yet if the crowd be judge of fit and just,
And kings are only officers in trust,
Then this resuming[69] covenant was declared
When kings were made, or is for ever barred.
If those who gave the sceptre could not tie
By their own deed their own posterity,
How then could Adam bind his future race?
How could his forfeit on mankind take place?
Or how could heavenly justice damn us all,
Who ne'er consented to our father's fall?
Then kings are slaves to those whom they command,
And tenants to their people's pleasure stand.
Add, that the power for property allowed
Is mischievously seated in the crowd;
For who can be secure of private right,
If sovereign sway may be dissolved by might?
Nor is the people's judgment always true:
The most may err as grossly as the few;
And faultless kings run down, by common cry,
For vice, oppression, and for tyranny.
What standard is there in a fickle rout,
Which, flowing to the mark, runs faster out?
Nor only crowds but Sanhedrins may be
Infected with this public lunacy,
And share the madness of rebellious times,
To murder monarchs for imagined crimes.
If they may give and take whene'er they please,
Not kings alone (the Godhead's images)
But government itself at length must fall
To nature's state, where all have right to all.[70]
Yet, grant our lords the people kings can make,

What prudent men a settled throne would shake?
For whatsoe'er their sufferings were before,
That change they covet makes them suffer more.
All other errors but disturb a state,
But innovation is the blow of fate.
If ancient fabrics nod, and threat to fall,
To patch the flaws, and buttress up the wall,
Thus far 'tis duty: but here fix the mark
For all beyond it is to touch our ark.[71]
To change foundations, cast the frame anew,
Is work for rebels, who base ends pursue,
At once divine and human laws control,
And mend the parts by ruin of the whole.
The tampering world is subject to this curse,
To physic their disease into a worse.
  Now what relief can righteous David bring?
How fatal 'tis to be too good a king!
Friends he has few, so high the madness grows:
Who dare be such, must be the people's foes.
Yet some there were, even in the worst of days;
Some let me name, and naming is to praise.
  In this short file Barzillai[72] first appears;
Barzillai, crowned with honour and with years.
Long since, the rising rebels he withstood
In regions waste, beyond the Jordan's flood:[73]
Unfortunately brave to buoy the State;
But sinking underneath his master's fate:[74]
In exile with his godlike prince he mourned;
For him he suffered, and with him returned.
The court he practised,[75] not the courtier's art:
Large was his wealth, but larger was his heart,
Which well the noblest objects knew to choose,
The fighting warrior, and recording Muse.
His bed could once a fruitful issue boast;
Now more than half a father's name is lost.
His eldest hope,[76] with every grace adorned,
By me (so Heaven will have it) always mourned,
And always honoured, snatched in manhood's prime
By unequal fates, and Providence's crime;
Yet not before the goal of honour won,
All parts fulfilled of subject and of son:
Swift was the race, but short the time to run.
O narrow circle, but of power divine,
Scanted in space, but perfect in thy line!
By sea, by land, thy matchless worth was known,
Arms thy delight, and war was all thy own:
Thy force, infused, the fainting Tyrians propped;
And haughty Pharaoh found his fortune stopped.[77]

O ancient honour! O unconquered hand,
Whom foes unpunished never could withstand!
But Israel was unworthy of thy name;
Short is the date of all immoderate fame.
It looks as Heaven our ruin had designed,
And durst not trust thy fortune and thy mind.
Now, free from earth, thy disencumbered soul
Mounts up, and leaves behind the clouds and starry pole:
From thence thy kindred legions mayst thou bring,
To aid the guardian angel of thy king.
Here stop, my Muse, here cease thy painful flight;
No pinions can pursue immortal height:
Tell good Barzillai thou canst sing no more,
And tell thy soul she should have fled before.
Or fled she with his life, and left this verse
To hang on her departed patron's hearse?
Now take thy steepy flight from heaven and see
If thou canst find on earth another he:
Another he would be too hard to find;
See then whom thou canst see not far behind.
Zadoc[78] the priest, who, shunning power and place,
His lowly mind advanced to David's grace.
With him the Sagan of Jerusalem,[79]
Of hospitable soul, and noble stem;
Him of the western dome,[80] whose weighty sense
Flows in fit words and heavenly eloquence.
The prophets' sons, by such example led,
To learning and to loyalty were bred:[81]
For colleges on bounteous kings depend,
And never rebel was to arts a friend.
To these succeed the pillars of the laws;
Who best could plead, and best can judge a cause.
Next them a train of loyal peers ascend;
Sharp-judging Adriel,[82] the Muses' friend;
Himself a Muse – in Sanhedrin's debate
True to his prince, but not a slave of state:
Whom David's love with honours did adorn,
That from his disobedient son were torn.
Jotham[83] of piercing wit, and pregnant thought;
Endued by nature, and by learning taught
To move assemblies, who but only tried
The worse a while, then chose the better side:
Nor chose alone, but turned the balance too;
So much the weight of one brave man can do.
Hushai,[84] the friend of David in distress;
In public storms of manly steadfastness:
By foreign treaties he informed his youth,
And joined experience to his native truth.

His frugal care supplied the wanting throne;
Frugal for that, but bounteous of his own:
'Tis easy conduct when exchequers flow,
But hard the task to manage well the low;
For sovereign power is too depressed or high,
When kings are forced to sell, or crowds to buy.
Indulge one labour more, my weary Muse,
For Amiel:[85] who can Amiel's praise refuse?
Of ancient race by birth, but nobler yet
In his own worth, and without title great:
The Sanhedrin long time as chief he ruled,
Their reason guided, and their passion cooled:
So dexterous was he in the crown's defence,
So formed to speak a loyal nation's sense,
That, as their band was Israel's tribes in small,
So fit was he to represent them all.
Now rasher charioteers the seat ascend,
Whose loose careers[86] his steady skill commend:
They, like the unequal ruler of the day,[87]
Misguide the seasons, and mistake the way;
While he withdrawn at their mad labour smiles,
And safe enjoys the sabbath of his toils.
These were the chief, a small but faithful band
Of worthies, in the breach who dared to stand,
And tempt the united fury of the land.
With grief they viewed such powerful engines bent
To batter down the lawful government:
A numerous faction, with pretended frights,
In Sanhedrins to plume the regal rights;
The true successor from the court removed;
The Plot, by hireling witnesses, improved.
These ills they saw, and, as their duty bound,
They showed the king the danger of the wound;
That no concessions from the throne would please,
But lenitives fomented the disease;
That Absalom, ambitious of the crown,
Was made the lure to draw the people down;
That false Achitophel's pernicious hate
Had turned the Plot to ruin Church and State;
The council violent, the rabble worse;
That Shimei taught Jerusalem to curse.
With all these loads of injuries oppressed,
And long revolving in his careful breast
The event of things, at last, his patience tired,
Thus from his royal throne, by Heaven inspired,
The godlike David spoke: with awful fear
His train their Maker in their master hear.
'Thus long have I, by native mercy swayed,

My wrongs dissembled, my revenge delayed:
So willing to forgive the offending age;
So much the father did the king assuage.
But now so far my clemency they slight,
The offenders question my forgiving right.
That one was made for many, they contend;
But 'tis to rule; for that's a monarch's end.
They call my tenderness of blood,[88] my fear;
Though manly tempers can the longest bear.
Yet, since they will divert my native course,
'Tis time to show I am not good by force.
Those heaped affronts that haughty subjects bring,
Are burdens for a camel, not a king.
Kings are the public pillars of the State,
Born to sustain and prop the nation's weight;
If my young Samson will pretend a call
To shake the column, let him share the fall:
But O that yet he would repent and live!
How easy 'tis for parents to forgive!
With how few tears a pardon might be won
From nature, pleading for a darling son!
Poor pitied youth, by my paternal care
Raised up to all the height his frame could bear!
Had God ordained his fate for empire born,
He would have given his soul another turn:
Gulled with a patriot's name, whose modern sense
Is one that would by law supplant his prince;
The people's brave, the politician's tool;
Never was patriot yet, but was a fool.
Whence comes it that religion and the laws
Should more be Absalom's than David's cause?
His old instructor,[89] ere he lost his place,
Was never thought indued with so much grace.
Good heavens, how faction can a patriot paint!
My rebel ever proves my people's saint.
Would *they* impose an heir upon the throne?
Let Sanhedrins be taught to give their own.[90]
A king's at least a part of government,
And mine as requisite as their consent;
Without my leave a future king to choose,
Infers a right the present to depose.
True, they petition me to approve their choice;
But Esau's hands suit ill with Jacob's voice.
My pious subjects for my safety pray;
Which to secure, they take my power away.
From plots and treasons Heaven preserve my years,
But save me most from my petitioners!
Unsatiate as the barren womb or grave;

God cannot grant so much as they can crave.
What then is left, but with a jealous eye
To guard the small remains of royalty?
The law shall still direct my peaceful sway,
And the same law teach rebels to obey:
Votes shall no more established power control –
Such votes as make a part exceed the whole:
No groundless clamours shall my friends remove,
Nor crowds have power to punish ere they prove;
For gods and godlike kings their care express,
Still to defend their servants in distress.
O that my power to saving were confined!
Why am I forced, like Heaven, against my mind,
To make examples of another kind?
Must I at length the sword of justice draw?
O cursed effects of necessary law!
How ill my fear they by my mercy scan!
Beware the fury of a patient man.
Law they require, let Law then show her face;
They could not be content to look on Grace,
Her hinder parts, but with a daring eye
To tempt the terror of her front and die.
By their own arts, 'tis righteously decreed,
Those dire artificers of death shall bleed.
Against themselves their witnesses will swear,
Till viper-like their mother Plot they tear;
And suck for nutriment that bloody gore,
Which was their principle of life before.
Their Belial with their Belzebub will fight;
Thus on my foes, my foes shall do me right.
Nor doubt the event; for factious crowds engage,
In their first onset, all their brutal rage.
Then let 'em take an unresisted course;
Retire, and traverse, and delude their force;
But, when they stand all breathless, urge the fight,
And rise upon 'em with redoubled might;
For lawful power is still superior found;
When long driven back, at length it stands the ground.'
He said. The Almighty, nodding, gave consent;
And peals of thunder shook the firmament.
Henceforth a series of new time began,
The mighty years in long procession ran:
Once more the godlike David was restored,
And willing nations knew their lawful lord.

Notes

The poem is accompanied by minimal notation. A fuller commentary is given in Philip Roberts, editor, *Absalom and Achitophel* (1973) or James Kinsley, editor, *The Poems of John*

Dryden (4 volumes, 1958). The numbers in brackets refer to the lines of the poem.

1 (7) 'Israel's monarch': King Charles II, subsequently referred to as David.

2 (11) 'Michal': Queen Catherine of Braganza.

3 (18) 'Absolon', i.e. Absalom: the Duke of Monmouth, illegitimate son of Charles II, born in 1649.

4 (34) 'Annabel': Anne, Countess of Buccleuch.

5 (39) 'Amnon's murder': probably a reference to the attack on Sir John Coventry in December 1670 because, unlike the biblical Absalom, Monmouth had not committed a murder.

6 (42) 'Sion': London.

7 (44) 'proves': tests.

8 (45) 'The Jews': the English.

9 (51) 'Adam-wits': like Adam, they wanted that which was forbidden.

10 (57–8) 'Saul . . . Ishbosheth': Oliver and Richard Cromwell.

11 (59) 'Hebron': Scotland.

12 (62) 'humour': wayward fancy.

13 (66) 'State': republic.

14 (72) 'dishonest': abhorrent, shameful.

15 (82) 'The Good Old Cause': the republican ideals of the Commonwealth period.

16 (85) 'Jerusalem': London.

17 (86) 'Jebusites': Roman Catholics.

18 (88) 'the chosen people': the Protestant English.

19 (108) 'that Plot': the 'Polish Plot', revealed in the summer of 1678.

20 (118) 'Egyptian': French; 'rites': Roman Catholicism.

21 Lines 119–121 refer to transubstantiation.

22 (124) 'sacrificer': priest.

23 (127) 'stews': brothels (notice the proximity to 'the court').

24 (128–9) 'Hebrew priests . . .': Anglican clergymen who feared for their fleece or tithes.

25 (138) 'hostile humour': corrupt liquid.

26 (150) 'Achitophel': Anthony Ashley Cooper, Earl of Shaftesbury (1621–83); Shaftesbury had been a royalist in the civil war, had then served the Protectorate, and was one of Charles II's leading ministers 1670–73.

27 (175) 'the Triple Bond': the Triple Alliance of 1668 between Sweden, Holland and England.

28 (177) 'fitted Israel . . .': subversion by France (but Shaftesbury was not in fact guilty of this).

29 (188) 'an Abbethdin': a judge – Shaftesbury was Lord Chancellor November 1672–November 1673.

30 Line 197: i.e. there would have been one psalm less.

31 Line 213: Dryden could not know that Charles II was to declare himself a Catholic on his deathbed.

32 Lines 220–27: Dryden argues that Shaftesbury was using the movement to replace James, Duke of York as heir to the throne with Monmouth to establish limits to the monarch's power.

33 (251) 'or . . .or': either . . .or.

34 (264) 'Gath': Brussels.

35 (270) 'Jordan's sand': Dover beach.

36 (281) 'Pharaoh': Louis XIV of France.

37 (344) 'Prevents': anticipates.

38 (353) 'brother': James, Duke of York.

39 (390) 'Sanhedrin': Parliament.

40 Lines 417–18: The period 1649–53 is compared to Israel under the Judges. In January 1649 the Commons declared, 'The people are, under God, the original of all just power.'

41 (453) 'The . . . vulgar': the common people.

42 (461) 'Prevail': avail.

43 (513) 'Solymaean rout': the London mob.

44 (517) 'Ethnic plot': the Popish Plot. (Ethnic here means Gentile.)
45 (519–20) 'Hot Levites . . .': the non-conformist ministers ejected in 1662.
46 (525) 'Aaron's race': the priesthood.
47 (544) 'Zimri': George Villiers, second Duke of Buckingham (1628–87) author and politician.
48 (571) 'Commonwealth's-men': republicans.
49 (574) 'Balaam': the Earl of Huntingdon, a supporter of Shaftesbury until 1681.
50 (574) 'Caleb': the Whig Earl of Essex, who committed suicide in 1683 after being implicated in the 'Rye House' plot.
51 (575) 'Nadab': Lord Howard of Esrick, a'Whig and a former sectary.
52 (581) 'Jonas': Sir William Jones, attorney-general, prosecutor for the Popish Plot.
53 (585) 'Shimei': Slingsby Bethel, Whig sheriff of London in 1680.
54 (595) 'vare': staff of office.
55 (598) 'The sons of Belial' in the Bible (Judges 19. 22–5) were immoral drunks; reference is also made to the fact that the Whig leaders stayed at Balliol College during the Oxford Parliament (March 1681).
56 (617) 'Rechabite': the Rechabites (Jeremiah 35) did not drink.
57 (632) 'Corah': Titus Oates, chief witness of the 'Popish plot'.
58 Lines 633–5: the brazen serpent used by Moses to save the people of Israel (Numbers 21.6–9).
59 (644) 'Levite': an Anglican clergyman – which Oates had been.
60 Line 649: a ruddy shining face.
61 Lines 658–9: Oates claimed the degree of Doctor of Divinity from the University of Salamanca.
62 (676) 'Agag's murder': presumably a reference to the execution of the Catholic Viscount Stafford in December 1680.
63 (697) 'Hybla': honey.
64 (705) 'Egypt and Tyrus': France and Holland.
65 (710) 'Bathsheba': the Duchess of Portsmouth, Charles II's French mistress.
66 (729–30) 'his progress . . .': Monmouth's progress through the west country, July–September 1680.
67 (738) 'Issachar': Thomas Thynne of Longleat, a Whig.
68 (750) 'Endangered . . .': Oates had tried to implicate the Duke of York and the Queen (both Catholics) in the 'Popish Plot'.
69 (767) 'resuming': continuous through a succession of kings.
70 (794) 'nature's state . . .': as in Thomas Hobbes's *Leviathan* Book 1, Chapter 13.
71 (804) 'our ark': the ark of the Covenant which God made with Israel.
72 (817) 'Barzillai': the Duke of Ormonde, Lord Lieutenant of Ireland under Charles I and Charles II.
73 (820) 'Jordan's flood': the Irish Sea.
74 (822) 'his master's fate': the execution of Charles I.
75 (825) 'practised': frequented.
76 (831) 'His eldest hope': Ormonde's heir, Thomas Earl of Ossory, died in 1680.
77 Lines 842–3: Ossory had made his reputation in the wars against the Dutch and the French.
78 (864) 'Zadoc': William Sancroft, Archbishop of Canterbury from 1678.
79 (866) 'Sagan of Jerusalem': Henry Compton, Bishop of London from 1675.
80 (868) 'Him of the western dome': John Dolben, Dean of Westminster.
81 Lines 870–71 refer to Westminster school where Dryden was educated.
82 (877) 'Adriel': John Sheffield, Earl of Sheffield, later Marquess of Normanby, Dryden's patron; the *Aeneid* was dedicated to him, see p. 325.
83 (882) 'Jotham': George Savile, the 'Trimmer', see Biographical Index, p. 388.
84 (888) 'Hushai': Laurence Hyde, Clarendon's second son.
85 (899) 'Amiel': Edward Seymour, the Speaker of the House of Commons 1673–8.
86 (909) 'loose careers': careering about, wandering all over the place.
87 (910) 'the unequal ruler of the day': Phaeton, Apollo's son, who drove the horses of the sun too near the earth.
88 (947) 'tenderness of blood': unwilling to shed blood.

89 (971) 'His old instructor': Shaftesbury.
90 (976) 'to give their own': to stick to their legal function which does not include nominating the heir to the throne.

135 Tragedy and the Epic

[*Source*: George Watson, editor (1962) *John Dryden, Of Dramatic Poesy and Other Critical Essays*, pp. 227–9.]

[From the dedication to John Sheffield, Marquess (later Duke) of Normanby, prefaced to the *Aeneid* in *The Works of Virgil, Translated into English Verse* (1697). Normanby, a patron of Dryden's and an author himself, is the 'Adriel' of *Absalom*, line 877.]

To raise, and afterwards to calm the passions, to purge the soul from pride, by the examples of human miseries, which befall the greatest; in few words, to expel arrogance, and introduce compassion, are the great effects of tragedy.[1] Great, I must confess, if they were altogether as true as they are pompous. But are habits to be introduced at three hours' warning? Are radical diseases so suddenly removed? A mountebank may promise such a cure, but a skilful physician will not undertake it. An epic poem is not in so much haste: it works leisurely; the changes which it makes are slow; but the cure is likely to be more perfect. The effects of tragedy, as I said, are too violent to be lasting. If it be answered that, for this reason, tragedies are often to be seen, and the dose to be repeated, this is tacitly to confess that there is more virtue in one heroic poem than in many tragedies. A man is humbled one day, and his pride returns the next. Chemical medicines are observed to relieve oftener than to cure: for 'tis the nature of spirits to make swift impressions, but not deep. Galenical decoctions,[2] to which I may properly compare an epic poem, have more of body in them; they work by their substance and their weight. It is one reason of Aristotle's to prove that tragedy is the more noble because it turns in a shorter compass; the whole action being circumscribed within the space of four-and-twenty hours. He might prove as well that a mushroom is to be preferred before a peach, because it shoots up in the compass of a night. A chariot may be driven round the pillar in less space than a large machine, because the bulk is not so great. Is the Moon a more noble planet than Saturn because she makes her revolution in less than thirty days, and he in little less than thirty years? Both their orbs are in proportion to their several magnitudes; and consequently the quickness or slowness of their motion, and the time of their circumvolutions, is no argument of the greater or less perfection. And besides, what virtue is there in a tragedy which is not contained in an epic poem, where pride is humbled, virtue rewarded, and vice punished; and those more amply treated than the narrowness of the drama can admit? The shining quality of an epic hero, his magnanimity, his constancy, his patience, his piety, or whatever characteristical virtue his poet gives him, raises first our admiration; we are naturally prone to imitate what we admire; and frequent acts produce a habit. If the hero's chief quality be vicious as, for example, the choler and obstinate desire of vengeance in Achilles, yet the moral is instructive: and besides, we are informed in the very proposition of the *Iliads*[3] that this anger was pernicious, that it brought a thousand ills on the Grecian camp. The courage of Achilles is proposed to imitation, not his pride and disobedience to his general, nor his brutal cruelty to his dead enemy, nor the selling of his body to his father. We abhor these actions while we read them; and what we abhor we never imitate. The poet only shews them, like rocks or quicksands, to be shunned.

By this example, the critics have concluded that it is not necessary the manners of the hero should be virtuous. They are poetically good, if they are of a piece: though where a character of perfect virtue is set before us, 'tis more lovely; for there the whole hero is to be imitated. This is the Æneas of our author [Virgil]; this is that idea of perfection in an epic poem which painters and statuaries have only in their minds, and which no hands are able to express. These are the beauties of a god in a human body. When the picture of Achilles is drawn in tragedy, he is taken with those warts, and moles, and hard features by those who represent him on the stage, or he is no more Archilles; for his creator Homer has so described him. Yet even thus he appears a perfect hero, though an imperfect character of virtue. Horace paints him after Homer, and delivers him to be copied on the stage with all those imperfections. Therefore they are either not faults in a heroic poem, or faults common to the drama. After all, on the whole merits of the cause, it must be acknowledged that the epic poem is more for the manners, and tragedy for the passions. The passions, as I have said, are violent; and acute distempers require medicines of a strong and speedy operation. Ill habits of the mind are like chronical diseases, to be corrected by degrees and cured by alternatives; wherein, though purges are sometimes necessary, yet diet, good air, and moderate exercise have the greatest part. The matter being thus stated, it will appear that both sorts of poetry are of use for their proper ends. The stage is more active; the epic poem works at greater leisure, yet is active too, when need requires; for dialogue is imitated by the drama from the more active parts of it. One puts off a fit like the quinquina [quinine], and relieves us only for a time; the other roots out the distemper, and gives a healthful habit. The sun enlightens and cheers us, dispels fogs, and warms the ground with his daily beams; but the corn is sowed, increases, is ripened, and is reaped for use in process of time, and in its proper season. I proceed from the greatness of the action to the dignity of the actors; I mean to the persons employed in both poems. There likewise tragedy will be seen to borrow from the epopee; and that which borrows is always of less dignity, because it has not of its own. A subject, 'tis true, may lend to his sovereign; but the act of borrowing makes the king inferior, because he wants, and the subject supplies. And suppose the persons of the drama wholly fabulous, or of the poet's invention, yet heroic poetry gave him the examples of that invention, because it was first, and Homer the common father of the stage. I know not of any one advantage which tragedy can boast above heroic poetry, but that it is represented to the view as well as read, and instructs in the closet as well as on the theatre. This is an uncontended excellence and a chief branch of its prerogative; yet I may be allowed to say, without partiality, that herein the actors share the poet's praise. Your Lordship knows some modern tragedies which are beautiful on the stage, and yet I am confident you would not read them. Tryphon the stationer[4] complains they are seldom asked for in his shop. The poet who flourished in the scene is damned in the ruelle [fashionable reception]; nay more, he is not esteemed a good poet by those who see and hear his extravagances with delight. They are a sort of stately fustian and lofty childishness. Nothing but nature can give a sincere pleasure; where that is not imitated, 'tis grotesque painting; the fine woman ends in a fish's tail.

Notes

1 'effects of tragedy': based on Aristotle, *Poetics*, Chapter VI: 'A tragedy is an imitation of an action . . . with incidents arousing pity and fear, to purge us of these emotions.'

2 'Galenical decoctions': the vegetable cures favoured by physicians who adhered to the views of the Greek physician Galen, rather than to the new chemical remedies of the Paracelsians.

3 '*Iliads*': Homer's *Iliad* I. 1–2.

4 'Tryphon': presumably Jacob Tonson who published most of Dryden's works from 1679. The original Tryphon was a Greek bookseller in Augustus's Rome.

SECTION TWENTY ONE: SCIENTIFIC DEVELOPMENTS

[In this section we examine some aspects of the important English contribution to the 'scientific revolution' of the seventeenth century. The Royal Society, established at the Restoration, brought together scientists with a variety of backgrounds and attitudes, along with gentlemen who had a more amateur interest in new discoveries. The Society was probably more significant as a publicizer of new work than as a stimulator and organizer of research. The Anglican cleric Thomas Sprat, in his officially sponsored and approved account of the Society, traced its origins back no further than the late 1650s (extract 137); but the accounts of the mathematician John Wallis (extracts 141–3) suggest that its foundation was the culmination of a longer process going back at least to the 1640s. Some of the approaches shared by many of the Society's members can be briefly highlighted. There was the attack on the Aristotelian or 'peripatetic' philosophy, coupled with admiration for Bacon and for the experimental method (extracts 136 and 144). Many agreed with Boyle on the utility of science, a utility that had a religious as well as a practical dimension (extract 145). Finally there was the widespread desire to dissociate science from religious radicalism (extracts 136 and 140) and from scepticism in religion (extracts 145 and 149). For some of the reasons for this see Section Fifteen above.

In this period the most eminent of the Fellows of the Society was Isaac Newton, one of the most influential scientists of any age. His scientific work is represented by his early experiments on light (extract 146) and two extracts from the immensely significant *Principia* (147 and 148). We have tried to avoid the mistake of presenting Newton anachronistically as a modern, 'rational' scientist in a twentieth-century mould. There is unfortunately no space to illustrate Newton's preoccupation with alchemical research, but we include ample evidence of his interest in theology and biblical scholarship (extracts 149–151).]

136 Joseph Glanvill: The New Philosophy

[*Source*: Joseph Glanvill (1661) *The Vanity of Dogmatising*, pp. 178–9 and 186–7.]

The Aristotelian philosophy is inept for new discoveries; and therefore of no accommodation to the use of life. That all arts and professions are capable of maturer improvements cannot be doubted by those who know the least of any. And that there is an America of secrets, and unknown Peru of nature, whose discovery would richly advance them, is more than conjecture. Now while we either sail by the land of gross and vulgar doctrines, or direct our inquiries by the cynosure of mere abstract notions, we are not likely to reach the treasures on the other side the Atlantic: the directing of the world the way to which, is the noble end of true philosophy. That the Aristotelian physiology cannot boast itself the proper author of any one invention, is pregnant evidence of its infecundous [infertile] deficiency, and 'twould puzzle the schools to point at any considerable discovery made by the direct, sole manuduction [guidance] of peripatetic principles. Most of our rarities have been found out by casual emergency, and have been the works of time and chance, rather than of philosophy. What Aristotle hath of experimental knowledge in his books of animals, or elsewhere, is not much transcending vulgar observation; and yet what he hath of this, was never learnt from his hypotheses, but forcibly fetch'd in to suffrage [add support] to them. And 'tis the observation of the noble St Alban [Francis Bacon], that that philosophy is built on a few vulgar experiments . . . .

But, because the fooleries of some affected novelists have discredited new discoveries, and render'd the very mention suspected of vanity at least, and in points divine, of heresy; it will be necessary to add, that I intend not the former discourse in favour of any new-broach'd conceit in divinity: for I own no opinion there, which cannot plead the prescription of above sixteen hundred. There's nothing I have more sadly resented, than the frenetic whimsies with which our age abounds, and therefore am not likely to patron them. In theology, I put as great a difference between our new lights, and ancient truths, as between the sun, and an unconcocted, evanid [vanishing away] meteor. Though I confess, that in philosophy I'm a seeker, yet cannot believe, that a sceptic in philosophy must be one in divinity. Gospel-light began in its zenith and, as some say the sun, was created in its meridian strength and lustre. But the beginnings of philosophy were in a crepusculous [dim] obscurity, and it's yet scarce past the dawn. Divine truths were most pure in their source, and time could not perfect what eternity began: our divinity, like the grandfather of humanity, was born in the fullness of time, and in the strength of its manly vigour; but philosophy and arts commenced embryos, and are completed by time's gradual accomplishments.

The Royal Society

(a) Thomas Sprat

137 The Origins of the Society

[*Source*: Thomas Sprat (1667) *The History of the Royal Society of London*, pp.53–8.]

It was therefore some space after the end of the civil wars at Oxford, in Dr Wilkins[1] his lodgings, in Wadham College, which was then the place of resort for virtuous and learned men, that the first meetings were made, which laid the foundation of all this that follow'd. The University had, at that time, many members of its own, who had begun a free way of reasoning; and was also frequented by some gentlemen, of philosophical minds, whom the misfortunes of the kingdom, and the security and ease of a retirement amongst gown-men, had drawn thither.

Their first purpose was no more, than only the satisfaction of breathing a freer air, and of conversing in quiet, one with another, without being engag'd in the passions and madness of that dismal age. And from the institution of that assembly, it had been enough, if no advantage had come, but this: that by this means, there was a race of young men provided, against the next age, whose minds receiving from them, their first impression of sober and generous knowledge, were invincibly arm'd against all the enchantments of enthusiasm.[2] But what is more, I may venture to affirm, that it was in good measure, by the influence, which these gentlemen had over the rest, that the University itself, or at least, any part of its discipline and order, was saved from ruin. And from hence we may conclude, that the same men have now no intention of sweeping away all the honour of antiquity in this their new design: seeing they employ'd so much of their labour, and prudence, in preserving that most venerable seat of ancient learning, when their shrinking from its defence would have been the speediest way to have destroy'd it. For the truth of this, I dare appeal to all uninterested men, who knew the temper of that place; and especially to those who were my own contemporaries there, of whom I can name very many, whom the happy restoration of the Kingdom's peace, found as well inclin'd to serve their Prince, and the Church, as if they had been bred up in the most prosperous condition of their country. This was undoubtedly so. Nor indeed could it be otherwise: for such spiritual frenzies, which did then bear rule, can never stand long before a clear, and a deep skill in nature. It is also impossible that they, who converse much with the subtlety of things, should be deluded by such thick deceits. There is but one better charm in the world, than real philosophy, to allay the impulses of the false spirit, and that is, the blessed presence, and assistance of the true.

Nor were the good effects of this conversation only confined to Oxford: but they have made themselves known in their printed works, both in our own, and in the learned language, which have much conduc'd to the fame of our nation abroad, and to the spreading of profitable light at home. This I trust, will be universally acknowledg'd, when I shall have nam'd the men. The principal, and most constant of them, were Dr Seth Ward, the present Lord Bishop of Exeter, Mr Boyle, Dr Wilkins, Sir William Petty, Mr Matthew Wren, Dr Wallis, Dr Goddard, Dr Willis, Dr Bathurst, Dr Christopher Wren, Mr Rooke,[3] besides several others, who join'd themselves to them, upon occasions. . . .

For such a candid and unpassionate company, as that was, and for such a gloomy season, what could have been a fitter subject to pitch upon, than natural philosophy? To have been always tossing about some theological question, would have been to have made that their private diversion, the excess of which they themselves dislik'd in the public; to have been eternally musing on civic business, and the distresses of their country, was too melancholy a reflection: it was nature alone, which could pleasantly entertain them, in that estate. The contemplation of that, draws our minds off from past or present misfortunes, and makes them conquerors over things, in the greatest public unhappiness; while the consideration of men, and human affairs, may affect us with a thousand various disquiets: that never separates us into mortal factions; that gives us room to differ, without animosity; and permits us to raise contrary imaginations upon it, without any danger of a civil war.

Their meetings were as frequent as their affairs permitted; their proceedings rather by action than discourse, chiefly attending some particular trials in chemistry or mechanics; they had no rules nor method fix'd; their intention was more to communicate to each other their discoveries, which they could make in so narrow a compass, than a united, constant, or regular inquisition . . . .

Thus they continued without any great intermissions, till about the year 1658. But being then call'd away to several parts of the nation, and the greatest number of them coming to London, they usually met at Gresham College,[4] at the Wednesdays and Thursdays lectures of Dr Wren and Mr Rooke, where there join'd with them several eminent persons of their common acquaintance: the Lord Viscount Brouncker, the now Lord Brereton, Sir Paul Neile, Mr John Evelyn, Mr Henshaw, Mr Slingsby, Dr Timothy Clark, Dr Ent, Mr Ball, Mr Hill, Dr Croone,[5] and divers other gentlemen whose inclinations lay the same way. This custom was observ'd once, if not twice a week, in term time, till they were scatt'red by the miserable distractions of that fatal year [1659–60]; till the continuance of their meetings might have made them run the hazard of the fate of Archimedes,[6] for then the place of their meeting was made a quarter for soldiers. But (to make haste through those dreadful revolutions, which cannot be beheld upon paper, without horror, unless we remember that they had this one happy effect, to open men's eyes to look out for the true remedy) upon this follow'd the King's return; and that, wrought by such an admirable chain of events, that if we either regard the easiness, or speed, or blessed issue of the work, it seems of itself to contain variety, and pleasure enough, to make recompense for the whole twenty years melancholy that had gone before. This I leave to another kind of history to be describ'd. It shall suffice my purpose, that philosophy had its share in the benefits of that glorious action: for the Royal Society had its beginning in the wonderful pacific year, 1660. So that, if any conjectures of good fortune from extraordinary nativities hold true, we may presage all happiness to this undertaking.

Notes

1 Dr Wilkins: John Wilkins, see Biographical Index, p. 390.
2 'enthusiasm': religious radicalism.
3 'Dr Seth Ward . . .Mr Rooke': for Seth Ward, Robert Boyle, John Wilkins, John Wallis see Biographical Index; for Christopher Wren see pp. 364–372; William Petty, Professor of Anatomy at Oxford 1651–2, but best known as the pioneer of the science of statistics; Matthew Wren, son of a Laudian bishop and cousin of Christopher; Wren wrote against James Harrington's *Oceana* in the 1650s, and became Clarendon's secretary after the Restoration; Jonathon Goddard, a physician and close associate of Oliver Cromwell, Warden of Merton College Oxford 1651–60 and Professor of Physic at Gresham College from 1655; Thomas Willis, physician and medical researcher; Ralph Bathurst, physician and clergyman; Laurence Rooke, astronomer, Professor of Astronomy at Gresham College 1652–7, and Professor of Geometry there from 1657 until his death in 1662. Several of these men were based at Wadham College, Oxford, where Wilkins was Warden 1648–59.
4 'Gresham College': founded by the merchant Sir Thomas Gresham in the late sixteenth century. It consisted of seven Professors – of geometry, astronomy, physic, theology, music, law and rhetoric – who were required to give public lectures for the benefit of the people of London.
5 'the Lord Viscount Brouncker . . . Dr Croone': William, Viscount Brouncker, Irish mathematician and first president of the Royal Society; William, Lord Brereton, Sir Paul Neile, John Evelyn (the diarist) and Henry Slingsby were all gentlemen with an amateur interest in science; Mr Henshaw could be either the physician Nathaniel, or his brother Thomas, a scientific author and diplomat: both were prominent early members of the Royal Society; Timothy Clarke, George Ent and William Croone were all physicians; Croone was also Professor of Rhetoric at Gresham College and the first Registrar of the Royal Society; William Ball, astronomer, Treasurer of the Royal Society 1662–3; Abraham Hill, London merchant, Treasurer of the Royal Society 1663–5.
6 'the fate of Archimedes': the mathematician Archimedes was killed in 212 B.C. in Syracuse, when the city was besieged and captured by the Romans.

138 The Membership of the Society

[*Source*: Sprat (1667) *The History of the Royal Society*, pp.67–9.]

They diligently search out, and join to them, all extraordinary men, though but of ordinary trades. And that they are likely to continue this comprehensive temper hereafter, I will show by one instance: and it is the recommendation which the King himself was pleased to make, of the judicious author of *The Observations on the Bills of Mortality*;[1] in whose election, it was so far from being a prejudice, that he was a shop-keeper of London, that his Majesty gave this particular charge to his Society, that if they found any more such tradesmen, they should be sure to admit them all, without any more ado. From hence it may be concluded, what is their inclination towards the manual arts, by the careful regard which their founder and patron has engag'd them to have for all sorts of mechanic artists.

But though the Society entertains very many men of particular professions, yet the far greater number are gentlemen, free and unconfin'd. By the help of this, there was hopeful provision made against two corruptions of learning, which have been long complain'd of, but never remov'd: the one, that knowledge still degenerates to consult present profit too soon; the other, that philosophers have been always masters and scholars, some imposing and all the other submitting, and not as equal observers without dependence.

The first of these may be call'd, the marrying of arts too soon, and putting them to generation, before they come to be of age; and has been the cause of much inconvenience. It weakens their strength; it makes an unhappy disproportion in their increase, while not the best, but the most gainful of them flourish; but above all, it diminishes that very profit for which men strive. It busies them about possessing some petty prize, while nature itself, with all its mighty treasures, slips from them . . . .

The second error, which is hereby endeavour'd to be remedied, is that the seats of knowledge have been for the most part heretofore not laboratories, as they ought to be, but only schools, where some have taught, and all the rest subscrib'd. The consequences of this are very mischievous. For first, as many learners as there are, so many hands and brains may still be reckon'd upon as useless: it being only the masters' part to examine and observe, and the disciples' to submit with silence to what they conclude. But besides this, the very inequality of the titles of teachers and scholars does very much suppress and tame men's spirits; which though it should be proper for discipline and education, yet is by no means consistent with a free philosophical consultation. It is undoubtedly true, that scarce any man's mind is so capable of thinking strongly in the presence of one whom he fears and reverences, as he is when that restraint is taken off.

Note

1 'the judicious author . . .': John Graunt, the merchant and statistician whose *Observations* was published in 1662.

139 The Society and the English Language

[*Source*: Sprat (1667) *The History of the Royal Society*, pp.111–13.]

There is one thing more, about which the Society has been most solicitous, and that is, the manner of their discourse; which, unless they had been very watchful to keep in due temper, the whole spirit and vigour of their design had been soon eaten out by the luxury and redundance of speech. The ill effects of this superfluity of talking have already overwhelm'd most other arts and professions; insomuch, that when I consider the means of happy living, and the causes of their corruption, I can hardly forbear recanting what I said before, and concluding that eloquence ought to be banish'd out of all civil societies, as a thing fatal to peace and good manners. To this opinion I should wholly incline, if I did not find that it is a weapon which may be as easily procur'd by bad men as good; and that, if these should only cast it away, and those retain it, the naked innocence of virtue would be upon all occasions expos'd to the armed malice of the wicked. This is the chief reason that should now keep up the ornaments of speaking in any request, since they are so much degenerated from their original usefulness. They were at first, no doubt, an admirable instrument in the hands of wise men, when they were only employ'd to describe goodness, honesty, obedience, in larger, fairer and more moving images; to represent truth, cloth'd with bodies, and to bring knowledge back again to our very senses, from whence it was at first deriv'd to our understandings. But now they are generally chang'd to worse uses: they make the fancy disgust the best things, if they come sound and unadorn'd; they are in open defiance against reason, professing not to hold much correspondence with that, but with its slaves, the passions; they give the mind a motion too changeable and bewitching to consist with right practice. Who can behold, without indignation, how many mists and uncertainties these specious tropes and figures have brought on our knowledge? How many rewards, which are due to more profitable and difficult arts, have been still snatch'd away by the easy vanity of fine speaking? For now I am warm'd with this just anger, I cannot withhold myself from betraying the shallowness of all these seeming mysteries, upon which we writers and speakers look so big. And, in few words, I dare say that, of all the studies of men, nothing may be sooner obtain'd than this vicious abundance of phrase, this trick of metaphors, this volubility of tongue, which makes so great a noise in the world. But I spend words in vain, for the evil is now so inveterate that it is hard to know whom to blame, or where to begin to reform. We all value one another so much upon this beautiful deceit; and labour so long after it in the years of our education, that we cannot but ever after think kinder of it than it deserves. And indeed, in most other parts of learning, I look on it to be a thing almost utterly desperate in its cure; and I think it may be plac'd amongst those general mischiefs, such as the dissension of Christian princes, the want of practice in religion, and the like, which have been so long spoken against, that men are become insensible about them, everyone shifting off the fault from himself to others; and so they are only made bare common places of complaint. It will suffice my present purpose to point out what has been done by the Royal Society towards the correcting of its excesses in natural philosophy, to which it is, of all others, a most professed enemy.

They have therefore been most rigorous in putting in execution the only remedy that can be found for this extravagance: and that has been a constant resolution to reject all the amplifications, digressions and swellings of style; to return back to the primitive purity and shortness, when men deliver'd so many things almost in an equal number of words. They have exacted from all their members a close, naked, natural way of speaking, positive expressions, clear senses, a native easiness, bringing all things as near the mathematical plainness as they can; and preferring the language of artisans, countrymen and merchants before that of wits or scholars.

140 The Society and the Church of England

[*Source*: Sprat (1667) *The History of the Royal Society*, pp.270–71.]

The true and certain interest of our Church is to derive its doctrine from the plain and unquestion'd parts of the word of God, and to keep itself in a due submission to the civil magistrate. The extremes which it opposes are implicit faith and enthusiasm; and it is a great mistake, if men think it cannot be maintain'd against these, but by the mutual arguments of its enemies: that it cannot withstand the separatists but by the authority of the Church of Rome; nor dissent from the Church of Rome but on the tenents [tenets] of the separatists. The grounds on which it proceeds are different from both: and they are no other but the rights of the civil power, the imitation of the first uncorrupt churches, and the Scripture expounded by reason; from whence may be concluded, that we cannot make war against reason, without undermining our own strength, seeing it is the constant weapon we ought to employ.

From this I will farther urge, that the church of England will not only be safe amidst the consequences of a rational age, but amidst all the improvements of knowledge, and the subversion of old opinions about nature, and introduction of new ways of reasoning thereon. This will be evident, when we behold the agreement that is between the present design of the Royal Society, and that of our Church in its beginning. They both may lay equal claim to the word 'Reformation', the one having compass'd it in religion, the other purposing it in philosophy. They both have taken a like course to bring this about, each of them passing by the corrupt copies, and referring themselves to the perfect originals for their instruction, the one to the Scripture, the other to the large volume of the creatures. They are both unjustly accus'd by their enemies of the same crimes, of having forsaken the ancient traditions, and ventur'd on novelties. They both suppose alike, that their ancestors might err, and yet retain a sufficient reverence for them. They both follow the great precept of the Apostle, of trying all things. Such is the harmony between their interests and tempers. It cannot therefore be suspected that the Church of England, that arose on the same method, though in different works; that heroically pass'd through the same difficulties, that relies on the same Sovereign's authority, should look with jealous eyes on this attempt, which makes no change in the principles of men's consciences, but chiefly aims at the increase of inventions about the works of their hands.

(b) John Wallis on the Origins of the Society

141 1678

[*Source:* John Wallis (1678) *A Defence of the Royal Society*, pp. 7–8. All three Wallis accounts are printed in Margery Purver, *The Royal Society: Concept and Creation* (1967).]

[Wallis wrote this account in the course of a controversy with Dr William Holder, the brother-in-law of Christopher Wren. The dispute mainly concerned rival claims to have pioneered methods of teaching the deaf to speak, but Wallis also challenged Holder's view that the Royal Society had developed from meetings held at John Wilkins's lodgings in Oxford, just before the Restoration.]

I take its first ground and foundation to have been in London, about the year 1645 (if not sooner) when the same Dr Wilkins, then chaplain to the Prince Elector Palatine in London, Dr Jonathon Goddard, Dr Ent, now Sir George Ent, Dr Glisson, Dr Scarburgh, now Sir Charles Scarburgh, Dr Merret,[1] with myself and some others met weekly (sometimes at Dr Goddard's lodgings, sometimes at the Mitre in Wood Street, hard by) at a certain day and hour, under a certain penalty and a weekly contribution for the charge of experiments, with certain rules agreed amongst us. Where, to avoid diversion to other discourses and for other reasons, we barred all discourses of divinity, of state affairs and of news (other than what concern'd our business of philosophy) confining ourselves to philosophical inquiries, and such as related thereunto, as physic, anatomy, geometry, astronomy, navigation, statics, mechanics, and natural experiments. We there discoursed the circulation of the blood, the valves in the veins, the Copernican hypothesis, the nature of comets and new stars, the attendants on Jupiter, the oval shape of Saturn, the inequalities and selenography of the moon, the several phases of Venus and Mercury, the improvement of telescopes and grinding of glasses for that purpose (wherein Dr Goddard was particularly engaged, and did maintain an operator in his house for that purpose), the weight of the air, the possibility or impossibility of vacuities, and nature's abhorrence thereof, the Torricellian experiment in quicksilver, the descent of heavy bodies and the degrees of acceleration therein, with others of like nature.[2] Some of which were then but new discoveries, and others not so generally known and embraced as now they are.

These meetings we removed soon after to the Bull-head in Cheapside, and, in term time, to Gresham College[3] where we met weekly at Mr Foster's[4] lecture (then Astronomy Professor there); and after the lecture ended repaired sometimes to Mr Foster's lodgings, sometimes to some other place not far distant, where we continued such inquiries, and our numbers increased.

About the years 1648, 1649, some of our company were removed to Oxford, (first Dr Wilkins, then I, and soon after, Dr Goddard); whereupon our company divided. Those at London (and we, when we had occasion to be there) met as before. Those of us at Oxford, with Dr Ward (now Bishop of Salisbury), Dr Petty (now Sir William Petty), Dr Bathurst, Dr Willis,[5] and many others of the most inquisitive persons in Oxford met weekly, for some years, at Dr Petty's lodgings on the like account; to wit, so long as Dr Petty continued in Oxford, and for some while after, because of the conveniencies we had there (being the house of an apothecary) to view and make use of drugs and other like matters, as there was occasion.

Our meetings there were very numerous and very considerable. For, beside the diligence of persons, studiously inquisitive, the novelty of the design made many to resort thither; who, when it ceased to be new, began to grow more remiss, or did pursue such inquiries at home.

We did afterwards (Dr Petty being gone for Ireland, and our numbers growing less) remove thence. And, some years before his Majesty's return, did meet, as Dr Holder observes, at Dr Wilkins' lodgings in Wadham College.

But before the time he [i.e. Dr Holder] mentions, those set meetings ceased in Oxford, and were held at London. Where, after the death of Mr Foster, we continued to meet at Gresham College, as before, at Mr Rooke's[6] lecture (who succeeded Mr Foster); and from thence repaired to some convenient place, in or near that College. And so onward, till the fire of London caused our removal to Arundel House; from whence we are since returned to Gresham College again.

In the meanwhile our company at Gresham College, being much again increased by the accession of divers eminent and noble persons upon his Majesty's return, we were, about the beginning of the year 1662, by his Majesty's grace and favour, incorporated by the name of the Royal Society etc.

All this while, Dr Wilkins and Dr Goddard, through all these changes, continued those meetings [at Oxford], and had a great influence on them, from the first original, till the days of their death; and some others of us, to this day.

Notes

1 'Dr Wilkins . . . Dr Merret': for Wilkins see Biographical Index, p. 390; for Goddard p. 332, Note 3; for Ent p. 332, Note 5; Francis Glisson, Charles Scarburgh and Christopher Merret were all physicians; Glisson was Professor of Physic at Cambridge from 1636 until his death in 1677; Scarburgh became one of Charles II's doctors.

2 'We there discoursed . . .of like nature': the most important of the group's discussions were based on the work of William Harvey who had revealed the circulation of the blood in 1628, the sixteenth-century Polish astronomer Copernicus, and the Italian scientist Galileo (1564–1642). In 1643, the Italian Torricelli had shown how a vacuum could be obtained with an experiment using a barometer containing mercury.

3 'Gresham College': see p. 332, Note 4.

4 'Mr Foster': Samuel Foster (d. 1652), mathematician and astronomer; Professor of Astronomy at Gresham College 1636 and 1641–52.

5 'Dr Ward . . .Dr Willis': for Ward see Biographical Index, p. 389; for Petty, Bathurst and Willis p. 332, Note 3.

6 'Mr Rooke': see p. 332, Note 3.

142 1697

[*Source*: Thomas Hearne, editor (1725) *Peter Langtoft's Chronicle* volume one, pp.CLXI–CLXIV.]

[This description of the origins of the Society formed part of 'Dr Wallis's Account of Some Passages of his Own Life' which he wrote for the Oxford scholar and collector Dr Thomas Smith.]

About the year 1645, while I lived in London (at a time when, by our civil wars, academical studies were much interrupted in both our universities) beside the conversation of divers eminent divines, as to matters theological, I had the opportunity of being acquainted with divers worthy persons, inquisitive into natural philosophy and other parts of humane learning, and particularly of what hath been called the New Philosophy, or Experimental Philosophy.

We did by agreement, divers of us meet weekly in London on a certain day, to treat and discourse of such affairs. Of which number were Dr John Wilkins (afterward Bishop of Chester), Dr Jonathon Goddard, Dr George Ent, Dr Glisson, Dr Merret (Doctors in physic), Mr Samuel Foster, then Professor of Astronomy at Gresham College, Mr Theodore Haak (a German of the Palatinate, and then resident in London who I think, gave the first occasion, and first suggested those meetings) and many others.[1]

These meetings we held sometimes at Dr Goddard's lodgings in Wood Street, or some convenient place near, on occasion of his keeping an operator in his house for grinding glasses for telescopes and microscopes; and sometime at a convenient place in Cheapside, sometime at Gresham College or some place near adjoining.

Our business was (precluding matters of theology and state affairs) to discourse and consider of philosophical enquiries, and such as related thereunto: as physic, anatomy, geometry, astronomy, navigation, statics, magnetics, chemics, mechanics, and natural experiments, with the state of these studies, as then cultivated, at home and abroad. We there discoursed of the circulation of the blood, the valves in the veins, the *venae lactae* [or] the lymphatic vessels, the Copernican hypothesis, the nature of comets and new stars, the satellites of Jupiter, the oval shape (as it then appeared) of Saturn, the spots in the sun, and its turning on its own axis, the inequalities and selenography of the moon, the several phases of Venus and Mercury, the improvement of telescopes and grinding of glasses for that purpose, the weight of air, the possibility or impossibility of vacuities and nature's abhorrence thereof, the Torricellian experiment in quicksilver, the descent of heavy bodies, and the degrees of acceleration therein, and divers other things of like nature.[2] Some of which were then but new discoveries, and others not so generally known and embraced as now they are, with other things appertaining to what hath been called the New Philosophy; which, from the times of Galileo at Florence, and Sir Francis Bacon (Lord Verulam) in England, hath been much cultivated in Italy, France, Germany and other parts abroad, as well as with us in England.

About the year 1648, 1649, some of our company being removed to Oxford (first Dr Wilkins, then I, and soon after Dr Goddard) our company divided. Those in London continued to meet there as before (and we with them, when we had occasion to be there); and those of us at Oxford, with Dr Ward (since Bishop of Salisbury), Dr Ralph Bathurst (now President of Trinity College in Oxford), Dr Petty (since Sir William Petty), Dr Willis (then an eminent physician in Oxford),[3] and divers others, continued such meetings in Oxford; and brought those studies into fashion there; meeting first at Dr Petty's lodgings, in an apothecary's house, because of the convenience of inspecting drugs and the like, as there was occasion; and after his [Petty's] remove to Ireland, though not so constantly, at the lodgings of Dr Wilkins, then Warden of Wadham College. And after his [Wilkins's] removal to Trinity College in Cambridge, at the lodgings of the Honourable Mr Robert Boyle,[4] then resident for divers years in Oxford.

Those meetings in London continued, and, after the King's return in

1660, were increased with the accession of divers worthy and honourable persons; and were afterwards incorporated by the name of the Royal Society, etc. and so continue to this day.

Notes

1 'Of which number . . .'; for Wilkins see Biographical Index, p. 390; Goddard p. 332 Note 3; Ent p. 332 Note 5; Glisson and Merret p. 338 Note 1, Foster, p. 338, Note 4. Theodore Haak was an exile from the Palatinate, settled in England from 1625; he was a close associate of Samuel Hartlib and other Puritan reformers and had contacts with many European scholars. For Gresham College see p. 332, Note 4.
2 'Our business was . . .': for the nature of these discussions see p. 338, Note 2.
3 'with Dr Ward . . .': for Ward see Biographical Index, p. 389; for Bathurst, Petty and Willis, p. 332, Note. 3
4 'Robert Boyle': see Biographical Index, p. 381.

143 1700–1701

[*Source*: Bodleian Library, Oxford, Ms Savile 57, p.7.]

[In this account Wallis was writing against Lewis Maidwell who petitioned Parliament in 1700 for funds to start a technical academy in London. Wallis argued that the universities already provided adequate scientific education and so he now, like Sprat, emphasized the debt the Royal Society owed to the University of Oxford.]

It is also more that [than is meant] fifty [years] ago, since divers of the best rank amongst us, when the University began to be a little settled after the disturbance of a long civil war, with many other inquisitive persons, did, by common agreement, meet weekly; and made it their business to inquire into, and promote, mechanical experiments, and other pieces of experimental philosophy, and, what they call the New Philosophy. Which meetings afterward were divided: part of them continuing their meetings here; and part of them, removing to London, laid the foundation of what is now called the Royal Society, at Gresham College.[1] And the like meeting[s], though with some intermission, have been here[2] pursued to good purpose.

Notes

1 'Gresham College': see p. 332, Note 4.
2 'meetings . . . here': Wallis is referring to the Oxford Philosophical Society, founded by topographer Robert Plot in 1683.

* * * * * * * * * * *

144 Robert Hooke: Experimental Philosophy

[*Source*: Robert Hooke (1665) *Micrographia*, from the 'Preface', not paginated.]

It is the great prerogative of mankind above other creatures, that we are not only able to behold the works of nature, or barely to sustain our lives by them, but we have also the power of considering, comparing, altering, assisting, and improving them to various uses. And as this is the peculiar privilege of human nature in general, so is it capable of being so far advanced by the helps of art and experience, as to make some men excel others in their observations, and deductions, almost as much as they do beasts. By the addition of such artificial instruments and methods, there may be, in some manner, a reparation made for the mischiefs and imperfection mankind has drawn upon itself by negligence and intemperance, and a wilful and superstitious deserting the prescripts and rules of nature, whereby every man, both from a deriv'd corruption, innate and born with him, and from his breeding and converse with men, is very subject to slip into all sorts of errors.

The only way which now remains for us to recover some degree of those former perfections seems to be by rectifying the operations of the sense, the memory and reason; since upon the evidence, the strength, the integrity and the right correspondence of all these, all the light, by which our actions are to be guided, is to be renewed, and all our command over things is to be established . . . .

All the uncertainty and mistakes of human actions proceed either from the narrowness and wandering of our senses, from the slipperiness or delusion of our memory, from the confinement or rashness of our understanding, so that 'tis no wonder that our power over natural causes and effects is so slowly improv'd, seeing we are not only to contend with the obscurity and difficulty of the things whereon we work and think, but even the forces of our own minds conspire to betray us.

These being the dangers in the process of human reason, the remedies of them all can only proceed from the real, the mechanical, the experimental philosophy, which has this advantage over the philosophy of discourse and disputation, that whereas that chiefly aims at the subtlety of its deductions and conclusions, without much regard to the first groundwork, which ought to be well laid on the sense and memory; so this intends the right ordering of them all, and the making them serviceable to each other.

The first thing to be undertaken in this weighty work is a watchfulness over the failings, and an enlargement of the dominion of the senses.

To which end it is requisite, first, that there should be a scrupulous choice, and a strict examination of the reality, constancy and certainty of the particulars that we admit: this is the first rise whereon truth is to begin, and here the most severe and most impartial diligence must be employed; the storing up of all, without any regard to evidence or use, will only tend to darkness and confusion. We must not therefore esteem the riches of our philosophical treasure by the number only, but chiefly by the weight; the most vulgar instances are not to be neglected, but above all, the most instructive are to be entertain'd; the footsteps of nature are to be trac'd, not only in her ordinary course, but when she seems to be put to her shifts, to make many doublings and turnings, and to use some kind of art in endeavouring to avoid our discovery.

The next care to be taken, in respect of the senses, is a supplying of their infirmities with instruments, and, as it were, the adding of artificial organs to the natural; this in one of them has been of late years accomplished with prodigious benefit to all sorts of useful knowledge, by the invention of optical glasses. By the means of telescopes, there is nothing so far distant but may be represented to our view; and by the help of microscopes, there is nothing so small as to escape our inquiry; hence there is a new visible world discovered to the understanding. By this means the heavens are open'd, and a vast number of new stars, and new motions, and new productions appear in them, to which all the ancient astronomers were utterly strangers. By this the earth itself, which lies so near us, under our feet, shows quite a new thing to us, and in every little particle of its matter, we now behold almost as great a variety of creatures, as we were able before to reckon up in the whole universe itself.

It seems not improbable, but that by these helps the subtlety of the composition of bodies, the structure of their parts, the various texture of their matter, the instruments and manner of their inward motions, and all the other possible appearances of things, may come to be more fully discovered; all which the ancient Peripatetics were content to comprehend in two general and (unless further explained) useless words of matter and form. From whence there may arise many admirable advantages, towards the increase of the operative, and the mechanic knowledge, to which this age seems so much inclined, because we may perhaps be enabled to discern all the secret workings of nature, almost in the same manner as we do those that are the productions of art, and are manag'd by wheels, and engines, and springs, that were devised by human wit.

In this kind I here present to the world my imperfect endeavours; which though they shall prove no other way considerable, yet, I hope, they may be in some measure useful to the main design of a reformation in philosophy, if it be only by showing that there is not so much requir'd towards it, any strength of imagination, or exactness of method, or depth of contemplation (though the addition of these, where they can be had, must needs produce a much more perfect composure) as a sincere hand and a faithful eye to examine and to record the things themselves as they appear . . . .

If once this method were followed with diligence and attention, there is nothing that lies within the power of human wit (or which is far more effectual) of human industry, which we might not compass; we might not only hope for inventions to equalise those of Copernicus, Galileo, Gilbert, Harvey[1] and of others, whose names are almost lost, that were the inventors of gunpowder, the seaman's compass, printing, etching, graving, microscopes, etc., but multitudes that may far exceed them: for even those discoveries seem to have been the products of some such method, though but imperfect; what may not be therefore expected from it if thoroughly prosecuted? Talking and contention of arguments would soon be turn'd into labours; all the fine dreams of opinions, and universal metaphysical natures, which the luxury of subtle brains has devis'd, would quickly vanish, and give place to solid histories, experiments and works. And as at first, mankind fell by tasting of the forbidden tree of knowledge, so we, their posterity, may be in part restor'd by the same way, not only by beholding and contemplating, but by tasting too those fruits of natural knowledge, that were never yet forbidden.

From hence the world may be assisted with variety of inventions, new matter for sciences may be collected, the old improv'd, and their rust rubb'd away; and as it is by the benefit of senses that we receive all our skill in the works of nature, so they also may be wonderfully benefited by it, and may be guided to an easier and more exact performance of their offices; 'tis not unlikely, but that we may find out wherein our senses are deficient, and as easily find ways of repairing them.

The endeavours of skilful men have been most conversant about the assistance of the eye, and many noble productions have followed upon it; and from hence we may conclude, that there is a way open'd for advancing the operations, not only of all the other senses, but even of the eye itself; that which has been already done ought not to content us, but rather to encourage us to proceed further, and to attempt greater things in the same and different ways . . . .

This was undertaken in prosecution of the design which the Royal Society has propos'd to itself. For the members of the assembly, having before their eyes so many fatal instances of the errors and falsehoods, in which the greatest part of mankind has so long wandered, because they reli'd upon the strength of human reason alone, have begun anew to correct all hypotheses by sense, as seamen do their dead reckonings by celestial observations; and to this purpose it has been their principal endeavour to enlarge and strengthen the senses by medicine, and by such outward instruments as are proper for their particular works. By this means they find some reason to suspect that those effects of bodies, which have been commonly attributed to qualities, and those confess'd to be occult, are perform'd by the small machines of nature, which are not to be discern'd without these helps . . . . And the ends of all these enquiries they intend to be the pleasure of contemplative minds, but above all, the ease and dispatch of the labours of men's hands. They do indeed neglect no opportunity to bring all the rare things of remote countries within the compass of their knowledge and practice. But they still acknowledge their most useful informations to arise from common things, and from diversifying their most ordinary operations upon them. They do not wholly reject experiments of mere light and theory; but they principally aim at such, whose applications will improve and facilitate the present way of manual arts. And though some men, who are perhaps taken up about less honourable employments, are pleas'd to censure their proceedings, yet they can show more fruits of their first three years wherein they have assembled, than any other Society in Europe can for a much larger space of time.

Notes

1 'Copernicus . . . Harvey': Nicolaus Copernicus (died 1543), Polish astronomer who put forward a heliocentric theory of the universe. Galileo Galilei (1564–1642), Italian astronomer and physicist, a strong supporter of Copernican theories. William Gilbert (died 1603), physician to Elizabeth I and James I, published his theories on magnetism in 1600. William Harvey (died 1657) explained the circulation of the blood in a work published in 1628; Harvey acted as physician to the royalist army during the civil war.

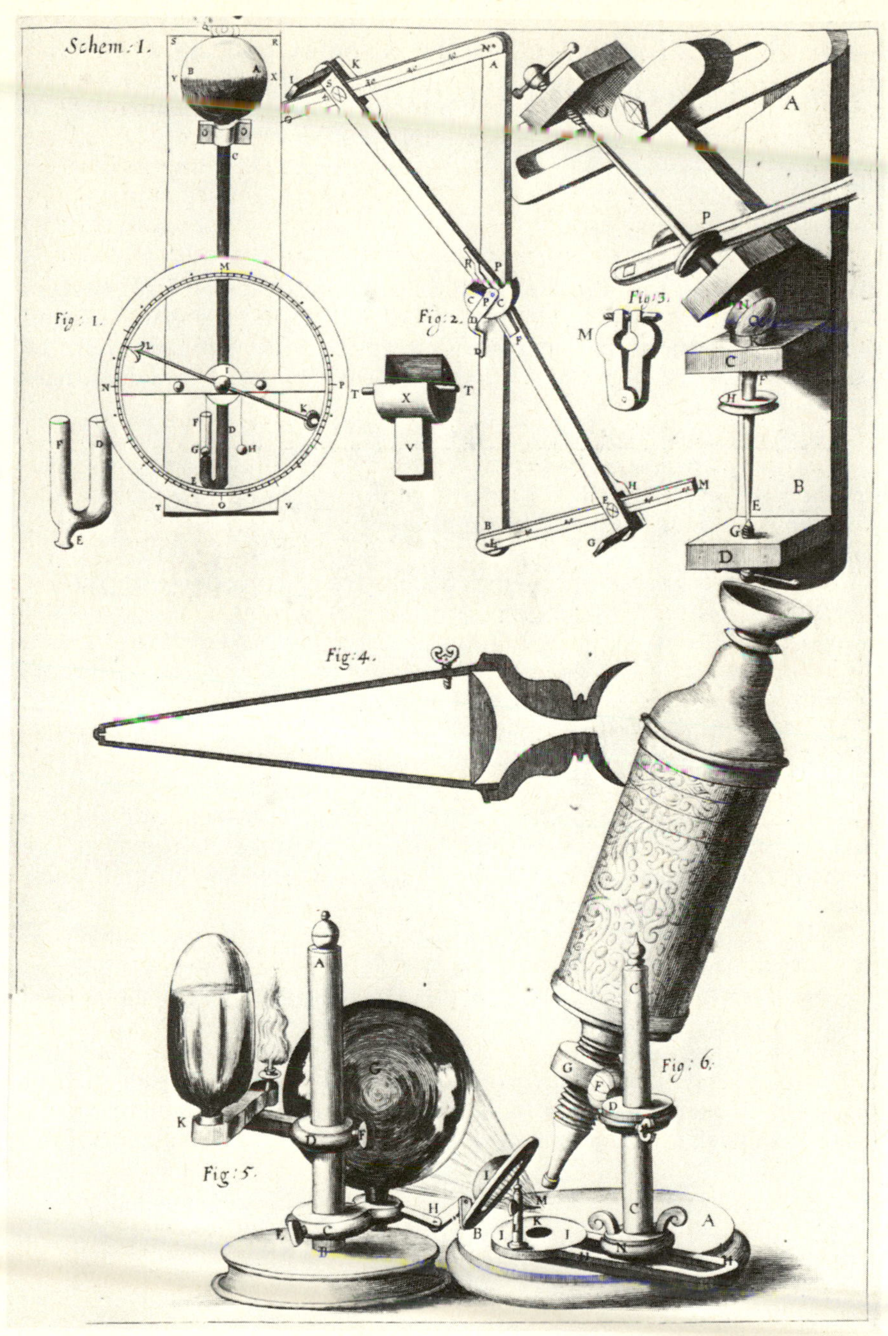

Microscope illustration from Robert Hooke, Micrographia (1665) (Bodleian Library)

145 Robert Boyle: The Usefulness of Experimental Philosophy

[*Source*: Robert Boyle (1671) *Some Considerations Touching the Usefulnesse of Experimental Naturall Philosophy*, the second tome, preamble, no pagination.]

It was suggested, that the uses would not prove despicable . . . such as the improvement of the minds of men, and, especially, the assisting them to understand the works of God, and thereby engage them to admire, praise and thank him for them. Besides these, I say, there may be other uses: . . .

I It may afford materials for the history of nature . . .

II It may afford some instructions, advices, and hints to promote the practical or operative part of natural philosophy in divers particulars, wherein men have been either not able, or not solicitous, to assist the curious.

III It may enable gentlemen and scholars to converse with tradesmen and benefit themselves (and perhaps the tradesmen too) by that conversation; or at least, it will qualify them to ask questions of men that converse with things, and sometimes to exchange experiments with them.

IV It may serve to beget a confederacy and an union between parts of learning, whose possessors have hitherto kept their respective skills strangers to one another; and by that means may bring great variety of observations and experiments of differing kinds into the notice of one man, or of the same persons; which how advantageous it may prove towards the increase of knowledge, our illustrious Verulam [Francis Bacon] has somewhere taught us.

V It may contribute to the rescuing natural philosophy from that unhappy imputation of barrenness, which it has so long lain under . . .

VI And which is the main of all, it may serve by positive considerations and directions to rouse up the generality of those that are any thing inquisitive, and both loudly excite and somewhat assist the curiosity of mankind; from which alone may be expected a greater progress in useful learning, and consequently greater advantages to men, than in the present state of human affairs will be easily imagin'd.

Isaac Newton

146 On Experiments in Light

[*Source*: *The Philosophical Transactions of the Royal Society of London*, first published 1672; here taken from the abridgement by Charles Hutton, George Shaw and Richard Pearson (1809) volume one, pp.678–81, and 683–6.]

[This account was sent by Newton in a letter of 6 February 1672 to the editor of the *Philosophical Transactions* of the Royal Society, who published it the same month.]

[1] Sir,
To perform my late promise to you I shall without further ceremony acquaint you, that in the beginning of the year 1666 (at which time I applied myself to the grinding of optic glasses of other figures than spherical) I procured a triangular glass prism, to try therewith the celebrated phenomena of colours. And for that purpose having darkened my chamber, and made a small hole in my window shuts, to let in a convenient quantity of the sun's light, I placed my prism at his entrance, that it might be thereby refracted to the opposite wall. It was at first a very pleasing diversion to view the vivid and intense colours produced thereby; but after a while applying myself to consider them more circumspectly, I was surprised to see them in an oblong form; which, according to the received laws of refraction, I expected would have been circular. They were terminated at the sides with straight lines, but at the ends, the decay of light was so gradual, that it was difficult to determine justly what was their figure; yet they seemed semicircular.

[2] Comparing the length of this coloured spectrum with its breadth, I found it about five times greater; a disproportion so extravagant, that it excited me to a more than ordinary curiosity of examining from whence it might proceed. I could scarce think, that the various thickness of the glass, or the termination with shadow or darkness, could have any influence on light to produce such an effect; yet I thought it not amiss, first to examine those circumstances, and so tried what would happen by transmitting light through parts of the glass of divers thicknesses, or through holes in the window of divers sizes, or by setting the prism without, so that the light might pass through it, and be refracted before it was terminated by the hole; but I found none of those circumstances material. The fashion of the colours was in all these cases the same.

[3] Then I suspected, whether by any unevenness in the glass, or other contingent irregularity, these colours might be thus dilated. And to try this, I took another prism like the former, and so placed it, that the light, passing through them both, might be refracted contrary

ways, and so by the latter returned into that course from which the former had diverted it. For, by this means, I thought the regular effects of the first prism would be destroyed by the second, but the irregular ones more augmented, by the multiplicity of refractions. The event was, that the light, which by the first prism was diffused into an oblong form, was by the second reduced into an orbicular one, with as much regularity as when it did not at all pass through them. So that, whatever was the cause of that length, it was not any contingent irregularity. . . .

[4] Then I began to suspect whether the rays, after their trajection through the prism, did not move in curve lines, and according to their more or less curvity tend to divers parts of the wall. And it increased my suspicion, when I remembered that I had often seen a tennis ball, struck with an oblique racket, describe such a curveline. For, a circular as well as a progressive motion being communicated to it by that stroke, its parts on that side, where the motions conspire, must press and beat the contiguous air more violently than on the other, and there excite a reluctancy and reaction of the air proportionably greater. And for the same reason, if the rays of light should possibly be globular bodies, and by their oblique passage out of one medium into another acquire a circulating motion, they ought to feel the greater resistance from the ambient ether,[1] on that side where the motions conspire, and thence be continually bowed to the other. But notwithstanding this plausible ground of suspicion, when I came to examine it, I could observe no such curvity in them. And besides (which was enough for my purpose) I observed, that the difference between the length of the image and diameter of the hole, through which the light was transmitted, was proportionable to their distance.

[5] The gradual removal of these suspicions, at length led me to the *experimentum crucis*, [crucial experiment] which was this: I took two boards, and placed one of them close behind the prism at the window, so that the light might pass through a small hole, made in it for the purpose, and fall on the other board, which I placed at about 12 feet distance, having first made a small hole in it also, for some of that incident light to pass through. Then I placed another prism behind this second board, so that the light, trajected through both the boards, might pass through that also, and be again refracted before it arrived at the wall. This done, I took the first prism in my hand, and turned it to and fro slowly about its axis, so much as to make the several parts of the image, cast on the second board, successively pass through the hole in it, that I might observe to what places on the wall the second prism would refract them. And I saw, by the variation of those places, that the light tending to that end of the image, towards which the refraction of the first prism was made, did in the second prism suffer a refraction considerably greater than the light tending to the other end. And so the true cause of the length of that image was detected to be no other, than that light consists of rays differently refrangible, which, without any respect to a difference in their incidence, were, according to their degrees of refrangibility, transmitted towards divers parts of the

wall. . . .

[6] I shall now proceed to acquaint you with another more notable difformity [diversity of form] in its rays, wherein the origin of colours is unfolded: concerning which I shall lay down the doctrine first, and then, for its examination, give you an instance or two of the experiments, as a specimen of the rest. The doctrine you will find comprehended and illustrated in the following propositions:

1 As the rays of light differ in degrees of refrangibility, so they also differ in their disposition to exhibit this or that particular colour. Colours are not qualifications of light, derived from refractions, or reflections of natural bodies (as it is generally believed) but original and connate properties, which in divers rays are diverse. Some rays are disposed to exhibit a red colour, and no other; some a yellow, and no other; some a green, and no other; and so of the rest. Nor are there only rays proper and particular to the more eminent colours, but even to all their intermediate gradations.

2 To the same degree of refrangibility ever belongs the same colour, and to the same colour ever belongs the same degree of refrangibility. The least refrangible rays are all disposed to exhibit a red colour, and contrarily, those rays which are disposed to exhibit a red colour, are all the least refrangible: so the most refrangible rays are all disposed to exhibit a deep violet-colour, and contrarily, those which are apt to exhibit such a violet colour, are all the most refrangible. And so to all the intermediate colours, in a continued series, belong intermediate degrees of refrangibility. And this analogy betwixt colours, and refrangibility, is very precise and strict; the rays always either exactly agreeing in both, or proportionally disagreeing in both.

3 The species of colour, and degree of refrangibility proper to any particular sort of rays, is not mutable by refraction, nor by reflection from natural bodies, nor by any other cause, that I could yet observe. When any one sort of rays has been well parted from those of other kinds, it has afterwards obstinately retained its colour, notwithstanding my utmost endeavours to change it. I have refracted it with prisms, and reflected it with bodies, which in day-light were of other colours; I have intercepted it with the coloured film of air interceding two compressed plates of glass; transmitted it through coloured mediums, and through mediums irradiated with other sorts of rays, and diversely terminated it; and yet could never produce any new colour out of it. It would, by contracting or dilating, become more brisk, or faint, and by the loss of many rays, in some cases very obscure and dark; but I could never see it change in specie.

4 Yet seeming transmutations of colours may be made, where there is any mixture of divers sorts of rays. For in such mixtures, the component colours appear not, but, by their mutual allaying each other, constitute a middling colour. And therefore, if by refraction, or any other of the aforesaid causes, the difform rays, latent in such a mixture, be separated, there shall emerge colours different from the colour of the composition. Which colours are not new generated, but

only made apparent by being parted; for if they be again entirely mixed and blended together, they will again compose that colour, which they did before separation. And for the same reason, transmutations made by the convening of divers colours are not real; for when the difform rays are again severed, they will exhibit the very same colours, which they did before they entered the composition; as you see, blue and yellow powders, when finely mixed, appear to the naked eye green, and yet the colours of the component corpuscles are not thereby really transmuted, but only blended. For, when viewed with a good microscope, they still appear blue and yellow interspersedly.

5 There are therefore two sorts of colours. The one original and simple, the other compounded of these. The original or primary colours are, red, yellow, green, blue, and a violet-purple, together with orange, indigo, and an indefinite variety of intermediate gradations.

6 The same colours in specie with these primary ones may be also produced by composition: for a mixture of yellow and blue makes green; of red and yellow makes orange; of orange and yellowish green makes yellow. And in general, if any two colours be mixed, which in the series of those, generated by the prism, are not too far distant one from another, they by their mutual alloy compound that colour, which in the said series appears in the midway between them. But those which are situated at too great a distance, do not so. Orange and indigo produce not the intermediate green, nor scarlet and green the intermediate yellow.

7 But the most surprising and wonderful composition was that of whiteness. There is no one sort of rays which alone can exhibit this. It is ever compounded, and to its composition are requisite all the aforesaid primary colours, mixed in a due proportion. I have often with admiration beheld, that all the colours of the prism being made to converge, and thereby to be again mixed as they were in the light before it was incident upon the prism, reproduced light, entirely and perfectly white, and not at all sensibly differing from a direct light of the sun, unless when the glasses I used were not sufficiently clear; for then they would a little incline it to their colour.

8 Hence therefore it comes to pass, that whiteness is the usual colour of light; for, light is a confused aggregate of rays indued with all sorts of colours, as they are promiscuously darted from the various parts of luminous bodies. And of such a confused aggregate, as I said, is generated whiteness, if there be a due proportion of the ingredients; but if any one predominate, the light must incline to that colour; as it happens in the blue flame of brimstone; the yellow flame of a candle; and the various colours of the fixed stars.

9 These things considered, the manner how colours are produced by the prism, is evident. For, of the rays constituting the incident light, since those which differ in colour, proportionally differ in refrangibility, they by their unequal refractions must be severed and dispersed into an oblong form in an orderly succession, from the least refracted scarlet, to the most refracted violet. And for the same reason it is that

objects, when looked upon through a prism, appear coloured. For the difform rays, by their unequal refractions, are made to diverge towards several parts of the retina, and there express the images of things coloured, as in the former case they did the sun's image upon a wall. And by this inequality of refractions they become not only coloured, but also very confused and indistinct.

10 Why the colours of the rainbow appear in falling drops of rain, is also from hence evident. For those drops which refract the rays disposed to appear purple, in greatest quantity to the spectator's eye, refract the rays of other sorts so much less, as to make them pass beside it; and such are the drops on the inside of the primary bow, and on the outside of the secondary or exterior one. So those drops, which refract in greatest plenty the rays apt to appear red, towards the spectator's eye, refract those of other sorts so much more, as to make them pass beside it: and such are the drops on the exterior part of the primary, and interior part of the secondary bow.

11 The odd phenomena of an infusion of *lignum nephriticum*,[2] leaf gold, fragments of coloured glass, and some other transparently coloured bodies, appearing in one position of one colour, and of another in another, are on these grounds no longer riddles. For, those are substances apt to reflect one sort of light, and transmit another; as may be seen in a dark room, by illuminating them with similar or uncompounded light. For then they appear of that colour only, with which they are illuminated, but yet in one position more vivid and luminous than in another, accordingly as they are disposed more or less to reflect or transmit the incident colour.

12 From hence also is manifest the reason of an unexpected experiment, which Mr Hooke, somewhere in his micrography[3] relates to have made with two wedge-like transparent vessels, filled the one with red, the other with a blue liquor: namely, that though they were severally transparent enough, yet both together became opaque; for, if one transmitted only red, and the other only blue, no rays could pass through both.

13 I might add more instances of this nature; but I shall conclude with this general one, that the colours of all natural bodies have no other origin than this, that they are variously qualified to reflect one sort of light in greater plenty than another. And this I have experimented in a dark room, by illuminating those bodies with uncompounded light of divers colours. For, by that means, any body may be made to appear of any colour.

Notes

1 'ether': a universally pervasive material, which Newton believed to be the medium through which forces can act.

2 'infusion of *lignum nephriticum*': an aqueous extract of wood used to treat kidney diseases. It is yellow by transmitted light, blue by reflected light; a phenomenon identified as 'luminescence emission' by Stokes in 1852.

3 'Mr Hooke . . .': for Robert Hooke, see Biographical Index, p. 384, for an extract from his *Micrographia* see p. 341.

147 Rules of Reasoning in Natural Philosophy

[*Source*: Sir Isaac Newton (1729) *The Mathematical Principles of Natural Philosophy*, translated by Andrew Motte, volume two, pp.202–5.]

RULE I

We are to admit no more causes of natural things than such as are both true and sufficient to explain their appearances.

To this purpose the philosophers say that Nature does nothing in vain, and more is in vain when less will serve; for Nature is pleased with simplicity, and affects not the pomp of superfluous causes.

RULE II

Therefore to the same natural effects we must, as far as possible, assign the same causes.

As to respiration in a man and in a beast; the descent of stones on Europe and in America; the light of our culinary fire and of the sun; the reflection of light in the earth, and in the planets.

RULE III

The qualities of bodies, which admit neither intension nor remission of degrees, and which are found to belong to all bodies within the reach of our experiments, are to be esteemed the universal qualities of all bodies whatsoever.

For since the qualities of bodies are only known to us by experiments, we are to hold for universal all such as universally agree with experiments; and such as are not liable to diminution can never be quite taken away. We are certainly not to relinquish the evidence of experiments for the sake of dreams and vain fictions of our own devising; nor are we to recede from the analogy of Nature, which uses to be simple, and always consonant to itself. We no other way know the extension of bodies than by our senses, nor do these reach it in all bodies; but because we perceive extension in all that are sensible, therefore we ascribe it universally to all others also. That abundance of bodies are hard, we learn by experience; and because the hardness of the whole arises from the hardness of the parts, we therefore justly infer the hardness of the undivided particles not only of the bodies we feel but of all others. That all bodies are impenetrable, we gather not from reason, but from sensation. The bodies which we handle we find impenetrable, and thence conclude impenetrability to be an universal property of all bodies whatsoever. That all bodies are moveable, and endowed with certain powers (which we call the *vires inertiae*) [inertial powers] of persevering in their motion, or in their rest, we only infer from the like properties observed in the bodies which we have seen. The extension, hardness, impenetrability, mobility, and *vis inertiae* of the whole, result from the extension, hardness, impenetrability, mobility, and *vires inertiae* of the parts; and thence we conclude the least particles of all bodies to be also all extended, and hard, and impenetrable, and moveable, and endowed with their proper *vires inertiae*. And this is the foundation of all philosophy. Moreover, that the divided but contiguous particles of bodies may be separated from one another, is matter of observation; and, in the particles that remain undivided, our minds are able to distinguish yet lesser parts, as is mathematically demonstrated. But whether the parts so distinguished, and not yet divided, may, by the powers of Nature, be actually divided and separated from one another, we cannot certainly determine. Yet, had we the proof of but one experiment that any undivided particle, in breaking a hard and solid body, suffered a division, we might by virtue of this rule conclude that the undivided as well as the divided particles may be divided and actually separated to infinity.

Lastly, if it universally appears, by experiments and astronomical observations, that all bodies about the earth gravitate towards the earth, and that in proportion to the quantity of matter which they severally contain; that the moon likewise, according to the quantity of its matter, gravitates towards the earth; that, on the other hand, our sea gravitates towards the moon; and all the planets mutually one towards another; and the comets in like manner towards the sun; we must, in consequence of this rule, universally allow that all bodies whatsoever are endowed with a principle of mutual gravitation. For the argument from the appearances concludes with more force for the universal gravitation of all bodies than for their impenetrability; of which, among those in the celestial regions, we have no experiments, nor any manner of observation. Not that I affirm gravity to be essential to bodies: by their *vis insita* [innate power] I mean nothing but their *vis inertiae*. This is immutable. Their gravity is diminished as they recede from the earth.

RULE IV

In experimental philosophy we are to look upon propositions collected by general induction from phenomena as accurately or very nearly true, notwithstanding any contrary hypotheses that may be imagined, till such time as other phenomena occur, by which they may either be made more accurate, or liable to exceptions.

This rule we must follow, that the argument of induction may not be evaded by hypotheses.

148 The Law of Gravitation

[*Source*: Sir Isaac Newton (1729) *The Mathematical Principles of Natural Philosophy*, translated by Andrew Motte, volume two, p. 392.]

Hitherto we have explained the phenomena of the heavens and of our sea by the power of gravity, but have not yet assigned the cause of this power. This is certain, that it must proceed from a cause that penetrates to the very centres of the sun and planets, without suffering the least diminution of its force; that operates not according to the quantity of the surfaces of the particles upon which it acts (as mechanical causes use to do), but according to the quantity of the solid matter which they contain, and propagates its virtue on all sides to immense distances, decreasing always in the duplicate proportion of the distances. Gravitation towards the sun is made up out of the gravitations towards the several particles of which the body of the sun is composed; and in receding from the sun decreases accurately in the duplicate proportion of the distances as far as the orb of Saturn, as evidently appears from the quiescence of the aphelions of the planets; nay, and even to the remotest aphelions of the comets, if those aphelions are also quiescent. But hitherto I have not been able to discover the cause of those properties of gravity from phenomena, and I frame no hypotheses: for whatever is not deduced from the phenomena is to be called an hypothesis; and hypotheses, whether metaphysical or physical, whether of occult qualities or mechanical, have no place in experimental philosophy. In this philosophy particular propositions are inferred from the phenomena, and afterwards rendered general by induction. Thus it was that the impenetrability, the mobility, and the impulsive force of bodies, and the laws of motion and of gravitation, were discovered. And to us it is enough that gravity does really exist, and acts according to the laws which we have explained, and abundantly serves to account for all the motions of the celestial bodies, and of our sea.

149 Newton to Bentley

[*Source*: *Four Letters from Sir Isaac Newton to Doctor Bentley* (1756), pp.1–11.]

[In 1692, Richard Bentley, a young clergyman and classical scholar, delivered the first series of lectures established under the will of Robert Boyle. The theme of his lectures was 'A Confutation of Atheism', and the last three, collectively entitled 'A Confutation of Atheism from the Origin and Frame of the World', drew heavily on Newton's *Principia*.

Before publishing his lectures, Bentley wrote to Newton seeking clarification on certain points. Only Bentley's last letter survives but Newton's four replies are extant. This is the first of them, written from Cambridge 10 December 1692.]

When I wrote my treatise about our system [The *Principia*], I had an eye upon such principles as might work with considering men for the belief of a deity, and nothing can rejoice me more than to find it useful for that purpose. But if I have done the public any service this way, it is due to nothing but industry and patient thought.

As to your first query, it seems to me that if the matter of our sun and planets, and all the matter of the universe, were evenly scattered throughout all the heavens, and every particle had an innate gravity towards all the rest, and the whole space, throughout which this matter was scattered, was but finite; the matter on the outside of this space would by its gravity tend towards all the matter on the inside, and by consequence fall down into the middle of the whole space, and there compose one great spherical mass. But if the matter was evenly dispersed throughout an infinite space, it could never convene into one mass, but some of it would convene into one mass and some into another, so as to make an infinite number of great masses, scattered at great distances from one to another throughout all that infinite space. And thus might the sun and fixed stars be formed, supposing the matter were of a lucid nature. But how the matter should divide itself into two sorts, and that part of it, which is fit to compose a shining body, should fall down into one mass and make a sun, and the rest, which is fit to compose an opaque body, should coalesce, not into one great body like the shining matter, but into many little ones; or if the sun at first were an opaque body like the planets, or the planets lucid bodies like the sun, how he alone should be changed into a shining body, whilst all they continue opaque, or all they be changed into opaque ones, whilst he remains unchanged, I do not think explicable by mere natural causes, but am forced to ascribe it to the counsel and contrivance of a voluntary agent.

The same power, whether natural or supernatural, which placed the sun in the centre of the six primary planets, placed Saturn in the centre of the orbs of his five secondary planets, and Jupiter in the centre of his four secondary planets, and the earth in the centre of the moon's orb; and therefore had this cause been a blind one, without contrivance or design, the sun would have been a body of the same kind with Saturn, Jupiter and the earth, that is, without light and heat. Why there is one body in our system qualified to give light and heat to all the rest, I know no reason, but because the author of the system thought it convenient; and why there is but one body of this kind I know no reason, but because one was sufficient to warm and enlighten all the rest. For the Cartesian hypothesis of suns losing their light, and then turning into comets, and comets into planets, can have no place in my system, and is plainly erroneous; because it is certain that as often as they appear to us, they descend into the system of our planets, lower than the orb of Jupiter, and sometimes lower than the orbs of Venus and Mercury, and yet never stay here, but always return from the sun with the same degrees of motion by which they approached him.

To your second query, I answer that the motions which the planets now have could not spring from any natural cause alone, but were impressed by an intelligent agent. For since comets descend into the region of our planets, and here move all manner of ways, going sometimes the same way with the planets, sometimes the contrary way, and sometimes in cross ways, in planes inclined to the plane of the ecliptic, and at all kinds of angles, 'tis plain there is no natural cause which could determine all the planets, both primary and secondary, to move the same way and in the same plane, without any considerable variation: this must have been the effect of counsel. Nor is there any natural cause which could give the planets those just degrees of velocity, in proportion to their distances from the sun, and other central bodies, which were requisite to make them move in such concentric orbs about those bodies. Had the planets been as swift as comets, in proportion to their distances from the sun (as they would have been, had their motion been caused by their gravity, whereby the matter, at the first formation of the planets, might fall from the remotest regions towards the sun) they would not move in concentric orbs, but in such eccentric ones as the comets move in. Were all the planets as swift as Mercury, or as slow as Saturn, or his satellites; or were their several velocities otherwise much greater or less than they are, as they might have been had they arose from any other cause than their gravities; or had the distances from the centres about which they move been greater or less than they are with the same velocities; or had the quantity of matter in the sun, or in Saturn, Jupiter and the earth, and by consequence their gravitating power been greater or less than it is; the primary planets could not have revolved about the sun, nor the secondary ones about Saturn, Jupiter and the earth, in concentric circles as they do, but would have moved in hyperbolas, or parabolas, or in ellipses very eccentric. To make this system therefore, with all its motions, required a cause which understood, and compared together, the quantities of matter in the several bodies of the sun and planets, and the gravitating powers resulting from thence; the several distances of the primary planets from the sun, and of the secondary ones from Saturn, Jupiter, and the earth; and the velocities with which these planets could revolve about those quantities of matter in the central bodies; and to compare and adjust all these things together, in so great a variety of bodies, argues that cause to be not blind and fortuitous, but very well skilled in mechanics and geometry.

To your third query, I answer that it may be represented that the sun may, by heating those planets most which are nearest to him, cause them to be better concocted, and more condensed by that concoction. But when I consider that our earth is much more heated in its bowels below the upper crust by subterraneous fermentations of mineral bodies than by the sun, I see not why the interior parts of Jupiter and Saturn might not be as much heated, concocted, and coagulated by those fermentations as our earth is; and therefore this various density should have some other cause than the various distances of the planets from the sun. And I am confirmed in this opinion by considering, that the planets of Jupiter and Saturn, as they are rarer than the rest, so they are vastly greater, and contain a far greater quantity of matter, and have many satellites about them; which qualifications surely arose not from their being placed at so great a distance from the sun, but were rather the cause why the creator placed them at great distance. For by their gravitating powers they disturb one another's motions very sensibly, as I find by some late observations of Mr Flamsteed,[1] and had they been placed much nearer to the sun and to one another, they would by the same powers have caused a considerable disturbance to the whole system.

To your fourth query, I answer that in the hypothesis of vortices,[2] the inclination of the axis of the earth might, in my opinion, be ascribed to the situation of the earth's vortex before it was absorbed by the neighbouring vortices, and the earth turned from a sun to a comet; but this inclination ought to decrease constantly in compliance with the motion of the earth's vortex, whose axis is much less inclined to the ecliptic, as appears by the motion of the moon carried about therein. If the sun by his rays could carry about the planets, yet I do not see how he could thereby effect their diurnal motions.

Lastly, I see nothing extraordinary in the inclination of the earth's axis for proving a deity, unless you will urge it as a contrivance for winter and summer, and for making the earth habitable towards the poles; and that the diurnal rotations of the sun and planets, as they could hardly arise from any cause purely mechanical, so by being determined all the same way with the annual and menstrual motions, they seem to make up that harmony in the system, which, as I explained above, was the effect of choice rather than chance.

There is yet another argument for a deity, which I take to be a very strong one, but till the principles on which it is grounded are better received, I think it more advisable to let it sleep.

Notes

1 'Mr Flamsteed': John Flamsteed (1646–1719) first Astronomer Royal.

2 'the hypothesis of vortices': the theory of the French philosopher Descartes who held that the universe was filled with a fluid, constantly rotating, through which the stars and planets swirled round in vortices, much as a stick rotates in a whirlpool.

[Newton's study of the Bible was as rigorous and as dedicated as his scientific work. He was particularly concerned with the prophetic books of Daniel and of Revelation (The Apocalypse): in F.E. Manuel's words, 'Newton wrestled with the meaning of these books from early manhood until his death'. These two extracts are from manuscript treatises, written at Cambridge in the 1670s and 1680s, and now in the Newton Collection in Jerusalem. In both passages Newton's repetitions and stylistic changes have been omitted.]

150 Rules for Interpreting the Words and Language in Scripture

[*Source*: F.E. Manuel (1974) *The Religion of Isaac Newton*, pp.116–19.]

[Part of an unfinished treatise on Revelation]

1 To observe diligently the consent of Scriptures and analogy of the prophetic style, and to reject those interpretations where this is not duly observed. Thus if any man interpret a beast to signify some great vice, this is to be rejected as his private imagination because according to the style and tenor of the Apocalypse and of all other prophetic Scriptures a beast signifies a ... body politic and sometimes a single person which heads that body, and there is no ground in Scripture for any other interpretation ....

2 To assign but one meaning to one place of Scripture ... (For a man cannot be obliged to believe more meanings of a place than one. If the place be intended literally he is not obliged to believe any mystical sense, but if mystically, he is not obliged to believe the literal sense. And if two meanings seem equally probable he is obliged to believe no more than in general that one of them is genuine until he meet with some motive to prefer one side.

Yet this rule is not so to be understood but that the same thing may have divers meanings but then each meaning is to be collected from a different ... passage or circumstance of Scripture. As when of anything done under the Law we collect the literal truth ... out of the Old Testament and a mystical meaning ... out of the New. Or understand the heads of the beast both of mountains and kings out of Revelation 17. 9, 10. Or consider the number of the beast as it is the number of his name, Rev. 13. 17, as it is apposite to the number of the churches, Rev. 7. 4, and 21. 17, and as it is the type of some iniquity, Rev. 19. 2.)[1]

... Unless it be perhaps by way of conjecture, or where the literal sense is designed to hide the more noble mystical sense as a shell the kernel ... from being tasted either by unworthy persons, or until such time as God shall think fit. In this case there may be for a blind, a true literal sense, even such as in its way may be beneficial to the church. But when we have the principal meaning: if it be mystical we can insist on a true literal sense no farther than by history or arguments drawn from circumstances it appears to be true; if literal, though there may be also a by-mystical sense yet we ... can scarce be sure there is one without (divine authority for it and)[1] some further arguments for it than a bare analogy. Much more are we to be cautious in giving a double... mystical sense. There may be a double one, as where the heads of the beast signify both mountains and kings, Apocalypse, 17. 9, 10 .... But without divine authority or at least some further argument than the analogy and resemblance and similitude of things, we... cannot be sure that the prophecy looks more ways than one. Too much liberty in this kind savours of a luxuriant ungovernable fancy and borders on enthusiasm.[2]

3 To keep as close as may be to the same sense of words, especially in the same vision, ...(unless where the propriety of the language or other circumstances plainly require a different signification [as] in divers places Scripture itself declares that there is a double meaning ...)[1] and to...prefer those interpretations where this is best...observed....Thus if a man interpret the beast to signify a kingdom in one sentence and a vice in another when there is nothing in the text that does argue any change of...sense, this is to be rejected as... no genuine interpretation. So if a man in the same or contemporary visions where the earth and sea or the earth and waters stand related to one another shall interpret the earth to signify sometimes the dition [command] of a kingdom as in the first trumpet in [Revelation] chapter 12 where the dragon came down to the inhabitants of the earth and sea; sometimes councils, as where the earth helped the woman; and sometimes only a low estate, as where...the dragon was cast into the earth or the two horned beast rose out of the earth, this wavering is not readily to be acquiesced in, but such an interpretation to be... endeavoured after as retains the same signification of earth in all cases. So in the vision of the whore, chapters 17 and 18, to take the kings of the earth... over which the woman or great city reigned... for any other than the kings of the earth which committed fornication with her, ch. 17.2, and 18. 3, 9, and lamented her fall, ch. 18. 9, 10, that is for any other than the 10 kings or horns... of the beast she reigned over, is not congruous. So in the vision of the whore, chapters 17 and 18 to take kings of the earth in... one sense ch. 17. 2, and ch. 18. 3, 9, and in another ch. 17, 18 is not harmonious.

4 To... choose those interpretations which are most according to the literal meaning of the Scriptures unless where the tenor and circumstances of the place plainly require an allegory. Thus if the wound by a sword should be interpreted of a spiritual wound, or if the battle at the seventh trumpet and vial expressed by the concourse of armies and by a hail storm with other meteors should be... interpreted of a spiritual battle; since there is nothing in the text to countenance such an interpretation it ought to be rejected as a fantasy, where note that the usual signification of a prophetic figure is in the application of this rule, to be accounted equipollent to the literal meaning of a word whenever it appears that the prophets speak in their figurative language. As if they describe the overthrow of nations by a tempest of hail, thunder, lightning and shaking of the world, the usual signification of this figure is to be esteemed the proper and direct sense of the place as much as if it

had been the literal meaning, this being a language as common amongst them as any national language is amongst the people of that nation.

5 To acquiesce in that sense of any portion of Scripture as the true one which results most freely and naturally from the use and propriety of the language and tenor of the context in that and all other places of Scripture to that sense. For if this be not the true sense, then is the true sense uncertain, and no man can. attain to any certainty in the knowledge of it. Which is to make the Scriptures no certain rule of faith, and so to reflect upon the spirit of God who dictated it.

He that without better grounds than his private opinion or the opinion of any human authority whatsoever, shall turn Scripture from the plain meaning to an allegory or to any other less natural sense declares thereby that he reposes more trust in his own imaginations or in that human authority than in the Scripture (and by consequence that he is no true believer).[1] And therefore the opinion of such men how numerous soever they be, is not to be regarded. Hence is it, and not from any real uncertainty in the Scripture that commentators have so distorted it; and this hath been the . . . door through which all heresies have crept in and turned out the ancient faith.

Notes

1 The passages in round brackets were deleted by Newton.
2 'enthusiasm': religious radicalism, with a strong emphasis on emotional experience.

151 Of the World to Come

[*Source*: Manuel (1974) *The Religion of Isaac Newton*, pp.132–6.]

It's a received opinion that this judgement shall be accompanied with a conflagration of the world; and some hearing that in the future world the wolf shall lie down with the lamb, and all beasts shall become gentle and harmless, and the earth become fuller of rivers and more fruitful, and the light of the sun and moon be much increased, and the royal city be as it were of jewels and gold like clear glass, have conceived that an amendment of the whole frame of nature shall ensue that conflagration. But these fancies have been occasioned by understanding in a vulgar and literal sense what the prophets writ in their own mystical language. For the conflagration of the world in their language signifies the consumption of kingdoms by war, as you may see in Moses, where God thus describes the desolation of Israel: 'I will . . .provoke them to anger with a foolish nation. For a fire is kindled in mine anger and shall burn unto the lowest hell and shall consume the earth with her increase and set on fire the foundations of the mountains. I will heap mischiefs upon them. I will spend mine arrows upon them. They shall be burnt with hunger and devoured with burning heat and with bitter destruction,' Deuteronomy 32.22. But in the . . . day of judgement there is also a literal conflagration of the world politic in the lake of fire and to those that are cast into it, a conflagration also of the world natural, the heaven and earth, where they are being on fire and the elements melting with fervent heat. And whilst the Apostle Peter tells us that none but the wicked shall suffer . . . in this conflagration and that this is a time of refreshing to the godly, I cannot take it for a conflagration of any considerable part of this . . .globe whereby the rest of the habitable world may be annoyed. And if the world natural be not burnt up, there is no ground for such a renovation thereof as they supposed. The glorious sun and moon, multiplied rivers and copious vegetables of the new world are its kings and people, the peaceable and harmless beasts its peaceable kingdoms, and the new Jerusalem that . . . spiritual building in Sion whereof the chief corner stone is . . .Christ, and the rest of the stones and gold are the saints, 1 Peter 2. 4, 5, 6; particularly the city and streets of pure gold are the holy people purged from the wicked as gold is refined from dross, Isaiah, 1. 25, 28. 16, Malachi, 3. 2. The 12 foundations are the 12 Apostles . . . Isaiah, 3. 26, 60. 18, and the 12 gates the elders of the tribes. For the names of the Apostles and tribes are written on them. Gates are put for elders because the elders judged in them, and these gates . . . and foundations are of pearls and precious stones to denote them kings and princes. For great and valuable men are known by rich and precious ornaments . . . .

If you desire to know the manner of this city on earth and of the war of Gog and Magog you may see them both described by Ezekiel chapters 38 and 39 . . . where he represents how the Jews after their return from captivity dwell safely and quietly upon the mountains of Israel in unwalled towns without either gates or bars to defend them until they are grown very rich in cattle and gold and silver and goods, and Gog of the land of Magog stirs up the nations round about, Persia and Arabia and Africa and the northern nations of Asia and Europe against them to take a spoil, and God destroys all that great army, that the nations may from thenceforth know that the . . . Jews went formerly into captivity for their sins but now since their return are become invincible by their holiness.

We have hitherto considered the new Jerusalem as a city of mortals only: but whilst Christ is the chief corner stone of this city, whilst he rules the nations with a rod of iron and gives power over them to the saints risen from the dead (Apocalypse 2. 26) and makes them kings over the earth (ch. 1.6 and 5.10) and gives them to eat of the tree of life which is in the midst of the paradise of God and to enter in through the gates into the city (ch. 2. 7 and 22. 14) and writes upon them the name of this . . .new Jerusalem (ch. 3. 12); this city must be understood to comprehend as well Christ and the children of the resurrection as the race of mortal Jews on earth. It signifies not a material city but the . . .body politic of all those who have dominion over the nation whether they be the saints in heaven or their mortal vice regents on earth and therefore the Apostle Paul in his Epistle to the Hebrews, chapter 11 understands it of the saints in heaven, and in Galatians, 4. 26 calls it Jerusalem which is above. Hence this city is not only long and broad as other cities are, but rises high from the earth into heaven. Hence also the dimensions of the sides thereof are double to those of the terrestrial Jerusalem described by Ezekiel: for understanding which, you are to know that the prophets have written of superficial and solid measure as well as of linear. Ezekiel tells us that the oblation, which was 25,000 cubits in length and as much in breadth, shall be five and twenty thousand, and calls it four square. So John tells us that the wall of this city was 144 cubits according to the art of measuring used by men, that is 12 cubits high and 12 cubits broad, and so in square measure, 144 cubits. For he had told us a little before that this wall was great (that is broad) and high, and now he gives the measures of . . . it according to those dimensions. Ezekiel had put the wall of his temple six cubits high and six cubits broad (Ezek. 40.5) and John puts the measure of his wall double. And as the Angel in . . . the Apocalypse measured the wall by a superficial measure so he measured the city by solid measure, for John saith that he measured the city with the reed, twelve thousand furlongs, the length, the breadth and the height of it are equal.[1] The last words show that the measure of 12000 furlongs respects all the three dimensions and so is a solid measure. Whence the cubit root of 12000 furlongs (will be the side of the city and this side will be repeated four times, will be the compass thereof below, which by my computation is 91 4/7 furlongs or in round numbers ninety furlongs, that is thirty six thousand cubits reckoning four hundred Jewish cubits to a Jewish furlong as authors teach. And the half of this compass being eighteen thousand cubits is the compass of Ezekiel's city. Ezek. 48. 35)[2] that is 22 894/1000 furlongs of 9157 cubits . . . will be the side of this city, and this side, if you take the round number of 9,000 cubits, is double to the side of Ezekiel's city which was only 4500 cubits, Ezek. 48. 16, 32. As the linear dimensions of the temple under the Kings were double to those of the tabernacle under the Judges, so those of the city under the King of Kings are double to those of the city under the Kings.

But whilst this doubled city is the inheritance of the saints, both mortal and immortal, we are not to conceive that Christ and the children of the resurrection shall reign over . . . the nations after the manner of mortal kings or converse with mortals as mortals do with one another; but rather as Christ after his resurrection continued for some time on earth invisible to mortals unless . . . upon certain occasions when he thought fit to appear to . . . his disciples: so it is to be conceived that at his second coming he and the children of the resurrection shall reign invisibly unless when they shall think fit upon any extraordinary occasions to appear. And as Christ after some stay in or near the regions of this earth ascended into heaven so after the resurrection of the dead it may be in their power . . . to leave this earth at pleasure and accompany him into any part of the heavens, that no region in the whole universe may want its inhabitants. For Christ at his second coming must . . . rule the nations with a rod of iron and reign till he hath put down all rule and all authority and power and when he hath put all enemies under his feet (the last whereof is death, to be conquered in these regions) he shall deliver up the kingdom to God the father, 1 Corinthians 15. 24; that is he shall withdraw himself from it and depart into the heavens. For when the martyrs and prophets live again they may reign here with Christ a thousand years till all the nations, Gog and Magog be subdued and the dominion of the new Jerusalem be established and death be vanquished by raising the rest of the dead (those who do not live again until . . . the thousand years be finished) and all this time they may be in the same state of happiness in or near these regions as afterwards when they retire into the highest heavens.[Revelation, Chapter 20].

Notes

1 For John's description of the 'holy Jerusalem' see Revelation 21. 10–27.

2 The passage in brackets was deleted by Newton.

SECTION TWENTY-TWO: SIR CHRISTOPHER WREN, 1632–1723

[We saw in the last section that Christopher Wren was one of the founders of the Royal Society and as a young man Wren was known as a scientific prodigy, especially for his work in geometry and astronomy. In 1649 Wren went to study at Wadham College, Oxford, then under John Wilkins, but his background was very different from most of the Wadham scientists': he was the nephew of the Laudian Bishop Matthew Wren, and son of another high churchman, Christopher Wren, Dean of Windsor. Wren was Gresham Professor of Astronomy 1657–61, and Savilian Professor of Astronomy at Oxford 1661–73. By this last date, however, architecture had become Wren's chief career although he kept up his scientific interests and was President of the Royal Society 1681–3. Wren's mathematical talents and his taste for drawing and for visible results (he produced the illustrations for Hooke's *Micrographia* – extract 144) provided a sound background to the career for which he is best known. His first architectural projects date from the early 1660s when he designed the Sheldonian Theatre, Oxford, and cooperated with his uncle in the building of the chapel at Pembroke College, Cambridge. Within days of the Great Fire of 1666, Wren presented Charles II with a plan for the rebuilding of London, and he was one of the architects most involved in the remaking of the City (as was Robert Hooke). In 1669 Wren became Surveyor of the King's Works, and he held this post until 1718, through all the upheavals of the later seventeenth century. As this long tenure suggests, Wren remained aloof from the political controversies of his day. He undertook many royal commissions, such as the building of the Royal Hospital Chelsea in the 1680s and the rebuilding at Hampton Court (1689–95) and was responsible for many university buildings; but it is chiefly for his London churches, and, of course, for St Paul's that he is now remembered. Wren had rebuilt or repaired some fifty of London's churches by 1690, most of the work being done in the 1670s. St Paul's occupied most of his working life as an architect, from the early proposals for the cathedral's repair (extract 152) until 1710 when the new construction was more or less complete. Wren submitted the first of a series of designs for a new St Paul's in 1669, and the actual building work began in 1675. Towards the end of his life, Wren drew on this experience in his advice to a younger generation of architects (extract 153). His comments were occasioned by the Act of 1711 for building fifty new churches in the Cities of London and Westminster. Many of these churches were designed by Nicholas Hawksmoor who had been Wren's clerk and protégé.]

152 Wren's Report on Old St Paul's after the Fire

[*Source*: *The Thirteenth Volume of the Wren Society* (1936), pp.20–22.]

[St Paul's was severely damaged in the Great Fire of September 1666. (For Pepys' description of the start of the fire see p. 280.) This report was sent by Wren to the Dean and Chapter of St Paul's some time before February 1667.]

What time and weather had left entire in the old, and art in the new repaired parts of this great pile of Paul's, the late calamity of the fire hath so weakened and defaced that it now appears like some antique ruin of 2000 years standing, and to repair it sufficiently will be like the mending of the *Argo Navis*,[1] scarce anything will at last be left of the old.

The first decays of it were great, from several causes first from the original building itself, for it was not well shaped and designed for the firm bearing of its own vault, how massy soever the walls seemed to be . . .nor were the materials good, for it seemed to have been built out of the stone of some other ancient ruins, the walls being of two several sorts of free-stone and those small, and the core within was ragstone cast in rough, with mortar and putty, which is not a durable way of building, unless there had been that peculiar sort of banding, with some through-courses, which is necessary in this kind of filling work, but was omitted in this fabric. This accusation belongs chiefly to the west, north and south parts. The choir was of later and better work, not inferior to most Gothic fabrics of that age. The tower, though it had the effects of an ill manner of building and small stones and filling work, yet was it more carefully banded and cramped with much iron.

A second reason of the decays, which appeared before the last fire, was in probability the former fire which consumed the whole roof in the reign of Queen Elizabeth [1561]. The fall of timber then upon the vault was certainly one main cause of the cracks which appeared in the vault and of the spreading out of the walls above ten inches in some places from their true perpendicular, as it now appears more manifestly. This giving out of the walls was endeavoured to be corrected by the artist of the last repairs[2] who placed his new case of Portland stone truly perpendicular, and if he had proceeded with casing it within the whole had been tolerably corrected, but now even this new work is gone away from its perpendicular also, by this second fall of the roof in this last fire. This is most manifest in the northwest aisle.

These second ruins are they that have put the restoration past remedy; the effects of which I shall briefly enumerate.

First. The portico is totally deprived of that excellent beauty and strength which time alone and weather could have no more overthrown than the natural rocks; so great and good were the materials and so skilfully were they laid after a true Roman manner. But so impatient is the Portland stone of fire that many tons of stone are scaled off, and the columns flawed quite through.

Next, the southwest corner. One of the vast pillars of the body of the church with all that it supported is fallen.

All along the body of the church the pillars are more given out than they were before the fire; and more flawed towards the bottom by the burning of the goods below, and the timbers fallen from above.

This farther spreading of the pillars within hath also carried out the walls of the aisles, and reduced the circular ribs of the vaults of the aisles to be of a form which to the eye appears distorted and compressed, especially in the northwest aisle of the body of the church.

The tower and the parts next about it have suffered the least, for these by reason that the walls lying in form of a cross give a firm and immovable butment [support] each to other, and they stand still in their position and support their vaults, which shows manifestly that the fall of the timber alone could not break the vaults unless where the same concussion had force enough to make the walls also give out.

And this is the reason of the great desolation which appears in the new choir, for there the falling vaults, in spite of all the small buttresses, hath broke them short or dislocated the stouter of them, and overthrowing the north wall and pillars, and consequently the vaults of the northeast aisle, hath broken open the vaults of St Faith's[3] (though those were of very great strength); but irresistible is the force of so many thousand tons, augmented by the height of the fall.

Having shown in part the deplorable condition of our patient, we are to consult of the cure if possible art may effect it, and herein we must imitate the physician who, when he finds a total decay of nature, bends his skill to a palliation, to give respite for a better settlement of the estate of the patient. The question is then where best to begin this kind of practice, that is to make a choir for present use.

It will worst of all be effected in the new choir for there the walls and pillars being fallen, it will cost a large sum to restore them to their former height, and before this can be effected the very substruction and repair of St Faith's will cost so much, that I shall but fright this age with the computation of that which is to be done in the dark before anything will appear for the use desired.

The old choir seems to some a convenient place, and that which will be most easily effected, because the vault there looks firm or easily reparable as far as to the place where was once the old pulpit. But this design will not be without very material objections. First, the place is very short and little between the stone screen and the breach, and only capable of a very little choir, not of an auditory; and if the auditory be made without, yet secondly all the adjacent places are under the ruins of a falling tower, which every day throws off smaller scales, and in frost will yield such showers of the outside stones (if no greater parts come down with tempests) that the new roofs, yet to be made, will be broken up, if no further mischiefs ensue. Thirdly, you are to make such a dismal procession through ruins to come thither that the very passage will be a penance. Fourthly, this cannot be effected without considerable expense of making four partition walls to the top to sever this part on every side from the ruins, and covering with timber and lead these four short parts of the cross next the tower, and covering the tower also: that is, if you make room for the auditory as well as the choir, the choir itself being very little.

These ways being found inconvenient and expenseful, either of taking out a part where the new choir was, or where the old choir is, with the parts west, north and south, next the tower, as far as the vaults stand; it remains that we seek it in the body of the church, and this is that which I should humbly advise as the properest and cheapest way of making a sufficient choir and auditory after this manner.

I would take the lesser north and south doors for the entrances and leaving two intercolumniations eastward, and three or four westward, I would there make partition walls of the fallen stone upon the place; the east part above the doors may be contrived into a choir, the west into the auditory. I would lay a timber roof as low as the bottoms of the upper windows, with a flat fretted ceiling, the lead saved out of the burning will more than cover it. Of iron and of pavement there is enough for all uses. The roof, lying low, will not appear above the walls, and since we cannot mend this great ruin we will not disfigure it, but that it shall still have its full motives to work if possible upon this or the next ages; and yet within it shall have all convenience and light (by turning the second storey of arches into windows) and a beauty durable to the next two centuries of years, and yet prove so cheap that between three and four thousand pounds shall effect it all in one summer.

And having with this ease obtained a present cathedral, there will be time to consider of a more durable and noble fabric to be made in the place of the tower and eastern parts of the church, when the minds of men, now contracted to many objects of necessary charge, shall by God's blessings be more widened after a happy restoration both of the buildings and wealth of the city and nation. In the meanwhile, to derive, if not a stream, yet some little drills of charity this way, or at least to preserve that already obtained from being diverted, it may not prove ill advice to seem to begin something of the new fabric. But I confess this cannot well be put in execution without taking down all that part of the ruins, which whether it be yet seasonable to do, we must leave to our superiors.

[On the back of the letter is an endorsement from the surveyors.]

A report touching the decays of the walls and piers on the north and south aisles at the west end of the Cathedral of St Paul's London.

We find the walls to be of a sufficient strength to sustain the weight of the roof intended to be laid thereon. But the second pillars on the south side next to it, which are fallen down, are so much decayed and perished by the fire that it is necessary to case them and to build the pillar which is fallen down which will be a great strength and support to all the whole aisle on the south side of the church. 26 February 1667.

Notes
1 '*Argo Navis*': the ship in which Jason and the Argonauts sailed in search of the golden fleece.
2 'the last repairs': those supervised by Inigo Jones in the 1630s.
3 'St Faith's: the parish church sited in St Paul's crypt.

153 Upon the Building of the National Churches

[*Source*: *The Ninth Volume of the Wren Society* (1932), pp.15–18.]

Since providence, in great mercy, has protracted my age to the finishing the Cathedral church of St Paul and the parochial churches of London, in lieu of those demolished by the Fire (all which were executed during the fatigues of my employment in the service of the crown, from that time to the present happy reign);[1] and being now constituted one of the Commissioners for Building, pursuant to the late Act, fifty more churches in London and Westminster, I shall presume to communicate briefly my sentiments . . .

1 First, I conceive the churches should be built, not where vacant ground may be cheapest purchased in the extremities of the suburbs, but among the thicker inhabitants for convenience of the better sort, although the site of them should cost more; the better inhabitants contributing most to the future repairs and the ministers and officers of the church, and charges of the parish.

2 I could wish that all burials in churches might be disallowed, which is not only unwholesome, but the pavements can never be kept even nor pews upright; and if the churchyard be close about the church, this also is inconvenient because the ground being continually raised by the graves, occasions in time a descent by steps into the church which renders it damp and the walls green, as appears evidently in all old churches.

3 It will be enquired, where then shall be the burials? I answer, in cemetries seated in the outskirts of the town . . . In these places, beautiful monuments may be erected, but yet the dimensions should be regulated by an architect and not left to the fancy of every mason, for thus the rich, with large marble tombs, would shoulder out the poor; when a pyramid, a good bust, or statue on a proper pedestal will take up little room in the quarters and be properer than figures lying on marble beds. . . .

4 As to the situation of the churches, I should propose they be brought as forward as possible into the larger and more open streets, not in obscure lanes, nor where coaches will be much obstructed in the passage. Nor are we, I think, too nicely to observe east or west in the

position unless it falls out properly. Such fronts as shall happen to lie most open in view should be adorned with porticos both for beauty and convenience; which, together with handsome spires or lanterns rising in good proportion above the neighbouring houses (of which I have given several examples in the city of different forms) may be of sufficient ornament to the town, without a great expense for enriching the outward walls of the churches in which plainness and duration ought principally, if not wholly, to be studied.

When a parish is divided, I suppose it may be thought sufficient, if the mother-church has a tower large enough for a good ring of bells, and the other churches smaller towers for two or three bells; because great towers and lofty steeples are sometimes more than half the charge of the church.

5 I shall mention something of the materials for public fabrics. It is true, the mighty demands for the hasty works of thousands of houses at once, after the fire of London, and the frauds of those who built by the great, have so debased the value of materials that good bricks are not to be now had without greater prices than formerly, and indeed, if rightly made, will deserve them; but brickmakers spoil the earth in the mixing and hasty burning till the bricks will hardly bear weight; though the earth about London, rightly managed, will yield as good brick as were the Roman bricks (which I have often found in the old ruins of the City) and will endure in our air beyond any stone our Island affords which unless the quarries lie near the sea are too dear for general use: the best is Portland or Roche Abbey stone, but these are not without their faults. The next material is the lime: chalk lime is the constant practice, which, well mixed with good sand, is not amiss though much worse than hard stone lime. The vaulting of St Paul's is a rendering as hard as stone: it is composed of cockle-shell lime well beaten with sand; the more labour in the beating, the better and stronger the mortar. I shall say nothing of marble, though England, Scotland and Ireland afford good, and of beautiful colours, but this will prove too costly for our purpose unless for altar pieces. In windows and doors Portland stone may be used, with good bricks and stone quoins. As to roofs, good oak is certainly the best because it will bear some negligence. The churchwardens' care may be defective in speedy mending drips: they usually whitewash the church and set up their names, but neglect to preserve the roof over their heads. It must be allowed that the roof being more out of sight, is still more unminded. Next to oak is good yellow deal which is a timber of length and light and makes excellent work at first, but if neglected will speedily perish; especially if gutters (which is a general fault in builders) be made to run upon the principal rafters, the ruin may be sudden. Our sea service for oak, and the wars in the north sea,[2] make timber at present of excessive price. I suppose ere long, we must have recourse to the West Indies where most excellent timber may be had for cutting and fetching. Our tiles are ill made, and our slate not good; lead is certainly the best and lightest covering, and being of our own growth and manufacture, and lasting, if properly laid,

for many hundred years is without question the most preferable; though I will not deny but an excellent tile may be made to be very durable, our artisans are not yet instructed in it and it is not seen done to inform them.

6 The capacity and dimensions of the new churches may be determined by a calculation. . . .Now if the churches could hold each 2000, it would yet be very short of necessary supply. The churches therefore must be large, but still, in our reformed religion, it should seem vain to make a parish church larger than that all who are present can both hear and see. The Romanists, indeed, may build larger churches: it is enough if they hear the murmur of the mass and see the elevation of the host, but ours are to be fitted for auditories. I can hardly think it practicable to make a single room so capacious with pews and galleries as to hold above 2000 persons, and all to hear the service and both to hear distinctly and see the preacher. I endeavoured to effect this in building the parish church of St James's Westminster which, I presume, is the most capacious, with these qualifications, that hath yet been built; and yet, at a solemn time, when the church was much crowded, I could not discern from a gallery that 2000 were present. In this church I mention, though very broad, and the middle nave arched up, yet there are no walls of a second order, nor lanterns, nor buttresses, but the whole roof rests upon the pillars as do also the galleries; I think it may be found beautiful and convenient and, as such, the cheapest of any form I could invent.

7 Concering the placing of the pulpit, I shall observe . . .a moderate voice may be heard 50 feet distant before the preacher, 30 feet on each side and 20 behind the pulpit and not this, unless the pronunciation be distinct and equal, without losing the voice at the last word of the sentence, which is commonly emphatical and if obscured spoils the whole sense. A Frenchman is heard further than an English preacher because he raises his voice and not sinks his last words. I mention this as an insufferable fault in the pronunciation of some of our otherwise excellent preachers which schoolmasters might correct in the young as a vicious [defective] pronunciation, and not as the Roman orators spoke: for the principal verb is in Latin usually the last word and if that be lost, what becomes of the sentence?

8 By what I have said, it may be thought reasonable that the new church should be at least 60 feet broad and 90 feet long besides a chancel at one end and the belfry and portico at the other. These proportions may be varied but to build more room than that every person may conveniently hear and see is to create noise and confusion. A church should not be so filled with pews but that the poor may have room enough to stand and sit in the alleys, for to them equally is the gospel preached.

It were to be wished there were to be no pews, but benches, but there is no stemming the tide of profit and the advantage of pew keepers; especially too, since by pews, in the chapels of ease, the minister is chiefly supported. It is evident these fifty churches are not enough for the present inhabitants and the town will continually grow, but it is to be hoped that hereafter more may be added, as the wisdom of the government shall think fit, and therefore the parishes should be so divided as to leave room for sub-divisions, or at least for chapels of ease.

I cannot pass over mentioning the difficulties that may be found in obtaining the ground proper for the sites of the churches among the buildings, and the cemetries in the borders without the town; and therefore I shall recite the method that was taken for purchasing in ground at the north side of St Paul's cathedral where in some places the houses were but eleven feet distant from the fabric, exposing it to the continual danger of fires.

The houses were seventeen, and contiguous, all in leasehold of the Bishop, or Dean alone, or the Dean and Chapter, or the Petty Canons, with divers undertenants. First we treated with the superior landlords who being perpetual bodies were to be recompensed in kind, with rents of the like value for them and their successors, but the tenants in possession for a valuable consideration, which to find what it amounted to, we learned by diligent inquiry what the inheritance of houses in that quarter were usually held at. This we found was fifteen years purchase at the most, and proportionably to this, the value of each lease was easily determined in a scheme, referring to a map. These rates, which we resolved not to stir from, were offered to each; and to cut off much debate, which may be imagined everyone would abound in, they were assured that we went by one uniform method, which could not be receded from.

We found two or three reasonable men who agreed to these terms; immediately we paid them and took down their houses. Others who stood out at first, finding themselves in dust and rubbish, and that ready money was better as the case stood than to continue paying rent, repairs and parish duties, easily came in. The whole ground at last was cleared and all concerned were satisfied and their writings given up. The greatest debate was about their charges for fitting up their new houses to their particular trades: for this we allowed one year's purchase and gave leave to remove all their wainscot, reserving the materials of the fabric only. This was happily finished without a judicatory or jury although in our present case we may find it perhaps sometimes necessary to have recourse to Parliament.

Notes

1 'the present happy reign': the date of this letter is uncertain, but this passage suggests it was written shortly after the accession of George I in 1714.

2 'the wars in the north sea': the Great Northern War of 1700–21 which mainly involved the Baltic powers.

SECTION TWENTY-THREE: JOHN LOCKE, 1632–1704

[This volume ends, appropriately, with extracts from John Locke's *Essay Concerning The True Original, Extent and End of Civil Government* (1689) (extracts 154–7). This work, the second of Locke's *Two Treatises of Government*, was published shortly after the Revolution that brought William and Mary to the throne, and originated in Locke's close involvement in the political controversies of the 1670s and 1680s. The *Essay*'s significance stretches far beyond our period, however, for the general principles concerning the basis of political authority drawn by Locke from his immediate situation, were regarded as the foundation of the English system of government in the eighteenth century and exercised great influence on the American Revolutionaries and the European 'Enlightenment'.

John Locke was born into a Somerset gentry family with Puritan leanings: his father fought for Parliament during the civil war. In 1652 he went to Christ Church College, Oxford, then under John Owen, the Independent divine. He remained at Christ Church into the 1660s, studied medicine, and was moderately successful in his academic career. In 1666, after a chance meeting, Locke performed a successful operation on Anthony Ashley Cooper (later Earl of Shaftesbury – Dryden's Achitophel) who suffered from a chronic liver complaint. In 1667 he moved into Cooper's household as his personal physician and tutor to his grandchildren. Locke became a Fellow of the Royal Society in 1668 and formed a close friendship with Robert Boyle who shared Locke's political and religious views. After 1672 when Shaftesbury became Lord Chancellor, Locke obtained several civil service posts, the most important being that of Secretary to the Council of Trade. The association with Shaftesbury was of crucial importance in Locke's life. His personal papers show little sign of great interest in political or philosophical matters before 1666, and many of his writings began as policy statements prepared for his mentor. *A Letter Concerning Toleration* (1689), for example, derived from an 'Essay on Toleration' drafted for Shaftesbury in 1667.

Locke acted as Shaftesbury's right-hand man during the Exclusion Crisis, and after Shaftesbury's exile was involved in Whig plots against Charles II's government. In 1683 Locke himself fled to Holland and in 1684 he was formally expelled from Christ Church. After 1689, Locke again held government office, for example as a member of the Board of Trade from 1696, but, more importantly, he exercised immense informal influence as the leading Whig intellectual. His major works on education, toleration and money appeared in the years following the

Revolution. *An Essay Concerning Humane Understanding* (1690), Locke's general philosophical work, and his first acknowledged publication, made him internationally famous.

It used to be thought that the *Two Treatises* were written in 1688 to justify the Revolution and the Settlement, but it has now been demonstrated that they were composed in 1679–80 at the height of the Exclusion Crisis. Their specific purpose was to answer the divine right arguments of Sir Robert Filmer, published in their extended form in *Patriarcha* (1680). (See extract 54 for an example of Filmer's ideas.) The first treatise, probably the second to be written, was entirely devoted to a critique of Filmer, while the second was Locke's positive statement on the issue of political obligation, which was of urgent concern to Shaftesbury and his allies at this time. The work is thus, 'an Exclusion Tract, not a Revolution Pamphlet'.[1] While Locke was in exile, the manuscript was left with friends, and more than half of it seems to have disappeared. Locke only acknowledged he had written the *Two Treatises* in his will, but his authorship was widely suspected in his lifetime.

Note

1 Peter Laslett, editor, *John Locke: Two Treatises of Government* (Second edition, 1967) Introduction.]

154 The State of Nature

[*Source*: *Social Contract: Essays by Locke, Hume, Rousseau* (1947 The World's Classics); extract 154: pp. 4–8; extract 155: pp. 73–4, 80–1, 83; extract 156: pp. 101–3; extract 157: pp. 106–9.]

. . .

3 Political power, then, I take to be a right of making laws with penalties of death, and consequently all less penalties, for the regulating and preserving of property, and of employing the force of the community in the execution of such laws, and in the defence of the commonwealth from foreign injury; and all this only for the public good.

4 To understand political power aright, and derive it from its original, we must consider what state all men are naturally in, and that is, a state of perfect freedom to order their actions, and dispose of their possessions and persons, as they think fit, within the bounds of the law of nature, without asking leave, or depending upon the will of any other man.

A state also of equality, wherein all the power and jurisdiction is reciprocal, no one having more than another; there being nothing more evident, than that creatures of the same species and rank, promiscuously born to all the same advantages of nature, and the use of the same faculties, should also be equal one amongst another without subordination or subjection, unless the Lord and Master of them all should by any manifest declaration of his will, set one above another, and confer on him, by an evident and clear appointment, an undoubted right to dominion and sovereignty. . . .

6 But though this be a state of liberty, yet it is not a state of licence: though man in that state have an uncontrollable liberty to dispose of his person or possessions, yet he has not liberty to destroy himself, or so much as any creature in his possession, but where some nobler use than its bare preservation calls for it. The state of nature has a law of nature to govern it, which obliges every one; and reason, which is that law, teaches all mankind, who will but consult it, that, being all equal and independent, no one ought to harm another in his life, health, liberty, or possessions. For men being all the workmanship of one omnipotent and infinitely wise Maker; all the servants of one sovereign Master, sent into the world by his order, and about his business; they are his property, whose workmanship they are, made to last during his, not one another's pleasure; and being furnished with like faculties, sharing all in one community of nature, there cannot be supposed any such subordination among us, that may authorize us to destroy one another, as if we were made for one another's uses, as the inferior ranks of creatures are for ours. Every one, as he is bound to preserve himself, and not to quit his station wilfully, so, by the like reason, when his own

preservation comes not in competition, ought he as much as he can to preserve the rest of mankind, and not, unless it be to do justice on an offender, take away or impair the life, or what tends to the preservation of the life, the liberty, health, limb, or goods of another.

7 And that all men may be restrained from invading others' rights, and from doing hurt to one another, and the law of nature be observed, which willeth the peace and preservation of all mankind, the execution of the law of nature is in the state put into every man's hands, whereby every one has a right to punish the transgressors of that law to such a degree as may hinder its violation. For the law of nature would, as all other laws that concern men in this world, be in vain if there were nobody that, in the state of nature, had a power to execute that law, and thereby preserve the innocent and restrain offenders. And if any one in the state of nature may punish another for any evil he has done, every one may do so. For in that state of perfect equality, where naturally there is no superiority or jurisdiction of one over another, what any may do in prosecution of that law, every one must needs have a right to do.

155 The Beginning of Political Societies

. . .

89 Wherever therefore any number of men are so united into one society, as to quit everyone his executive power of the law of nature, and to resign it to the public, there and there only is a political or civil society. And this is done wherever any number of men, in the state of nature, enter into society to make one people, one body politic, under one supreme government, or else when anyone joins himself to and incorporates with any government already made. For hereby he authorizes the society, or, which is all one, the legislative thereof, to make laws for him, as the public good of the society shall require, to the execution whereof his own assistance (as to his own decrees) is due. And this puts men out of a state of nature into that of a commonwealth, by setting up a judge on earth with authority to determine all the controversies and redress the injuries that may happen to any member of the commonwealth; which judge is the legislative, or magistrates appointed by it. And wherever there are any number of men, however associated, that have no such decisive power to appeal to, they are still in the state of nature. . . .

95 MEN being, as has been said, by nature all free, equal, and independent, no one can be put out of this estate and subjected to the political power of another, without his own consent, which is done by agreeing with other men, to join and unite into a community for their comfortable, safe, and peaceable living, one amongst another, in a secure enjoyment of their properties, and a greater security against any that are not of it. This any number of men may do, because it injures not

the freedom of the rest; they are left, as they were, in the liberty of the state of nature. When any number of men have so consented to make one community or government, they are thereby presently incorporated, and make one body politic, wherein the majority have a right to act and conclude the rest. . . .

99 Whosoever therefore out of a state of nature unite into a community, must be understood to give up all the power necessary to the ends for which they unite into society to the majority of the community, unless they expressly agreed in any number greater than the majority. And this is done by barely agreeing to unite into one political society, which is all the compact that is, or needs be, between the individuals that enter into or make up a commonwealth. And thus, that which begins and actually constitutes any political society is nothing but the consent of any number of freemen capable of a majority, to unite and incorporate into such a society. And this is that, and that only, which did or could give beginning to any lawful government in the world.

156 The Obligation of Obedience

. . .

119 Every man being, as has been showed naturally free, and nothing being able to put him into subjection to any earthly power, but only his own consent, it is to be considered what shall be understood to be a sufficient declaration of a man's consent to make him subject to the laws of any government. There is a common distinction of an express and a tacit consent, which will concern our present case. Nobody doubts but an express consent of any man, entering into any society, makes him a perfect member of that society, a subject of that government. The difficulty is, what ought to be looked upon as a tacit consent, and how far it binds, i.e., how far any one shall be looked on to have consented, and thereby submitted to any government, where he has made no expressions of it at all. And to this I say, that every man that hath any possession or enjoyment of any part of the dominions of any government, doth thereby give his tacit consent, and is as far forth obliged to obedience to the laws of that government during such enjoyment as any one under it; whether this his possession be of land to him and his heirs for ever, or a lodging only for a week; or whether it be barely travelling freely on the highway; and in effect it reaches as far as the very being of any one within the territories of that government.

120 To understand this the better, it is fit to consider that every man when he at first incorporates himself into any commonwealth, he, by his uniting himself thereunto, annexes also, and submits to the community those possessions which he has, or shall acquire, that do not already belong to any other government. For it would be a direct contradiction for any one to enter into society with others for the

securing and regulating of property, and yet to suppose his land, whose property is to be regulated by the laws of the society, should be exempt from the jurisdiction of that government to which he himself, the proprietor of the land, is a subject. By the same act, therefore, whereby anyone unites his person, which was before free, to any commonwealth, by the same he unites his possessions, which were before free, to it also; and they become, both of them, person and possession, subject to the government and dominion of that commonwealth as long as it hath a being. Whoever therefore, from thenceforth, by inheritance, purchase, permission, or otherwise enjoys any part of the land so annexed to, and under the government of that commonwealth, must take it with the condition it is under, that is, of submitting to the government of the commonwealth, under whose jurisdiction it is, as far forth as any subject of it.

121 But since the government has a direct jurisdiction only over the land, and reaches the possessor of it (before he has actually incorporated himself in the society) only as he dwells upon and enjoys that, the obligation anyone is under, by virtue of such enjoyment, to submit to the government, begins and ends with the enjoyment; so that whenever the owner, who has given nothing but such a tacit consent to the government, will, by donation, sale, or otherwise, quit the said possession, he is at liberty to go and incorporate himself into any other commonwealth, or to agree with others to begin a new one, *in vacuis locis* [in empty places] in any part of the world they can find free and unpossessed. Whereas he that has once, by actual agreement and any express declaration, given his consent to be of any commonweal, is perpetually and indispensably obliged to be and remain unalterably a subject to it, and can never be again in the liberty of the state of nature; unless, by any calamity, the government he was under comes to be dissolved, or else by some public acts cuts him off from being any longer a member of it.

157 The Ends of Political Society and Government

. . .

127 Thus mankind, notwithstanding all the privileges of the state of nature, being but in an ill condition while they remain in it, are quickly driven into society. Hence it comes to pass, that we seldom find any number of men live any time together in this state. The inconveniencies that they are therein exposed to by the irregular and uncertain exercise of the power every man has of punishing the transgressions of others, make them take sanctuary under the established laws of government, and therein seek the preservation of their property. 'Tis this makes them so willingly give up every one his single power of punishing, to be exercised by such alone as shall be appointed to it amongst them; and

by such rules as the community, or those authorized by them to that purpose, shall agree on. And in this we have the original right and rise of both the legislative and executive power, as well as of the governments and societies themselves. . . .

131 But though men when they enter into society give up the equality, liberty, and executive power they had in the state of nature into the hands of the society, to be so far disposed of by the legislature as the good of the society shall require; yet it being only with an intention in everyone the better to preserve himself, his liberty, and property (for no rational creature can be supposed to change his condition with an intention to be worse), the power of the society, or legislative constituted by them can never be supposed to extend farther than the common good, but is obliged to secure every one's property by providing against those three defects above-mentioned[1] that made the state of nature so unsafe and uneasy. And so whoever has the legislative or supreme power of any commonwealth is bound to govern by established standing laws, promulgated and known to the people, and not by extemporary decrees; by indifferent and upright judges, who are to decide controversies by those laws; and to employ the force of the community at home only in the execution of such laws, or abroad to prevent or redress foreign injuries and secure the community from inroads and invasion. And all this to be directed to no other end but the peace, safety, and public good of the people.

Note

1 'three defects above-mentioned': the defects in the state of nature were the lack of 'an established, settled, known law', of a 'known and indifferent judge' and of a 'power to execute judgments' (Sections 124–6).

BIOGRAPHICAL INDEX

This index gives brief biographical information on the authors of extracts, with some exceptions: joint authors of cooperative works (extracts 11, 63, 90) and the drafters of official documents such as constitutional programmes or legislative measures have been excluded; biographies of some authors have been incorporated in section introductions or headnotes – where this is the case, a cross-reference is given.

Lancelot Andrewes (1555–1626) extract 125
Bishop of Chichester (1605–9), Ely (1609–19) and Winchester (1619–26); Privy Councillor 1616-26. Noted for his brilliant preaching and his learning, Andrewes was one of the scholars who worked on the Authorised Version of the Bible.

John Aubrey (1626–1697) extract 128
Antiquary and versatile scholar; from an impoverished Wiltshire gentry family. He published only one book in his lifetime but left a vast manuscript collection covering biography, topography and natural history. Aubrey's *Lives* and *The Natural History of Wiltshire* were first published in the nineteenth century.

Francis Bacon, Viscount St Albans (1561–1626) extract 4
From an eminent legal family, Lord Chancellor 1618–21 when he was impeached in Parliament for bribery. His major works on science and philosophy were *The Advancement of Learning* (1605, with an enlarged Latin edition in 1623); *Novum Organum* (1620); *New Atlantis* (1627). A small collection of his essays was published in 1597; the first complete edition appeared in 1625.

John Bastwick (1593–1654) extract 24
Bastwick trained as a doctor in Italy and practised medicine in Colchester, Essex, from 1623. Imprisoned by the High Commission in 1634 for a Latin treatise against episcopacy; while in prison wrote the *Letany* (1637) for which he was mutilated with Prynne and Burton. He was released in 1640; fought briefly in Parliament's army, and by the later 1640s had become a fierce opponent of religious and political radicals.

Richard Baxter (1615–1691) extracts 8, 47, 65, 74, 80, 116, 119
Born in Shropshire, received only a basic education. In 1641, on the invitation of some of the parishioners, became lecturer at Kidderminster but he was driven from there by royalists and settled in

Coventry. As chaplain to Coventry's garrison Baxter preached against separation and he was alarmed at the radicalism of some New Model soldiers when he preached to that army in 1645. He was a very moderate Parliamentarian; dubious about the Covenant and opposed to the Engagement to the Republic. In the 1650s as vicar of Kidderminster, he had some success in establishing moral discipline over his parishioners; in 1653 established the Worcester Association, a union of moderate ministers, an initiative that was followed by other areas. In 1660 he refused a Bishopric but lost his Kidderminster living. Attended the Savoy Conference, 1661, and after 1662 lived mainly in retirement although he continued to work for religious unity and suffered some spells of imprisonment, including eighteen months in 1685–6 after a trial conducted by Jefferies. Baxter was the author of about 130 books; the *Reliquiae* was produced by an editor from Baxter's manuscripts.

Immanuel Bourne (1590–1672) extracts 75, 79
Educated at Oxford; minister in London 1617–21 and at Ashover, Derbyshire, from 1621. A Derbyshire Justice of the Peace before the civil war. Neutral at the start of the war, but welcomed Parliament's victory after the royalists had forced him to flee to London. Bourne was a Presbyterian in the 1640s and 1650s, but conformed at the Restoration.

Robert Boyle (1627–1691) extract 145
Younger son of the Earl of Cork; Boyle had very broad scientific interests, and was an important figure in the Oxford experimental science group of the 1650s. 'Boyle's Law', published in 1662, developed from experiments on the air conducted with Robert Hooke. A devout Protestant, Boyle made provision in his will for an annual series of lectures to prove the truth of Christianity against 'infidels'; controversies within Christianity were to be avoided.

Sir Thomas Browne (1605–1682) extract 127
A merchant's son, educated at Oxford and on the continent, with medical degrees from Leyden and Oxford. From 1637, Browne lived at Norwich, becoming famous as a physician and for his wide scholarly interests. His best known work was *Religio Medici* written about 1635, first authorized publication 1643. Browne was knighted in 1671.

John Bryan (died 1676) extract 58
Warwickshire Presbyterian minister; preacher to Warwick Castle, a parliamentary garrison, during the civil war; ejected from his living in Coventry 1662.

Laurence Clarkson (1615–1667) extract 83
Born in Lancashire; extract 83 traces his development from Presbyterian to Ranter, and eventually to Muggletonian. In 1650 the Rump sentenced Clarkson to banishment for blasphemy, but the sentence

was not carried out. Died in a debtors' prison: he had lent money for the rebuilding of London after the Fire but the borrowers defaulted.

Thomas Collier (died 1691) extract 73
Particular Baptist author and preacher; a baptist before 1645, and an itinerant preacher in the 1640s and 1650s, mainly in the west country; an army preacher in the late 1640s. Collier wrote against the Quakers.

Oliver Cromwell (1599–1658) extracts 92, 98–100
From a Huntingdon gentry family; educated at Cambridge. M.P. for Cambridge in the Long Parliament; Captain of horse in Essex's army; then Colonel and Lieutenant General of horse under Manchester in the Eastern Association Army. Cromwell's quarrels with Manchester over religious and military matters were an important trigger of the Self-denying Ordinance of April 1645. Despite being an MP, Cromwell served in the New Model as Lieutenant General of horse, on a temporary commission, periodically renewed. Supported the army in its 1647 campaign for the redress of practical grievances, but kept Leveller agitation in check; involved in negotiations with the King, 1647. In 1649–50, as military commander and Lord Lieutenant, began the reconquest of Ireland. In June 1650, became Commander in Chief of the Army in England on Fairfax's resignation; defeated the Scots at Dunbar, September 1650, and exactly a year later defeated Charles II and his Scots army at Worcester. Forcibly dissolved the Rump, April 1653, and in December 1653, after the failure of the 'Barebones' Parliament, became Lord Protector under the Instrument of Government. By the Humble Petition and Advice of May 1657, Cromwell received power to nominate his successor and to create an upper house in Parliament.

William Davenport (1586–1655) extract 60
Head of an ancient and moderately important Cheshire gentry family; tried to remain neutral in the civil war, but suffered sequestration by the parliamentary authorities.

William Dell (died 1669) extract 107
Leading army preacher in the Eastern Association Army, and then in the New Model. Master of Gonville and Caius College, Cambridge, 1649–60. Ejected from a Bedfordshire living 1662. Dell rejected tithes, an ordained ministry and any form of state church; and worked for religious toleration. He was a republican and supported social reform.

Sir Edward Dering (1598–1644) extract 35
Kentish gentleman; scholar and antiquary. In the Long Parliament Dering supported the first moves for religious reform, but opposed the Grand Remonstrance and defended episcopacy. A royalist in the civil war, but was rapidly disillusioned and early in 1644 Dering was the first royalist to compound for his estates and was pardoned by Parliament.

John Donne (1572–1631) extract 126
London merchant's son; Donne's mother was a Catholic but Donne conformed. A successful court career was wrecked by a secret marriage and he suffered poverty until he entered the Church in 1615. Reader at Lincoln's Inn, 1616; Dean of St Paul's, 1621. Most of his poetry was published posthumously in 1633; his *Sermons* appeared in three volumes, 1640, 1649, 1660.

John Dryden – see p. 291

Thomas Edwards (1599–1647) extracts 64, 86
Presbyterian minister. Puritan preacher in Cambridge and London before the civil war and suffered suspension by Laud. Edwards supported Parliament in the war but fiercely opposed religious and political radicals as his *Gangraena* (3 parts 1646) shows. Died in Holland, having fled there to avoid his opponents.

Sir Robert Filmer (1588?–1653) extract 54
From an established Kent gentry family. Took no part in the civil war but was imprisoned 1643–5 because of his well-known royalist views. His political writings circulated in manuscript among his neighbours long before their publication. *Patriarcha*, his most important work, was written probably about 1648 and published in 1680.

George Fox (1624–1691) extract 78
Founder of the Quaker movement. Son of a Leicestershire weaver, with little education. Worked as an apprentice shoemaker and shepherd until his disgust with the established clergy led him to begin preaching in the mid-1640s. From this period Fox travelled continually on missionary journeys in England and abroad. Imprisoned eight times, including one period of three years, 1663–6. After 1660 Fox gave the Quakers a stable organization that enabled them to survive persecution.

Joseph Glanvill (1636–1680) extract 136
Chaplain to Francis Rous, the Cromwellian Provost of Eton in the 1650s, but conformed in 1660 and obtained preferment in the Church of England. Chaplain to Charles II from 1672. Fellow of the Royal Society from 1664; author of several religious and philosophical works.

William Goffe – see p. 218

Godfrey Goodman (1583–1656) extract 20
Bishop of Gloucester from 1625; briefly opposed the 1640 Canons – submitted after being imprisoned by Laud. One of the bishops impeached in 1641, and spent his later years in retirement. Goodman was widely suspected of 'popery' and professed adherence to the Roman Catholic faith in his will.

Robert Greville, Lord Brooke (1608–1643) extract 27
Adopted heir of the poet and politician, Fulke Greville. Brooke was the most radical of the Parliamentarian peers; refused to help Charles I against the Scots, and supported religious toleration. Killed at Lichfield while commanding Parliament's forces in the West Midlands.

Thomas Hall (1610–1665) extracts 71, 76
Minister at Kings Norton, Worcestershire, from the 1630s until his ejection in 1662. In the 1650s he was a member of the Presbyterian Classis, based at Kenilworth, Warwickshire, and wrote several pamphlets against the radical sectaries.

James Harrington – see p. 235

William Harrison (1534–1593) extract 3
Historian and clergyman, serving mainly in Essex. Canon of Windsor from 1586. His *Description of England* was first published in 1577 with an enlarged edition in 1588.

William Hartley (?–?) extract 72
We know little of Hartley's life. Wrote two pamphlets against an established ministry (1649, 1651) and one arguing that all believers would be saved (1650). From these pamphlets it seems he lived at Stony Stratford, Buckinghamshire; had served in Parliament's army, and preached in Buckinghamshire and Northamptonshire. He was probably a layman: a William Hartley was a Justice of the Peace in Buckinghamshire, 1653, and was described by a hostile witness as 'a sorry shopkeeper, but a fierce Anabaptist'.

Hezekiah Haynes – see p. 213

George Herbert (1593–1633) extract 69
Younger son of a dominant Welsh border family. Had a successful academic career at Cambridge and sought court favour until about 1626. Thereafter Herbert lived in retirement, entered the church and obtained a Wiltshire living in 1630. *The Temple*, Herbert's collected religious poetry, was published shortly after his death, *The Country Parson*, his major prose work, in 1652.

Robert Hooke (1635–1703) extract 144
Experimental scientist of great versatility and originality; curator of experiments at the Royal Society from 1662; and a talented architect. However, many of his projects remained half-completed and he frequently quarrelled with fellow scientists (notably Newton).

Philip Hunton (1604?–1682) extract 52
Schoolmaster and minister in Wiltshire until his ejection in 1661. Provost of Cromwell's new university college at Durham 1657–60.

Author of three tracts on mixed monarchy, published 1643–5.

Edward Hyde (1609–1674), Earl of Clarendon from 1661 – extracts 12, 19, 22, 26, 28, 30, 37, 43–6, 57, 62
Trained as a lawyer. Supported the early reforms of the Long Parliament, but a supporter of the King from autumn 1641. Privy Councillor from 1643; wrote many of Charles I's public declarations 1642–5, presenting moderate, constitutionalist arguments. As adviser to the exiled Charles II, opposed the King's links with Presbyterians and Catholics. Appointed Lord Chancellor, 1658, and kept the post at the Restoration. Clarendon was unpopular with Charles's younger ministers, and in the country as a whole, especially during the second Dutch war. He was dismissed by Charles in 1667 and impeached by Parliament; spent the rest of his life in exile in France. His daughter married James, Duke of York, and was the mother of Queens Mary and Anne. His *History of the Rebellion* was begun in 1646, and completed after 1667; first published in three volumes 1702–4. His *Life* – a continuation of the *History* – was first published in 1759.

James VI and I (1566–1625) extract 10
King of Scotland 1567, on the abdication of his mother Mary, Queen of Scots; King of England, 1603. Main works of political theory: *Basilikon Doron* (1599); *True Law of Free Monarchies* (1603). His collected works were published in 1616.

Ben Jonson (1572–1637) extracts 16, 17
Now chiefly remembered as the author of plays like *Volpone*, *Bartholemew Fair* and *The Alchemist* (first performed 1606–14); but Jonson himself was proudest of his non-dramatic poetry. Collaborated with Inigo Jones on court masques from 1605; awarded a royal pension, 1616. Collected *Works* (plays and poetry) published 1616, with a further two-volume collection 1640–41.

Ralph Josselin – see p. 115

Gregory King (1648–1712) extract 2
A Herald from 1677; worked also as an engraver, mapmaker and surveyor; best known for his statistical work, begun in 1695. This work was not published in King's lifetime although extracts appeared in the writings of the political economist Charles Davenant. In the early eighteenth century King was associated with Robert Harley and worked for various public accounting bodies.

Hanserd Knollys (1599?–1691) extract 122
Prominent 'Particular Baptist'. Schoolmaster and clergyman in Lincolnshire in the 1630s; became a separatist and was in New England 1638–42. On his return to England, worked as a schoolteacher and a preacher in Parliament's army. Pastor to various London congregations from

1645. Extract 122 describes his sufferings after the Restoration.

Thomas Knyvett (1596–1658) extract 48
Norfolk gentleman who also held office in the Royal Mint and was in financial trouble before 1642. Briefly imprisoned after being implicated in an abortive royalist rising at Lowestoft, March 1643, but the intervention of the Earl of Manchester and Oliver Cromwell prevented the sequestration of his estates.

John Locke – see p. 373

Edmund Ludlow (1617?–1692) extracts 105, 117
Wiltshire gentleman; officer in Parliamentarian army; staunchly republican M.P. in the Long Parliament from 1646, and regicide. Lieutenant General and Parliamentary Commissioner in Ireland, 1651, but withdrew from office on Cromwell's assumption of personal power. Supported the overthrow of Richard Cromwell and tried to prevent the Restoration. After 1660 lived in exile in Switzerland where his *Memoirs* were written. Encouraged by the Revolution, Ludlow returned to England in 1689 but quickly withdrew when threatened with arrest.

William Medley (active 1654–1683) extract 106
Fifth monarchist, son-in-law of Thomas Venner; described 1661 as the scribe and accountant of the movement. Imprisoned 1657–9 for his part in the 1657 'Venner Plot'. London agent for the Dutch 1672–4; Medley was living in Holland, 1682, when he had contact with the exiled Shaftesbury.

Edward Moore (1635?–1678) extract 7
From an ancient Lancashire family living near Liverpool; son of the regicide John Moore, who was M.P. for Liverpool in the Long Parliament. Edward kept the family estates in 1660 through the influence of his wife's family, and became a baronet in 1675.

James Nayler (1617–1660) extract 77
From a Yorkshire yeoman family; served in Parliament's army and became a preacher. A Quaker from 1651; preached to Quaker meetings in the north and in London and was frequently in trouble with local ministers and magistrates. Nayler quarrelled with the more restrained Fox, 1656. In October 1656, entered Bristol in a manner recalling Christ's entry into Jerusalem; tried by Parliament for blasphemy; sentenced December 1656 to imprisonment, whipping and branding. Released September 1659, died soon afterwards.

Sir Isaac Newton (1642–1727) extracts 146–151
Son of a Lincolnshire yeoman; educated at Trinity College, Cambridge. In 1665–6, while confined to Lincolnshire by the plague, laid the

foundations of his work on gravitation, light and mathematics. Lucasian Professor of Mathematics at Cambridge, 1669. Newton's work on gravitation was laid aside until the 1680s when his theories were perfected and published in his greatest work, *Philosophiae Naturalis Principia Mathematica* (1687). Prominent in the opposition at Cambridge to James II's appointment of Catholics to academic positions; Whig MP for the University in the Convention of 1689. Newton had a lifelong interest in alchemy and spent much time on theological studies. Master of the Royal Mint, 1699; knighted 1705; President of the Royal Society from 1703 until his death.

Richard Overton (?–?) extracts 31, 32, 84, 85
Possibly the son of a Leicestershire clergyman and educated at Cambridge; the style of his early works suggests a link with the theatre. Most of Overton's early pamphlets were religious satires directed first against the bishops and then against the Presbyterians. *Man's Mortality* (1644) argued that the soul died with the body. Led the 1646 agitation against Lilburne's imprisonment and was himself imprisoned by the Lords, August 1646–September 1647. Leveller leader 1646–9; author of many Leveller pamphlets. Imprisoned March–November 1649. Overton's later life is obscure, but he was involved in Leveller–royalist plots, 1655; arrested 1659; and threatened with arrest 1663. Most of his works were published anonymously.

Henry Parker (1604–1652) extract 53
Younger son of a Sussex knight, educated at Oxford and Lincoln's Inn. Secretary to Essex's army during the civil war; secretary to the Merchant Adventurers' Company at Hamburg 1646–9. Died in Ireland serving in a similar capacity with the English army. Author of many political tracts – *Jus Populi* (1644) is the best known.

Thomas Patient (died 1666) extract 82
Ordained as a Church of England minister, but went to New England in the 1630s and became a Baptist. On his return in 1644, became joint pastor with William Kiffin of a leading Baptist church in London, and helped to write the Particular Baptist 'Confession of Faith' (1644). Preacher in Ireland 1650–1660; died of the plague.

Samuel Pepys (1633–1703) extract 129
Son of a London tailor; educated at Cambridge; entered the service of his kinsman, Edward Montagu, later Earl of Sandwich, in the 1650s. Through Sandwich obtained posts in the naval administration after 1660; the most important naval official by the late 1660s. His association with James, Duke of York, led to brief imprisonment and temporary loss of office during the Popish Plot, but became Secretary of the Admiralty, 1683. He retired in 1689. Fellow of the Royal Society 1665, President 1684. Pepys's diary, written in shorthand and covering 1660–69, was first published in the nineteenth century.

John Pym (1584–1643) extracts 14, 36
From a moderately wealthy Somerset gentry family, but had no real local base. Receiver for Crown lands 1607–38; patronized by the Earl of Bedford from 1624. Sat in all Parliaments from 1621, but not a leading member until the Short Parliament. Member of the Providence Island Company 1630s, with other 'opposition' figures. Strongly anti-Catholic and anti-Laudian. Played a major part in the early reforms of the Long Parliament, in the framing of the Grand Remonstrance, and in Parliament's moves to assume control of military power after the Irish Rebellion. Organized the financial and administrative measures of 1642–3, that enabled Parliament to fight the civil war. Pym worked to keep Parliament united, and died shortly after securing the Scottish alliance.

John Rogers (1627–1665?) extract 81
A fifth monarchist by 1652 although he had earlier supported Presbyterianism and then Independency. Preacher in Dublin 1650–52; imprisoned 1655–7 and 1658 for opposition to Cromwell's government. Took refuge in Holland 1660–62; qualified there as a doctor.

George Saville (1633–1695) Marquess of Halifax from 1682 – extracts 130, 131
From a great Yorkshire family; his father was a royalist during the civil war. Privy Councillor from 1672 until his dismissal in 1676; opponent of Charles II's pro-French policies. Hostile to popery but led the struggle against the Exclusion Bill, proposing a regency instead (he was the 'Jotham' of *Absalom and Achitophel*). Returned to office 1679, but had little influence in the 1680s. Dismissed by James II, 1685, for his opposition to the repeal of the Test Acts. Corresponded with William of Orange before 1688 but was not involved in the moves to bring William to England. After James's flight led the pressure to make William king. In office 1689–90, but returned to opposition at the end of his life, fearing the expansion of the monarchy's powers.

John Selden (1584–1654) extracts 18, 23, 41, 49, 56
Trained as a lawyer, but better known as an antiquarian. Imprisoned 1629–31 for his role in the 1628 Parliament. A very moderate Parliamentarian during the civil war, but stayed in the Long Parliament until secluded at Pride's Purge. Publications include *History of Tithes* (1617) which denied the clergy's divine right to tithes; and *Mare Clausum* (1636) which supported English claims to control the seas against the Dutch. *Table Talk* was a posthumously published collection of his conversations, as recorded by a secretary.

Thomas Sprat (1635–1713) extracts 137–140
Educated at Wadham College, Oxford, during Wilkins's headship; became a clergyman in 1660 and was patronized by the Duke of Buckingham. Dean of Westminster 1683; Bishop of Rochester 1684.

Member of James II's Ecclesiastical Commission 1686–8. Fellow of the Royal Society from 1663. A High Church Tory by inclination although he tended to support the *status quo*.

John Stow (1525–1605) extract 5
Antiquary. A London tailor until about 1570; thereafter concentrated on his historical work. His great *Survey* was first published 1598 with an enlarged edition, 1603.

Moses Wall (? – ?) extract 114
Little is known about this contact of John Milton. Probably served as chaplain to the Earl of Warwick 1643–4, and was associated with the Puritan educational reformer Samuel Hartlib. Disapproved of the Protectorate.

John Wallis (1616–1703) extracts 141–3
Wallis became a clergyman in 1640, and became famous as Parliament's chief code-breaker during the civil war. Savilian Professor of Geometry at Oxford, 1649; kept the post at the Restoration. One of the Presbyterian representatives at the Savoy Conference 1661. His mathematical work provided a basis for Newton to develop.

William Walwyn (1600–?) extract 70
Son of a Worcestershire gentleman; grandson of a bishop; a London trader belonging to the Merchant Adventurers' Company. In the early 1640s Walwyn wrote pamphlets advocating freedom of conscience and came into conflict with the Presbyterians. Leveller leader from 1647; imprisoned March–November 1649. Little is known of his later life although he was practising medicine in 1660.

Seth Ward (1617–1689) extract 110
Astronomer, mathematician and clergyman. Lost his Cambridge fellowship, 1644, for opposition to the Covenant, but Savilian Professor of Astronomy at Oxford from 1649, living at Wadham College. Resigned this post in 1660 and entered the Church. Bishop of Exeter, 1662; Bishop of Salisbury, 1667. Ward favoured a more comprehensive Church of England but was a determined harrier of non-conformists in his dioceses.

John Webster (1610–1682) extract 108
Clergyman and schoolmaster in Yorkshire before the civil war. Surgeon in Parliament's army during the second civil war. Studied chemistry under a Hungarian alchemist in the 1630s; in the 1650s he abandoned the ministry for chemistry and alchemy. Published a work attacking the belief in witchcraft, 1677.

Edward Whalley – see p. 217

John Wilkins (1614–1672) extract 109
As warden of Wadham College, Oxford, 1648–59, made it a centre of scientific learning. Married Cromwell's sister, 1656. Master of Trinity College, Cambridge, 1659, but replaced at the Restoration. Wilkins then turned to the Church, becoming Bishop of Chester, 1668. Lenient in his policies towards dissenters; opposed the 1670 Conventicles Act. Author of many religious, mathematical and astronomical works. One of the most important figures in the foundation of the Royal Society.

Sir Thomas Wilson (1560?–1629) extract 1
Had a versatile career as diplomat, foreign correspondent, spy, author and (1606–29) keeper of the public records. In none of these roles was he conspicuously successful. Employed as a companion to Sir Walter Ralegh in the Tower, 1618, with the object of securing incriminating evidence against Ralegh.

Gerrard Winstanley – see p. 187

Charles Worsley – see p. 215

Sir Christopher Wren – see p. 364

INDEX

Index

Note: an italic page reference indicates an entry in the biographical index

Index by Ann Edwards